SPACE AND REVOLUTION

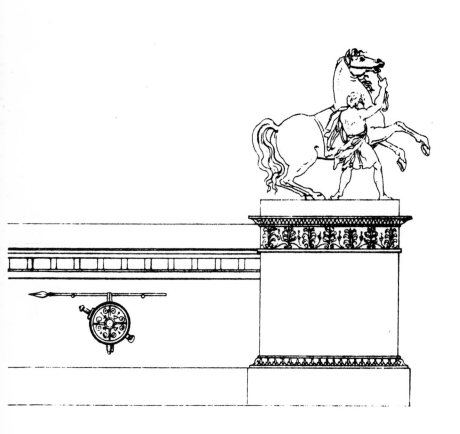

SPACE AND REVOLUTION

Projects for
Monuments, Squares, and
Public Buildings in France
1789-1799

James A. Leith

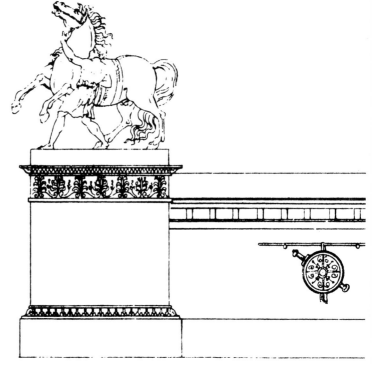

McGill-Queen's University Press

MONTREAL & KINGSTON · LONDON · BUFFALO

© McGill-Queen's University Press 1991
ISBN 0-7735-0757-4

Legal deposit third quarter 1991
Bibliothèque nationale du Québec

Printed in Canada on acid-free paper

This book has been published with the help of a grant from
the Canadian Federation for the Humanities,
using funds provided by the Social Sciences and
Humanities Research Council of Canada.

Composed by Metrotype Graphics Ltd. in
Adobe Garamond

Designed by Miriam Bloom, Expression Communications

Canadian Cataloguing in Publication Data

Leith, James A., 1931–

Space and revolution

Includes bibliographical references.
ISBN 0-7735-0757-4

1. Public buildings – France – History – 18th century. 2. Monuments –
France – History – 18th century. 3. Architecture and state – France –
History – 18th century. 4. France – History – Revolution, 1789–1799.
I. Title.

NA1046.L44 1990   725′.0944   C90-090442-9

To the memory of
my mother, father, and brother

CONTENTS

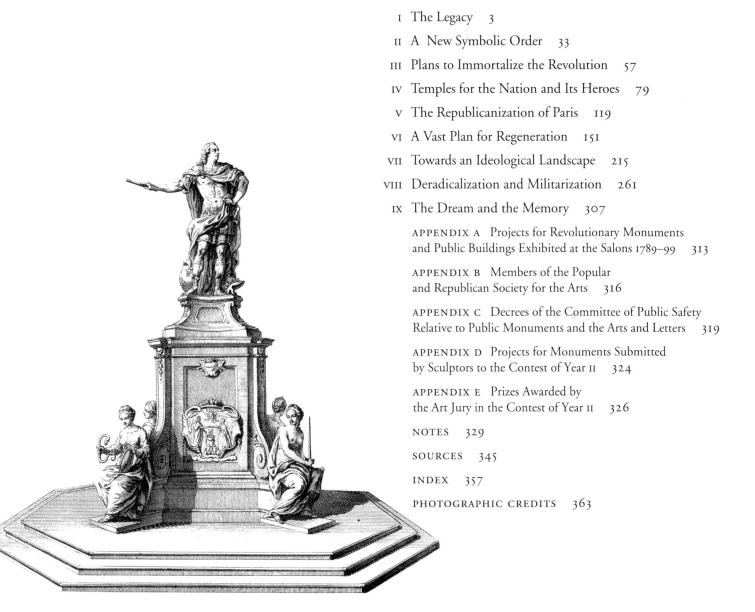

FIGURES

IV TEMPLES FOR THE NATION AND ITS HEROES

VII TOWARDS AN IDEOLOGICAL LANDSCAPE

VIII DERADICALIZATION AND MILITARIZATION

IX THE DREAM AND THE MEMORY

ACKNOWLEDGMENTS

I WOULD LIKE FIRST OF ALL to thank the various bodies that have funded the research that made this study possible. The Advisory Research Committee of the School of Graduate Studies and Research at my own university, Queen's University in Kingston, Ontario, Canada, provided me with "seed money" to begin the project. The Social Sciences and Humanities Research Council of Canada made possible a number of summer research excursions to collections in France, England, and North America. The project, however, would have been prolonged greatly without two years free from teaching and administration provided by a Research Fellowship granted by the Killam Program of the Canada Council.

I would like to thank M Giles Lefebvre, who, as associate director of the Canada Council, intervened on my behalf to gain access to thirty-odd revolutionary designs "discovered" in 1984 in a public collection in Paris about which I was not informed despite a visit after they were identified and to which I was refused immediate access when I learned about them. Others who intervened to obtain access to this and other collections were Mme Nicole Villa Sébline, then Bibliothécaire-en-chef of the Louvre; M G.-H.-J. Duquay, Ministre d'Affaires Culturelles of the Canadian Embassy in Paris; and Mme Adrienne Clarkson, then Agente Générale de l'Ontario in France.

I am otherwise very much indebted to a number of librarians and curators in Paris: Mme Laure Beaumont of the Département des Estampes of the Bibliothèque Nationale; Mlle Danielle Le Nan and Mlle Aline Locker of the Département des Périodiques of the same library; Mme Jacqueline Sanson of the Service Photographique also of the same library; Mme Nicole Felkay of the Cartes et Plans section of the Archives Nationales; Mme Lafitte-Larnaudie, the curator of archives of the Institut National; and M J.-P. Willesme of the Musée Carnavalet. M Werner Szambien, a researcher in architectural history with the Conseil National de la Recherche Scientifique, guided me to some sources in Germany that I might have missed.

Since most cities in the departments of France have departmental archives, municipal archives, a municipal library, an art museum, and specialized collections as well, it is impossible to thank all those who assisted me in the provinces. However, a few individuals were exceptionally helpful: M Xavier Lavagne in Aix, M Jacques Foucard-Boville in Amiens, Mme Annie Scottez in Lille, M Lacave in Montpellier, M Daniel Samson in Nantes, and M Baronte in Toulon.

In Canada Claudette Hould of the Université du Québec à Montréal has given me invaluable assistance. Several scholars and librarians at my own university have been especially helpful as well: Michèle Lalancette of the Department of History; Pierre du Prey of the Department of Art; Joan Hansen of the Art Library; and Anthony Riley of the German Department, who helped me to obtain photographs from Munich and Weimar.

Finally, I would like to thank Sharon Judd for her invaluable help in preparing the text for publication.

SPACE AND REVOLUTION

Boullée. Project for a cenotaph to Newton. (Figure 20)

I

THE LEGACY

T HIS BOOK IS NOT A HISTORY of art or architecture as such in France from 1789 to 1799, useful and enlightening though such a study might be; rather it is an attempt by a historian to analyse how the French revolutionaries attempted to use monuments, squares, and public buildings as instruments in their efforts to create a new order. Historians of the French Revolution have recently expanded the scope of what needs to be encompassed in any analysis of this upheaval, which in so many ways opened the modern era. They have emphasized the need not only to examine the political events and institutional changes but to look at all aspects of the new political culture – the rhetoric, the symbols, the rituals, the novel ways in which people related to each other, the involvement of new groups in politics, and so on. In the period since the Second World War there have been new studies of art, music, theatre, and festivals, all of which were integral parts of the revolutionary political culture. There have also been some studies of architecture,[1] but there has been no study comparable to that of Anatole Kopp on Soviet architecture and urbanism in the 1920s[2] or those by Barbara Miller Lane[3] and Robert R. Taylor[4] of Nazi architecture and urbanism in the 1930s.

Revolution might be defined simply as an effort to use force or the threat of force to achieve an abrupt change in the existing order. Such attempts vary greatly in nature and depth. There is the abortive revolution, which is suppressed before it has accomplished very much. There is the palace revolution or coup, in which one group ousts another and takes its place without changing much else, although sometimes extensive changes may follow. Then there is the political revolution, in which some groups previously excluded from power aim at achieving increased representation or influence. Also there is the social revolution, in which the leaders attempt to alter the very social structure and the relation of various social groups to each other. Or there is the economic revolution, not in the sense of a change in the system of production or in technology but in the sense of an attempt to change control over or ownership of the means of production. But revolution in the deepest sense of the word involves many of these meanings and more: the attempt to impose a whole new paradigm on society. This in turn involves changing citizens' attitudes, values, and beliefs – in short, creating a novel sort of individual suited to the new order.

If this definition is correct, revolution in the deepest meaning of the word obviously requires re-education of the masses, consequently a concerted program of persuasion or propaganda. There are two basic kinds of propaganda, one that might be called agitational propaganda, and another that might be called integrational propaganda. The former is used primarily to discredit and dislodge some group, party, or class and what it stands for. It is essentially negative, striving to arouse gut resentment, especially sheer hatred. It often aims at stirring up the populace, provoking demonstrations and violence. However, once revolutionaries have succeeded in seizing power, they are prone to shift to propaganda that is no longer aimed at inciting opposition but at engendering support for the novel order, at integrating the masses around the new leaders and institutions. Of course these two sorts of propaganda often operate simultaneously, the campaign to undermine the old regime being combined with the effort to rally people around the new objectives. Nevertheless, there is a shift in emphasis as the revolutionaries seek to consolidate the new regime.

The use of the word "propaganda" in this study must be made clear at the beginning. There are two assumptions about the term that have become widespread as the result of the propaganda disseminated by Nazi Germany, Stalinist Russia, and other twentieth-century regimes. The first assumption is that propaganda is usually organized by the state. While this is often true, it is by no means always the case. In Old Regime France alone one can think of important movements that employed propaganda but were not organized by the central government – indeed were often opposed by it. Some of the intellectuals in eighteenth-century France waged a campaign against the dogmas and authority of the Catholic church, a campaign that was an anathema to the monarchical government.[5] Voltaire, who played a leading role in this effort to crush *l'infâme*, as he called it, was a skilled propagandist, using essays, short stories, plays, and poems to get his message across. Because his ideas were offensive to the government, Voltaire had to pass the last part of his life at Ferney near the Swiss border, across which he could flee if need arose. Later, on the eve of the Revolution pamphleteers such as the Abbé Sieyès, who campaigned for greater representation for the Third Estate or commoners, were propagandists outside of government control. In the contemporary world one could cite many other examples of voluntary, non-governmental organizations that employ propaganda in favour of civil rights, against nuclear weapons, in support of women's rights, and so on.

The second widespread assumption is that propaganda involves the calculated dissemination of lies or distortions. This too has often been the case: Goebbels frequently spread falsehoods to promote the Nazi cause, as did his contemporary Stalin and other modern leaders. Admittedly, propaganda only presents one side of a case, since its aim is to arouse ardent support for a cause, but this does not mean that propagandists always consciously disseminate lies and distortions. The Catholic church, which gave us the term "propaganda" when it established the Congregation for the Propagation of the Faith in 1622, did not think it was propagating untruths. Voltaire believed he was attacking real superstitions and abuses when he lampooned the Catholic church and revealed religions in general. Also, on the eve of the Revolution the pamphleteers who attacked the power of the First and Second Estates, the clergy and the nobility, on behalf of the commoners of the Third Estate thought that they were making fair and justifiable claims. Likewise, concerned citizens who campaign for the rights of blacks, for the freedom of women to choose abortions, or against the slaughter of seal pups obviously believe in their causes. In this study, therefore, the word is used to mean any attempt to turn people against something or to rally them around something else, whether this effort is made by government leaders or by individuals wishing to support a particular cause.

Closely related to the use of agitational and integrational propaganda are other revolutionary processes that also have negative and positive dimensions: the process of delegitimization or desacralization of the old order, followed by relegitimization or resacralization of the new one. The first process attempts to strip away the aura of legitimacy and sanctity surrounding the old ruler and institutions. In Old Regime France the legitimacy of rule by the king was not only based on inheritance of authority through the male line but also on the claim that he ruled by the grace of God, a claim affirmed on coins and the seals of state. The coronation reinforced this belief when the new heir was anointed with oil from the Sainte Ampoule, the Holy Ampulla, said to have been brought down from heaven by a dove to anoint Clovis. At first the French revolutionaries did

not repudiate the king as head of state, although they added consent of the nation to the grace of God, but they soon began to treat the figure of Liberty and revolutionary symbols with reverence. Then, when they overthrew the monarch and executed him, an act that combined patricide with regicide, they had to try further to surround the new institutions and ideals with an aura of legitimacy and sanctity. Although the French Revolution is often interpreted as a stage in the secularization of society, Frenchmen were so used to religious terms and rituals that they continued to use them to establish the claims of the new order.

In applying these techniques of agitational and integrational propaganda, or delegitimization and relegitimization, revolutionary leaders can use monuments and architecture in a number of basic ways. By sanctioning or promoting the destruction of existing monuments and the eradication of old symbols and inscriptions on public buildings, revolutionary leaders can give to the public a vivid example of the repudiation of the old order. Then they can promote the conversion of old buildings or the erection of new structures that will represent the pre-eminence of the revolutionary movement or the new regime. These edifices, old and new, can be used to communicate messages to the public by means of low-reliefs, statues, and inscriptions. "Grand monuments should make great impressions," declared a member of an art jury at the peak of the Revolution; "the walls must speak; maxims should turn our buildings into moral textbooks."[6] Even without such statuary and inscriptions, buildings could convey a message by their style, size, and positioning.

The positioning of the monument or building links it to urban planning. In addition to choosing prominent sites for revolutionary monuments, attention can be focused on them and people can be directed towards them by the layout of streets, boulevards, and squares. Moreover, the squares and buildings can be designed to accommodate revolutionary ceremonies such as parades, spectacles, and rallies. At the same time leaders can demonstrate their concern for the welfare of the citizenry by promoting public facilities such as spacious parks, broader streets, plentiful fountains, bath-houses, hospitals, libraries, schools, theatres, museums, and so on. Some modern revolutionary movements have promoted housing that would not only be healthier and more comfortable but would lead to a new way of life – for instance, the apartments designed by the early Bolsheviks to promote communal living. The French revolutionaries used most, if not all, of these techniques.

Knowing by hindsight that a great upheaval was to take place in France during the final decade of the eighteenth century, the historian is tempted to show that all trends led up to that event. Yielding to this temptation

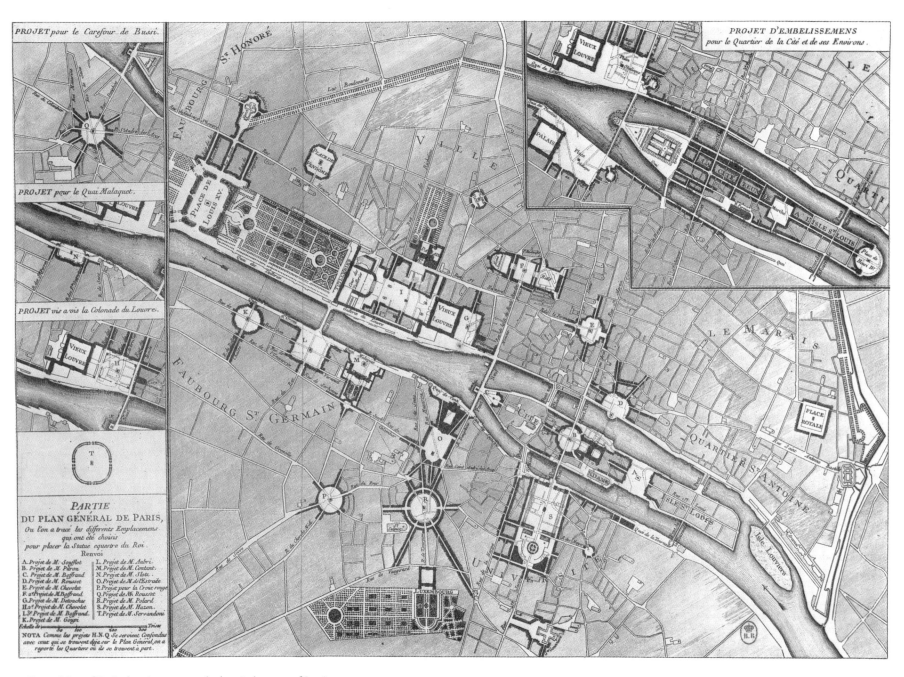

1 Patte. Map of Paris showing proposed *places* in honour of Louis xv.

STATUE DE LOUIS XV A NANCI,

Composée et Exécutée en Bronze par M. Guibal.

Plan du Piédestal.

Echelle de 4 Toises pour le Piédestal.

2 Guibal and Cyfflé. Statue of Louis xv in Nancy.

obscures the fact that contemporaries had a sense of choice, the opportunity to make decisions, the chance to select various avenues to the future. And once revolution broke out, again not everything that happened was necessarily inevitable. Once more actors felt that they had some freedom to shape events, that they were not merely subject to great impersonal forces. In looking at the developments in the old regime on the eve of the Revolution, it is therefore probably better to analyse a number of trends from which revolutionary leaders could choose what they thought would be useful to them or that they thought they could adapt to their needs. In this way we can do justice to continuities without denying groups and individuals their role in making their own history. Our intention here is to call attention to some of the major legacies from which the revolutionaries could make their selection. The repertory of ideas on which they could draw was rich and complex; we can only highlight some of the most important elements.

For this study one of the most important legacies of the eighteenth century was the evolving nature of the public square. Public squares in French and other European cities are now so much a part of the urban landscape that we are apt to forget that their advent was an important stage in the history of urbanism. Medieval cities grew up in a haphazard fashion in which open spaces were often accidental rather than the result of conscious planning. Even the great cathedrals that dominated the horizons of such cities usually had very little space around them to set them off and to allow the public to get an overall view of them, especially to encompass their rich façades. In many cases the space in front and around them is the result of later planning, usually involving the destruction of ancient buildings that had cluttered their surroundings.[7] As authorities in the seventeenth and eighteenth centuries became increasingly conscious of the possibility of planning urban space, a number of spacious public squares were created, often with the surrounding buildings planned to provide a uniform frame for the monument in the centre.

In Paris the earliest such planned public squares tended to be enclosed areas cut into or added to the old matrix of streets and alleys, enclosures visible only from a restricted number of angles. The Place Dauphine, created in the reign of Henry IV, is a triangular *place* at the western end of the Ile de la Cité in the centre of the Seine, with the statue of the king outside the apex next to the Pont Neuf. The square is only visible through the opening in the apex or after one enters it through one of the inconspicuous openings at the other end. In this case the statue is visible from the square only if one is aligned with it exactly through the opening in the apex. The Place Royale, now called the Place des Vosges, ordered built in 1605 by Henry IV, is another enclosure largely cut off from the maze of streets in the Marais district of old Paris. One has to enter the square from almost hidden passages in the corners in order to get a view of it. The octagonal Place Louis-le-Grand, now known as the Place Vendôme, with the monument in the centre, is likewise visible from the outside only if one is in line with the entrances at either end. Then one can see the monument, originally Louis XIV on horseback and now a towering column in honour of Napoleon, but one cannot see the framework of the surrounding buildings. These early squares were thus to a large extent cut off from the surrounding city.

During the eighteenth century the public square tended to be conceived of as more open and more linked to its setting. This could be achieved by creating the square on the banks of a river, as was done at the Place Royale in Bordeaux, now the Place de la Bourse, which is open along the Garonne. The greatest square created in the century, the Place Louis XV in Paris, now rechristened the Place de la Concorde, is open on three sides, but especially along the Seine. One can view it and the monument in the centre, originally a statue of the king but now an obelisk, from the other side of the river or from the bridge leading to the square from the Left Bank. The square is also quite visible from the Tuileries Garden to the east and the Champs-Elysées to the west. Other squares created in the second half of the eighteenth century, such as the Place Stanislas in Nancy or the Place Royale in Reims, are opened up by entrances on three or four sides.

The radiating square, the kind with streets fanning out in different directions, is the most closely linked to the surrounding city. This shape, which owed much to the classical formal garden with paths diverging from a statue or fountain, had already appeared in Paris with construction of the Place des Victoires, which was inaugurated in 1686. The radiating square grew increasingly popular as the eighteenth century wore on, as we can see from Pierre Patte's map showing squares in honour of Louis XV that had been proposed by various architects (Figure 1).[8] Several are circular, others semicircular. The revolutionaries would later find this shape especially attractive since it links the square to its neighbourhood both physically and psychologically, and at the same time makes the monument in the centre visible from a number of angles. The Place de l'Etoile, where the Arc de Triomphe can be seen from a dozen avenues that abut on the square, is a familiar example of a later application of this principle.

As the conception of the public square evolved, so too did that of the monument in the centre or nearby. The statues of kings erected in

3 Bouchardon. Statue of Louis XV in Paris.

the seventeenth century often showed them as conquerors, looming over the rivals they had defeated. Even the statue of the most popular of French kings, that of Henry IV sculpted by Pierre de Francheville, which was inaugurated next to the Place Dauphine in 1614, showed the king on horseback with chained figures at his feet. Similarly, the statue of Louis XIV by Martin Van den Bogaert, known as Desjardins, for the Place des Victoires showed the king being crowned by Victory, again with four captive effigies around the base. During the Enlightenment, these images of the ruler as conqueror came under attack. In *Le Siècle de Louis* XIV Voltaire tried to excuse the chained figures by claiming that they could represent vices suppressed just as well as nations conquered, but admitted that it would have been preferable to see free and happy citizens in their place.[9] In his *Dictionnaire géographique* Jean-Joseph Expilly wrote that "in the present century one prefers to transmit to posterity monuments to goodness and beneficence."[10]

In response to the new expectations of the Enlightenment there was a significant change in the depiction of the king: the ruler was portrayed less as a military conqueror and more as a benevolent legislator.[11] For the Place Stanislas in Nancy, Barthélémy Guibal and Paul-Louis Cyfflé did a statue of Louis XV in 1755 with allegorical figures representing Clemency, Force, Justice, and Prudence around the pedestal (Figure 2).[12] Then, for the new Place Louis XV in Paris, Edme Bouchardon did a statue, inaugurated in 1763, showing the king on horseback but much less imperious than that of his predecessor on the Place Louis-le-Grand (Figure 3). Jean-Baptiste Pigalle later completed the monument with figures at the base similar to those in Nancy, except that Peace replaced Clemency, which was appropriate since the Seven Years' War had just ended.[13] Even more significant was the statue of the same king by Pigalle for the new Place Royale in Reims, a statue inaugurated in 1765 (Figure 4).[14] There the king was shown on foot, accompanied by a woman leading a lion by its mane, to signify the Gentleness of Government, and by a male figure representing a Citizen, seated in a contemplative pose with a purse in his hand and sack of grain at his side. This tendency to represent the king as a beneficent ruler was to continue into the Revolution, when it was hoped that Louis XVI would become the father of his people. When the king became discredited and overthrown, the allegorical figures could be moved up to replace him atop the pedestal.

Not only was the portrayal of the monarch in the centre of royal squares evolving in keeping with the ideals of the Enlightenment, but at the same time the idea was emerging that he should share public space with great men. Although the king would still be the focal point, he would be encircled by men who had served him and the nation well. Planners

believed that such public recognition of outstanding individuals would inspire others to emulate them. Behind this idea of the *place d'émulation* was a growing sense of national patriotism that became evident after the middle of the eighteenth century, especially a sense of pride in the distinguished citizens the nation had produced.[15] Books about French heroes with titles such as *Plutarque français, Histoire du patriotisme français*, or *Annales pittoresques de la vertu française* became increasingly common after the mid-century. Two of the proposals submitted to the contest in 1748 for a new square in Paris in honour of Louis XV, the contest that produced the one now called Place de la Concorde, embodied the impulse to associate the king with great men.

The architect and scenographer Jean-Jérôme Servandoni proposed an amphitheatre on the outskirts of Paris to accommodate royal festivities – celebrating marriages, births, victories, and peace treaties – which were already developing into large-scale public events. We shall discuss the significance of the amphitheatre later; here it is important to note that while there was to be a statue of the king in the centre, there were also to be statues of worthy Frenchmen at intervals around the periphery. As Pierre Patte pointed out in his book on monuments in honour of Louis XV, the message was that the king was the focal point, the source from which everything emanated and to which everything returned.[16] It was significant, however, that great men were to share his glory, even if only the reflected glory around the circumference, like planets illuminated by the light of the sun. The crowd gathered on the surrounding benches was to identify with these heroes and to emulate them.[17] Several pedestals were to be left vacant purposely in order to arouse the ambition to occupy them some day, an idea we shall find repeated often later in the century.

This idea of a *place d'émulation* was not limited to the outskirts of Paris. For the same contest of 1748 Patte himself proposed an analogous scheme for the Pont Neuf, the bridge in the very heart of old Paris that joins the Left and Right banks of the Seine, cutting across the western tip of the Ile de la Cité (Figure 5). It was near the spot where the bridge traverses the end of the island that the statue of Henry IV stood. The bridge features semicircular exedras on each side that project out over the water. Patte proposed to display bronze statues of great Frenchmen on these protrusions. At the same time he suggested cutting a semicircular square into the apex of the *place* with a statue of Louis XV atop a column in the centre, placed so that it would face that of Henry. Once again the king would appear in the centre, this time with rows of great men to his left and right. As Richard Etlin has pointed out, the Abbé Laugier subsequently extended the idea of honouring great men to the whole city.[18] He

4 Pigalle. Statue of Louis xv in Reims.

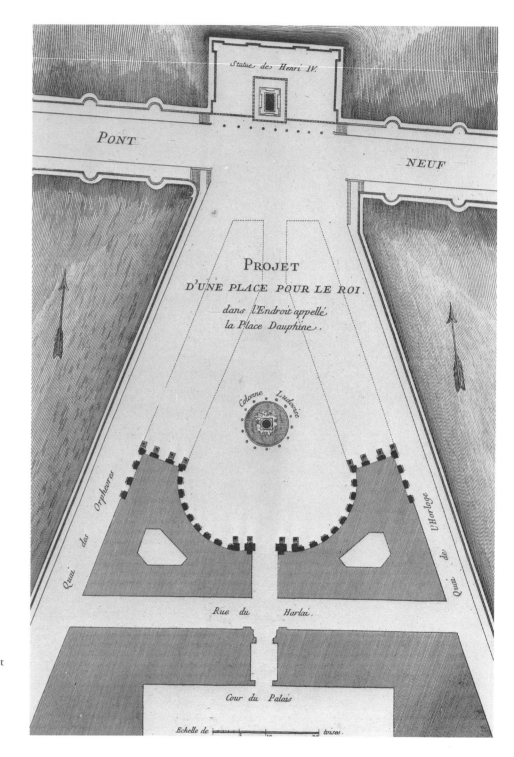

5 Patte. Plan for the point of the Ile de la Cité and the Pont
   Neuf.

proposed that all public buildings have halls dedicated to illustrious men. The entire city would in this way be turned into a history textbook aimed at inspiring great deeds, an interesting precedent for revolutionaries.

At the same time architects were designing various squares for different sites throughout Paris in honour of Louis XV, another architect was proposing a striking entrance to the city that would honour great men. Nicolas-Henri Jardin, a *pensionnaire* of the French Academy in Rome as winner of the Grand Prix in architecture in 1741, proposed a sepulchral chapel in 1747 and a triumphal bridge the following year, which both were to be located at the edge of the city (Figures 6, 7). The bridge was to acclaim the hero returning to the city, and the chapel with its surrounding cemetery was to commemorate the celebrated dead.[19] From the country a broad avenue lined with mausoleums, all honouring the worthy dead, was to lead to the chapel. It was to be set in a circular *place*, the two halves of which would suggest the meeting of country and city. The half next to the country was to be ringed with cypress trees encompassing a row of funerary monuments, while the half next to the city was to contain a covered promenade crowned with statues. The idea of a modern Via Appia, the Roman route lined with the tombs of patricians, and that of a grandiose entrance to the city were both to produce several variants before the end of the century.

Jardin's project for a sepulchral chapel surrounded by monuments and statues was one sign of changing attitudes towards death and the cemetery.[20] In the last half of the eighteenth century there was a widespread revulsion against the lugubrious Christian cemetery, featuring images of Death, in favour of a more humanistic conception of a burial ground. Like many of the projects for royal squares, those for cemeteries frequently arranged space so as to honour great men as well as the king, implying that through greatness one could transcend death. For example, the design by Léon Dufourny, awarded a Prix d'émulation by the Academy in 1778, featured a cenotaph to Henry IV in the centre of a courtyard framed by a segmented columnar screen on three sides (Figures 8, 9).[21] The openings in this screen were to lead into chapels honouring great men that would form exedra-like projections along the exterior walls. The entrance to the quadrangle from the large forecourt was to be flanked by two winged figures representing Fame, one with a trumpet, the other with a wreath of Immortality. The proposal to confer a non-Christian version of immortality on outstanding men was one that revolutionaries could adapt easily for their purposes.

The desire to honour great men as well as the king in cemeteries,

triumphal bridges, grandiose entrances, and public squares produced projects in the provinces as well as Paris. One of the best-documented cases concerned the ongoing planning for the Place du Peyrou in Montpellier, completed in 1776. Originally the architects, Jean-Antoine Giral and Jacques Donnat, had intended to complement the statue of Louis XIV in the centre with allegorical figures on the periphery,[22] but in 1771 the Comte de Faugères wrote a memorial in which he proposed to place around the square statues of great men who had served the king well.[23] This proposal won the approval of the local Estates, which charged the architect Jean-Arnaud Raymond with executing it.

The new program combined moral goals, a taste for history, and the emerging new concept of the nation. Faugères argued that the century of Louis XIV had been a great one for the Nation (he used a capital N) because the king had known how to encourage greatness. The aim was not just to exalt royal power by commemorating glorious achievements. Faugères had another goal in mind: "It is to stimulate emulation and ambition in all those who combine the fire of genius with outstanding talents in some field, whatever it might be, by arousing the glorious hope of being placed in a similar decoration and of being numbered among the great men of the century. The soldier, the magistrate … will bring his son to this square to show him what honours he might aspire to in whatever calling he may have chosen."[24] Faugères wanted these outstanding men to be portrayed realistically in French costumes according to the fashion of the period in which they lived. He dreamt of an ensemble of no fewer than forty personages, either statues on foot or busts in low-relief, accompanied by trophies.

Faugères envisaged statues on the large pedestals already in place on the four corners of the square, accompanied by genii holding medallions bearing busts in low-relief of other heroes. Generals and admirals would occupy the large pedestals on the height of the square which struck the eye of anyone entering it, making the statues pendants to that of the king. Ministers and magistrates would occupy the large pedestals at the other end of the square. Busts of other great men would take their places around the perimeter. We know that Faugères' project was discussed in Paris and excited the interest of several sculptors, including Pigalle and Caffiéri. While one cannot speak of a contest, the records reveal that a project by Raymond was selected among those of several artists. He was asked to have made a full-size plaster model of his design for a pair of two great military leaders of the age of Louis XIV, Condé and Turenne, which was then put in place so that experts could judge the effect. Claude-Michel Clodion came to

Elevation en Perspective d'vne Chapelle Sepulcrale.

6 Jardin. Project for a sepulchral chapel.

Projet d'vn Pont Triomphal.

7 Jardin. Project for a triumphal bridge.

8, 9 Dufourny. Project for a cemetery. *Above*: elevation; *right*: ground-plan.

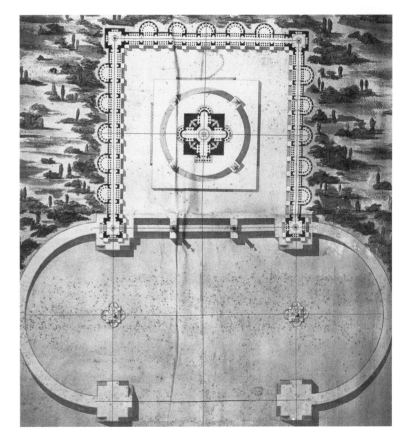

Montpellier to make this model, which he finished in November 1778, and a public debate followed.[25]

In 1780 an agreement was reached by which Raymond consented to certain changes suggested by Clodion. The statues of Condé and Turenne were to be six feet tall, executed in Carrara marble. The location of the design is now unknown, but an old photograph of it survives (Figure 10). The side of the pedestal facing the square was to be decorated with a figure of Glory in low-relief, while the other sides were to be ornamented with trophies and a tablet bearing an inscription. Clodion contracted to finish the group within three years. This deal served as the model for agreements with Augustin Pajou, Pierre Julien, and Jean-Guillaume Moitte. Whereas Clodion was to work in Paris, these sculptors agreed to come to work in Montpellier, where huge blocks of marble were to be delivered. Each of the artists was to make a preliminary model in terra cotta. The honorary curator of the Favre Museum in Montpellier has uncovered the ones by Pajou and Moitte. Pajou, the father-in-law of Clodion, was to do a group of Colbert and Duquesne, accompanied by a low-relief representing the Genius of Navigation (Figure 11). Moitte was to do statues of two great bishops, Fénelon and Bossuet, with a low-relief portraying Eloquence (Figure 12). Julien was to portray two jurists, Guillaume de Lamoignon and the Chancellor d'Aguesseau, with a low-relief portraying Justice.

Altogether around the king in the corners of the square there were to be four pairs of great men.

The project to decorate the Place de Peyrou in Montpellier was overtaken by the Revolution. Meanwhile, at the centre of France there was an important government program to honour great men and excite emulation among contemporaries. In 1774 the Comte d'Angiviller became director-general of buildings, in effect a sort of minister of fine arts. The new minister began to use royal patronage to direct painting towards noble historical themes, including episodes from French history, and to commission statues of famous Frenchmen. Between 1775 and the coming of the Revolution twenty-eight such statues were commissioned, all but one of which were completed and displayed in the biennial *salons* in the Louvre. The choice of these national heroes was conservative: ten were military commanders on land or sea; eleven were writers, philosophers, scholars, or orators, but only Rollin and Montesquieu were from the eighteenth century; three were magistrates; and one was a philanthropist and one an artist. Only one of these men was from the Middle Ages, two from the sixteenth century, seven from the reigns of Henry IV and Louis XIII, but no fewer than fifteen were from the reign of Louis XIV.[26] The radical thinkers of the eighteenth century, such as Rousseau, Voltaire, and Diderot, were conspicuously absent.

Already there was the ambition to create a national shrine by grouping such statues in one place. D'Angiviller's original idea was to place them along the great gallery of the Louvre. In the print department of the Bibliothèque Nationale there is also a design for the interior of a French museum, classified among the works of Etienne-Louis Boullée and dated at the very beginning of the Revolution (Figure 13).[27] Recently this has been attributed to Lubersac de Livron and dated 1783. It shows a sumptuous hall intended to contain ancient and modern masterpieces plus statues of great Frenchmen. A statue of Louis XVI was to mark the centre, while the other statues were to be placed against the columns encircling the hall. The arrangement proposed for public squares was thus brought indoors. The grandiose museum designed by Boullée in 1783, featuring a Temple of Fame in the centre to accommodate statues of great men, reveals a similar objective (Figures 14, 15).[28] These projects represent a transition from the program of d'Angiviller to the Pantheon created in the early years of the Revolution.

As the conception of the *place*, the central monument, and complementary statues all evolved in the last half of the century, so did that of the public building. The new conception of the public building in turn reflected the changing values of the literate classes during the heyday of

10 Raymond. Group of Condé and Turenne for the Place du Peyrou in Montpellier.

11 Pajou. Model of a group of Colbert and Duquesne for
the Place du Peyrou in Montpellier.

the Enlightenment, when desire for happiness on earth became more pronounced. Social utility became one of the chief measuring-rods for assessing
social institutions and human creations of all kinds. Utility was one of
the basic concepts pervading the *Encyclopédie*, the great repository of the
knowledge of the age and organ of the enlightened thinkers, seventeen
volumes of text published between 1751 and 1765, with four more volumes
of text added in 1776 and 1777. The emphasis on utility was clear in the
article "Fonction," where the Duc d'Aumont defined "function" as an action
corresponding to the purpose of an organ,[29] but an action that could also
be applied to morals and the arts. Since architecture is the most functional
of the arts, this notion was especially applicable to it. The projects prescribed in the sixties, seventies, and eighties for competitions among
students in the Académie Royale d'Architecture reflect the growing emphasis on buildings that would improve the quality of life. There were still
projects for palaces and churches, but they were outnumbered by projects
for hospitals, markets, schools, theatres, libraries, fountains, baths, and
amphitheatres. By continuing this trend the revolutionaries could show
that they had the interests of the public at heart.[30]

The nascent idea of functionalism demanded a rethinking of the very
nature of architecture. Just as thinkers of the period tried to understand
language and society by going back to their origins, some thinkers went
back to the hypothetical primitive hut, whose utility provided a criterion
for judging subsequent architectural inventions.[31] It was no longer
enough for an architect to achieve beauty by creating pleasing proportions
and three-dimensional shapes. Increasingly he had to combine his search
for pleasing geometrical forms with consideration for the dictates of society
and the environment. The objectives of social improvement and social
control had to be taken into consideration in laying out ground-plans and
dividing up space. There was already an inkling of the twentieth-century
notion of the architect as a social engineer. The new considerations are
evident in the designs by various architects for prisons, public baths, hospitals, and factories, but they can be seen best of all in Claude-Nicolas
Ledoux's plan for a whole factory village in Chaux (Figure 16). This centre
for the production of salt, which was built between 1774 and 1779, was
laid out so that the managers could easily oversee the whole operation,
workers could move freely from one part to another, both people and salt
would be sheltered from the elements, the living quarters would engender a sense of community, and winds would be able to freshen the air.[32]

It is surprising that some studies of the emergence of social purpose
in architecture have not paid more attention to the amphitheatre as an
instrument for creating certain relationships among the people assembling

in it, whether in an indoor auditorium or in a vast outdoor enclosure.[33] We have seen that Servandoni proposed a vast amphitheatre on the outskirts of Paris capable of accommodating huge crowds during national festivals, but there were many such projects. The programs for competitions among students in the Académie Royale d'Architecture frequently called for immense amphitheatres, hippodromes, or circuses. For example, in 1769 Jean-Jacob Guerne won a prize for facilities in which to celebrate the marriage of a prince, including a semicircular amphitheatre facing a Temple to Hymen;[34] in 1781 Jean-Nicolas Sobre won a prize for buildings on a waterfront to accommodate a festival celebrating peace, again with a semicircular amphitheatre;[35] in 1782 Charles-François Callet won a prize for a vast circus in which to stage games in celebration of the birth of a prince;[36] in 1783 Antoine-Laurent-Thomas Vaudoyer won a prize for a menagerie of a prince with a large arena in the centre (Figure 17);[37] and in 1787 Reverchon won a prize for an immense hippodrome.[38] Not only was the frequency of such projects for outdoor facilities increasing on the eve of the Revolution, but indoor amphitheatres occurred in plans for a riding-school in 1759, a medical school in 1775, and a building to house the academies in 1786.[39] Also, amphitheatres had actually been built in the Halle au Blé and the Ecole de Chirurgie.

The designs by Etienne-Louis Boullée for an immense coliseum for l'Etoile at the west end of the Champs-Elysées are especially revealing, although their precise date is uncertain (Figures 18, 19).[40] The designs seem related to the plans for amphitheatres submitted by students in the Academy of Architecture and other such plans in the 1760s, 1770s, and 1780s. In his notes Boullée also alludes to certain festivals staged in Paris where only one one-hundredth of the population of the city could participate, obviously allusions to celebrations in the final decades of the old regime. Yet the notes are full of the spirit of the early Revolution.[41] Perhaps the designs date from the 1780s, while the notes were written later. Boullée praised the Roman Coliseum as one of the most beautiful in Italy because its mass formed a majestic and impressive whole, but he felt that its decoration was not in keeping with good architecture and that it did not fulfil its purpose completely. Instead, therefore, of confining himself to simple restorations, he decided to create a new design suited to contemporary needs.[42] Like some other plans of the period, his designs called for a huge amphitheatre, in this case with large radiating entrances under low vaults, ringed with peristyles and flanked by Trojan-like columns.

In his notes Boullée emphasized the political, social, and moral benefits of mass celebrations staged in a huge enclosure. Here he referred to a series of papers read to the Academy of Inscriptions and Belles-Lettres

12 Moitte. Model of a group of Bossuet and Fénelon for the Place du Peyrou in Montpellier.

13 Lubersac de Livron. Projected French museum.

14, 15 Boullée. Project for a museum. *Above*: elevation; *below*: view of the interior.

16 Ledoux. View of the factory village of Chaux.

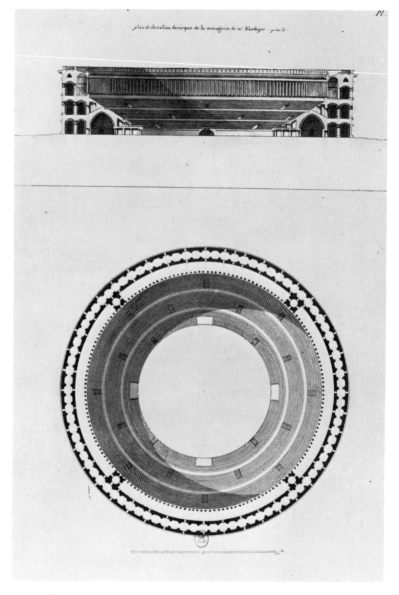

17 Vaudoyer. Project for an arena in the menagerie of a prince.

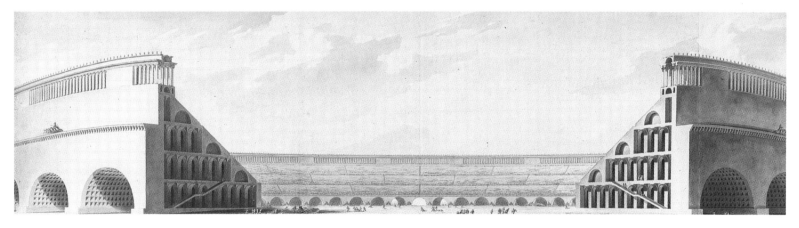

18, 19 Boullée. Project for a coliseum. *Above*: view of the exterior; *below*: view of the interior.

in 1781 by the Abbé Brotier, who had analysed at length the political use the Romans had made of circuses. It was the circus, not the theatre, the abbé had argued, that had been at the heart of Roman life. It was at the circus that the Romans rallied in time of adversity, and it was there that they had celebrated their victories.[43] Inspired by this prototype, Boullée envisaged festivals in contemporary France where up to three hundred thousand citizens would gather in a vast amphitheatre where no one could escape the view of the crowd. There athletic contests would be held, prizes awarded by academies would be distributed, distinguished authors would be crowned, and outstanding farmers would be honoured. "Thus it seems to me," wrote Boullée, "that through such truly national celebrations, organized to uplift the soul, we would succeed in bringing back a sense of morals."[44]

As the idea grew that public buildings should serve the people, so too did the notion that they could educate the people as well. There were some authors such as the historian and philosophe Marc-Antoine Laugier who treated architecture purely as structure. He traced all the basic elements of architecture back to the structure of the primitive hut: the upright supports were the beginnings of columns; the horizontal members were the first entablatures; and the sloping roof beams created rudimentary pediments.[45] Most philosophes and architects, however, believed that architecture was much more than structure; it was a kind of language, a system of signs. Like other languages it consisted of conventions, many of them derived from classical antiquity, but it could also employ universal stereometric forms and the natural effects of light and shade. By manipulating these signs one could convey ideas of rank, indicate the use of a building, and arouse emotions. In contrast to Laugier, Jean-Louis Viel de Saint-Maux contended that all the elements of architecture were originally symbolic.[46]

Belief in the symbolic and educational role of architecture was reinforced by the proliferation of Masonic lodges in the last half of the eighteenth century. As Anthony Vidler has pointed out, over 120 architects belonged to various lodges.[47] Among these Masonic architects were some who were to be very active in the revolutionary decade – Alexandre-Théodore Brongniart, Jacques Cellérier, Jean-François Chalgrin, Jean-Jacques Lequeu, Bernard Poyet, Quatremère de Quincy, Jean-Baptiste Rondelet, and Charles de Wailly. For Masons God was the Great Architect, the lodge itself was modelled on Solomon's temple in Jerusalem, and building was a metaphor for the re-establishment of a natural social order. "Artisans of our own happiness," stated the Masonic writer Couret de Villeneuve in 1748, "we work on Plans traced by Nature and compassed by Reason, to construct a moral universe, the model of which, executed in the first ages of the world, we have preserved by the universal ideas of the [Masonic] Order."[48] Not only were Masonic symbols – pyramids, equilateral triangles, carpenter's levels, starry vaults, and all-seeing eyes – to become widespread, but the emphasis on regeneration and on communal life would draw on their rituals and lodges, both to be promoted by architecture.

In discussing how architects in the later eighteenth century tried to make buildings communicate to the public, modern historians have often used the term "architecture parlante."[49] Contemporaries, however, usually spoke of giving buildings a distinctive "caractère." By their size, shape, materials, and decoration, buildings could convey their purpose to the public. Etienne-Louis Boullée argued that architecture should be a kind of poetry, using imagery based on a profound study of nature to display the function of each building. In an introductory section of his notes addressed to those who cultivate the arts, he emphasized this view: "That is my belief. Our buildings – and our public buildings in particular – should be to some extent poems," he argued; "the impression they make on us should arouse in us sensations that correspond to the function of the building in question."[50] Then, in the section on "caractère" that followed in his notes, he urged architects to make judicious use of all the means at their disposal so that each building would arouse only those sensations that were related to its purpose.[51]

Boullée's projects show how he tried to give each structure an appropriate character. He designed a cenotaph to Newton in the form of a giant sphere pierced with apertures so as to turn it into a sort of planetarium, reminding the viewer of how the great scientist had explored the motion of the planets and the stars (Figure 20). His design for a Palace of Justice featured prisons in the form of pavilions on the four corners in order to provide "an imposing image of vices overcome by the weight of justice."[52] Claude-Nicolas Ledoux carried the idea of giving each building a suitable character to extremes. One of his woodcutters' houses was made out of horizontal logs rising out of a square base. The interior of his workshop for coopers was organized as a series of circles with a round hole in the centre, reminding the workers constantly of the hoops with which they bound barrels together. His proposed quarters for engineers of the Loüe River took the form of a horizontal cylinder, turning the building into a sort of drain-pipe, allowing the engineers to survey the river as it coursed through their residence. His houses of pleasure for Paris and Chaux featured phallic shapes. When the Revolution erupted in 1789 the idea of imposing a distinctive character on buildings could be applied to National Assemblies, temples to revolutionary ideals, and public monuments.

In the attempt to give buildings a suitable *caractère* there were new stylistic trends available to architects in the closing decades of the Old Regime. One of these has been labelled "neoclassical" by modern art historians. Artists had, of course, been exploiting classical prototypes since the Renaissance, but there were many aspects of classical architecture that had not been fully known or exploited. Knowledge of its principles had been derived chiefly from the one text available, the treatise by Vitruvius, who reduced architectural design to the rule of orders. Architectural remains

20 Boullée. Project for a cenotaph to Newton.

had been largely interpreted according to that rule, but gradually a wider knowledge of classical architecture had accumulated. Renewed enthusiasm for classical antiquity was stirred by excavations of Roman ruins at Pompeii and Herculaneum and by the beginnings of archaeological research in Greece by James Stewart and Nicholas Revett in 1751. By the 1760s there was no longer any question of keeping to Vitruvian rules. "We read Vitruvius without understanding him," wrote the architect Marie-Joseph Peyre in 1765; "though the Romans confined themselves to following five orders, they were more attached to the principles which they laid down for the general proportions of *solids* and *voids*."[53]

The return to antiquity was also related to a powerful reaction against the rococo style, which had flowered in the reign of Louis XV, and the values associated with it. After the mid-century there was a rejection of rococo curves, curlicues, and subtleties in favour of a more severe and chastened classical style. A similar trend can be seen in the decorative arts, sculpture, painting, and architecture. In architecture there was a process of purification and clarification. This trend towards a simpler, more severe style would appeal to planners during the Revolution, with their desire

to emulate the early Romans and to turn Paris into a modern Rome. Neoclassical artists also sought to ground their art on principles that would appeal not just to people in one country at a particular time but to all people at all times.[54] Such desire for universality was also ideally suited to a revolution that claimed to be for all the world, even though it was led by France. This universalism existed in tension with the rising national patriotism we called attention to earlier.

There was also a shift away from the rococo conception of architecture as primarily a matter of creating intimate informal environments on a small scale to a taste for designing huge public buildings in imposing settings. This shift in scale was not just the result of newly discovered Roman remains but of looking in a new way at buildings that had been available for all to see since the Renaissance. For instance, when Peyre went to Italy in 1751 as the first winner of the Prix de Rome, he studied the most impressive buildings constructed by the Roman emperors, which he named as the Baths of Diocletian, Caracalla, and Titus, the Palace of the Emperors and the Villa of Hadrian. The effect of re-examining these buildings can be seen in the design he submitted to the annual contest of the

21 Boullée. Project for a cenotaph to
Turenne.

Accademia di San Luca for a large cathedral set in a huge circular colonnade, with palaces joined to the outside rim of this enclosure on two sides. When he published his studies a dozen years later he included designs for an immense building for academies and a grandiose palace for a sovereign.[55] "We are beginning to realize," he wrote, "that the monuments of the ancients were in a much grander and much more imposing style than anything which has been done ever since."[56]

Those who could not go to Rome could study the engravings of its buildings by Piranesi, which not only replaced the rococo image of antiquity but suggested new concepts of architectural space and mass.[57] The predilection for *le grandeur* can be seen in the programs laid down for contests among the students of the Académie d'Architecture and the resulting designs in the 1760s, 1770s, and 1780s. The trend towards ever more imposing buildings can be seen too in the progressive enlargement of the dome in successive designs by Jacques-Germain Soufflot in the same period for the new church of Ste-Geneviève in Paris.[58] The dome was so large that almost as soon as its construction was begun in 1776 two of the piers were discovered to be cracking. The argument over how to strengthen the supports or to lighten the dome continued through the

next two decades. The search for grandeur can perhaps be seen best of all in the plans by Boullée in the 1780s for an even more imposing royal palace at Versailles, a huge metropolitan church, and an opera complex on the Place du Carrousel between the Louvre and the Tuileries, as well as the immense museum containing a Hall of Fame and the gigantic coliseum we have already discussed. This "megalomania," as one art historian has called it,[59] would also appeal to revolutionaries anxious to impress the masses.

Related to this search for imposing architecture was the stylistic trend that grew out of neoclassicism but went beyond it, the trend that is best exemplified in the designs by Boullée, Ledoux, and Lequeu. Emil Kaufmann labelled these three "revolutionary" architects, and some other architectural historians have adopted the term.[60] Had the French Revolution not erupted during the lifetimes of these architects, they would probably have been called "avant-garde" rather than revolutionary. The term suggests that they and their designs had an affinity to the Revolution, but none of them proved to be very revolutionary in the social and political sense after 1789. Boullée did do some designs of public buildings early in the Revolution, then retreated to the sidelines and was attacked as a member of a reactionary clique during the Terror.[61] Ledoux was imprisoned at the peak of the Revolution, a fate not very surprising for a man whose best-known works under the Old Regime were customs gates around Paris for use by the hated tax farmers. And Lequeu entered some projects in the contest opened by the Commitee of Public Safety in the spring of 1794, but later wrote "drawing to save me from the guillotine" on the back of one of them.[62] This should warn us that artists who make radical innovations in painting or architecture do not necessarily support radical change in society.

This is not to deny that Boullée, Ledoux, and Lequeu often broke radically from baroque and rococo. They often violated the well-balanced harmony among the various parts, which was part of the traditional canon, in order to establish the autonomy of the parts. They also repudiated animism, which had given birth to so many caryatides and Atlantes in baroque and rococo works, in order to exploit the qualities of the materials themselves. Their search for plainness and monumentality often seems to link them to twentieth-century architects. Above all they utilized basic stereometric forms – cubes, spheres, pyramids, cylinders, and cones – in a new way. It was this employment of stereometric forms that could be used effectively in the design of revolutionary buildings in the political and social sense of the adjective. Boullée's plans early in the Revolution for a National Assembly and a municipal palace or city hall put the taste for massive cubes into practice. Also, his use of the sphere in his project for a Newton memorial provided a prototype for various spheric or hemispheric *temples décadaires*, Temples to Equality, and Temples to Immortality during the Revolution. And the pyramid he used in his design for a cenotaph for Turenne was to be used repeatedly in funerary monuments for revolutionary martyrs and soldiers who had died for the Fatherland (Figure 21).

Besides bequeathing the idea of buildings dedicated to the service of the public, the notion of giving such buildings a distinctive *caractère*, and the stylistic trends that would assist in this task, the Old Regime passed on precedents for some specific projects promoted by the Revolution. The most important of these were plans to level the Bastille and to use the site to erect a monument, create one or more new squares, and provide various public facilities. For example, in 1783 the *Courier du Bas-Rhin* published excerpts from a forthcoming book by Simon-Nicolas-Henri Linguet recounting the injustice and cruelty of incarceration in the prison where the author had recently spent nineteen months. Linguet was sure that Louis XVI would terminate such evils when they were revealed to him. The newspaper then proceeded to put forward a proposal that it thought would

22 Linguet. Frontispiece of his *Mémoires sur la Bastille*.

be supported by every good Frenchman, indeed by every citizen of the world: to liberate those imprisoned in the Bastille, judge them according to the law, raze the walls of the prison, and put in its place a monument to the king. Such a monument to the destruction of the Bastille would, the editor urged, do more to immortalize his memory than the most glorious victories and dazzling conquests.[63]

Taking up this suggestion, Linguet published a design for such a monument as the frontispiece of his book (Figure 22).[64] It shows a statue of

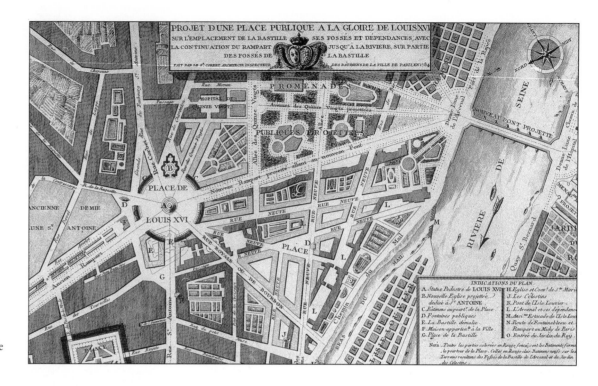

23 Corbet. Plan for the site of the Bastille
in 1784.

the king standing next to the crumbling walls of the prison. He extends his arms in goodwill towards some of the prisoners he has just released. On the pedestal one sees the inscription that the journal had proposed:

TO LOUIS XVI ON THE SITE OF THE BASTILLE

In the background lightning strikes the clock-tower of the prison, evidently suggesting divine condemnation. On the wall is a declaration by the king that once the secret punishments that had taken place there no longer served to uphold public order by example, they had become useless to his justice. Underneath the frontispiece the king is quoted as saying to the liberated prisoners, "Be free, live." A year later an architect named Corbet, an inspector of buildings for the City of Paris, designed a radiating square honouring Louis XVI on the site, with a church dedicated to St Antoine on the eastern side (Figure 23).[65] The plan included a park, public fountains, port facilities, and a new bridge across the Seine. Also there are fragments in the Archives Nationales of two alternative plans for the site, again showing radiating squares, tree-lined avenues, port facilties, and a bridge linking the Right and Left banks (Figures 24, 25).[66] One plan provides for a huge new hospital.

Planning for the area around the Louvre created another precedent for the revolutionaries. For example, Maille Dussausoy, who called himself "a disinterested citizen," published a two-volume work in 1767 in which he proposed turning the palace into a political and cultural centre.[67] At the same time he envisaged it as the place where great Frenchmen would be honoured. He cited the Capitol in Rome as the kind of centre he had in mind. As long as the Republic had endured, the Romans had continued to embellish it; as soon as a great man brought glory to his Fatherland, his statue was placed there. "The Capitol was like a Temple of Immortality," Dussausoy declared; "every citizen aspired to be admitted there."[68] He proposed to turn the old Louvre into a new city hall, with the proviso that the academies continue to be housed there as well. Also he proposed that various cultural facilities be located there – the archives, the royal collection of art, and the royal library. At the same time he called for creation of a spacious square in front of the peristyle around which would be constructed a new Hôtel du Clergé and a Hôtel des Bâtiments du Roi. To the west of the Louvre he envisaged a series of public buildings, palaces, and mansions stretching all the way to the Etoile. This ensemble would be more impressive than any monuments in antiquity and would attract visitors away from Italy. Significantly, Dussausoy also wanted spaces in which public festivals could be staged.

Eighteenth-century thinkers believed that monuments and public buildings could provide useful instruments for re-educating the masses because they had what seems to us an exaggerated belief in the potency of images of all kinds.[69] The widespread idea of John Locke that the human mind was not only empty at birth of any innate ideas but also free from any evil propensities meant that everything in the mind came from external sensations. Human nature appeared malleable: one could create the kind of subject or citizen one desired by manipulating all the sensations that impinged on the mind, especially on that of the unspoiled child. Adherents of this sensationist psychology consequently had confidence in the power of education defined in the broadest sense possible.[70] When Helvétius declared "Education can do everything,"[71] he did not mean that instruction in school could shape the sort of citizenry one wanted but that proper instruction combined with the right sort of books, plays, festivals, music, images, and so on could do so. This included public buildings and monuments. Sensationist psychology often entailed a belief that humans were attracted to pleasant sensations and repelled by unpleasant ones, a fact that could be exploited to engender actions that would win social approval. This belief in the possibility of creating a *nouvel homme* lay behind the cultural programs of the Revolution.

In addition to the changing notion of the public building and its social purpose, the last half of the eighteenth century also bequeathed the vision of the whole city replanned to make it healthier and more beautiful. The contention that the city, especially a teeming one like Paris, was a centre of disease and debauchery was a common one in the later eighteenth century. Rousseau in particular did much to convey a negative picture of the city in comparison with the countryside, and even more with unspoiled nature. He never got over his disappointment when he entered Paris for the first time. He had imagined a city as beautiful as it was large, with fine streets and imposing buildings, but he found narrow streets, dingy houses, filthiness, and poverty. Later experience convinced him that the city was the centre of vicious competition and artificial manners. The big city was an anthill, the abyss of the human species, breeding infirmities of the body and vices of the soul.[72]

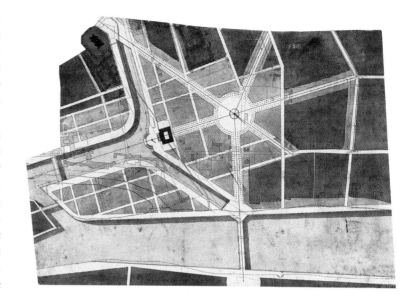

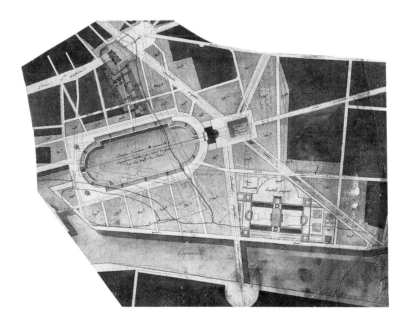

24, 25 Anonymous. *Above*: plan for the site of the Bastille; *below*: alternative plan for the site of the Bastille.

As usual Rousseau went further than most writers, but they often agreed that as it existed the big city was unattractive and unhealthy. Many, however, believed that it was not necessary to tolerate the city as it was: it could be transformed through enlightened planning. A host of writers called for urban renewal, including Maille Dussausoy, Marc-Antoine Laugier, Pierre Patte, and Voltaire.[73] They called for spacious squares, wider streets, sewage systems, numerous fountains, and green oases. Cemeteries, abbatoirs, and hospitals could be moved out of the centre of the city so that there would be less danger of pollution. Streets radiating out from squares distributed across the city would allow fresh air to penetrate all neighbourhoods. Public baths and swimming facilities would improve the cleanliness and physical fitness of the inhabitants. Broad avenues cutting through the old city would aid communication and stimulate commerce. Above all, some of the greenery of the countryside could be transported into the city in the form of tree-lined boulevards and public parks. There were so many proposals for improvements that Viel de Saint Maux suggested facetiously that buildings be put on rollers so that they could be moved about to facilitate planning.[74]

Planners now aspired not only to plan a particular monument, square, or building but to replan the city as a whole. In 1765 Laugier, for example, called for an overall plan for the city of Paris in which entrances, streets, squares, and bridges would be linked together.[75] The map of Paris that Patte published shortly afterward, showing all the proposed squares in honour of Louis xv imposed on the old city, envisaged redeveloping the whole city to a considerable extent. Then, just as the Revolution was breaking out, Charles de Wailly exhibited plans at the biennial *salon* at the Louvre that proposed transforming the area around the Louvre, the Faubourg Saint-Honoré, the Champs-Elysées, the islands at the heart of the city, and much of the Left Bank (Figure 26).[76] By supporting such comprehensive urban planning any regime, whether monarchical or revolutionary, could show that it had the welfare of its citizens at heart. Moreover, the intention of improving the urban environment and infrastructure was often combined with the goal of making Paris into the most impressive city in the world, the Rome of modern times. This too was an ambition that revolutionaries could take up and to which they could give a new meaning.

In replanning the old city or designing new suburbs there were already precedents for imposing a progressive political stamp on the urban landscape. Public squares already had a political significance: they were *places royales*, reminding subjects of the territorial scope of royal power, but following French intervention in what proved to be a successful war of independence in the thirteen English colonies on the Atlantic seaboard of North America, planners sometimes organized space to commemorate this revolution. For example, in Bordeaux the architect Victor Louis, in conjunction with an aristocrat promoter, presented a plan to demolish the old fortress known as the Château Trompette on the banks of the Garonne and to subdivide the site (Figure 27). He proposed to create a semicircular *place* on the river with a statue of Louis XVI in the centre.[77] Thirteen streets were to radiate out from this square, each honouring one of the new American states. These streets were to be linked by a colonnade around the periphery of the square, forming triumphal arches at the entrance to each of them. The plan won royal approval in 1785 but ran into a number of obstacles resulting in legal suits that were still not settled when the Revolution erupted.[78]

There was a similar plan to develop an area in Paris that was also to commemorate the successful struggle of the English colonies for independence. François-Joseph Bélanger drew up alternative plans for developing the fief of the Comte d'Artois north of the Champs-Elysées, where a street at present bears the name of the count. One version speaks of the "plan for a new America," and the other for a new "City of the Adelphs" (Figure 28). Both plans feature a Place Franklin in the centre of a grid and streets named after Washington, Lafayette, Vergennes, Rochambeau, and d'Estaing.[79] Franklin had become the object of a veritable cult after his arrival as American plenipotentiary in December 1776. Scientist, inventor, moralist, and champion of human rights – he seemed to embody many of the ideals of the Enlightenment. Prints of his likeness appeared with the Latin motto underneath ERIPUIT COELO FULMEN SCEPTRUMQUE TIRANNIS: "He snatched fire from the heavens and the sceptre from the tyrant."[80] The other proposed street names were also connected to the American Revolution. Lafayette had offered the Americans his services even before the French alliance with the Americans; the Comte de Vergennes had negotiated the treaty; the Comte d'Estaing had led the French fleet; and the Vicomte de Rochambeau had commanded the French forces that landed at Newport in 1780.

The idea of using the names of streets and squares to convey a message to the public had already led some authors to propose imposition of a system of nomenclature on urban space. The Abbé Etienne Teisserenc had put forward such a scheme, which combined the objective of utility with an expression of nationalism.[81] Like many thinkers later on, he attacked the absurdity of many of the names in Paris and the repetition of the same ones for different streets. He proposed to turn the city into a sort of map of France so that the inhabitants would get the sense of the whole country and visitors from the provinces would feel as though they lived in the city.

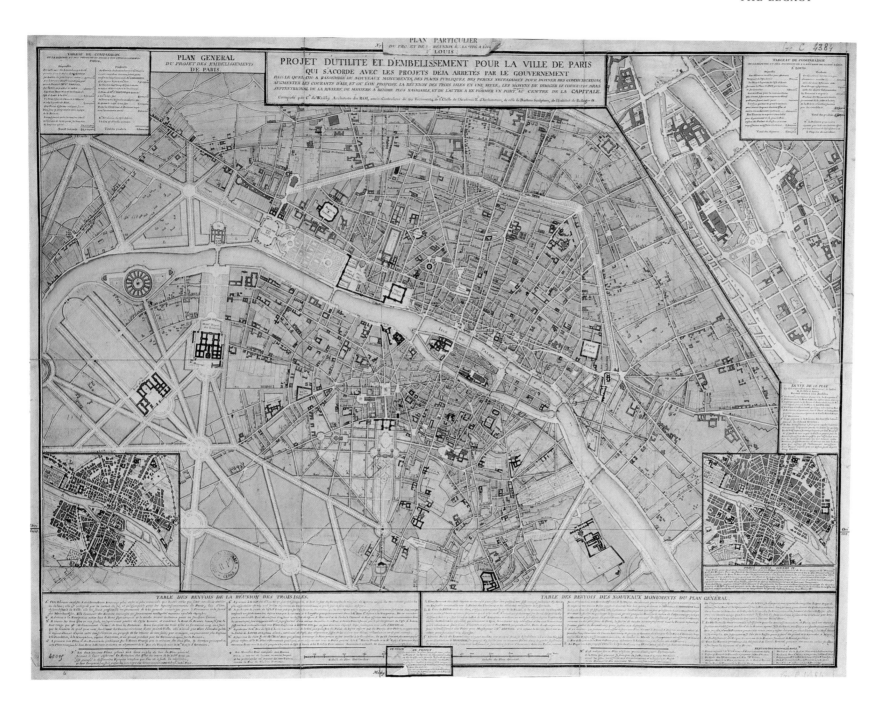

26 De Wailly. Plan for urban renewal in Paris.

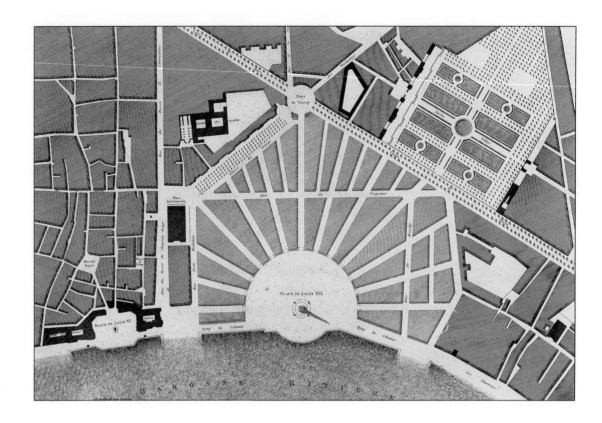

27 Louis. Plan for the site of the Château
Trompette in Bordeaux.

Sections would be named after provinces and the streets after important cities and towns in those provinces. Street signs on all the corners would indicate the province, the name of the city after which the street was named, and the number of leagues it was from Paris. To make the transition easier, the author provided a list of a thousand new names derived from cities and towns, a description of them, and the old names, complete with cross-references.

Teisserenc went even further. He wanted signs on shops and other establishments likewise to convey a message. The subjects of all *enseignes* would be drawn from history, literature, or the tools of various crafts. Signs derived from historical events would include the date: for instance, a merchant might use a sign featuring the Battle of Fontenoy in 1747 (naturally, only victories would be used in this way). One could do the same with the names of kings, saints, famous men, and so on. Such signs could become a form of public instruction and an inspiration to citizens:

"If the notices were prescribed for such reasons by public authority, how many men who are forgotten and are only known through history books will as it were come alive among us, and by their memory cause us to follow in their footsteps, and to merit the same honour."[82] Teisserenc's project was still conservative. It included kings and saints, but the idea of street names and signs as educational tools could be adapted readily to serve various ideological objectives.

Behind many of these developments, such as celebrating the great men whom France had produced, turning Paris into the most impressive capital of the world, or teaching the geography of the country by nomenclature, lay the burgeoning national patriotism to which we have alluded before. Other signs of increasing national sentiment were the increased use of words such as *patrie, patriotisme, nation* and *national*; demands for a national system of education;[83] the call for national subjects in historical painting;[84] the appearance of plays glorifying episodes in French history;

and the spate of patriotic poems that appeared during the Seven Years War and the American War of Independence. Various authors began to campaign to have all inscriptions rendered in French rather than Latin. Also, there was a mounting demand to create a national gallery in the Louvre that would make Paris the rival and successor to Rome.[85]

The growing sense of national unity and pride in the later eighteenth century was the result of the convergence of a number of factors. The long association of most of the kingdom under a common government had gradually created a feeling of community, at least among the better-educated classes. Repeated wars with other countries had further engendered a sense of identity. Roads and canals had knit the country more closely together. Mail had increased dramatically, carrying correspondence, books, and periodicals from the centre. By the last half of the century the central government was increasingly impinging on the life of local communities. Moreover, literate Frenchmen could take pride in the great prestige that French language and culture enjoyed in Europe. The rising national patriotism that resulted from all these factors and was intensified by the Revolution erupting on the national stage was to have a pronounced effect on art, architecture, and city planning: the desire to use these arts as instruments for creating a new order was intermingled with the ambition to make France, with Paris as the focal point, the artistic leader of the world.

There were clearly numerous developments concerning space from which revolutionaries could choose or which they could develop further in their effort to regenerate France and create a new citizenry. Recent research has shown that the political discourse and rhetoric of the Revolution grew out of the political debates during what turned out to be the closing decades of the Old Regime.[86] Thomas Crow has argued that the dramatic innovations made in painting by Jacques-Louis David grew out of debate about the role of art provoked by the public exhibitions in the Louvre, and that the painter's bold style exemplified in *The Oath of the Horatii* in 1785, *The Death of Socrates* in 1787, and *The Lictors Returning to Brutus the Bodies of His Sons* in 1789 were related to the blunt rhetoric of radical pamphleteers who attacked the court, the aristocracy, and the Academy of Painting and Sculpture.[87] It could be argued in a similar way that, although few if any of the architects and authors we have discussed anticipated revolution, their ideas about monuments, squares, and public space likewise set the stage for revolutionary projects, to which we now turn. ▲

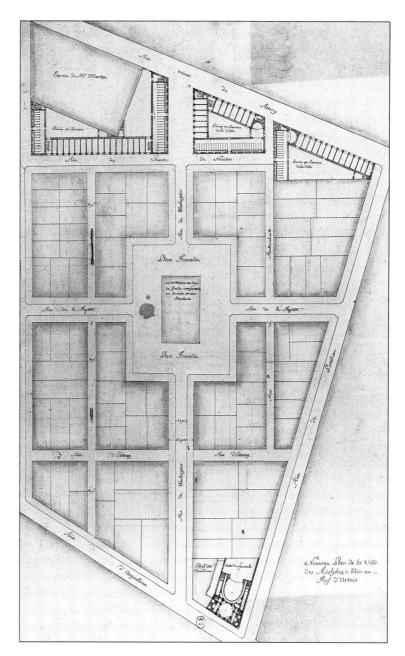

28 Bélanger. Plan for the *fief d'Artois* in Paris.

Ici l'on Danse.

Vue de la Decoration et Illumination faite sur le Terrein de la Bastille pour le jour de la Fête de la Confédération Française le 14 Juillet 1790.

Decoration of the site of the Bastille for the Federation in 1790. (Figure 48)

II

A NEW SYMBOLIC ORDER

SINCE DURKHEIM MANY ANTHROPOLOGISTS have shown that in primitive societies different cosmologies not only reflect but reinforce various social structures.[1] Using rituals and symbols, such cosmologies mask, legitimate, and sanctify power. Other social scientists have extended this analysis to modern societies as well.[2] Many of these scholars have called attention to the importance of a centre in various world-views as the point from which power radiates out and to which people give their allegiance. This centre may be a person, an institution, a sacred symbol, or all of these together. One could argue that there was such a cosmology in Old Regime France, with a vital centre that helped to uphold both the social and the political order.

Socially the symbolic order represented and sustained a hierarchical order. At the base of society, the Third Estate or commoners were generally characterized by their plain dress and lack of distinctive emblems. The Second Estate or noblemen were distinguished by their titles, swords, and coats of arms. The First Estate or clergy included commoners as well as nobles, but the top levels were distinguished by their insignia. At the apex, the king was surrounded by rituals and symbols that made manifest his supreme status. The coronation, at which he was annointed with oil from the Holy Ampulla, made clear that he ruled by the grace of God. So too did the great royal seal.[3] That of Louis XVI shows the king enthroned, crowned, and encircled by the chain of a knightly order. He holds a sceptre in his right hand and a Hand of Justice in the other. The legend reads: LOUIS XVI PAR LA GRACE DE DIEU ROY DE FRANCE ET NAVARRE. The reverse side features the royal coat of arms, a cartouche decorated with three fleurs-de-lis, again surrounded by the chain of orders

and held up by two angels. The three lilies associated the monarchy with the Trinity. The royal palace, triumphal arches, and statues of the king in royal squares all reinforced monarchical status.

Not only was the king at the top of the social hierarchy but in theory he was absolute, the only public person. Of course he was expected to consult his ministers and was subject to the influence of courtiers, but in the end he had the right to decide on matters concerning *la chose publique*. The vignettes that served as the headings of laws made clear their source. Sometimes the image of the king appeared, but usually only the symbols of his power were displayed – the royal coat of arms, the crown, the sceptre, and the Hand of Justice.[4] Complementary symbols were added depending on the subject of the laws. For instance, the headings of military legislation bristled with weapons, and judicial decrees exhibited Justice with her scales, fasces representing state power, and perhaps an all-seeing eye.

The *lit de justice* gave ceremonial expression to royal absolutism: if the courts refused persistently to register a law, the king could appear in person to order obedience to his will. Theoretically that was the final word. The belief that the king alone should decide public policy was reiterated right to the end of the Old Regime. In 1781, when Necker argued that the king in his council would be well advised to rule in conformity with enlightened public opinion, Vergennes in a letter reminded the king of his absolute power: "The Monarch speaks, everyone else belongs to the people which obeys."[5]

Both the social and the political aspects of the Old Regime were undermined in the eighteenth century and then destroyed by the Revolution, making necessary a new symbolic order. On the social side the philosophes helped to undermine the ideological basis of the hierarchical social structure, contrasting it with the state of nature, although because they feared social upheaval and were themselves often beneficiaries of the existing system, they hesitated to carry their theories to a logical conclusion. The repeated discussions of the origins of inequality by learned societies in the course of the century showed an uneasiness about gross inequalities in society. Then in the seventies documents coming out of the American Revolution such as the Virginia Declaration of Rights suggested the possibility of a society without a legalized hierarchy. Meanwhile, members of the upper levels of the Third Estate often blurred the juridical line between commoners and nobles by acquiring mansions, buying seigneurial property, purchasing government posts, and "living nobly" – that is, abandoning commercial activity. The line between well-to-do commoners and nobles thus became increasingly anachronistic. Then in 1789, following urban and rural insurrections, the Declaration of the Rights of Man affirmed that all men were equal in rights and that only distinctions based on social utility were legitimate. The idea of a kingdom of subjects divided by privileges inherited from history was replaced by that of a nation of citizens united by rights derived from nature. The old symbolic order became obsolete.

At the same time the political aspect of the old order was undermined. In the course of the eighteenth century open conflicts took place among the literate and politically aware sections of the public over Jansenism, the right to confession, fiscal policy, the fate of the Jesuit order, and the power of the courts. In these conflicts newspapers, pamphlets, and remonstrances published by the courts all competed for support. French-language journals published outside the country but distributed inside it made a mockery of royal censorship. In the end the royal government itself was forced to play the game by appealing to public opinion in the preambles to laws, pamphlets by its hirelings, and subsidized newspapers. In this emerging political culture public opinion rather than the royal will was becoming the basis of legitimacy. The pamphlet war provoked by the final crisis of the Old Regime and the convocation of the Estates General revealed how far the new political culture had developed, although as yet there was no national representative assembly in which public opinion could influence decision-making. The meeting of the Estates General and its subsequent transformation into a National Assembly gave the public a way of manifesting its will. This event was both the culmination of a long process and a new beginning. Politically as well as socially, a revised symbolic system was needed.

The birth of the new political culture was accompanied by a great emotional swell. Historians in recent decades have emphasized the importance of material factors, especially the decline in real wages, the rise in the cost of bread, and the burdens borne by the peasants, in provoking the revolutionary upheaval, but one cannot account for the events without also taking into account the hopes and dreams of a new world that inspired many of the actors. The calling of the Estates General for the first time in one hundred and seventy-five years, its transformation into a Constituent Assembly, the suppression in principle of feudal remnants in the countryside, the adoption of a statement of natural rights as a preamble to a constitution, and the beginning of measures to streamline the state and modernize the church all excited a hope for profound change. Many pamphleteers and journalists already used the word "régénération," a word with religious connotations, to describe the depth of change they hoped

for. A revolutionary faith was born that was destined to produce a series of sects and apostles down to our own day.[6]

The idea of the opening of a new era had already appeared in the American Revolution, expressed in the motto NOVUS ORDO SECLORUM, "a new order in time," inscribed on the Great Seal of the United States. The French revolutionaries expressed the same belief in a break with the past by starting to count the years from 1789 when rebirth had begun. "Year One of Liberty," "Year Two of Liberty," and so on began to appear on various publications. This idea of a new beginning was vividly expressed in the popular engravings of the period. Often broken shackles or yokes were shown lying on the ground, signifying the final end to servitude.[7] At the same time the sun, a very ancient symbol, was frequently used in a new way. Whereas Louis XIV had used the sun to represent himself as ascendant over the world, the revolutionaries used it to signify the dawn of a new era.[8] In the last decade of the *siècle des lumières*, in which light vanquishing darkness was the favorite metaphor for truth dispelling ignorance, it was now the Revolution that was often portrayed as the source of light.

The emotional swell of the early years of the French Revolution involved an upsurge of national feeling. As we have seen there had been a growing sense of national patriotism focused on the whole country in the last half of the eighteenth century, a feeling revealed in changes in vocabulary, projects for national historical paintings and statues, proposals for monuments and public buildings that would represent the prestige of France, and schemes for a national system of education. This mounting national sentiment was intensified by the calling of the Estates General and then the union of the three estates in a national legislature. The Declaration of the Rights of Man proclaimed that sovereignty was embodied in the Nation, and the new militia was called the National Guard. Subsequently the Assembly abolished the varied provincial institutions and substituted identical departments so that the whole nation would share common institutions. This devotion to *la patrie* was another reason why the old symbols became inadequate and new ones necessary.

The hope for a break with the past and the upsurge of national feeling was accompanied by the dual process that we have called delegitimization or desacralization, followed by relegitimization or resacralization. The negative side of this process was expressed in the destruction of the symbols that had helped to create an aura of legitimacy around the old social hierarchy. Popular engravings often showed swords, coats of arms, and croziers smashed, lying on the ground, and trampled under foot.[9] Following the abolition of aristocratic titles, there was a series of laws aimed at removing liveries, coats of arms, and other feudal emblems from public view. Since the monarchy still survived, some royal symbols were tolerated, although in 1790 Louis XVI was forced by the Assembly to change the inscription on his seal.[10] LOUIS XVI PAR LA GRACE DE DIEU ROY DE FRANCE ET NAVARRE was changed to LOUIS XVI PAR LA GRACE DE DIEU ET LA LOI CONSTITUTIONELLE DE L'ETAT ROI DES FRANÇOIS.[11] Just before the great Festival of Federation the same year, the Assembly decreed that all arrogant royal inscriptions and signs of servitude, such as the four chained figures around the statue of Louis XIV on the Place des Victoires, were to be removed as an affront to the dignity of the people.[12]

The positive side of this process, relegitimization and resacralization, also involved the use of symbols. Some of these were old symbols put to a new use – for instance, the Phrygian bonnet or Liberty cap, which went back to Roman times, when it had been worn by emancipated slaves. The fasces, the bundle of rods enclosing an axe, which lictors had carried before Roman magistrates, began to be used as a symbol of unity.[13] Sometimes the Phrygian bonnet and the fasces were shown radiating light like sacred objects.[14] One symbol, however, was particularly useful for giving an aura of sanctity to the new ideas – the equilateral triangle. Christians had used it to express the mysteries of the Trinity[15] and Masons to represent the Supreme Being, for whom past, present, and future are one.[16] Early in the Revolution this triangle was sometimes used to frame the three good kings, Louis XII, Henry IV and Louis XVI.[17] Most often, however, it was used to represent the union of the three formerly separate estates. For instance, one engraving shows a member of the clergy, a noble, and a commoner enclosed in an equilateral triangle.[18] The points are associated with the emblems of the three orders – a mitre, a cannon, and a plough. The inscription declares, "Better late than never." Later one finds the sacred triangle used on *assignats* to represent another trinity: "Nation, Law, and King."[19] Meanwhile, the tricolour cockade emerged as an emblem of devotion to the nation. The three colours were a sign of hoped-for unity of the king and his people – the white came from the royal livery, the red and blue from the city of Paris.

Such symbols as the Phrygian bonnet or the fasces were often held by or associated with allegorical figures. Usually these figures were female, largely for a simple reason: most abstract entities in French are feminine in gender from their Latin roots – la France, la Nation, la Liberté, l'Egalité, la Nature, la Raison, la Justice, and so on. Even Fatherland and Brotherhood are feminine in French. In any case, there was a long tradition of female allegorical figures. Most of these figures too were ancient ones that could be put to a new use. Various emblem books were available that provided a repertory of figures from which artists could draw.[20] In fact it was because such figures were familiar that they could be used effectively. "Allegory is a kind of language which ought to be common to a number of persons, and which is founded on accepted usage," La Combe de Prezel asserted in his *Dictionnaire iconologique* published in 1756, quoting from an earlier work by de Piles.[21]

The central allegorical figure early in the Revolution was that of Liberty. La Combe described Liberty as a divinity celebrated by the ancient Greeks and Romans. The fact that she had a religious aura about her made her especially useful in the process of legitimizing and sacralizing the new order. La Combe pointed out that she had been traditionally depicted as a Roman woman, dressed in a white robe, holding a sceptre in one hand and a bonnet in the other. Sometimes instead of a sceptre she held a rod, reminding the viewer of the one with which the magistrate touched slaves to signify their liberation. At other times Liberty was shown holding a club just like Hercules, or with a broken yoke at her feet.[22] She had already become conspicuous more than a decade before the outbreak of the revolution, at the time of the American War of Independence.[23] After 1789 she became still more prominent, although for a time she existed alongside the king. Gradually she became more autonomous, especially as the Revolution grew more radical.

Among the repertory of allegorical figures there was one conspicuous male whom we have already mentioned: Hercules. This demigod, usually wearing a lion-skin and carrying a club, was likewise a legacy of classical antiquity. Traditionally he had been associated with French kings as a symbol of power, intelligence, and virtue. It was under the heading "Heroic Virtue" that Cesare Ripa discussed Hercules in his famous guide to allegorical figures.[24] On the eve of the Revolution and soon after its eruption we find him associated with Louis XVI. In fact we even find the king holding a club just like Hercules.[25] Very soon, however, we see Hercules becoming more independent and increasingly associated with the power of the people. He appears on allegorical engravings, on flags of the National Guard, on certificates of members of the guard, and on the diplomas given to the conquerors of the Bastille.[26]

It was in this emotional climate of rebirth and nationalism that architects produced their projects. Their motives were no doubt mixed. There was, of course, fame and fortune to be gained if the designer's project was adopted by the government. As royal and aristocratic patronage declined, the revolutionary government became the main hope for employment, but there was also the satisfaction of contributing to the revolutionary cause, to human progress. Most of the designers can be called propagandists. They spoke repeatedly of propagating, celebrating, and commemorating the ideas and accomplishments of the Revolution. For example, in proposing a "Colonne de la Liberté" for the esplanade in Montpellier, the architect Demoulin emphasized how it would educate the young and warn all citizens of the dangers of disunity: "On it all our children will learn their duty, it will be a living lesson for them. If ever the seeds of division threaten their tranquility, it will be a source of dread and reproach. At the sight of it, what citizen will not feel personal hatreds die away in the breast, will not be stirred up by the desire for peace and union, will not sacrifice his personal resentments to the general good and the happiness of all which results from it."[27] Such architects clearly sought to contribute to what we have called integrational propaganda, the type designed to rally the people around the new ideals and institutions, but they were not propagandists in the derogatory sense in which the word is often used today. They were not trying to mislead or delude the masses. Their projects and pamphlets exude enthusiasm for the revolutionary faith.

The first opportunity for architects to create structures in the service of the Revolution came with the festivals that took place in the autumn of 1789 and the following year. These began as local rallies throughout France in which units of the National Guard and regular troops from neighbouring villages and towns swore to unite in the defence of the Revolution. Besides the oath, the other main ritual was the consecration of flags, but there were also parades, dances, bonfires, banquets, and fraternal embraces. The word "Federation," popularized by the American Revolution, gradually came to be applied to these ceremonies. Local rallies led to district and regional ones, and finally to the great national one in Paris on the first anniversary of the storming of the Bastille. The Federations demanded temporary props that would create special enclosures for citizens, provide focal points for rituals, and supports for symbols, inscriptions, and low-reliefs.

Such festivals were intended to be spectacles in which the people would be both spectators and actors. The planners had various models to draw on. They were naturally aware of church processions and royal festivals of the Old Regime. Royal celebrations of marriages, births, coronations, victories, and the inauguration of monuments had featured elaborate sets as well as fireworks, distribution of food and wine, various sporting events, and open-air dances.[28] In an age when education was still based on the works of classical antiquity, the planners were also recalling the Olympic games and Roman spectacles. Despite all these precedents, the revolutionaries hoped to create a new kind of festival in which there would be none of the animal fights, gladiatorial contests, or processions of chained captives that had degraded Roman festivals. Furthermore, the people themselves were to be involved, in a way befitting a society based on the participation of citizens. In his *Lettre à d'Alembert sur le théâtre*, Rousseau had made such involvement the essence of a popular festival: "Plant a post crowned with flowers in the centre of a site, assemble the people there and you will have a festival. Do even better: display the spectators as spectacle; make them actors themselves, make each of them see himself and love himself in the others, in order that all will be better united."[29]

In some Federations the setting was almost as simple as Rousseau had envisaged. In Montpellier there is no mention of any decor other than a simple altar erected on the esplanade at the edge of the city, but it apparently served as a focal point around which the soldiers and citizens could unite. "The city is brought together in front of the Altar of the Fatherland," declared the procurator of the commune; "all hearts are aflame with the sacred fire of patriotism, and we form only a single family."[30] In Strasbourg the architecture for the Federation of the departments of the Upper and Lower Rhine and neighbouring departments was almost as simple. There the focal point was provided by an unembellished altar, covered with a plain canopy, raised up on a crude mound constructed in the centre of the Plaine des Bouchers near the city (Figure 29).[31] Tall trees at the corners of the mound and a circle of flower-stands both reinforced this ceremonial centre and suggested the idea of rebirth. An engraving by the architect Dupuis, depicting the moment when the flags of the regular troops and the National Guard were blessed, shows that the field was framed by lines of soldiers and by makeshift stands on either side.

Although it was a small centre, Aix-en-Provence was the site of an impressive Festival of Federation on 14 July 1790. The fête there centred to a large extent on the broad avenue now called the Cours Mirabeau, an axis running from la Rotonde (now the Place de la Libération) eastward for about several hundred meters to what is now the Place Carnot (Figure 30).[32] An Altar of the Fatherland was erected near the thermal fountain on this avenue atop a platform with three steps leading up to it. Numerous clergy were grouped around this altar, led by the Abbé Rovère, who intoned a Te Deum. Facing the altar was an obelisk surmounted by a globe, on which was the inscription LONG LIVE THE NATION. In the middle of the obelisk was another inscription, LONG LIVE THE LAW, and further down LONG LIVE THE KING. The Nation thus appeared on top of this trinity, which embodied the aspirations of the early Revolution.

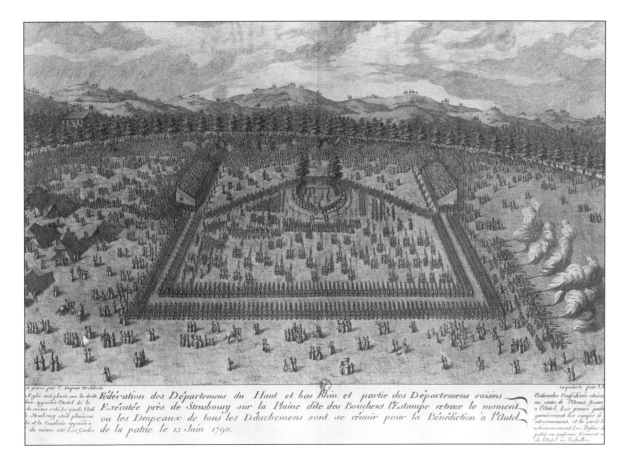

Fédération des Départemens du Haut et bas Rhin et partie des Départemens voisins Exécutée près de Strasbourg sur la Plaine dite des Bouchers l'Estampe retrace le moment ou les Drapeaux de tous les Détachemens vont se réunir pour la Bénédiction à l'Autel de la patrie. le 13 Juin 1790.

29 View of the Festival
of Federation
in Strasbourg in 1790.

VUE PERSPECTIVE DE LA FÊTE DU XIV JUILLET 1790 DONNÉS AU COURS A AIX
DÉDIÉE A SON AMI RIMBAUD. PAR SON TRES H. ET TRES OBEISSANT Serviteur

30 View of the Festival of Federation in Aix-en-Provence in 1790.

31 View of the Festival of Federation
in Amiens in 1790.

AUTEL DE LA PATRIE
Vue de láutel sur lequel s'est fait le Serment de la Fédération D'orleans,
qui a eu lieu le 9 May 1790.

32 Altar of the Fatherland in Orléans in 1790.

On each side of the obelisk was a colonnade that ended a short distance from the altar. Just in front of the obelisk were tiered benches covered with fabric to accommodate municipal officials. Thirty-two units of the National Guard were ranged in columns eight deep on one side of the aisle, the troops of the line on the other.[33] The tree-lined walkways and windows of the adjacent buildings created a sort of amphitheatre. The scene was captured for posterity by Joseph Regnault in a watercolour now in the Musée Arbaud in Aix.

The Festival of Federation at Aix underscores several significant features of such ceremonies early in the Revolution. Especially noteworthy is the mixture of religious and secular: priests played a conspicuous part, but the oaths that all the officers and men took individually were to the secular trinity. Already the revolutionaries had sensed how an existing feature of the urban landscape, in this case the broad axis of the Cours Mirabeau, could be decorated so as to serve a new purpose. Also conspicuous is the procession through the streets, which was to become a central feature of revolutionary festivals throughout France, asserting revolutionary control over urban space and causing the old streets to reverberate with new life. After the oath-taking, the officials and soldiers marched to the city hall, where the mayor made a speech and a portrait of Louis XVI was deposited. This portrait was another sign of the high hopes placed in the king at this time. It was the work of a talented young deaf and dumb artist. The painting was crowned with oak leaves and bore the inscription LOUIS XVI RESTORER OF FRENCH LIBERTY. During the oath-taking it was placed at the foot of the obelisk before being carried through the streets by one of the units of the National Guard to its destination in the city hall.[34]

Amiens was a medium-sized centre that produced impressive decor for the Festival of Federation staged there on two days, 13 and 14 July 1790. An open area known as La Hautoye on the edge of town served as the local Champ de Mars.[35] The decor was designed by a local architect called Limozin, aided by other local artists (Figure 31). The Altar of the Fatherland was raised upon a dodecagonal platform with obelisks in the four corners surmounted by vases spouting thick smoke. On the corner of the altar itself were incense burners, adding further to the mystical aura surrounding the scene. The decorations on the altar mixed traditional attributes of monarchy – a crown *fleurdelisée*, a sceptre, the Hand of Justice, and a globe bearing the arms of France – with symbols of the nascent order, above all the Book of the Constitution, inscribed with the three key nouns of the day: THE NATION, THE LAW, THE KING. At one side of the platform there was accommodation for officials. As in the festivals elsewhere, the event featured a procession, a Te Deum, speeches, and the oath to the new

trinity.[36] In order to perpetuate the memory of this grandiose ceremony, Limozin himself did a view of the scene, which he had engraved in Paris. This engraving has become very rare, but it seems to have inspired the lithograph by which Louis Duthoit illustrated the *Histoire d'Amiens* by Hyacinthe Dusevel.[37]

At Le Mans the centre of the local Federation, held on 4 July 1790, was a curious Altar of the Fatherland that mixed old religious symbols with new ones. The altar, holding a cross surrounded by candelabra, was placed on a square perron with steps leading up on all sides. This altar was covered by an elaborate canopy, the peak of which was decorated with a pedestal resting on horizontal fasces and supporting lions that in turn held up the royal coat of arms. A plaque on the entablature displayed two key words of the day – UNION and LIBERTY. The corners of the canopy were decorated with trophies. This cover was upheld by columns of "un ordre nouveau," as a letter to the *Chronique de Paris* called it, consisting of four thick cannon forty feet in height, encircled with chains and cannon balls. According to this report, at the moment the federative oath had been taken these chains were severed by blows of an axe, and as the debris fell to the ground the crowd cried out in exaltation, "We are free, we are brothers."[38] Such a ritual reinforced the idea of emancipation from bondage, but it did so in a symbolic fashion that avoided naming those guilty of having forged the chains.

In Orléans the Festival of Federation was primarily focused on the Matroi, the principal square of the city, although stands were also placed at main intersections to allow crowds to see the procession. On the Matroi a young architect called Lebrun created a large enclosure by placing barriers on the four sides.[39] For the middle of this enclosure he designed a temple in which was placed the Altar of the Fatherland that had already been used in a previous Federation on 9 May 1790. This stone altar in Roman style was quite different from a traditional Christian altar (Figure 32). On its four sides were inscribed the words FATHERLAND, LAW, KING, and FAITHFULNESS, each encircled with laurel and oak. These key words were separated by fasces.[40] The temple that enclosed this altar was composed of six pilasters supporting a parabolic dome. From the middle of each of these pilasters sprouted six trees whose branches formed a portico. Double garlands of flowers tied the trees to one another. During the fête officials entered the temple to swear the oath to king, country, and law with their hands raised over the altar. Ordinary soldiers marched around the enclosure, taking the oath as they passed in front of the temple.

Several features of this particular festival are noteworthy. Once again the repeated use of religious terms in accounts of the event reveals the civic

CONFÉDÉRATION DES DÉPARTEMENS DU NORD DE LA SOMME ET DU PAS DE CALAIS,
Faite à Lille le 14 Juillet 1790.

Dédié à Messieurs le Maire et Officiers Municipaux,
de la Ville de Lille.

33 View of the Festival of Federation in Lille in 1790.

religiosity that was already emerging in this early phase of the Revolution and would evolve later into a cult in competition with Christianity. Also significant was the intermixture of greenery with classical architecture in the central structure, representing the two ideals of the eighteenth century, nature and culture. "This edifice fulfilled the double purpose of presenting on the exterior a sacred temple composed of trees, branches, and flowers set in the middle of a camp," reported one observer, "and on the interior a temple in architecture whose taste and lightness is worthy of the century in which we live."[41] Finally, the role of women in this event was significant. A hundred women asked to participate and to take the oath on behalf of all their sex. The municipality set aside space specifically for them in the enclosure. Women clearly were coming to think of themselves as citizens, although male politicians were not ready to treat them as equals.

In larger centres the architectural props were more elaborate. For example, at Lille the local architect, François Verly, and his associate Biarez created an impressive setting for a Federation in which the departments of the Nord, the Somme, and the Pas de Calais all participated. The celebration took place on 6 June 1790 – that is, more than a month before the national one in Paris. Like their counterparts in the capital, the planners chose the esplanade of the Champ de Mars on the edge of the city, which offered a vast space in which to create an enclosure for a massive gathering, decorated with appropriate symbols (Figure 33). Four allegorical figures announced the entrance to an ideal space in which citizens would be purified and uplifted. The centre was demarked by an elevated altar, surrounded by classical tripods in which incense burned and flanked by obelisks that expressed elan and punctuated the perspective. The idea of a centre was important, not as the symbol of a static point but as a source of movement radiating out, a point of convergence and divergence at the same time. Further on there was another elevation, crowned with a temple sheltering a statue of Liberty. Along the entablature was a Latin inscription:

JUS POPULI RECUPERATUM

Two smaller temples faced the altar on either side of the enclosure.[42] The temple was destined to play a key role in revolutionary design, becoming the favourite way of celebrating a hero or ideal. As elsewhere, the oath-taking was followed by a series of lesser celebrations – civic banquets, fireworks, dances, illuminations, and processions.

The Federation at Lyon on 30 May 1790 provides another striking example of the use of architecture in a provincial festival. There the plan-

ners chose the Plaine des Brotteaux to accommodate the National Guard from the Rhône-et-Loire, neighbouring departments, and others as far away as Bretagne, altogether 50,000 troops, plus a 150,000 spectators. The centre consisted of a man-made rocky hillock down which water seemed to cascade and on which plants and shrubs seemed to have grown (Figure 34). On the four sides, each eighty feet wide, steps led up to four porticoes in the Doric style, leading to the interior. On one of the porticoes was the likeness of Diogenes, breaking the lamp with which he had sought an honest man and saying, "I looked for only one, and I found millions." This structure formed the Temple of Concord, which served as a giant Altar of the Fatherland. On its peak, seventy-two feet above the ground, stood a statue of Liberty, simple but imposing. In one hand she held a pike topped with a Liberty Bonnet, in the other civic crowns for the *Fédérés*.[43] This temple was the work of local artists, among them Cochet and Dunony, and Liberty was the creation of Joseph Chinard. Inspired by patriotism, they demanded no recompense.

The *Annales patriotiques et littéraires* relates that as soon as the oath was taken at the altar, a balloon was released in the direction of the rising sun. It was decorated with the new national colours and bore an inscription on its underside:

I WAS BORN UNDER DESPOTISM, I RISE UP UNDER LIBERTY

The reporter saw a favourable portent in its rise: "It seemed that its glorious ascent toward the star which illuminates us was the sign of our political redemption."[44] This balloon and the manner in which it was employed is an early example of the effort of the revolutionaries to link the Revolution symbolically to cosmic forces.

Even before the Festival of Federation took place in Paris on the first anniversary of the storming of the Bastille, there was an oath-taking that deserves attention. On 14 February 1790 the deputies of the nation, representatives of the Commune, presidents of the sections, and the commanders of the Parisian National Guard all gathered in Notre Dame to renew together the civic oath they had already taken individually.[45] An unsigned plan in the Bibliothèque Nationale shows how the interior of the cathedral was rearranged for this event (Figure 35).[46] The Altar of the Fatherland was placed at the end of the nave. Above it were inscribed the words GOD, THE LAW, and THE KING, a variant of the usual trinity of the period. Musicians occupied the benches in the apse, the deputies filled those in the north transept, and the representatives of the Commune sat on those in the south transept. About eight hundred members of the public

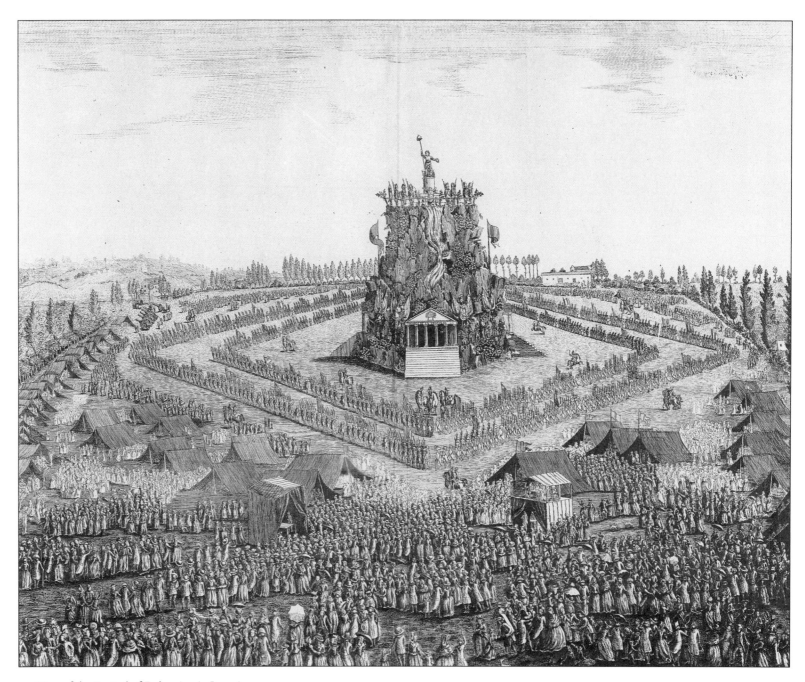

34 View of the Festival of Federation in Lyon in 1790.

occupied the benches parallel to the nave, except for the front rows, which were reserved for officers of the Parisian National Guard. The flags of the sixty battalions lined the centre aisle. The architect thus managed to create a sort of amphitheatre in the church, the kind of enclosure that was to become the favourite one for civic gatherings. Moreover, although the ceremony involved priests, a sermon, a mass, and a Te Deum, the patriotic cult had already moved into a church, a portent of things to come.

When it was decided to have a national Federation in the capital on 14 July 1790, the planners soon realized the problems involved in assembling thousands of troops, plus hundreds of thousands of spectators, all in one place. The royal extravaganzas of the Old Regime had not produced an adequate enclosure; consequently, numerous people had been crushed at the celebration of the marriage of the dauphin and Marie-Antoinette. There were, however, models available for such an enclosure. As we have seen, the architectural contests for the Prix de Rome had included plans for vast coliseums; several architects had designed such arenas for actual sites in Paris, and amphitheatres had been constructed in the Ecole de Chirurgie and the Halle au Blé. We have seen too that architects were convinced of the psychological advantages of assembling people in an enclave where they could see each other and share common emotions. Bernard Poyet reasserted this conviction at the time of the preparations for the national Federation. "Public festivals insired by lofty considerations of common interests," he argued, "have this special characteristic, that the sentiment of each person becomes that of all by a sort of electrification which people can scarcely resist."[47]

Since no existing enclosure could accommodate the vast crowds that were anticipated, the commission set up by the Constituent Assembly to prepare for the Federation realized that they would have to create one. After considering various possible sites, the planners chose the Champ de Mars because it was relatively close to the city, the surrounding rows of trees would provide a verdant frame, and the area could be enlarged by accommodating spectators on the hills of Passy and Chaillot across the river.[48] The site also had a sacred aura about it, since it recalled the field where the Frankish ancestors of the French had assembled long ago.

The final plans for the site were an amalgam of ideas put forward by Jean-Baptiste Blondel, Jacques Cellérier, Bernard Poyet, and the commissioners. All the proposals contained similar ingredients, a number of temporary structures built out of wood, plaster, and canvas, all painted to look like stone: an approach across a pontoon bridge on the Seine, a triumphal gateway into the Champ de Mars, a huge amphitheatre running the length of the field, a massive altar in the centre, and a pavilion at the

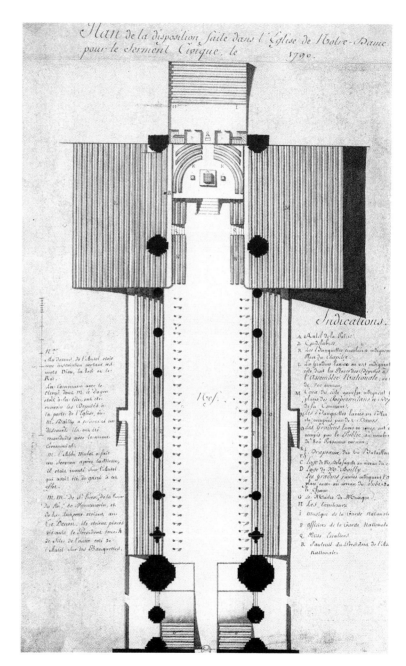

35 Notre-Dame in Paris decorated for an oath-taking in February 1790.

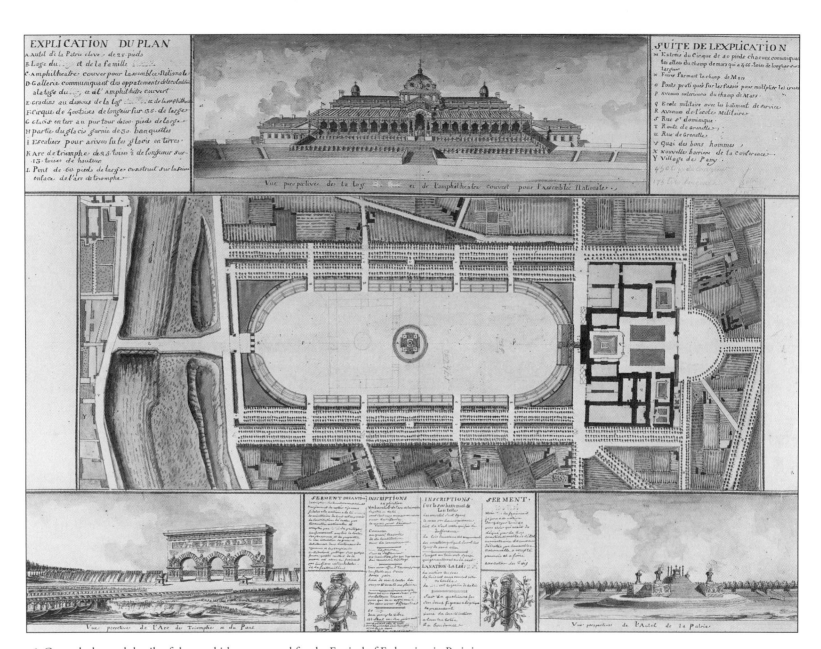

36 Ground-plan and details of the amphitheatre created for the Festival of Federation in Paris in 1790.

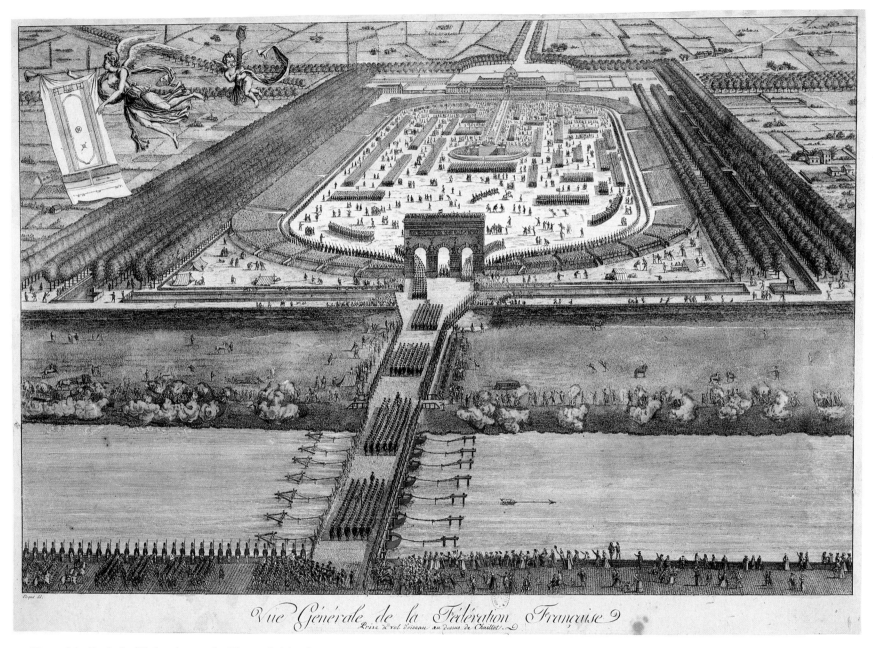

Vue Générale de la Fédération Française
Prise à vol d'oiseau au dessus de Chaillot.

37 View of the Festival of Federation on the Champ de Mars in 1790.

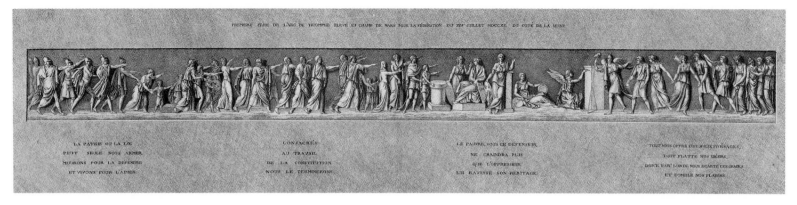

38 Frieze on the façade of the triumphal arch facing the Seine.

end in front of the Ecole Militaire for the deputies of the National Assembly and the king (Figures 36, 37). All classes participated in the construction of the giant circus. Contemporaries and later historians have recounted how preparation for the festival became a sort of festival itself. Families and corporations marched out to the site accompanied by fifes, drums, and flags. At times the workers sang a new refrain that appeared at the time, "Ça ira" (It'll all work out), expressing the optimism of the day.

The architecture of the national Federation was charged with symbolism. The bridge across the Seine, linking the Left and Right banks to the Champ de Mars, seemed to represent the new unity of all Frenchmen. The triumphal arch, with its three equal apertures, was decorated with low-reliefs and inscriptions celebrating not bloody victories but the conquest of liberty, the Constitution, and the Rights of Man. Verses added to the arch at the time of the festival rejoiced in this fact:

L'Arc de triomphe enfin n'inspire plus d'effroi;
Jadis il n'était que victoires sanglantes:
Et devant leurs tyrans, les nations tremblantes.
Il consacre aujourd'hui la liberté, la loi,

Et le contrat sacré du peuple avec son roi.
Romains, le feu chez vous a pu s'éteindre.
Celui de cet autel, du temps n'a rien à craindre:
Non, le feu de nos coeurs ne s'éteindra jamais,
Les Vestales sont les français.[49]

The friezes on both façades of this new-style triumphal arch were the work of the sculptor Jean-Guillaume Moitte. We know the subject matter of the frieze facing the river from an engraving by Félix Massard that was presented to the National Assembly (Figure 38).[50] The frieze announces the purposes of the Federation, the swearing of an oath by the regular troops, the National Guard, the deputies, Louis XVI, and citizens to uphold the constitution. It shows soldiers, women, and children, arms upraised like the Roman brothers in David's *Oath of the Horatii,* approaching the Altar of the Fatherland. Behind the altar stand female figures holding the Law and the coat of arms of France, without the traditional crown. On the right Mercury, holding a pike and a Liberty Bonnet, leads a group of men and women, many bearing trumpets, towards a pedestal on which Renown records events. The classical attire of the figures both gave the work a universal quality and linked contemporary events to the heyday of Rome.

We have even better reproductions of the frieze on the façade of the arch facing the Champs de Mars and the Ecole Militaire, thanks to an engraving by Massard and the close-ups published by the editor Joubert and presented to the Legislative Assembly (Figures 39–41).[51] On the left side of the frieze we see aristocracy and its agents among the ruins of the Bastille. Out of the rubble rises Liberty, armed with a sword and carrying a pike and a Liberty Bonnet, trampling a Hydra representing reaction. She directs prisoners, victims of arbitrary power, towards the Altar of the Fatherland, before which they prostrate themselves in gratitude. Towards the centre of the frieze Frenchwomen, imitating those of ancient Rome, deposit their jewels on the altar. Nearby is Abundance, who will replenish such sacrifices. Further to the right Renown leads the Chariot of the Law, drawn by lions symbolizing force, while the royal family and

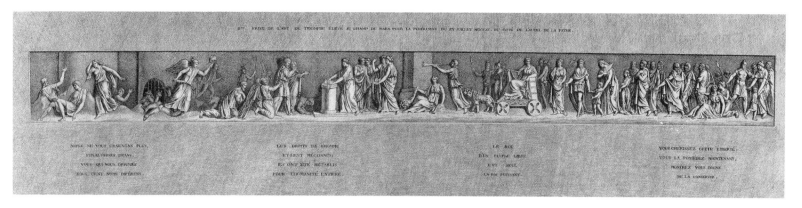

39 Frieze on the façade of the triumphal arch facing the Champ de Mars.

40, 41 Detail of the centre of the frieze facing the Champ de Mars. *Centre*: French women sacrificing their jewels and Renown leading the chariot of the Law; *below*: detail of the right-hand side of the frieze, showing Louis XVI and his family, accompanied by deputies and the National Guard, returning to Paris in October 1789.

42 The Altar of the Fatherland in the centre of the amphitheatre.

deputies follow behind, allegorically representing their return to Paris in October 1789. The National Guard directs the people, signifying that its mission was to maintain order and enforce the law.

The focal point of the vast amphitheatre was the civic altar elevated in the centre (Figure 42). The four broad staircases leading up the platform on each side signified that the altar was accessible to everyone. The equal faces of the altar itself pointed to all of France and the four corners of the world. Like the triumphal arch, the pillars on either side of the four stairways were laden with low-reliefs and inscriptions.[52] On one of the pillars facing the entranceway France was shown sitting on part of the globe, holding a cornucopia in her hands. Beside her were the attributes of the arts and sciences. On the other pillar on the same side a female figure radiating light dispelled clouds, disclosing the word CONSTITUTION. On each of the pillars fronting on the pavilion two rows of warriors were depicted facing each other, their hands raised over an altar, swearing the oath decreed by the National Assembly, which was inscribed underneath. On the pillar facing one side of the circus, six Renowns trumpeted the injunction inscribed there: "Reflect on the three sacred words of the Revolution: NATION, LAW, KING" (Figure 43). On the pillars on the other façade, four female Spirits were shown (Figure 44) inscribing these words:

> Mortals are equal; it is not birth, but
> virtue alone which makes the difference.

> Law in every state should be universal.
> Mortals, whoever they may be, are equal before it.

There was no canopy over this altar, so that there would be no barrier between the Supreme Being and his priests.

On the day of the Federation, as one passed through the imposing entrance to the great amphitheatre containing a sea of flags – the sixty standards of the Paris National Guard, the eighty-three flags of the departmental contingents, and the colours of the troops of the line – and throngs of spectators, one seemed to be entering a special space. "One does not feel that he is entering a field," reported one pamphleteer, "but rather another world."[53] In effect a vast outdoor cathedral had been created, significantly lacking the cruciform shape and the orientation of a traditional one, with the sky forming an immense dome. At the far end of the field, in the apse, so to speak, was the pavilion on which a throne had been placed for the "Citizen King," as some now called Louis XVI. His new status was expressed by the fact that an identical seat for the president of the National

Assembly had been placed to his right on exactly the same level. The two seats were flanked on either side by places for the national deputies and municipal officials, so that the representatives of the people formed one body.

The ceremonies staged in this setting reveal the mix of the old and new that characterized this phase of the Revolution. The banners of each contingent of the troops were blessed in turn at the altar. Following this, Talleyrand, leader of the new constitutional church, celebrated mass. Then Lafayette led the troops in an oath "to be faithful forever to the Nation, the Law, and the King," the trinity of the new regime. The crowd echoed this pledge. Finally, to underline that he too was now subject to the law, Louis XVI himself swore to uphold the constitution.

Since the event commemorated the storming of the Bastille, one might have expected a re-enactment of that event. There were several proposals for inclusion of such a skit. One writer had proposed an attack on a model of the Bastille erected on the Champ de Mars.[54] Pierre-François Palloy, the entrepreneur charged with demolition of the old prison-fortress, proposed that a model be carried through the streets and placed on the altar.[55] The king would then smash the model with a hammer as he took the oath to uphold the constitution. The planners rejected such proposals because they wished to minimize reminders of past conflicts in order to achieve unanimity. This festival and those that followed were examples of integrational propaganda, aimed at rallying the people around new ideas and institutions, not at reminding them of old divisions.

The ceremonies on the Champ de Mars were only part of the great celebration. Strategic sites throughout the city were decorated to accommodate banquets, dances, and athletic contests, which continued for a week. The new Halle au Blé, the garden of Ruggiery, and the summer Vauxhall were among the principal sites. On the Champs-Elysées each of the trees bore lanterns, which at night formed a chain running as far as the eye could see (Figure 45). Triangular frames, also bearing lights, announced the entrances to adjacent streets. In the centre of the avenue was a pyramid of lights topped with a crown. Orchestras arranged in an octagon played lively airs that invited citizens to dance and mingle regardless of class. The city hall too was decorated for the occasion (Figure 46). It was a "sacred place," as one observer called it, because it was there that the electors had first expressed the hopes of the nation.[56] On either side of the main doorway, panels were mounted, the one on the left showing the oath administered by Lafayette in the name of the nation, that on the right the oath taken by the king. Above the doorway was a huge sun whose rays were composed of little coloured lanterns. In the centre of the sun

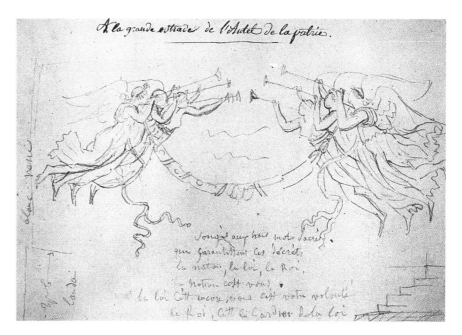

43 Sketch of the side of the Altar showing six Renowns trumpeting the "sacred words" Nation, Law, and King.

44 Sketch of the side of the Altar showing female Spirits recording the dictum "Mortals are equal … "

45 Illuminations of the Champs-Elysées for the Festival of Federation in 1790.

46 Illuminations of the City Hall for the Festival of Federation in 1790.

was inscribed the new trinity: NATION, LAW, KING. Underneath the frame was a square tablet bearing another inscription:

ALL CITIZENS ARE BROTHERS
ALL CITIZENS ARE SOLDIERS[57]

The emplacement of the statue of Henry IV near the Pont Neuf was the site of a special celebration the day after the Federation. The popular king had been bedecked with a tricolour scarf and surrounded with floral bouquets (Figure 47). His statue was flanked by two large painted poplars (etymologically, "trees of the people"), each decorated with giant medallions, one showing Lafayette presenting flowers to Henry on behalf of the National Guards, who were visible in the background, the other depicting the mayor offering the king another bouquet in the name of the people, likewise shown in the rear. Amid the poplars had been placed a rock with inscriptions honouring Henry and Louis XVI as two monarchs who loved their people. Nearby in the Place Dauphine a simple altar had been erected, decorated with stately candelabras. There a Te Deum was sung, followed by dancing that lasted into the night.[58]

Next to the Champ de Mars the most impressive decor was erected on the site of the Bastille (Figure 48).[59] As one pamphleteer pointed out, nothing could have inspired "a more profound or religious respect than the location of the Bastille." There eighty-three poles, or rather trees that had been transplanted, outlined the ground-plan of the recently demolished fortress. The eight bastions of the monument to despotism were draped with garlands of lights. Overhead was suspended an ornamented chandelier that diffused all the colours of the rainbow. At night all the lights created a starry vault, under which musicians played and people danced. At the centre of the site was an obelisk crowned with a Phrygian bonnet. At the entrance to this artificial grove was an inscription that underlined the contrast between the present spectacle and the memories that the place evoked:

HERE ONE DANCES AND LAUGHS

Another pamphleteer praised the planning committee for arranging a dance on land that needed to be purified, so that the pollution of the Old Regime would be trampled into the ground and the exhalation of despotism would be chased away by the people's songs and thanksgivings.[60] This notion of purifying a site by superimposing a new structure was to become a familiar one in the coming decade.

The enclosure created on the Champ de Mars for the great

47 Decoration of the statue of Henry IV on the
Pont Neuf for the Festival of Federation in 1790.

48 Decoration of the site of the Bastille for the
Federation in 1790.

49 View of the Festival of Federation in Paris in 1791.

Federation of 1790 continued to serve as the setting for subsequent festivals, but the decor was modified to suit changing circumstances. For the second anniversary of the taking of the Bastille, the architect J.-J. Lequeu was in charge of the embellishments. We have an engraving from Prudhomme's *Révolutions de Paris* (Figure 49)[61] and the plans of the architect in the Cabinet des Estampes of the Bibliothèque Nationale (Figures 50–52).[62] The Altar of the Fatherland was raised up on a circular dias that was decorated with troops holding their standards. The festival had degenerated into a military procession of the Parisian National Guard. The recent attempted flight of the king had raised inquietitude everywhere and ruled out popular rejoicing. The following year national volunteers passed through Paris and renewed the ceremony of Federation on 14 July. A Tree of Feudalism, loaded with crowns of counts and barons, chains of knightly orders, ermine cloaks, and coats of arms, was set aflame (Figure 53). The coat of arms of Lafayette crowned the tree; the general had fallen from popular favour since the massacre nearby of antimonarchical demonstrators by troops under his command on 17 July the previous year. Towards the Ecole Militaire there was a funerary obelisk to soldiers who had lost their lives on the frontier – perhaps the first monument to the common soldier.[63]

The great Festival of Federation was unquestionably an event of epochal significance. It became a model for the long series of *fêtes révolutionnaires* staged throughout the decade. Although it involved considerable spontaneous rejoicing, it was also the result of a conscious effort by the authorities of the day to curb and direct public enthusiasm. The revolutionary festival was to develop into one of the principal instruments of social control wielded by successive regimes. Each of these regimes in turn would use it to try to stop the Revolution, to consolidate it around the ideals and institutions on which the regime rested. Just as the Festival of Federation was an attempt to consolidate the achievements of the first year of the Revolution, so the Festival of Unity and Indivisibility would try to entrench the ideals of the new Republic, the Festival of the Supreme Being would try to reinforce the Robespierrist Republic of Virtue, and the cycle of *fêtes décadaires* under the Directory would seek to save the Constitution of Year III. Moreover, other festivals honouring martyrs, celebrating victories, and Pantheonizing famous men, each with a distinctive architectural decor, were to play an important role throughout the decade.

In her much acclaimed book *La Fête révolutionnaire* Mona Ozouf has argued that openness and horizontality were two principal features sought by planners in choosing space for revolutionary festivals.[64] This contention has been repeated by other historians,[65] but the evidence suggests that it is not completely accurate. The revolutionaries did prefer large

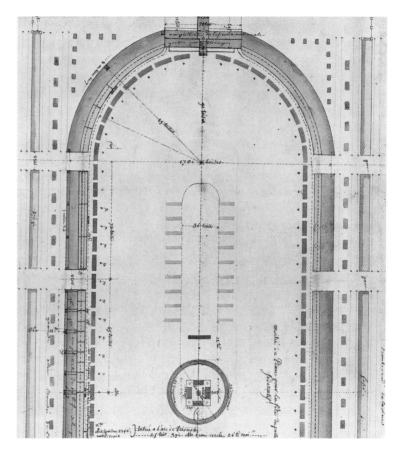

50 Lequeu. Plan for the Festival of Federation in Paris in 1791.

open-air spaces because of their closeness to nature and their capacity to hold huge crowds, but the surviving drawings or engravings show that these spaces were usually delimited in some way, by barriers, lines of troops, or stands around the perimeter. To a large extent festivals were instruments of social control, and crowds were more easily controlled in an enclosure of some kind than in an ill-defined space. At the same time the revolutionaries were opposed to partitions among citizens, but horizontality was not an end in itself. Whenever the revolutionaries planned permanent festival facilities, these invariably featured tiered benches, so that spectators would have an unobstructed view of each other and of the rituals taking place. Moreover, while planners preferred outdoor facilities, they were well aware that the weather was often inclement – it poured rain on the day

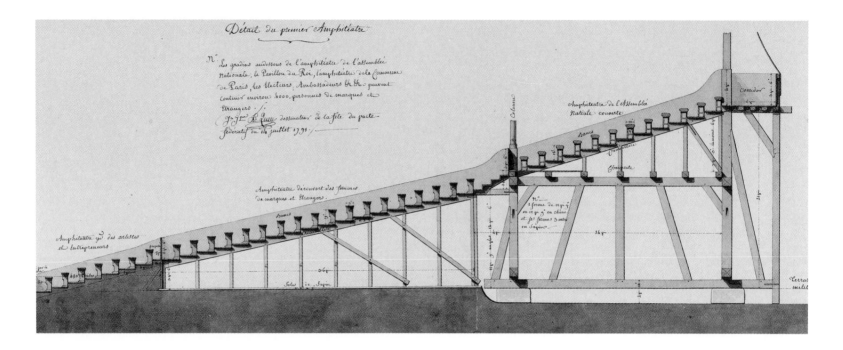

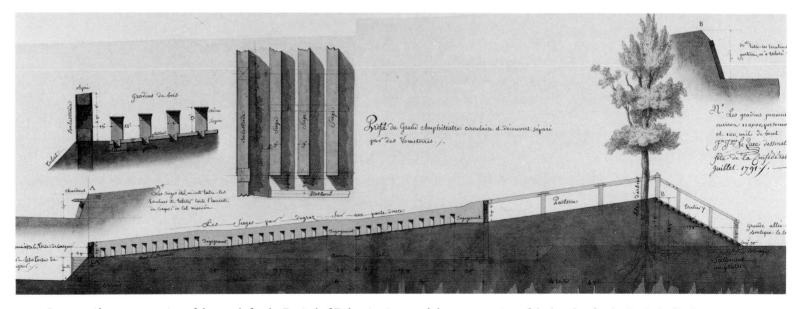

51, 52   Lequeu. *Above*: cross-section of the stands for the Festival of Federation in 1791; *below*: cross-section of the benches for the Festival of Federation in 1791.

53 View of the Federation in 1792, with the Feudal Tree burning in the foreground.

of the Festival of Federation in Paris – consequently, they planned covered arenas and *temples décadaires*. Ozouf does not discuss the numerous plans for such indoor spaces.

The Festival of Federation also reinforced the idea of the amphitheatre as the ideal enclosure for popular gatherings. Throughout the decade there were to be not only several projects to create permanent outdoor amphitheatres in granite and marble but many others to construct the same sort of enclosure in indoor arenas, revolutionary temples, primary assemblies, and large squares. The amphitheatre seemed more democratic than the hierarchical and compartmentalized space of the conventional theatre or the cruciform shape of the traditional church. It seemed the best shape to obscure social differences and to arouse shared emotions. At the same time it offered the authorities the opportunity to control and direct the masses, who, in a less definitely defined space, might get out of hand. Moreover, as we shall see later, the revolutionaries also preferred the amphitheatre as the best form for the assembly hall of the representatives of the people, who ideally were supposed to express the united will of the nation.

The Festival of Federation also revealed the possibility of giving a revolutionary appearance to the capital, and by extension to the whole country. The anonymous author of *Songe patriotique, ou le monument et la fête*, which appeared at the time of the festival, dreamed of the inauguration of a national monument on the anniversary of the Revolution seven years later.[66] He envisaged a monument on the site of the Bastille consisting of an immense quadrilateral pyramid three hundred feet high, crowned with a Temple of Liberty, dominating Paris. Vast staircases would lead inside to a sanctuary containing a statue of Liberty and a hall for the National Assembly. The outside would be covered with sculpture recalling the events of the Revolution and inscriptions recording important laws. This visionary monument would be constructed entirely of marble from all over France and would be made possible by donations from across the country. The author also anticipated a public contest for the design, judged by non-competing artists and citizens.[67] There are other portents of the future in his dream: at the inauguration the king is absent because of an indisposition, and no religious ritual takes place inside the sanctuary. "It is sacred, but not holy," explains the guide. During the festival, as the citizens watch a statue of Liberty exactly like the one in the sanctuary being carried down the Seine on a boat, the guide explains that such statues have been decreed for all of France. As we shall see in the next chapter, this dream was already shared by many planners. ▲

De Varenne. Project for a monument honouring Louis XVI. (Figure 64)

III

PLANS TO IMMORTALIZE THE REVOLUTION

THE ARCHITECTURAL DECOR OF THE FESTIVALS of Federation eloquently symbolized the advent of a new order, but such architecture was ephemeral, like stage sets designed for the life of a play. One could not satisfactorily represent the permanent accomplishments of a revolution, which was allegedly a turning-point in history, by plaster sculptures, wooden structures, and canvas painted to look like marble. From the time of the convocation of the Estates General, architects proposed works in granite, marble, and bronze. They contended that such works would provide ongoing instruction for citizens and transmit the achievements of the Revolution to posterity. *Immortaliser* was the verb favoured by many architects. In fact one planner, Armand-Guy Kersaint, argued that even if France should decline, as everything in nature tends to do eventually, ruins in bronze and stone would still convey the greatness of her achievements. Kersaint thus anticipated what Speer in our own century would call the "ruin value" of architecture.[1]

In the first years of the Revolution projects for permanent monuments mushroomed throughout France. For example, in December 1789 the city of Sens sent an address to the Constituent Assembly along with a patriotic gift of 14,000 livres. In its address the city announced that it was building a port on the Seine that would be decorated with an obelisk.[2] It asked the Assembly to consent to having the cornerstone laid in its honour and to have the names of all the deputies inscribed on it. The Assembly left these decisions entirely to the municipality. Two months later the press reported that eighty-eight new municipalities in Basse-Normandie, Maine, Anjou, and Bretagne had decided to send delegations to a patriotic festival in Ponthivy and "to order there the establishment of a public

monument erected in memory of the abolition of the limits and divisions of the provinces and consecrated as a tribute to the new constitution."[3] Moreover, there was a proposal to erect in each commune a triangular obelisk on which laws would be posted with great pomp.[4] Such projects would have been the first step in putting a new ideological stamp on the whole country.

Among many other projects for statues, columns, and squares,[5] some deserve a closer look, such as the one at Champ-deuil in Brie. On 1 August 1790, the seventeenth day of the Federation there, inhabitants inaugurated a monument in honour of Liberty to serve as a focal point for future festivals and a means of instructing citizens.[6] It was decorated with a Phrygian bonnet and revolutionary injunctions on all sides. The inscription on the second façade read: "Passerby, this is a bonnet of Liberty. On the same day each year the inhabitants will swear in a civic festival to die rather than abandon it." To mark the occasion the name Champ-deuil (Field of Mourning), which recalled the scourges of the past, was changed to Champ-Libre. This was one of the earliest incidents of the name-changing that was to become a mania later on across France and another way of giving space a new character.

The leaders in some cities already sought to give them a new ambiance, not by changing the names of a few squares or streets but by systematically imposing a new revolutionary nomenclature. In June 1790, following the suppression of hereditary nobility, the National Assembly suppressed all titles such as prince, duke, count, viscount, baron, knight, sire, and squire, and called for the eradication of visual aristocratic signs such as liveries and coats of arms.[7] Toulouse provides a striking example of a city that not only eradicated the last vestiges of feudal emblems but then proceeded to give revolutionary names to all of its fifteen sections – la Nation, la Loi, le Roi, la Constitution, Droits de l'Homme, la Liberté, la Fraternité, la Justice, l'Honneur, le Jeu de Paume, la Fédération, l'Alliance bordeloise, Département, District, and Commune. At the same time, names of streets, squares, and quais with feudal connotations were changed.[8] The new names provided a summary of the ideals and administrative changes of the early Revolution. This rechristening of spatial units was taken very seriously by contemporaries. "These changes are all the more important, that in banishing forever the memory of such ridiculous names, they recall other names which are the signs of the constitution and liberty," commented the *Annales patriotiques et littéraires*. Moreover, the National Assembly authorized cities, towns, villages, and parishes to which seigneurs had given their family names to revert to their ancient names.[9]

In Nantes a project for a monument initiated near the end of the

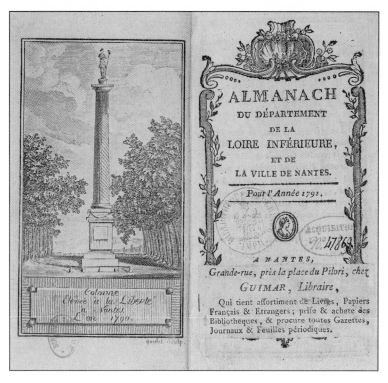

54 Column of Liberty in Nantes as imagined by an artist in 1791.

55 Crucy. Statue of Liberty proposed in Nantes in 1790.

Old Regime was updated to suit the new order. The city had recently been the site of remarkable urban development – the opening of a new quarter named after Graslin, the Hospice des Enfans-Trouvés, the Halle aux Grains, the Grand Théâtre, the Bourse, the Place Royale, the Cours des Capucins (now the Cours Napoléon), and the Quai Poissonnerie. Near the end of 1788 the architects of the city had decided to mark this extraordinary development by a column crowned with an effigy of Louis XVI to be situated between the two promenades in the city centre (Figure 54).[10] When the time arrived to lay the foundation stone, preparations were under way for the Festival of Federation. The column became linked to the Federation and was christened La Colonne de la Liberté. The municipal authorities issued an ordinance on 23 June 1790 stating that the inauguration would take place along with the Federation the next day.[11] At the festival an Altar of the Fatherland stood at the base of the projected column. There a mass was celebrated and the federative oath was sworn. There were the usual parade, banquet, and dancing, after which the procession returned to the column for the laying of the first stone.

At the site of the column M Douillard, an architect, made a speech. He pointed out that the site was the very place where the old walls had stood that formerly seemed to separate the city from the rest of France. It was the spot where the battle had been fought against ministerial despotism. Now it was the venue where regenerated Nantais had taken the civic oath. He continued: "The architects of this city, gathered here, have thought that, French and free, we ought, Messieurs and dear fellow-citizens, on the very spot which still testifies to the last grimace of aristocracy, raise up to Liberty, which until Louis XVI found no refuge in France, the first column of a temple which should have no limits except those of the universe."[12] Here again was the idea of symbolically reversing the meaning of a site. When Douillard had finished his speech, the senior architect present passed a trowel to the mayor, who passed it to the president of the department, who in turn passed it to the president of the district. Then the municipal officials, the heads of administrative bodies, and the military leaders all in turn tapped the stone with a hammer.

Following the plan that had been approved, the column was to be Doric in style, six feet in diameter, eighty-six feet tall, and surmounted by a statue of the king. A fasces, symbol of union and force, was to form the pedestal, which was to rise up on a granite plinth. The cornice was to be decorated with garlands of oak, linking Liberty Bonnets on the four corners. Originally it had been planned to engrave the circumstances that had given birth to the monument and the principal events of the Revolution on marble tables on the four sides of the pedestal, but after the inauguration it was decided to engrave the inscriptions on two copper plates. One of the inscriptions was dedicated to the fortunate revolution taking place in France, to Louis XVI as restorer of liberty, to the National Assembly, to the citizens of Nantes who had presented the first demand for rights, and to the young citizens who had gone to the aid of the Rennois on 29 January 1789. This long inscription ended with a list of the architects. The second inscription read in small capitals:

YEAR MDCCXC

SIXTEENTH YEAR OF THE REIGN OF LOUIS XVI THE BENEFICENT

KING OF THE FRENCH

RESTORER OF FRENCH LIBERTY[13]

Nantes was also the site of another very significant project. On 27 January 1789 two hundred young volunteers from Nantes marched to support their fellow patriots in Rennes. Early in 1790 Fournier de Custine proposed that a statue be placed on the Place Graslin to commemorate this event. On 11 May the municipal council approved his proposal.[14] The design by Mathurin Crucy, who had become municipal architect a few months before, featured a statue of Liberty, holding a Phrygian bonnet (Figures 55, 56).[15] On both sides soldiers are shown hailing her. Although on one side of the pedestal Louis XVI is praised as the "Restorer of French Liberty," the inscription on another side makes it clear that Liberty was the real object of devotion:

1790

MONUMENT ERECTED

TO LIBERTY

BY THE 14 COMPANIES

OF THE CORPS OF YOUNG CITIZEN

SOLDIERS OF NANTES

This may be the first proposal for a monument in which Liberty rather than the king would occupy the summit. A year later, soon after the royal family's abortive flight to Varennes – *not* after the overthrow of the monarchy, as a local historian claims[16] – the municipal council decided that Liberty should also replace the king atop the Column of Liberty.[17]

Even more intriguing is the example of the Column of Liberty erected in Montpellier (Figure 57).[18] This project was born at an extraordinary session of the local Jacobin Club on 2 December 1790, at which the National Guard of the city and the troops of the line from the nearby gar-

56 Crucy. Detail of the pedestal of the statue of Liberty proposed in Nantes in 1790.

ÉLÉVATION PERSPECTIVE DE LA COLONNE À LA LIBERTÉ ET À LA CONCORDE
que la société des amis de la constitution et de l'égalité de Montpel.ᵉ a fait
élever à ses fraix, sur la place de l'esplanade, en mémoire de la révolution
française, et de l'étroite afiliation qu'elle a contractée avec la garde-
nationale de la ville et les troupes de lignes formant la garnison.
La 2ᵉ face du piedestal est ornée du nom des grands hommes. La 3ᵐᵉ de la pierre de la Bastille. La 4ᵐᵉ de l'historique du monument.
Derriere la figure de la Liberté est un génie foulant aux pies un joug et s'apuiant sur la constitution.

57 Column of Liberty erected in Montpellier.

rison were special guests. In the enthusiasm of this fraternal meeting the architect Demoulin proposed that the sentiments of the assembly ought to be perpetuated in a durable form, a column on the Esplanade of the city. He envisaged the monument as a focal point around which the descendants of those at the assembly would swear every year to live free or die.[19] This column would be crowned with a statue of Liberty, holding in one hand a fasces out of which protruded a pike capped with a Phrygian bonnet, pointing with the other to this symbol of happiness. Behind the figure of Liberty there was to be a Genius leaning on the Constitution. At the base of the capital there would be one of the signs of the zodiac, a lion to recall that it was under its influence that Liberty had been conquered in July 1789. This is how the column appears in engravings that were sent to the National Assembly, the Jacobin Club, and all other such clubs in France, but contemporary reports record that on the completed monument Liberty held a shield on which was engraved NATION, LAW, KING.

This Column of Liberty offers one of the best examples of the effort to link the Revolution to the cosmos. Demoulin suggested that the site on the Esplanade should be designed as a great sundial, with the column so positioned that its shadow would fall on a line marked 14 July each year when the anniversary came around.[20] At a meeting of the club on 5 December 1790 a citizen named Scipion Vialard proposed to go one better. Pointing out that if only the shadow was used to announce each anniversary, only part of the crowd would be able to see it, he proposed that a cannon be placed at its base and a lense so arranged that the sun would ignite the powder without any human help. "I propose, therefore," he declaimed, "that this star should participate in our oath, and that by the concentration of its rays, it should announce with an explosion to all the citizens that the moment has arrived, and that it is the first actor in this imposing ceremony."[21] A clockmaker offered to make the mount for the lens and to place it so that it would ignite the powder. There was no mention of what would be done on an overcast day. A professor of mathematics later offered to lay out the sundial.[22]

The decorations proposed for the four faces of the pedestal are also revealing. The sketches with accompanying notes, apparently done in 1791 and now in the Municipal Archives, show a further attempt to link the monument to the cosmos (Figures 58–61).[23] On the side facing the rising sun was to be inserted one of the stones from the dungeons of the Bastille, on which would be engraved a Renown announcing the victory of the French people and the coming of the Revolution. The stone was to be surrounded by images of the weapons that the conquerors of the Bastille had used, and underneath was to be a broken yoke. On the north side

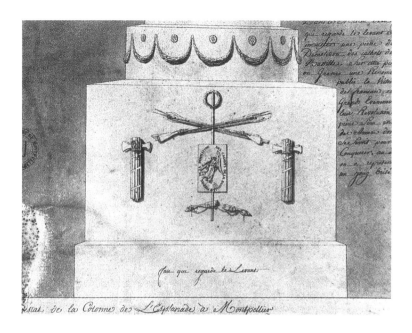

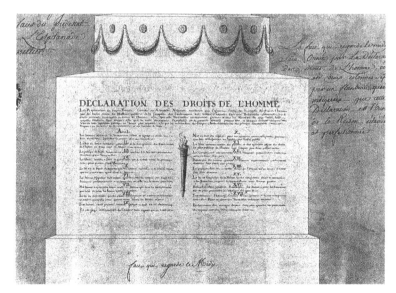

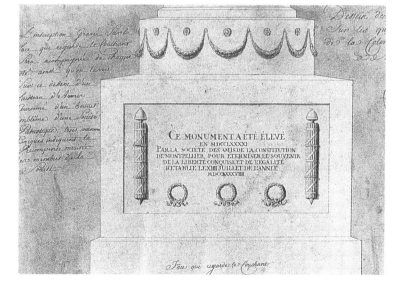

58, 59 Detail of the side of the pedestal of the Column of Liberty in Montpellier. *Above*: facing the rising sun; *below*: facing south.

60, 61 Detail of the side of the pedestal of the Column of Liberty in Montpellier. *Above*: facing north; *below*: facing the setting sun.

was to be a Glory, with an inscription in honour of great men. This was to be encircled by a serpent biting its tail, a symbol of Eternity, and further out by a ring of civic crowns, each bearing the name of one of the great men. On the south side were to be two columns listing the clauses of the Declaration of the Rights of Man, separated by a torch indicating that they were the product of Reason, enlightened and perfected. On the side towards the setting sun was to be inscribed the history of the monument. The position of the symbols and inscriptions was clearly as carefully thought-out as on a mediaeval cathedral.

The cornerstone was laid with great fanfare on 3 January 1791. There was a parade of municipal officials, commissioners of the Jacobin Club, and contingents of the National Guard from the city hall to the site where a huge crowd was gathered. Following speeches by one of the commissioners and the mayor, the architect Demoulin handed a trowel to the mayor, who laid the first stone amid cries of "Long live the Nation, long live the Law," and the blaring of trumpets and other instruments. A glass cylinder encased in lead, which was placed inside the foundation, contained a tricolour cockade, a medallion commemorating the Federation, seals of the various groups participating in the ceremony, a copy of the constitution of the Jacobin Club, minutes of the alliance of the club and the troops at which the column had been proposed, a copy of the Rights of Man, and an account of the ceremony. A warning written on parchment was deposited with these mementos: "If ever this monument becomes the prey of time, may this inscription urge our descendants to reconstruct it, and may those who attempt to destroy it be covered with ignominy."[24] This warning was also engraved on a lead plaque on the monument.

One local historian says that there is no evidence about the exact location of the site,[25] but a plan for realignment of streets during the Revolution shows it in the middle of the Esplanade between two basins at either end.[26] Another historian states that the column was not finished for several years,[27] but an invoice from the artist – unnamed – shows that the statue of Liberty for the summit was completed before the end of 1791.[28] Other invoices show that work continued, not to complete the column but to revise the symbols and inscriptions from time to time to make them conform to the ideological shifts of the Revolution. The records show too that the column served repeatedly as a symbolic centre for local rituals. At the ceremony celebrating the proclamation of the constitution in October 1791, the mayor, Durand, addressed the statue in an almost idolatrous fashion: "Yes, we shall maintain it [the constitution], it is under thy scrutiny that we swear to do so. Holy Liberty! It is at the feet of thy statue that we come to proclaim a constitution based on thee. From high on this column, thou attractest our hearts and our vows."[29] On 1 January 1792, when patriotic women had completed flags of free nations – America, England, France, and Poland – for the Temple of Liberty (the Jacobin meeting-place), the flags were paraded through the city, and each in turn was dipped in tribute to Liberty atop the column while guns and music sounded.[30]

In Saintes, a small town in the department of the Charente-Inférieure, the Jacobin Club trooped to the Place de la Liberté, formerly the Place Blair, on 8 July 1791 to lay the first stone of a monument to be erected at the expense of the club in honour of the Revolution.[31] The monument was to be a Doric column, two feet in diameter and thirty feet tall including the base, surmounted by a pike supporting a Liberty Bonnet. A bottle containing the Declaration of the Rights of Man was deposited in the foundation along with the date of the ceremony. The monument was to be completed by 14 July. It is still in place but is now crowned with a fleur-de-lis. Another design done in Saintes three months earlier may have been an alternative project for the same site or the centrepiece for a festival of Federation (Figure 62).[32] It features an obelisk, inscribed with the date 1789, with giant fasces on each corner atop a pedestal bearing another inscription anticipating the Robespierrist cult more than three years later:

UNDER THE AUSPICES

OF THE SUPREME BEING

THE FRENCH PEOPLE

FREE

A fascinating example of a monument in a provincial centre was the one erected by Joseph Sec, whom Michel Vovelle has called "a self-made man," at the entrance to his garden in the new suburb of Notre-Dame in Aix-en-Provence.[33] Sec had begun as an apprentice wood-worker but later acquired moderate wealth as a merchant of wood. The monument, which was completed near the end of the constitutional monarchy, is one of the few constructions of the French Revolution that is still in place, although some of the sculpture is badly deteriorated (Figure 63). It conveyed multiple meanings: it was at the same time a visual summary of the Judeo-Christian revelation, a sort of Masonic temple, a tribute to the French Revolution, and a memorial to Sec himself, who intended to be buried in the garden. It consists of a tiered structure decorated with nearly fifty low-reliefs and statues. Some recount events in the Old and New Testaments. Others allude to the Great Architect and the elements with which he worked. Still others relate to the confiscation of church prop-

62 Anonymous. Project for an obelisk in Saintes.

63 View of the Monument Sec in Aix-en-Provence, from a nineteenth-
century watercolour.

erty that served as backing for the *assignats*, the new paper money. And the panel depicting the young Christ in the workshop of Saint-Joseph, Sec's patron saint, is doubtless an invocation of his own career.

Although this complex iconography is difficult to decipher in detail, as it must have been at the time it was sculpted, its basic message is clear: freedom is based on the rule of law. When viewing it from the street, one sees on the left side an African and on the right a European, both dressed in classical attire.[34] They point theatrically to Moses, who is carrying a tablet on which one can still read, "Love God and love thy neighbour." Above Moses, crowning the pyramidal structure, is a large figure representing Law, a woman attired like Minerva, holding scales, a pike, and a fasces. She is flanked by flaming pots on the corners of the pedestal, which create a religious aura around her. Significantly, Law stands above a low-relief that originally bore the likeness of Louis XVI but later featured the image of Sec himself. In case the onlooker missed the message, several inscriptions affirmed the need to observe the law. Like the Festival of Law in Paris on 3 June 1792, the monument may have warned against excessive violence. The large panel in the centre of the base bore the main inscription:

1792 – YEAR IV OF LIBERTY
MONUMENT DEDICATED TO THE MUNICIPALITY OF
THE CITY, KEEPER OF THE LAW,
BY JOSEPH SEC

Paris was, of course, the object of most proposals to immortalize the Revolution. De Varenne was one of the first to call for a monument there (Figure 64).[35] The monarch was to be depicted in a very different manner from the statue of Louis XIV by Desjardins in the Place des Victoires, where the Sun King had been shown ascendant over chained figures representing his conquests. As we have seen, the monarch had already been largely demilitarized and turned into a beneficent legislator in the monument honouring Louis XV in Reims. In 1789 De Varenne proposed a monument that would depict Louis XVI as the Father of His People. The king was to be shown in royal attire welcoming three genii distinguished by their attributes – Agriculture, the Arts, and Commerce. The Genius of Commerce would be depicted presenting a medallion of Necker to the king. Alongside Louis was to be a statue of Henry IV, smiling and saying, "My son, the happiness of Peoples causes that of Kings." Louis XVI would reply, "My People and I constitute one only." On one side of the pedestal was to be the figure of a woman holding a fasces, symbol of Concord; on

64 De Varenne. Project for a monument honouring Louis XVI.

Sergent inv. & sculp. 1790.

PROJET D'UN MONUMENT ELEVÉ A L'HONNEUR DE LOUIS XVI.

Voté par les Citoyens du District de S. Jacques l'hôpital,
et présenté à l'Assemblée Nationale et aux Représentans de la Commune.

65 Sergent. Project for an obelisk in Paris honouring Louis XVI.

the other was to be a figure of Hercules, representing Force. On the front of the pedestal was to be a low-relief showing the three estates united, presenting the new constitution to the king. On the rear the names of all the deputies would be engraved in bronze to perpetuate their memory. This project, engraved by Moreau junior, was approved by the National Assembly in September 1789.[36]

The project proposed by the artist Antoine-François Sergent to the district assembly of Saint-Jacques l'Hôpital revealed the same high hopes early in the Revolution that Louis XVI would become the Father of His People (Figure 65).[37] Sergent was inspired by the speech the king had made when he appeared in the National Assembly on 4 February 1790. "May this day, when your Monarch comes to unite himself with you in the frankest and most intimate way, be a memorable epoch in the history of this Empire," he quoted Louis as saying. Sergent proposed that a huge marble obelisk be erected to commemorate the event. A medallion would be attached to the monument by a garland of oak leaves, with this inscription below:

MONUMENT ERECTED BY THE AFFECTION OF THE PEOPLE
TO THE FIRST CITIZEN KING

On the pedestal would be a figure in bronze relief representing History, holding a book on which she would be shown writing on one page, "Louis XVI proclaimed Restorer of French Liberty MDCCLXXXIX," and on the other, "Constitution accepted by the king." On one of the faces of the pedestal would be engraved the speech of the king to the Assembly, on the reverse side the Declaration of the Rights of Man. On one of the lateral faces would be a scene of the demolition of the Bastille, and on the other the civic oath taken by the people at the Altar of the Fatherland. So that children could read the inscriptions and educate themselves in their rights, there would be no balustrade or grille.

Since Sergent believed that it was in public squares that the annals of a nation should be recorded, he wanted his proposed obelisk to be set in a strategically located square. He suggested that it be erected on the Place Dauphine near the equestrian statue of Henry IV. Louis would be associated with that popular king, but Sergent wanted the nude enchained figures at Henry's feet stripped away because they gave a false impression of his character. Sergent also preferred this site because the young members of the new citizen army had established an artillery park nearby. Moreover, the plans for the embellishment of Paris called for a square in the vicinity that would lead to the Temple of Justice, where the National

Laws would be deposited. The monument to Louis XVI would thus be placed between the Sanctuary of the Laws and the boulevard de la Liberté: "This would place it in the midst of his most beautiful work." In advance the artist proposed an inscription for what he called the Temple de Thémis:

SANCTUARY OF NATIONAL LAWS.
OBEY PEOPLE AND MONARCHS

It was significant how often Sergent used religious terminology in referring to the setting. He proposed that this be the site where on 4 February of each year the king's speech would be read and young citizens and the National Guard would swear an oath. He concluded by pointing out that his monument would be unique, a monument erected by the people, unlike those raised up by monarchs in praise of themselves.

Most of the early monuments symbolizing a new era were to honour Louis XVI; however, an anonymous pamphleteer reminded the public that 2 August 1789 was the second centenary of the advent of Henry IV to the throne.[38] The author pointed out that the first centenary had passed without any monument to express the fond memory that the nation had of Henry. The pamphleteer proposed a monument to this king, who had been the benefactor not only of France but of all mankind. The monument was to consist of a vast rotunda, composed of a double series of columns with space in between forming a covered promenade. Trees would embellish the exterior. In the centre of the interior would be a classical altar supporting a statue of the king, posed like a good father among his children, dressed in the simple costume he liked to wear, and gesturing in welcome to even the lowest of his subjects. The author called on artists to compete in depicting the king in the statue, low-reliefs, and paintings because images were more effective than words. Henry would provide a model for the future kings of France: "It is there that the august child who must reign over France will educate himself about his duties, as soon as he will be able to know his relations with his subjects and his neighbours."

A number of artists proposed permanent monuments for the site of the great Festival of Federation. The project of Jean-Nicolas Sobre was typical of their aspirations.[39] His plan was to commemorate the festival, which he claimed was the most impressive in history, with a massive structure in the centre of the circus. The whole edifice was to sit on a square dias measuring two hundred and ten feet on each side. Forty steps would lead up the sides of this massive base. Along the faces of the base would be placed four altars to accommodate celebrations on anniversary days. On the faces of these altars would be inscribed the four oaths – the Tennis

Court Oath, that of the Fédérés in 1790, that of the clergy, and that of new magistrates. Over these inscriptions there would be low-reliefs illustrating the union of legislative and executive power, elections by the people, freedom of religion, and the abolition of privileges. Flanking the altars would be statues of famous liberators such as Voltaire, Mably, and Mirabeau. Underneath the dias were to be guardhouses for three or four thousand National Guards, watched over by vestals bearing sacred fire. From the immense base would tower a triumphal column one hundred and forty feet tall, encircled with bronze reliefs depicting the major events of the Revolution, and topped by a statue of Liberty. Hidden lamps around the base of this statue, visible for ten leagues, would announce celebrations, or warn that the Fatherland was in danger.

The terrain of the Bastille was naturally a favourite site for planners early in the Revolution. Apparently unaware of pre-revolutionary plans, several architects claimed to have been the first to propose a monument for this site. Davy de Chavigné claimed to have proposed such a monument honouring Louis XVI during the elections for the Estates General (Figure 66).[40] Under the engraving it says that it was designed in May 1789 and engraved in 1790, by which time the Bastille had been stormed and ordered demolished, making de Chavigné's proposal all the more appropriate. He proposed a towering column topped by the figure of Louis XVI. Low-reliefs would commemorate the deeds of the king in favour of liberty. The column was to be decorated with civic crowns honouring the citizens of the three orders and especially the two superior orders, who had renounced their privileges in favour of civic equality. At the four corners of the base were to be seated figures of France Liberty, Concord, and the Law. At the feet of these allegorical figures water would spout forth, not only representing the great rivers of France, but signifying that the benefits of the regime flowed out to all parts of the kingdom. Free-standing statues on lower pedestals surrounding the column were to represent the cities and colonies of France, all united in recognition of the king, the foremost friend of the people and restorer of liberty.

Joseph-Pierre Du Morier also claimed the honour of being the first to propose a monument to replace the old prison. In a letter to the *Moniteur* in May 1790 he reminded the public that he had made such a proposal when he had been among those chosen more than a year before to edit the *cahier* for the district of Notre-Dame.[41] The pamphlet to which he refers bears out his claim.[42] In it Du Morier made several demands for urban improvements. He called on the directors of buildings henceforth to consult the Commune about the construction of public buildings in Paris. He called too for construction of a bridge across the Seine from the

66 Davy de Chavigné. Project for a
column honouring Louis XVI, elevation.

Arsenal to the Left Bank, replacement of the wooden bridge between the two islands in the centre of the city, and eradication of all the architectural remnants of former barbarism, especially demolition of the Bastille, the fortress that had inflicted so much suffering on the victims of depotism under Louis XIV. "We would like a monument placed on this site which will inform the most distant posterity that this Bastille, having become a state prison under *Louis the Tyrant*, was destroyed under *Louis the Patriot*."[43] Du Morier, however, apparently did not produce a design for such a monument.

An architect by the name of Etienne-Louis-Denis Cathala also proposed a monument for the site of the Bastille early in the Revolution (Figures 67, 68). In a pamphlet accompanying his designs he said that he had served as one of the supervisors of the demolition of the prison-

fortress.[44] As a result of his experience, he reported, he had come up with two basic ideas. The first was to create a huge square from which the boulevards would be extended as far as the Seine, where a new bridge would be constructed over to the Left Bank. Unlike many other planners of the period, he preferred a quadrilateral *place*. He argued that a circular *place* was only acceptable when it was not divided into numerous segments, whereas his square would allow a number of entrances from different angles. He pointed out that the Romans had not created circular *places*. He had searched Italy in vain looking for examples. France was now imitating the popular government that had led Rome to greatness; she should imitate the Roman example in the arts as well.

The centrepiece of his proposed square was also inspired by the Romans, who had used columns rather than equestrian statues to

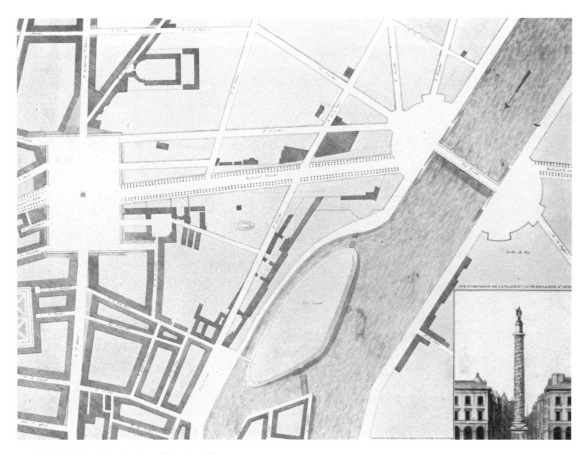

67 Cathala. Plan for the site of the Bastille.

68 Cathala. Detail of the column.

honour their heroes. He had found nothing more striking than Trajan's Column in Rome. The barbarians had not destroyed it because they had found it so imposing. He called for a column even larger than its model: the pedestal was to be nineteen feet high, the shaft more than twelve feet thick and one hundred feet in height, plus the statue of Louis XVI on the top. The low-reliefs spiraling upward, however, would depict the progress of the Revolution rather than military victories. Cathala clearly shared the eighteenth-century faith in the power of monuments to overawe and instruct the onlooker: "It is with these objectives in mind that I have proposed to erect a similar one [to Trajan's] in the centre of the square, one which will astonish posterity while impressing on it a sentiment of veneration. The enemies of the Revolution will not fail to come across this

project, the completion of which will speak to the eyes of the whole world, more than books which are over the heads of the people."[45]

Cathala's second basic idea was to exploit the ditches around the garden of the Arsenal to create a docking basin adjacent to the Seine. At the same time he would have improved the infrastructure of the district and inserted more greenery into the whole urban landscape. His plans show that he wanted to straighten and widen old streets, create new ones, and have them terminate in semicircular *places*. In his designs new streets and buildings are shown in red, and buildings to be suppressed are indicated with dotted lines. The broad boulevards – the boulevard Saint-Antoine and the new one leading to the river – are lined with trees. Also, like other planners of the day, his plans provide for useful facilities such as granaries, a hos-

69 Gatteaux. Proposal for the site of the Bastille.

pital, and wharfs. There are two versions of his proposal in the Archives Nationales, one with his proposed basin and one without it, both with elevations of the column in the lower right-hand corner.

An even more revealing example of the desire to perpetuate through monuments the memory of the coming of the Revolution was the grandiose proposal by Nicolas-Marie Gatteaux at the time of the Festival of Federation (Figures 69–73). Like Davy de Chavigné and Cathala, Gatteaux proposed a column for the site of the Bastille, this one to be over three hundred feet tall so that it would be visible from a great distance on all sides.[46] The artist hoped that, since it would be higher than any other monument in Paris, it would be the first structure that visitors would want to see. The capital of this column was to be ornamented with a balustrade. Above that was to be a trophy of war holding up a large shield bearing four lions, symbols of the earth, which in turn would support a globe covered with fleurs-de-lis, emblematic of France. On the very top was to be Liberty,

holding a palm in one hand and a bonnet in the other. The column itself was to be a giant fasces, composed of one lance from each department, tied together by garlands decorated with their coats of arms. The garland was to be composed of oak and laurel leaves, symbols of glory, force, and peace.

Atop the pedestal were to be several groups of figures, some human, others allegorical. One group was to feature Louis XVI, leaning on Justice, receiving from a minister in the guise of Counsel the writ summoning the Estates General. Another group was to portray Philosophy depositing her riches on the Altar of the Fatherland. A third group was to show a warrior, supported by Hercules and guided by Wisdom, marching towards Glory. Here again we find Hercules, the demigod who in the past had served French kings, now beginning a revolutionary career. The final group was to depict Truth showing a citizen how to achieve happiness and abundance.[47] The massive pedestal, raised up on a perron, was to form an Altar

70 Gatteaux. Column to consecrate the
Revolution.

71, 72 Gatteaux. Column to consecrate the Revolution.
Above: detail of the pedestal; *right*: detail of the crown.

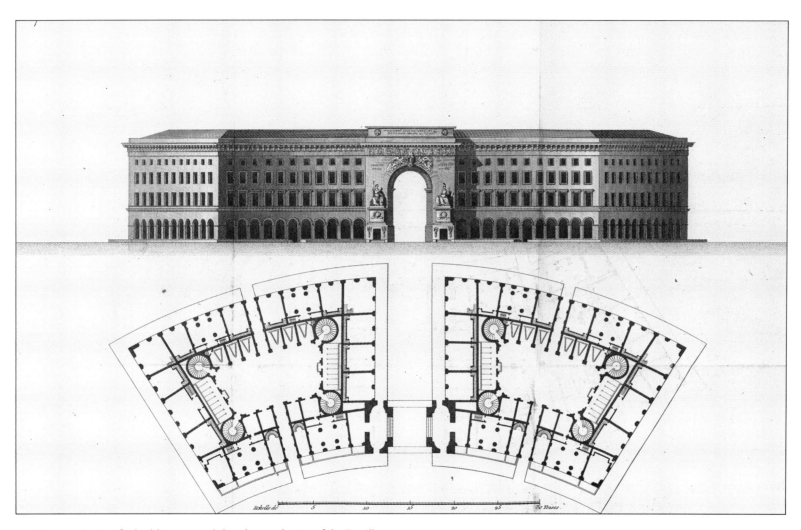

73 Gatteaux. Project for buildings around the *place* on the site of the Bastille.

temple dédié a la liberté

projetté Sur les ruines de la bastille; proposé par Souscription, l'autheur rénonçant a toute espece d'honnoraires et contribuant pour sa part, de la somme de 300ˢ.

74 Prieur. Project for a Temple dedicated to Liberty for the site of the Bastille.

of the Fatherland on which the constitution would be displayed in bronze. Inside there was to be a display of important legislation and a spiral staircase leading to the summit. All this was to be set in the centre of a huge circular square, ringed with uniform buildings from which six wide avenues would radiate. The monument was thus to be the focal point of an ideal French eighteenth-century *place* – that is, an open square linked strongly to the surrounding city.

Equally grandiose was the project for a Temple of Liberty by Prieur for the same site (Figure 74).[48] In the notes accompanying the engraving of his project he recalled how the Greeks and Romans had erected vast monuments to transmit to posterity a striking victory, a virtuous deed, or an extraordinary event. In comparison the French had constructed only monotonous squares, in most of which there appeared a proud despot sitting awkwardly on a corsair. The obligation to flatter the ruler had dictated the subject-matter to the artist. Prieur claimed that his proposed monument would therefore be unlike anything in existence and would be financed by a public subscription. He proposed four towers set on the ruins of the Bastille in a way that would recall the shape of the old fortress. On these towers he proposed to situate pedestals, each supporting a Genius in the form of a female in classical garb placing on an altar the bust of a great man who had earned the gratitude of his country. On the square base formed by each of these four towers would rise the temple itself.

The temple was to sit on a massive circular platform on which the names of those who contributed to its construction would be inscribed. Atop this circular base was to be the temple proper, consisting of a ring of Ionic columns constructed out of white marble. On the entablature there would be another larger inscription:

TEMPLE DEDICATED TO LIBERTY

In the centre of the circular interior there was to be an obelisk twice the height of the temple, topped with a statue of the king. On the faces of the obelisk inscriptions would record great achievements, especially those of the Revolution. On the circular cornice of the temple, genii, holding medallions of great men intertwined with garlands, would form another ring. One can judge the massiveness of the monument from the relative size of the carriage and the people shown in the engraving. The whole new structure would contrast sharply with the ruins of the old fortress representing former despotism. Again we have the ascendancy of a new order symbolized by the erection of a building or a statue on the ruins of an earlier one.

Just six months before the overthrow of the monarchy Pierre-François Palloy, the entrepreneur who had been in charge of the demolition of the Bastille, presented another ambitious scheme for the site to the Legislative Assembly (Figures 75–77).[49] At the same time he sent a pamphlet, illustrated with several plates, to all eighty-three departments, "in order to prod all artists in France into action for the welfare of the Fatherland."[50] Like several other planners we have discussed, he proposed a square with a towering column in the centre.[51] This Doric column was to be erected on one corner of the outline of the walls of the former prison-fortress, traced with black stones on the pavement of the square so that pedestrians would consciously trample it underfoot. The shaft was to rise out of a model of the Bastille, conveying the impression that it was crushing the old edifice. This replica was to sit in turn atop a rocky hillock formed out of debris from the demolished building. Inside this hillock were to be guardrooms, reservoirs for two fountains, and access to a spiral staircase leading to the summit. The column was to be crowned with a statue of Liberty, holding a pike capped with a bonnet in her right hand and the constitution in the other.

On the south edge of the square there were to be two auditoriums, one for theatrical productions, the other for public instruction. Commencing on the same edge there was to be a massive axis running along the old ditches of the Arsenal to the river-bank. Along the eastern side of this axis there was to be a tree-lined boulevard de la Liberté, abutting on a Pont de la Liberté connecting the Left and Right banks, a feature of all the plans for the area. Some of this axis was to be divided into blocks for residential and commercial development, but more than half the area was to consist of a National Garden. This green swath would match the Jardin des Plantes on the other side of the river, creating a huge verdant arch through the east end of the city. West of the garden old buildings and streets were to be suppressed to open another area for redevelopment. The thirty new streets were all to be named after civic virtues and revolutionary ideals.[52]

Part of the National Garden was to feature trees shaped to remind onlookers of the walls and towers of the Bastille. Alcoves in the greenery representing the eight towers were to shelter statues of Abundance, Equality, Force, Justice, Prudence, Truth, Union, and Victory. Inside the enclosure there was to be a massive mast ninety feet high, topped with a globe and a cock, symbol of vigilance. It would remind the onlooker of the height of the Bastille from the moats to the top of the towers. Every 14 July this reminder of the old prison-fortress was to be illuminated like the site of the Bastille during the Festival of Federation in 1790, and an inscription would repeat the theme of that first anniversary: "Here people dance" (Ici on danse). Another section of the park was to be decorated with a huge basin with a jet in the centre. Around the outer rim were to be statues of

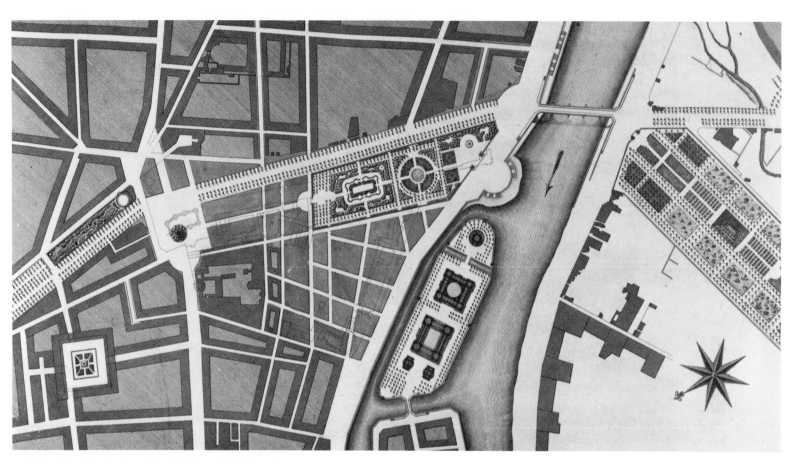

75 Palloy. Plan for the site of the Bastille and the Arsenal.

Franklin, Mably, Rousseau, and Voltaire. Nearer the river next to the semi-circular *place* was to be a statue of Louis XVI, later replaced by Minerva.[53]

Palloy's plan also called for new facilities along the river and the Ile Louvier, features which would demonstrate the concern of the new regime for the prosperity and health of the citizenry. An aqueduct was to service the whole area.[54] There was to be a dock at the south end of the broad axis from the Place de la Liberté and the Seine. Other port facilities were to line the river. On both banks there were to be large grain and flour depots to ensure supplies for the capital. On the island a modern arsenal was to be established with artillery depots, powder magazines, saltpetre works, and barracks for invalid soldiers. This arsenal was to be surrounded by

walls to provide protection to the adjacent city in case of accidental explosions. All these facilities were to be bordered with rows of trees. The plan once again shows the mix of residential development, improved communication, commercial facilities, green areas, and revolutionary ideology that typified many of the projects of the era.

In presenting his plan to the Assembly Palloy emphasized various advantages. The redevelopment of the area would create employment and promote the arts. He also appealed to the revolutionary ideal of equality, arguing that all sections of the capital should be developed evenly. It was unfair to give preference to the suburbs Saint-Honoré and Saint-Germain over those of Saint-Antoine and Saint-Marcel. In fact he proposed

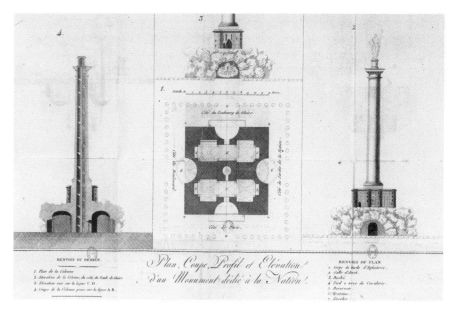

76, 77 Palloy. *Left*: column for the *place* on the site of the Bastille; *above*: details of the proposed column.

suppressing the very word *faubourg* so that there would be a single, unified city. Moreover, he argued that mixing social classes and improving living conditions would mollify discontent: "The well-off will find themselves mixed in with petty traders; the unfortunate class will feel themselves comforted … for disturbances arise only where the artisan is indigent, when he finds himself in a mass within too small confines. It is therefore in the interest of the government that all classes be spread throughout the city and that those in easy circumstances do not all build in the same district."[55]

Most of these projects for statues, columns, obelisks, and squares represented a symbolic order that still retained monarchical elements. It was an unstable mix. Although a great deal of gratitude had been directed towards Louis XVI early in the Revolution, the system could only last so long as he seemed willing to become a constitutional monarch reconciled

to the new order, a delicate task requiring skills that ran counter to his whole inheritance and upbringing. The queen too would have to support him in this task, if he was to succeed. Already in some projects Liberty, an abstract goddess still relatively unsullied by crimes committed in her name, had moved into the central position. Moreover, the Altar of the Fatherland was already evolving into an alternative to both the throne and the Christian altar as the focus of devotion. Before turning to the breakdown of this hybrid symbolic order, we must examine efforts to create a temple for the representatives of the Nation, sanctuaries for its heroes, and icons of the civic virtues demanded by the new order. ▲

Gilbert. Project for a National Assembly. (Figure 114)

IV

TEMPLES FOR THE NATION AND ITS HEROES

ONE COULD EXAMINE MANY OTHER PROPOSALS for monuments, but even more revealing were the proposals for an imposing building to house the representatives of the nation.[1] France had no completely satisfactory building for such a purpose because it had been a hundred and seventy-five years since there had been a convocation of the Estates-General. Conscious of the lack of a suitable building, the Royal Academy of Architecture in February 1789 set as the subject of its contest for students a building to accommodate the Estates General of a great nation.[2] The only design that seems to have survived is that of the prize-winner, Alexandre-Maximilien Le Loup or Lelong, a design now in the archives of the Institut de France (Figure 78).[3] This design is rather uninspired, but it is significant in that it shows three distinct but not completely separate areas for the three separate orders, although it also shows an amphitheatre where they could have met together on occasion. When the three traditional orders merged together into a single National (Constituent) Assembly in May 1789, such a plan was no longer suitable.

The Academy of Architecture recognized that the problem had not been solved when, in August 1790, it proposed as the subject for another contest a building to house National Assemblies.[4] Also conscious of the problem, numerous architects drafted plans. These designs, however, were aimed at much more than solving a practical problem. There was a need to create an impressive building that would provide a sacred space in which the representatives of the nation would assemble to pass the laws that were to be the foundation of a new society. It is significant that many of the designers called their proposed buildings temples. Formerly law had been surrounded by an aura of legitimacy and sanctity because it emanated from a king who ruled by the grace of God and who had been annointed at Reims by oil from the Sainte Ampoule. Now it was important to give laws emanating from the representatives of the nation their own aura of legitimacy and sanctity.

Before the Revolution the locus of power had been the palace in Versailles, about ten miles from the centre of Paris. The march of the market women and soldiers of the National Guard on 5–6 October compelled Louis XVI to move to Paris and the new National Assembly to follow suit. The king and the Assembly were henceforth to operate in the midst of "the people" as represented by the inhabitants of Paris, a shift that affected the whole subsequent course of the Revolution. The royal family took up residence in the Tuileries Palace, and the Assembly temporarily moved into the Archbishopric.[5] Soon it occupied the Manège, a former stable, which scarcely symbolized its role as the meeting-place of the representatives of the sovereign people. A permanent building was called for. Such a building would have to be made to stand out on the urban landscape while at the same time being linked to it. Architects were thus compelled to find or create an area large enough for a huge *place* or courtyard in the centre of which an immense legislative building would be clearly visible. To link it physically and psychologically to the adjacent city, architects had to place it on a great axis, at the focal point of radiating streets, or facing a garden or the Seine.

The Temple of the Nation had to accommodate more than just a legislature. It has often been asserted that the Revolution was a stage in the rise of the bourgeoisie, a claim that has been much contested in the last generation. Less controversial is the fact that the revolution was a stage in the rise of the modern bureaucratic state. As the representatives of the nation prepared legislation, investigated social problems, and took over responsibilities previously handled by the clergy, committees and officials proliferated. Moreover, since legislation henceforth had to be widely distributed among the citizenry, provision for printing presses was essential. Also, it was deemed desirable to preserve documents in archives adjacent to their source. This need for extensive space, however, could be used to advantage. Auxiliary buildings could be used to frame a massive courtyard, to encircle a spacious square, or to line adjacent streets. The overall mass of buildings could thus cater to the megalomania so evident in the projects of the later eighteenth century.[6]

The best-known design for a legislature is that of Boullée (Figures 79–81). As we have seen, architectural historians, influenced by the work of Emil Kaufmann, have grouped him with Ledoux and Lequeu as one

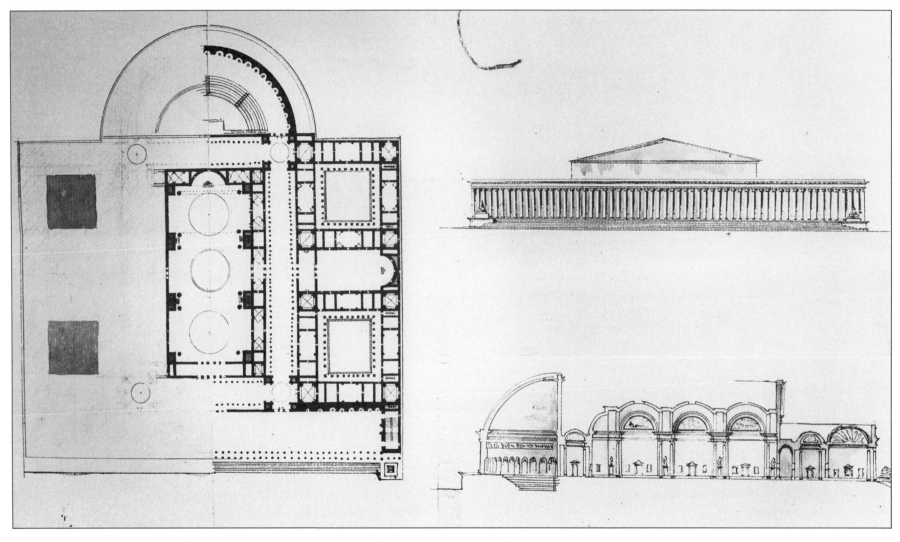

78 Le Loup. Plan, elevation, and longitudinal section for a building to house the Estates.

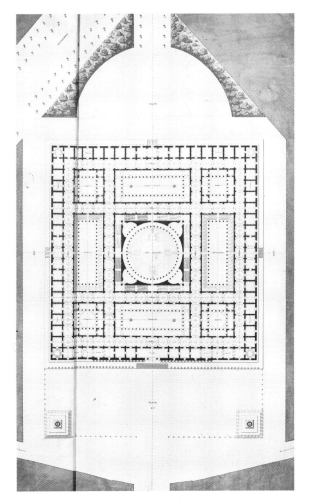

79, 80 Boullée. Project for a National Assembly. *Above*: elevation; *left*: ground-plan.

81 Boullée. Project for a National Assembly, cross-section.

of the "revolutionary architects" of the late eighteenth century, using the term in an aesthetic rather than a political sense. Although he was accused during the Terror with being a moderate or even a counter-revolutionary, he did design an immense National Assembly for the site of the Couvent des Capucins or the Place du Carrousel.[7] Pérouse de Montclos, author of an authorative work on Boullée, points out that the design and the architect's notes about it share many ideas with Kersaint's *Discours sur les monuments publics*, presented to the Legislative Assembly in February 1792. Pérouse de Montclos concludes that Boullée's design probably dates from about the same time.[8]

The project for a National Assembly, which he called a "Palace," provided an ideal opportunity for Boullée to apply his idea that architects should incorporate poetry into their buildings, above all when they were designing public monuments. With its massive cubic shape and its clean lines it was typical of his progressive style. It was to be crowned with a triumphal chariot of Liberty drawn by no fewer than twenty horses. The low-relief on the attic was to portray a revolutionary festival. The text of the Declaration of the Rights of Man was to be inscribed on the façade, making it speak to the public and announcing the function of the edifice. "I said to myself," Boullée wrote in his notes, "what image can arouse greater interest than the one which displays the Law, which is loved by all, since all desired it."[9] Along the two stylobates were to be seated figures representing the new departments, each holding a book of decrees, signifying the assent of the people to the work of the National Assembly. The edifice was to be flanked by two free-standing columns modelled on that of Trajan.

Inside the giant cube there was to be a circular assembly hall, surrounded by offices and committee rooms. This round amphitheatre that Boullée and others incorporated into their plans was destined to become the shape favoured by revolutionary architects for the meeting-place of the deputies of the nation. We can trace its evolution from a series of ground-plans by the architect Pierre-Adrien Pâris for the assembly hall in the Hôtel des Menus Plaisirs in Versailles designed to accommodate the Estates General in May 1789.[10] In the first plan the rectangular hall is divided so that the three orders would each have a distinct section: the clergy on the left of the plan but to the right of the podium, traditionally the place of honour; the nobility facing them on the other side; and the deputies of commoners across the end away from the podium (Figure 82). The second plan shows that when the three orders merged into a National Assembly, the architect replaced the separate sections with a continuous amphitheatre divided only by necessary aisles (Figure 83). This was the shape transferred to Paris when the National Assembly moved there

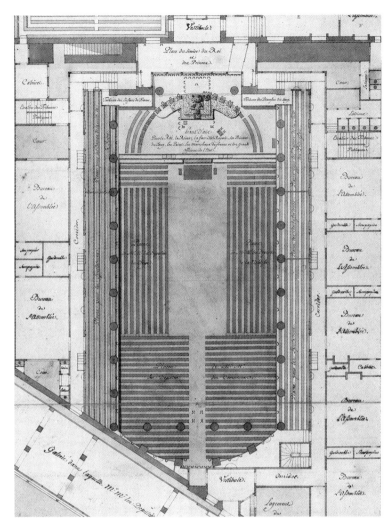

82 Pâris. Renovation of the Menus Plaisirs in Versailles to accommodate the three Estates.

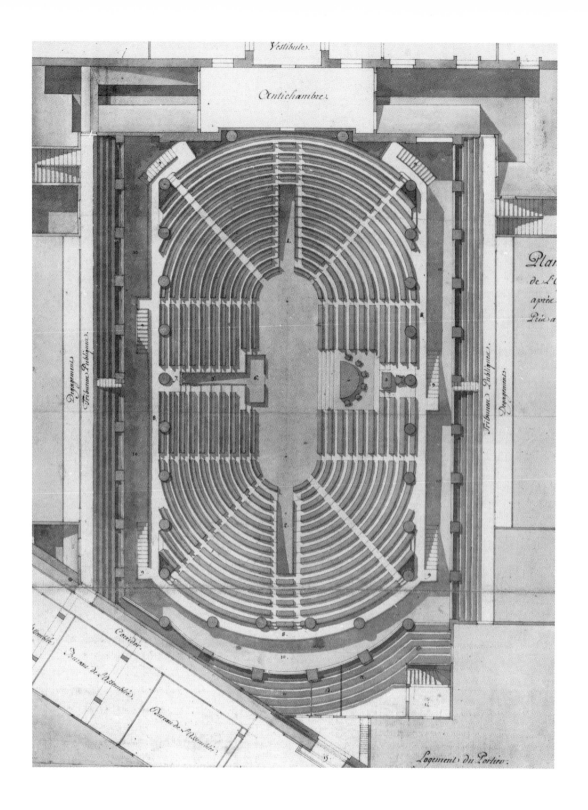

83 Pâris. Further renovation of the Menus
Plaisirs to accommodate the
Constituent Assembly.

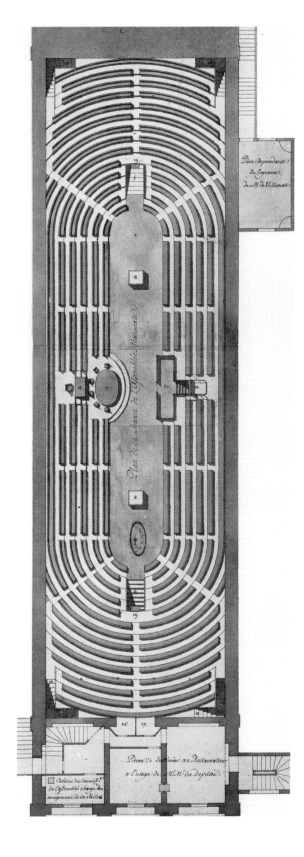

in October, as shown in a third plan (Figure 84). From then on the amphitheatre prevailed, whether oblong, circular, or semicircular.

The shape expressed a belief that played a key role in the new political culture. The revolutionaries rejected the possibility of a government party on one side facing an opposition party on the other. For the revolutionaries there could be only one public good, which all deputies should seek to express. This cannot be explained simply as a result of the influence of the idea of the general will as articulated by Rousseau. It was largely the product of the notion of sovereignty inherited from the Old Regime. Theoretically the king had embodied *la chose publique*, which he expressed in his single will. When authority was inverted and the nation became sovereign, the idea of a single will persisted, ruling out the legitimacy of political parties representing special interests. Although factions did emerge, the idea of a united will remained, expressed in the amphitheatre, which became the dominant shape of legislatures outside Britain and those colonies that remained under her control.[11] In addition, the circular or semicircular hall appealed to the taste for geometric shapes.

At about the same time, Boullée designed a Municipal Palace that was to serve a similar purpose to the National Assembly (Figures 85–7).[12] He claimed that in designing it he tried to take into account everything that was relevant and essential to such a building. "I told myself," he wrote in his notes, "that a Municipal palace was not merely a place for district magistrates, but that it belonged to all. It is in such a place that citizens give voice to their complaints and where they attend the most important debates."[13] In order to express the purpose of the building, he gave it a stark, virile character suited to republicans instead of the rich decor he had used on palaces for princes. On the four corners of the building there were to be quarters for armed forces, to emphasize the force of the law. Moreover, to proclaim the function of the building and to emphasize that it belonged to all, he provided countless apertures outside and numerous galleries inside so that a swarm of men could enter and leave freely without confusion.

Boullée explained that turning the building into a sort of beehive while also giving it a virile character posed aesthetic problems. On the one hand he had to incorporate many entrances, but at the same time he needed a smooth façade to give the virile appearance he sought. To solve this problem he increased the height of the building so that there would be a large bare space between the stories. The purpose of the building also

84 Pâris. Renovation of the Manège in Paris to accommodate the Constituent Assembly.

85, 86 Boullée. Project for a Municipal Palace.
Above: perspective view; *right*: ground-plan.

87 Boullée. Project for a Municipal Palace, cross-section.

led him to arrange the internal space in a way that followed the example of various Italian palaces, where the finest floor was on the highest level. This arrangement allowed him to open up the whole ground floor to the public. The main hall would occupy the centre, with waiting rooms and conference rooms arranged around it. Significantly, the hall resembles the circular meeting-place in his plan for a National Assembly. The whole upper floor was to be reserved for magistrates. Boullée's design thus reveals an acute awareness of the spacial imperatives of the new political culture.

Early in the Revolution the site of the Bastille attracted several designers of a National Assembly because of its symbolic significance and the extensive terrain when the adjacent arsenal was included. For example, the site inspired Mouillefarine, an obscure architect who described himself as a young man newly arrived from Troyes (Figures 88–93). He proposed using the terrain as the location for a complex of buildings, squares, boulevards, monuments, and even a new bridge across the Seine.[14] The focal point of the complex was to be the site of the Bastille, transformed into a spacious Place Nationale with a statue of Louis XVI in the centre and ringed with uniform buildings. From this circus seven streets were to fan out. Mouillefarine shared the preference for radiating squares that had developed in the eighteenth century and that we have seen already in the project

by Gatteaux. Besides five lesser streets, two of which were to be straightened, two wide tree-lined boulevards – the boulevard Saint-Antoine and the boulevard de la Liberté – were to fan out, transforming the neighbourhood and linking the complex to the rest of the city.

The broad axis running from the Place Nationale to the Seine, the boulevard de la Liberté, was to be lined with public buildings accommodating the militia, the mayoralty, and other government officials. It was to be punctuated by a spacious square, the Place de la Liberté. This square was to provide the setting for the National Assembly, a cross-shaped structure with four identical entrances on each side, symbolizing the fact that the Revolution had a message for the four corners of the world. The building was to be crowned by a temple honouring Liberty, consisting of a globe resting on a ring of columns, again signifying the world-wide significance of the Revolution. A huge figure of Mercury was to soar over a map of the world, heralding a new gospel. A ring of allegorical statues was to decorate the circular entablature. The centre of this edifice was to house a circular assembly hall, while the wings were to accommodate government offices constructed around inner courtyards.

The boulevard de la Liberté was to abut on a semicircular *place* on the banks of the river and the bridge across to the botanical gardens on

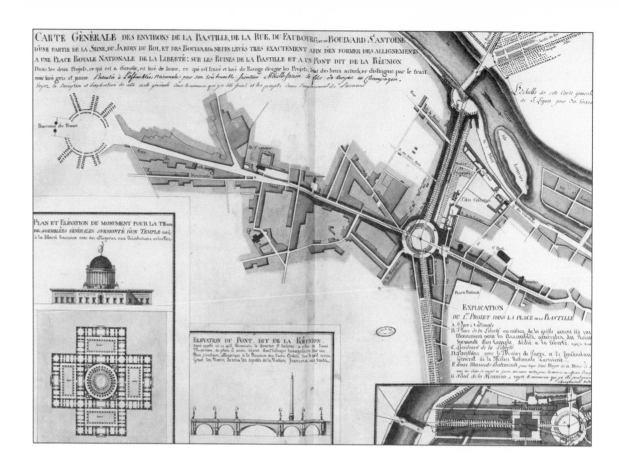

88 Mouillefarine. Plan for the site of
    the Bastille.

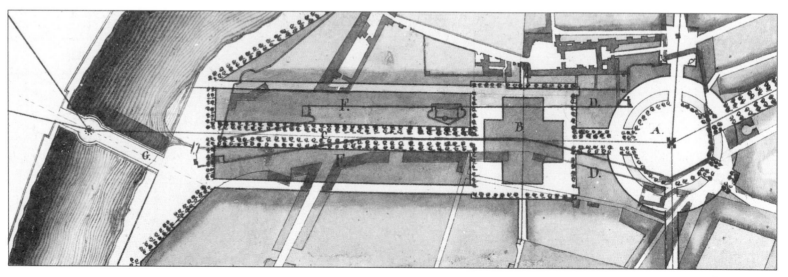

89 Mouillefarine. Detail of the axis from the Place Nationale to the Seine.

90 Mouillefarine. Project for a National Assembly, ground-plan.

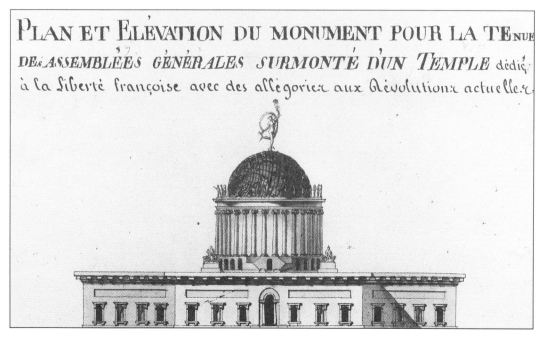

91 Mouillefarine. Project for a National Assembly, elevation.

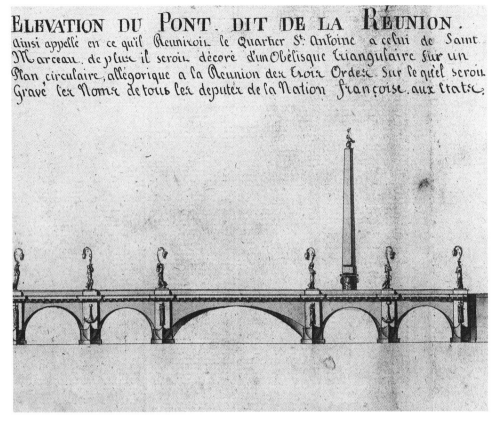

92 Mouillefarine. Pont de Réunion, elevation.

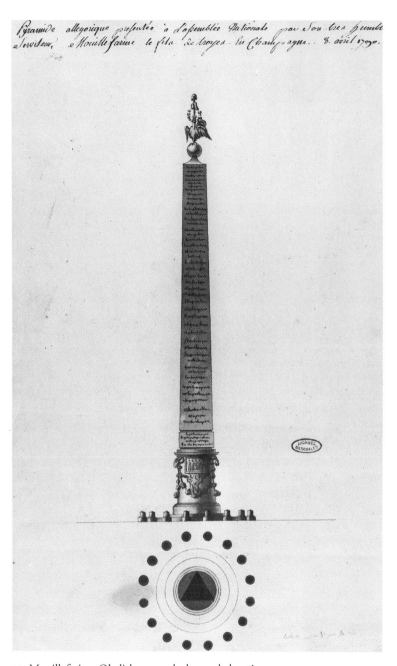

93 Mouillefarine. Obelisk, ground-plan and elevation.

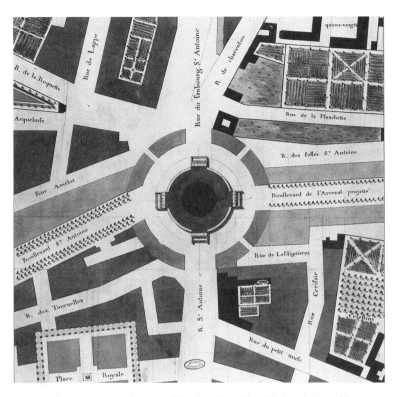

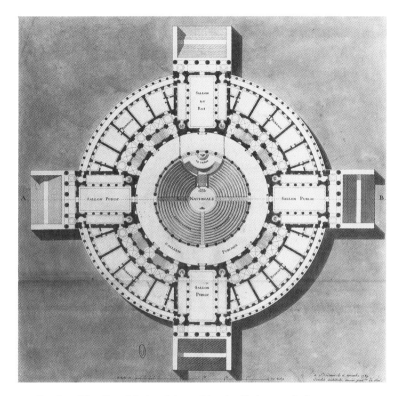

94 Combes. Square on the site of the Bastille with a National Assembly in the centre, ground-plan.

95 Combes. Plan for a National Assembly, detailed ground-plan.

the Left Bank. The name of this bridge, the Pont de Réunion, was intended to remind the public of the new unity among the three orders of the old society. Allegorical figures serving as lamp standards, fasces on the piers, and an obelisk were likewise to convey an ideological message. Moreover, the shape of the obelisk and its base were to reinforce this message. The obelisk was to form an equilateral triangle, which as we have seen was a shape that conveyed a sense of the sacred because it had been used by Christians to express the mystery of the Trinity and by Masons to denote the Supreme Being. In this case the triangle was to signify the equality of the three orders. The circular pedestal was to suggest unity and perpetuity. On the base, over an eagle, a low-relief was to depict citizens clasping hands around an altar. On the three faces of the obelisk were to be inscribed all the names of the deputies to the Constituent Assembly. On the peak was the familiar globe, a French cock, a pike, and a Phrygian bonnet.

An architect from Bordeaux, Louis Combes, was also attracted to

the site of the Bastille. His plan for the vacant site is especially revealing (Figures 94–8).[15] Like several others, he proposed a circular *place*, with broad avenues radiating out from it. In the centre was to be an imposing edifice to house the National Assembly. In the notes on his drawings Combes declared his belief in the symbolic role of architecture: "The Edifice destined for the sessions of the National Assembly ought to be a Majestic and durable Monument which could attest to posterity the importance and the grandeur of the Revolution which is taking place among us." His temple was to be a grand neoclassical structure unified by a ring of Ionic columns. There were to be four entrances, each featuring six Doric columns. Both the circular shape and the four entrances suggest again the idea of the Revolution transmitting its message in all directions.

It was in the decoration of the inner assembly hall that the symbolism of the edifice was to be most striking. Combes suggested that an Altar of the Fatherland should be placed in the centre of the hall, at which sacred

96, 97 Combes. Project for a National Assembly. *Above*: elevation; *below*: cross-section.

92

98 Combes. Project for a National Assembly, detail of the vault.

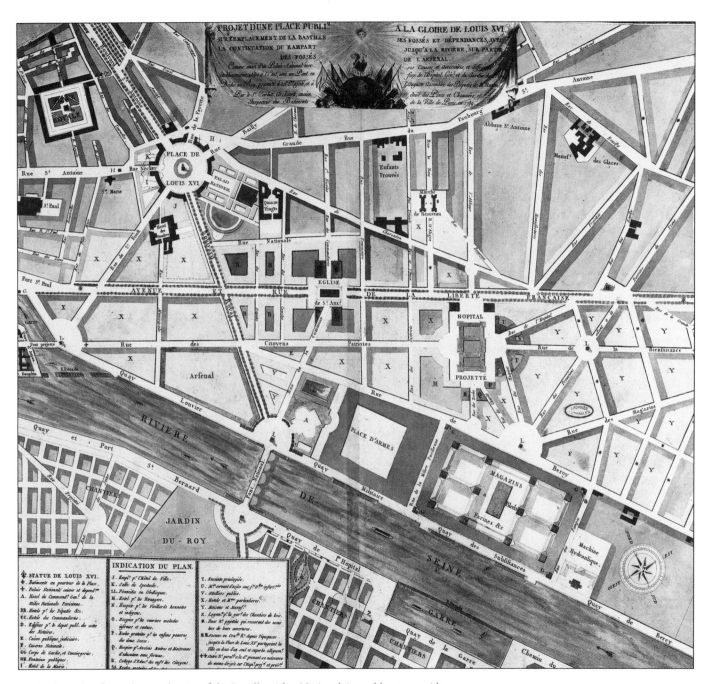

99 Corbet. Plan for a *place* on the site of the Bastille with a National Assembly on one side.

laws would be deposited and where oaths would be sworn. Overhead a vast hemispheric vault was to embrace the chamber. On it was to be reproduced the configuration of the stars and planets exactly as it had been on the night of 14–15 July 1789. The dawn would be shown breaking on the horizon. In the centre would soar a figure of Truth, holding a palm in one hand and a brilliant star in the other, the dazzling light dissipating the remaining clouds. A frieze atop the circular colonnade was to represent the signs of the zodiac. Obviously all these features were destined to emphasize the cosmic significance of the Revolution.

The architect Corbet, who, as we have seen already, had proposed a plan for the site of the Bastille in 1784, updated his project (Figures 99, 100). An engraving of his plan was announced in the *Gazette de France*, which spelled his name "Cerbet." In black and white it cost 2 livres, 8 sols, and in colour 3 livres.[16] The plan shows a huge Place Louis XVI, with a Palais National containing the Assembly on one side, and streets radiating out in all directions.[17] These streets bear the names of the leaders who still enjoyed popularity at the time – rue Necker, rue Lafayette, and rue Bailly. South of this radiating *place* is a huge artery, called the avenue de la Liberté Française, running westward from the Port Saint-Paul across the whole district. This artery goes around the church of Saint-Antoine, which is now isolated in the centre of a square framed by administrative buildings. Further south again is another lesser east-west avenue called the rue des Citoyens Patriotes. The plan features tree-lined boulevards, links from the Place Louis XVI to new squares on the Seine, and various public facilities – a new hospital, a college of the arts, a primary school, grain depots, workshops, docks, a hydraulic pump, a bridge across the Seine, and another to the Ile Saint-Louis. Obelisks and fountains also punctuate the landscape.

Architects were naturally attracted to the site of the Bastille as the site for a National Assembly because of the site's historic significance, but it was far from the fashionable area in the Faubourg Saint-Honoré and from the royal palace, which was still the centre of executive power. The suppression of monastic orders and the nationalization of church property opened up the possibility of clearing space for the Assembly nearer this centre. The architect Jean-Baptiste-Alphonse Lahure, about whom very little is known, proposed to place the National Assembly in a complex on formerly Capuchin land north of the Tuileries Garden, which would have the advantage of being visible from the terrace of the garden and of being situated on a street, the rue Nationale (now the rue de Rivoli), which would form an east-west axis linking the site to the city (Figures 101–3).[18] To the north the rue Saint-Honoré would provide another east-

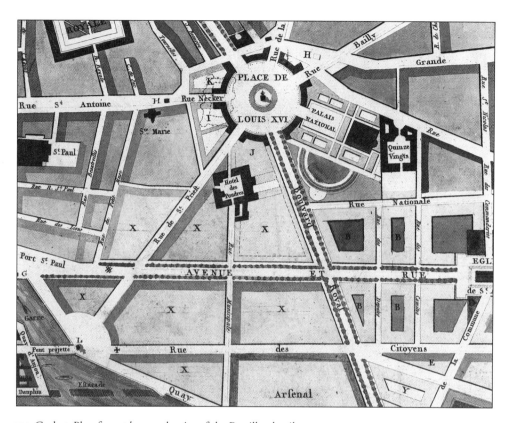

100 Corbet. Plan for a *place* on the site of the Bastille, detail.

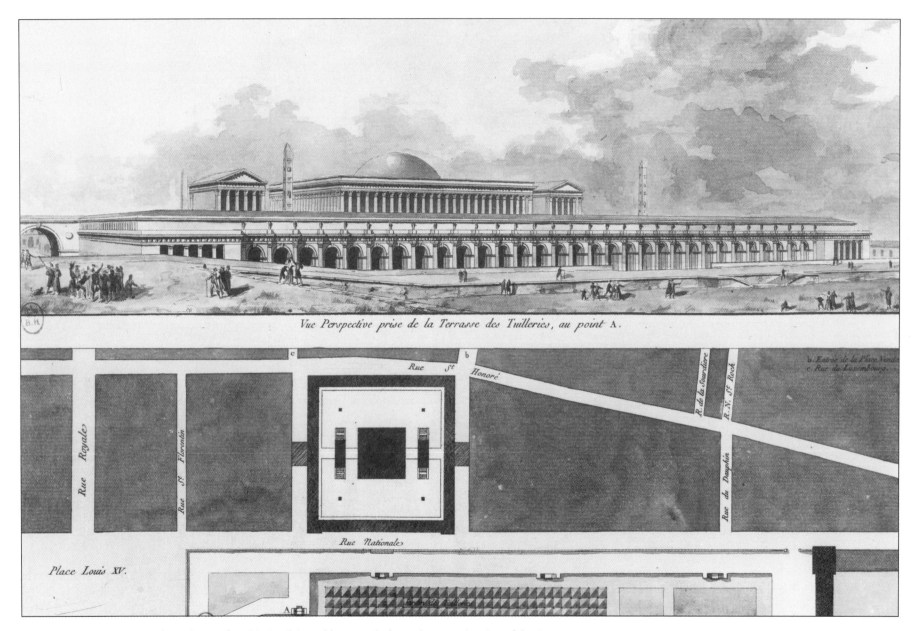

Vue Perspective prise de la Terrasse des Tuilleries, au point A.

101 Lahure. Project for a National Assembly, ground-plan and perspective view of the site.

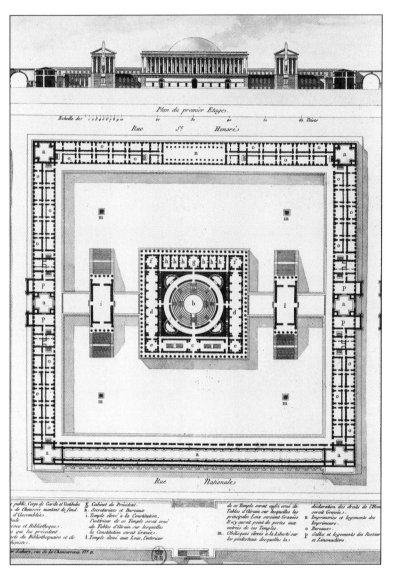

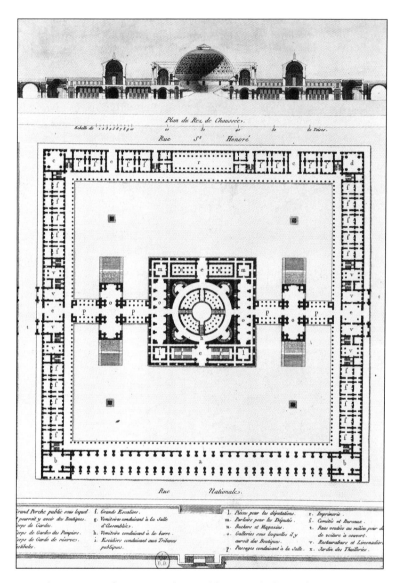

102 Lahure. Project for a National Assembly, first-floor plan of the enclosure and elevation of the hall and Temples.

103 Lahure. Project for a National Assembly, ground-plan and cross-section of the hall and Temples.

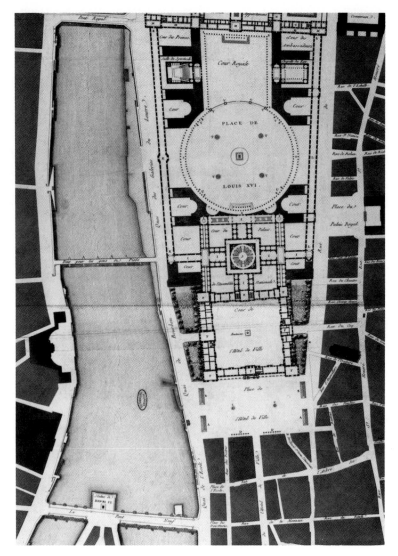

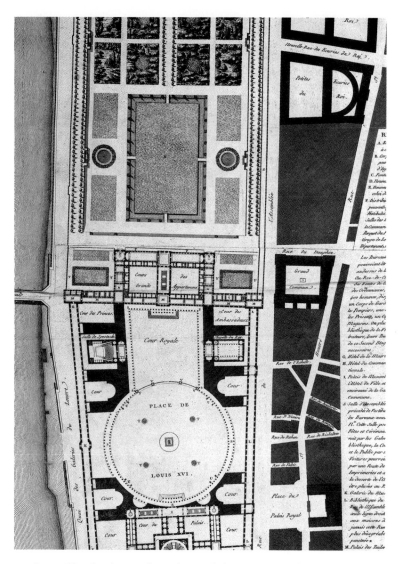

104 Poyet. Plan for the area from the rue de la Monnaie to the
Place Louis XV, lower section.

105 Poyet. Plan for the area from the rue de la Monnaie to the
Place Louis XV, middle section.

106 Poyet. Plan for the area from the rue de la Monnaie and the
    Place Louis xv, top section.

west line of communication. New streets on either side of the complex,
vaulted in the centre to provide protection from the elements for those
descending from carriages, would connect these two arteries.

The Assembly, with the usual amphitheatre in the centre, was to be
situated in a massive square edifice, encircled with Corinthian columns
and crowned with a dome. Also in this main building were to be the library,
archives, and offices. It was to be flanked on either side with temples, one
dedicated to the constitution, with the text engraved on bronze tablets
inside, the other dedicated to the laws, with the most important ones like-

wise engraved within. There could be no better example of the attempt
to sacralize the new order. "There would be no doors at the entrances to
these temples," the architect explained in the notes. Also, towards the four
corners of the courtyard there were to be four obelisks inscribed with the
Rights of Man. This courtyard was to be framed by two-storey buildings
accommodating guards, printing presses, stores, and restaurants. Along
the rue Nationale facing the Tuileries Garden was to be an arcade sheltering pedestrians. Unlike the royal palace at Versailles, the new National
Palace was to be meshed with the pulsating life of the capital.

Other planners used the desire for an impressive National Assembly
to push for completion of the Louvre, which in its unfinished state, and
with tawdry shops cluttering the area, seemed unworthy of the capital of
a great nation. Bernard Poyet, an architect who worked both for the king
and the city, was a strong advocate of developing the potential of the area
(Figures 104–6).[19] He proposed to build a northern wing to parallel the
one on the riverside. The latter was to house a museum, the former a library.
The old Louvre was to accommodate the city hall. To the west Poyet suggested a series of structures that would have created a revitalized city centre
– a building for the National Assembly, a huge circular Place Louis xvi
with four fountains around a statue of the king, a Cour Royale with a theatre
on one side and a chapel on the other, blocks of official residences, and
a rectangular park surrounded by a canal and flanked by basins. This axis
was to be continued westward with a dozen gardens laid out in rectan-
gles, but apparently informal within their borders, leading to the Place
Louis xv with four more fountains. Still farther west, the entrance to the
Champs-Elysées would lead to more gardens. The generous use of greenery and water would have reinforced the impression of rebirth.

This vast complex was designed to accommodate revolutionary activities and to symbolize the new era. The National Assembly and city hall
would counterbalance the royal palace at the other end of the two long
arms of the Louvre. The delicate balance of the constitutional monarchy
would be made explicit. In addition to uniting the political powers, with
its library, museum, theatre, and chapel, the complex would provide a cultural centre for the nation. Also, public festivals could be staged at the
National Assembly and on the great *place*, which would be readily accessible to the king, the national deputies, the municipal officials, and the
people. The statue of Louis xvi in the centre of the square was to be encircled by allegorical figures representing Liberty, Justice, Peace, and
Abundance. The four faces of the base were to be decorated with a view
of the Assembly, a scene showing the king accepting the constitution, an
engraving of the Rights of Man, and the text of the constitution. A huge

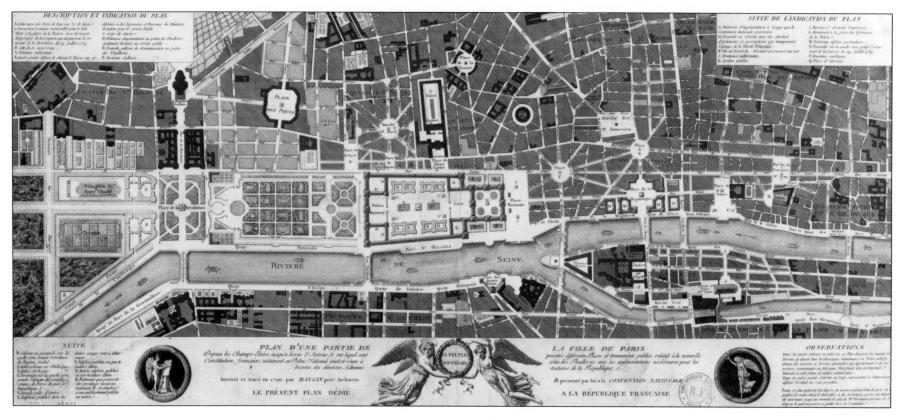

107 Mangin and Corbet. Plan for the area of the Louvre, the Tuileries Garden, and the Place Louis xv, right-hand section.

portal with openings twenty-four feet wide and Corinthian columns five feet in diameter were to lead from the square to the Assembly. Similiar porticoes would lead to other parts of the complex. Each column would support the effigy of a hero or a representative who had served his country well.

Two other architects, Jean-Charles Mangin and a colleague called Corbet, made completion of the Louvre part of the development of the whole Right Bank, from the church of Saint-Paul to the Champs-Elysées (Figure 107).[20] In their plan the Louvre was to be converted into a Palais National: "We say *Palace* because that is the name as suited to the Temple of equity, of regenerated laws, and of national happiness as to the asylum of Kings," the architects explained in their promotional pamphlet.[21] Linking

the palace of the people in the Louvre to the palace of the king in the Tuileries, the two planners argued, would not only create an impressive ensemble but would demonstrate architecturally that the monarch and the people were one. Mangin and Corbet contended that their ambitious scheme could be financed by the sale of church property and by a state lottery. It would create work for an immense crowd of artists and artisans. Related works would furnish employment for a century.[22]

The proposed political and administrative complex was to begin in front of the Palais National with a Place Nationale large enough to accommodate public festivals. The old palace was to be linked by two arms connecting it to an enlarged Tuileries Palace. Administrative buildings were to be built inside the large enclosure created in this way. In the centre of this space was to be a monument to the Nation, decorated with allegorical figures recounting the Revolution and its happy consequences. In the centre of the Cour Carrée, the heart of the old Louvre, there was to be a column, also embellished with attributes and inscriptions marking the advent of the age of liberty. Also, as in the plan by Poyet, there was to be provision for basins and green areas around the new Louvre and the Champs-Elysées, and next to these green areas were to be tree-lined promenades. The city would be regenerated by introducing some of the greenery of the countryside.

The plan also called for piercing and alignment of streets to create great axes improving communication. The rue Louis XVI running along the north side of the Louvre was to extend eastward across the city, like the modern rue Rivoli. The rue de la Monnaie was to extend the route across the Pont Neuf to intersect with the rue Louis XVI. Where the two arteries met Mangin and Corbet proposed a square decorated with an account of the embellishments of the city under the new regime. On the banks of the Seine north of the Pont au Change there was to be another large Place Louis XVI, anticipating the modern Place du Châtelet. This square was to feature a monument glorifying the king and the Revolution. Further north on the same axis was to be another square decorated with an obelisk commemorating how the king had "voluntarily" granted freedom to his people. Another obelisk was to embellish the Place de Grève. Other *places* were to be created in front of and north of the church of Saint-Gervais. The plan obviously expresses the optimism of the early Revolution, the hope that Louis XVI would become the father of his people, but it was a plan that could easily be updated as the Revolution moved on.[23]

Like Lahure, Pierre Rousseau, an inspector of royal buildings, advocated creating a huge complex on former monastic lands (Figures 108–10). He chose an area on the Left Bank framed by the Seine and the rue des Petits-Augustins, the rue Jacob, and the rue des Saints-Pères, the area around the present Ecole des Beaux-Arts.[24] Seven huge drawings in the Archives Nationales, an elevation in the Musée Carnavalet, and a ground-plan in the Bibliothèque Nationale reveal his dream.[25] There was to be a huge square, with obelisks at either end, on the riverside. Leading off from this square was to be an impressive entrance in the form of a triumphal arch in the middle of a long colonnade with pavilions at either end. Inside there was to be a vast court, at the far end of which would be the main building, containing a number of halls culminating in a semicircular auditorium with a public gallery. This hall was to be topped with

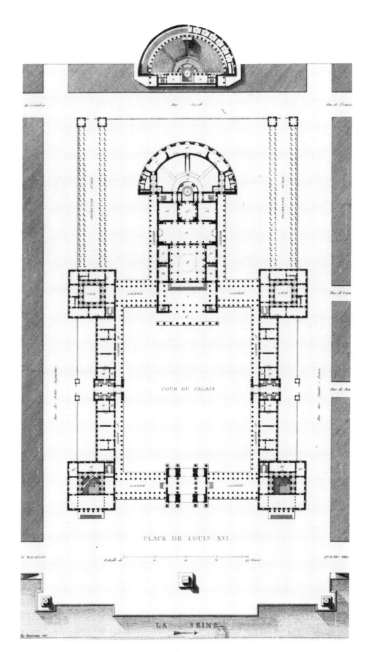

108 Rousseau. Project for a complex on the Left Bank, including a National Assembly, ground-plan.

109, 110 Rousseau. Project for a complex on the
Left Bank. *Above*: view of the main entrance;
right: assembly-hall, cross-section.

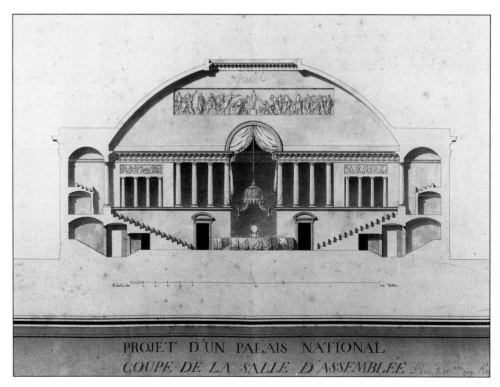

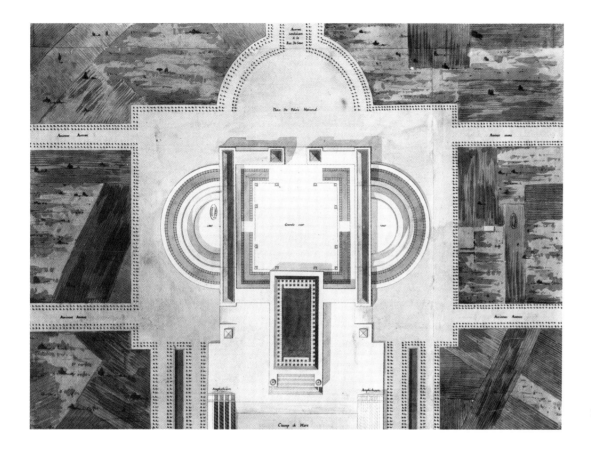

111 Thomas. Plan for a National Assembly on the site of the Ecole Militaire.

a dome pierced with an oculus on its peak. This vast complex was to be decorated with low-reliefs, inscriptions, and statues, inside and out. The adjoining streets were to be widened, and tree-lined promenades were to be created along the outer walls.

Other planners also favoured sites on the Left Bank. A lawyer named Giraud proposed a huge Place Patriotique, with a palace for the National Assembly, for the elevated site of the Place Saint-Michel (now the Place Edmond Rostrand), on which he advocated creating an even higher artificial mountain. "Where did Moses talk with the Divinity and receive the Tablets of the Laws?" he asked rhetorically. "Far from a muddy spot near a river, it was on a mountain."[26] The architect Thomas preferred locating the Assembly on the terrain occupied by the Ecole Militaire because the legislators would be reminded of their duties by a single glance at the Autel de la Patrie nearby, if ever they were in danger of being corrupted

(Figure 111).[27] The army officer Petit promoted the esplanade of the Invalides. To the north of an open space directly in front of the Invalides, there was to be a large garden or park, enclosed by government buildings, including an Assembly (Figures 112–13).[28] In the centre was to be a domed Temple of Liberty containing an Altar of the Fatherland and encircled by statues of famous men. Here the circular shape would suggest the message of liberty spreading in all directions like the ripples spreading from a pebble dropped into a pool. The axis commencing with the esplanade and garden was to be extended across the river to the Champs-Elysées. And Florentin Gilbert designed a legislature for an unspecified site, perhaps also the Left Bank (Figure 114).[29]

Most of these planners submitted their grandiose plans to the National Assembly, which usually commended them for their patriotism, then sent their plans to the archives. The fiscal problems that had precipitated the

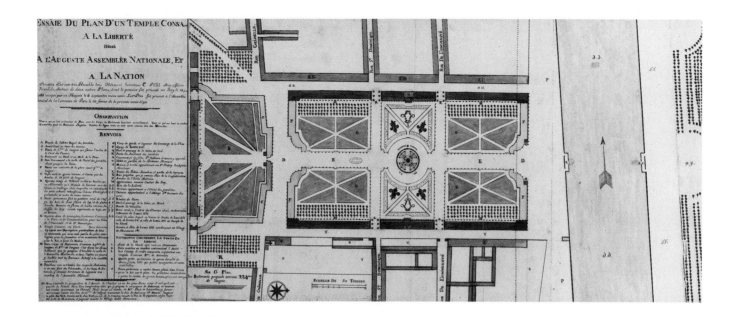

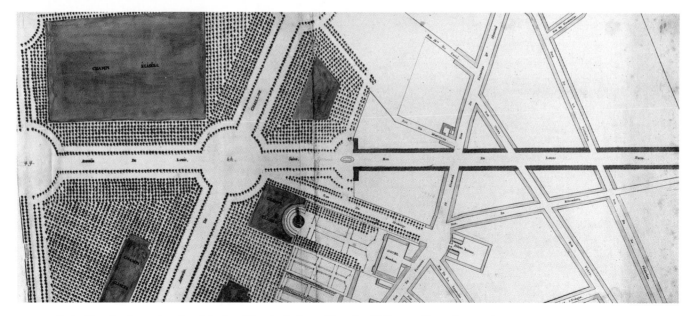

112, 113   Petit. Plan for the esplanade of the Invalides, including a Temple of Liberty. *Above*: first section; *below*: extension of the axis across the Seine.

114 Gilbert. Project for a National Assembly, perspective view.

Revolution militated against such vast projects. Designers were forced to lower their sights and consider how existing buildings, or partially completed ones, could be adapted for use as an Assembly. For example, the architect Thomas, who favoured the area of the Ecole Militaire, presented an alternative plan to expand the Palais de Justice in order to house the Assembly (Figure 115).[30] In the succession of plans there also seems to have been a shift away from the vicinity of the Tuileries Palace. As the king became increasingly unpopular, planners tended to choose sites distanced from the centre of his power. The unfinished church of the Madeleine seemed to meet both these contingencies: since the construction had begun, the cost of transforming it into a National Assembly would be less, and at the same time it was not too close to the court. Despite the restraints imposed by starting with a building already under way, Armand-Guy Kersaint was able to make it the centre of a bold plan of renewal (Figures 116–19).

The plan by Kersaint grew out of a report that he gave to the council of the Department of Paris on 15 December 1791, which ordered it entered in its proceedings, printed separately, and presented to the National Assembly and the king. The result was the brochure *Discours sur les monuments publics*, containing designs of each project by the architects Jacques-Guillaume Legrand and Jacques Molinos.[31] Kersaint argued that in order to create reverence for the laws, the legislature ought to be an impressive sanctuary. The uncompleted Madeleine, modelled on the Pantheon in Rome, could be used to meet this goal. Kersaint proposed to use the impressive portico as the entrance and to create a large circular structure, encompassing an inner garden, at the rear to house government offices. The hall itself was to consist of a semicircular amphitheatre facing the podium. On either side were to be statues of Rousseau and Voltaire, considered harbingers of the Revolution, and overhead medallions representing other great men. On the rear wall over the podium was to hang David's *Oath of the Tennis Court*. In the huge vault a figure of Renown, trumpeting the good news of the Revolution, was to soar over the globe, needless to say with France in the centre. Across the wall, on either side of David's painting, the constitution was to be displayed on ten tablets. Their number and shape were significant – the constitution was the new Decalogue.

Kersaint proposed other projects that would have put an ideological stamp on the capital and provincial cities – the completion of the Louvre to house a national gallery and national library, an immense stadium with a civic altar in the centre, and a series of monuments where heroes would

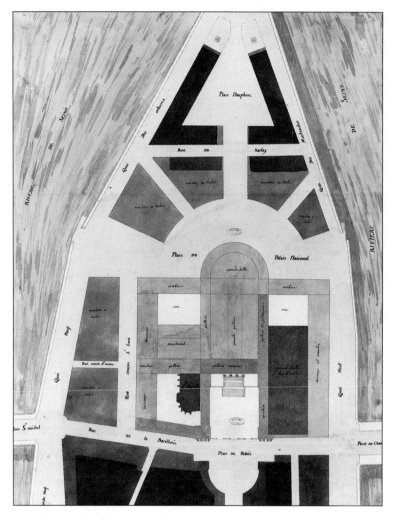

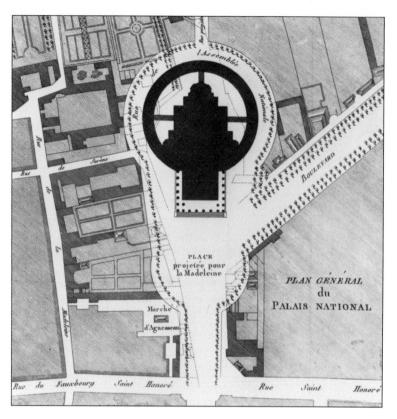

116 Kersaint, Legrand, and Molinos. Plan for the area around the unfinished Church of the Madeleine.

115 Thomas. Plan for a National Assembly adjacent to the Palais de Justice on the Ile de la Cité.

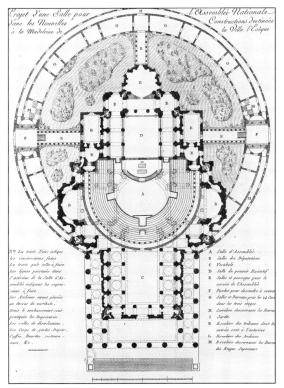

117, 118 Kersaint, Legrand, and Molinos. Project to complete the Madeleine as a National Assembly. *Above*: perspective view; *left*: National Assembly and government offices, ground-plan.

119 Kersaint, Legrand, and Molinos. National Assembly hall, cross-section.

120 Kersaint, Legrand, and Molinos. Project to convert the south wing of the Louvre into an art museum.

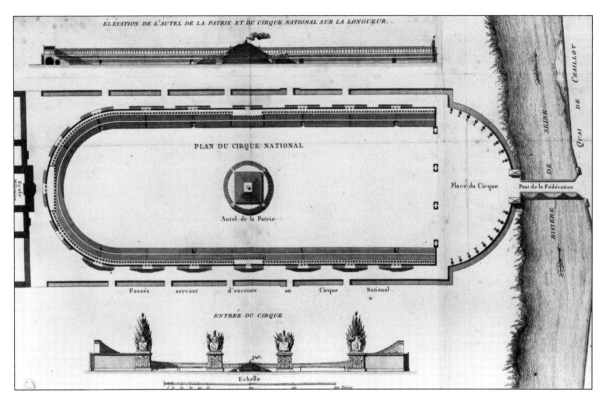

121 Kersaint, Legrand, and Molinos. Project for a vast *cirque* on the Champ de Mars, ground-plan, elevation, and cross-section.

be honoured and laws would be displayed throughout France (Figures 120–5). The name "prytanée," which he chose for these monuments, was significant. In ancient Athens the Prytaneum had been a public hall where a sacred fire was kept burning and where important ceremonies were staged. Kersaint and his architect colleagues advocated four different sizes of prytanea to suit locales of various degrees of importance throughout the nation. All were to be pentagonal to provide a space for displaying the enactments of all five levels of government – the monarchy, the National Assembly, the departments, the districts, and the municipalities. All of them were also to be surmounted by the symbols of unity and liberty, the fasces capped by a Phrygian bonnet. The larger ones were to contain a statue of a revolutionary hero, or a vacant pedestal to inspire youth to strive for such an honour. The largest prytaneum was to be erected on the site of the Bastille in such a way that one of the former cells would be clearly visible.

Again we have the triumph of the new regime over the old represented physically.

After the demand for monuments symbolizing the advent of the Revolution and for buildings to house the National Assembly, the next noteworthy theme was the demand for monuments or shrines to great Frenchmen. We have seen that as the Christian belief in the afterlife became less compelling, the notion of immortality through history gained strength. The most notable project to commemorate national heroes was spurred by the death of Mirabeau, who at the time was still considered a great patriot. On 3 April 1791 the executive of the Department of Paris proposed that his death might be turned into a lesson for posterity. Rochefoucauld, the spokesman of the department, reminded the Constituent Assembly that ancient peoples had used special monuments to keep alive the memories of their heroes, and proposed creation of a similar

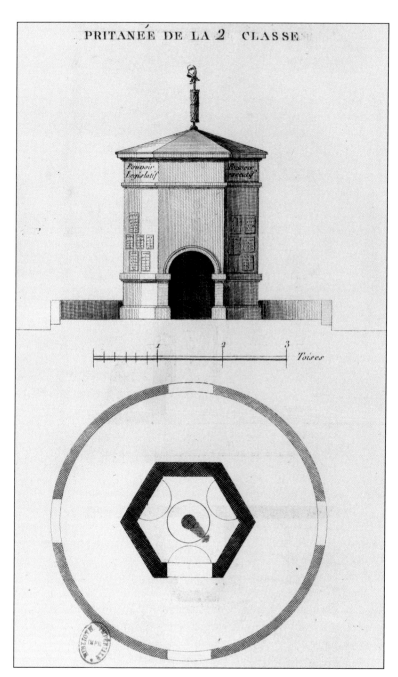

122 Kersaint, Legrand, and Molinos. Prytaneum of the first class.

123 Kersaint, Legrand, and Molinos. Prytaneum of the second class.

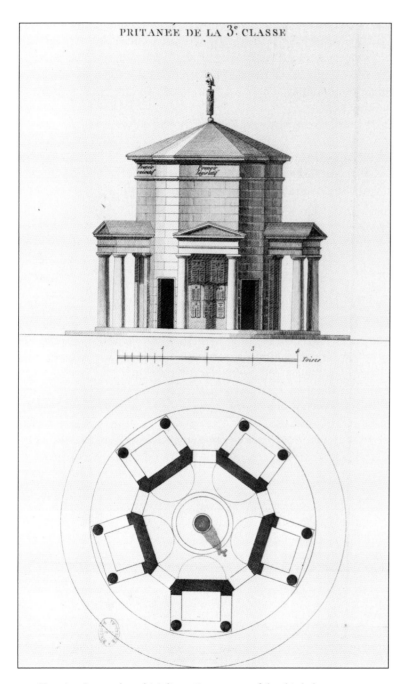

124 Kersaint, Legrand, and Molinos. Prytaneum of the third class.

125 Kersaint, Legrand, and Molinos. Prytaneum for the site of the Bastille.

126 Anonymous. View of Sainte-Geneviève converted into the Pantheon.

cult in France by converting the new church of Sainte-Geneviève into a national shrine "so that the temple of religion will become the temple of the fatherland; that the tomb of a great man will become the altar of liberty" (Figure 126).[32] The department proposed that the edifice should bear a huge inscription:

THE GRATEFUL FATHERLAND TO GREAT MEN

The grandiloquent neoclassical church designed by Jacques-Gabriel Soufflot was ideally suited to become a shrine to great Frenchmen. The Constituent Assembly placed Quatremère de Quincy in charge of the conversion of the church for its new purpose. Quatremère expected the shrine to stimulate youths to emulate the virtues, patriotism, and public service honoured there. "We propose to you," he wrote in his first report, "to adopt by preference, in the decoration of our philosophic pantheon, the emblems of that religion which is genuinely universal, to which all people should rally. That religion is morality."[33] In keeping with this new goal, Quatremère ordered the low-relief on the pediment representing the Triumph of the Faith by Coustou replaced by one depicting the Fatherland Crowning the Civic Virtues by Jean-Guillaume Moitte. The new low-relief showed France, clad in a long robe, with her arms outstretched, holding a civic crown in each hand. On her left Genius, in the form of a young winged male, seized the crown, while on the other side Virtue, in the guise of a modest young woman, awaited her turn. On the sides the attributes of the vices and passions lay crushed (Figure 127).[34]

Other images were likewise altered inside and out. The new images were to show on the one hand what *la patrie* did for the citizen and on the other what he owed to her in return. A drawing in the Carnavalet Museum shows how an anonymous artist envisaged the interior early in the Revolution (Figure 128).[35] It shows a group of sculptured figures under the dome. Diogenes, with the lamp at his feet with which he sought one virtuous man, points to a huge pedestal supporting a bust of Louis XVI, who is being crowned by Liberty. It is the new goddess, not the Christian God, who is consecrating the king. Busts of famous men line the walls, and medallions bearing the likenesses of others appear overhead. In the group of spectators to the right of the pedestal, a mother points out some of the great men to her child.

In a pamphlet published in 1792 before the overthrow of the monarchy, an author by the name of Charles Chaisneau explained even more clearly than Quatremère the way of thinking that lay behind the creation of the Pantheon.[36] Chaisneau argued that the hope of surviving death was a powerful human longing. Just as we strive to gain the admiration of our

Changemens projettés au Bas-relief du fronton de l'Eglise Ste Geneviève.

Esquisse du fronton dans son état présent.

1.re Série.
N.^{u.} 21

127 Baltard. Drawing of the fronton of the Pantheon before it was replaced.

fellow citizens while we are alive, so we aspire to be esteemed after we are gone. Such a hope was no longer a chimera now that the nation had demonstrated how it would honour its great men. The pleasant anticipation of this immortality could provide a powerful incentive to serving the Fatherland. A true patriot would feel demeaned by a monetary award but would be pleased to be honoured by a civic crown, a vase, or an inscription. Chaisneau anticipated some projects of the *gouvernement révolutionnaire* in Year II of the republic, in particular with his proposal for columns or obelisks, inscribed with the names of worthy citizens, next to the Altar of the Fatherland inside the Pantheon. Moreover, he called for an obelisk in tribute to virtuous citizens whose names were not known, an idea that implied what we might call the democratization of heroism.

Particularly significant was the religious fervour that the thought of visiting the Pantheon aroused in Chaisneau:

> Venerable Pantheon, I shall not die content if I have not penetrated into your holy enclave, if I have not prostrated myself before the remains of our tutelary spirits. Oh Rousseau! Oh Voltaire! My eyes fix themselves on your cherished image; at this sight my soul is penetrated with a religious sentiment; and if my voice dares to make itself heard, it will be to sing hymns in your honour, to swear in your presence and in your name TO LIVE FREE OR DIE.[37]

The beginning of the transformation of Sainte-Geneviève into the Pantheon was not the only scheme for immortalizing great Frenchmen. In the autumn of 1791 Mopinot de la Chapotte launched a proposal that

128 Anonymous. Proposal for decoration of the interior of the Pantheon around 1791.

was a direct sequel to the program for statues of great Frenchmen that d'Angiviller had launched for the Salon of 1777. Mopinot proposed to use the marble statues that had resulted from that program to decorate the new bridge across the Seine, from the Left Bank to the Place Louis xv.[38] The architect of the bridge, Jean-Rodolphe Perronet, backed the scheme.[39] In his memorandum to the government and his subsequent pamphlet Mopinot contrasted Louis XVI, who had commissioned the most eminent sculptors of the day to make statues of great men from all levels of society, with Louis XIV, who had not seen fit to honour those who had served him with statues like those erected to himself. Mopinot argued that statues in marble or bronze resisted the onslaughts of insects and weather. Even when broken by some violent upheaval, they retained some of their interest. Displayed on the bridge for all to see, these statues of great men would provide ongoing lessons in history, teach citizens how they should act, and give Paris a bridge even more magnificent than the San Angelico in Rome.

Another planner, Antoine-Laurent-Thomas Vaudoyer, contended that the Champs-Elysées was the best site to honour patriots.[40] Vaudoyer shared the belief in creating a special place for those who had served their country well, where every day citizens would receive a lesson in patriotism, but he did not think that the church of Sainte-Geneviève was suited for this purpose. Monuments in a sanctuary would distract from its real function. He also disagreed with the suggestion of putting Mirabeau's remains under the Altar of the Fatherland. The remains of such an illustrious citizen would divert attention from the oaths that were to be sworn there. The ancients had never placed mortals in the sanctuaries of their gods, and their Champ de Mars had never contained a sepulchre; they placed them along their most frequented routes. Consequently, Vaudoyer proposed placing French heroes along the great boulevard leading towards Neuilly, which he would rename the Voie de l'honneur. Simple allegorical monuments would line both sides, each recalling the most memorable episode in the life of a great man. Voltaire and Rousseau would occupy the first two places. At the end of his pamphlet Vaudoyer said that he was working on a suitable monument to Mirabeau for this sacred avenue.

Not all the advocates of the statuomania that erupted in the late eighteenth century wanted statues honouring real individuals; some called for allegorical figures to be placed throughout the city. For example, an advocate of various schemes of urban improvement, M.-C.-P. Le Sueur, presented such a scheme to the primary assembly of the Faubourg Saint-Denis in October 1790. The assembly encouraged him to have his project, "wisely conceived," printed.[41] Striking a note that was to be sounded fre-

quently throughout the decade, he complained that the names of sections were insignificant, unpleasant sounding, or the butt of jokes. He proposed to place in each district statues representing civic virtues with maxims on the bases by which the figures would address the public. If all wage-earners would contribute five sous per month, the sculptures would be ready in two years, making the city the rival of Athens. The project would get rid of bizarre names, encourage the arts, attract wealthy tourists, and provide an easy method of educating the public.

Le Sueur then proposed fifty-eight public virtues from which to choose – Concord, Constitution, Generosity, Justice, Reason, and so forth. The statue of Liberty illustrates his plan:

> LIBERTY
> Liberty and Emulation render man
> capable of the grandest achievements.
> Liberty does not consist in doing
> whatever one pleases, only what
> cannot do harm to others.[42]

Most of these allegorical figures were to be female because most abstract concepts are feminine in French. The figure representing the constitution would thank Frenchmen for bringing her into a happy existence, and warn them to adhere to the law and defend her against perverse men who sought to destroy her. Le Sueur's plan was an example early in the Revolution of the impulse to put an ideological stamp on the whole city.

Most of these ambitious projects under the Constituent and Legislative assemblies were aimed not only at commemorating the Revolution, creating a place of assembly for the national deputies, and honouring great Frenchmen but also at improving the city of man. Revolutionary leaders believed that they could demonstrate their concern for the welfare of the citizenry by pushing ahead with ideas for urban improvement that had been conceived under the Old Regime. In September 1791 the municipality of Paris called for plans to improve navigation on the Seine, communication between the islands, the supply of clean water, and other aspects of urban life.[43] The planners we have examined shared such objectives. They introduced into their projects provisions for spacious squares, wide boulevards, green oases, basins, and fountains. They also often included facilities to improve the economic infrastructure, such as better lines of communication, bridges, docks, warehouses, and canals.

The engineer Jean-Pierre Brullée typified this passion for urban

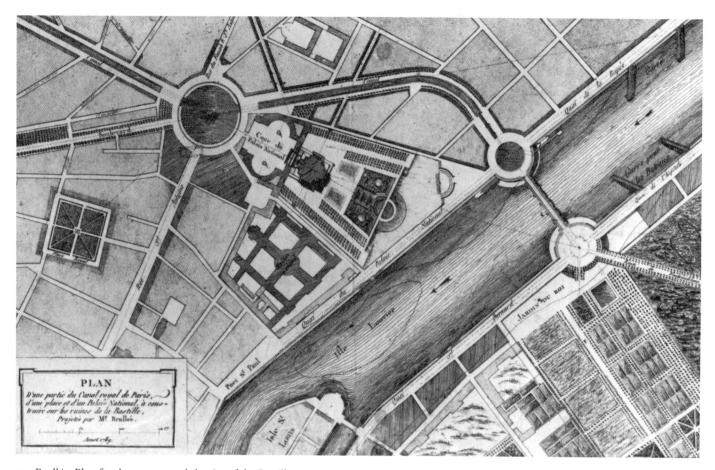

129 Brullée. Plan for the area around the site of the Bastille.

improvement. Beginning in 1789, he pressed the government to develop a canal from the northwest, terminating on a Place Nationale on the site of the Bastille, flanked by a National Palace and connected to port facilities on the Seine (Figure 129).[44] In June 1792, just as the government was finally drafting a proposal for the Place de la Bastille, Brullée appealed to the authorities to create a "Temple National" on the site, built out of stones from all departments, which would serve both as a monument to the Revolution and as a cultural centre. "This monument ... will embrace the most interesting goals for the advanced sciences," he argued; "it will be a temple of enlightenment and of national education."[45] This shrine would be surrounded by free schools teaching all the useful sciences and by accommodation for the professors. A bridge across the Seine would give the students access to the Jardin du Roi and the Cabinet d'histoire naturelle.

The fate of many of these projects for monuments, squares, and buildings depended on the success of the constitutional monarchy. That political system rested on a precarious compromise between the king and the new sovereign nation, a balance symbolized by the juxtaposition of the fleurs-de-lis and the new revolutionary symbols, or the coexistence of the figure of the king and that of the goddess Liberty. As Louis XVI's preference for the old order and his antagonism to the reforms of the Church imposed by the Revolution became clearer, the precarious balance began to totter.

Meanwhile, the constant agitation outside of the country by the *émigrés*, the refugees from the Revolution, created a constant state of anxiety. The flight to Varennes, in June 1791, by which the king and his family sought to escape the country, weakened the chances of the constitution even before it came into full operation in October of that year. The massacre of demonstrators against the king on the Champ de Mars in July aggravated the situation.

Reports in the press tell of growing animosity towards the symbols of monarchical power. On 18 July 1791 the *Annales patriotiques et littéraires* reported agitation in Paris following the king's flight and demands for his removal. The paper recounted how during the tumult on the streets and in the theatres the people called for the toppling of the statues of three tyrants – Louis XIII, Louis XIV, and Louis XVI – to be replaced by statues of outstanding citizens. The reporter approved: "This popular idea is grand and beautiful: it is very strange that as a matter of fact in the midst of revolution three crowned brigands have retained public monuments, raised up by the servitude and corruption of the court to three insolent and vile despots, who from the depths of the tomb where their crimes are buried still defy us with their insolent likenesses."[46] For the time being, it is interesting to note, far from demanding that the statue of Henry IV be toppled, the people draped it with a tricolour scarf and crowned him with a civic crown.

The fate of plans for the site of the Bastille typifies the outcome of so much planning. After a host of proposals, the Legislative Assembly on 27 June 1792 had finally approved a plan for the site, prompted by the proposal submitted earlier by Palloy, which we have already examined.[47] A Place de la Liberté was to be created, with a column supporting a statue of Liberty in the centre. A contest was opened to select the best design. The project inspired one citizen, a septuagenarian lawyer from Rouen named Duquesney, to resubmit a quatrain he had proposed for the monument three years before:

> Ici despotisme a trouvé son tombeau
> Pour briser d'anciens fers il falloit des prodiges
> Le Parisien se change en Peuple nouveau
> Il s'arme … les Sept-Tours n'offrent plus de vestiges.[48]

On 14 July the foundation was laid with much fanfare. Two iron boxes were deposited in the foundation, one containing the Declaration of the Rights of Man, the other portraits of the presidents of the Constituent and Legislative assemblies along with that of Louis XVI, coins, and assig-

nats.[49] This project came to naught. The following year the Convention ordered the boxes smashed publicly and the fragments sent to the archives "as documents of history."[50]

The outbreak of war with Austria in April 1792 brought more strain than the system could bear. Suspicion that the court sympathized with the counter-revolutionary powers, and the threat of a purge of revolutionaries if the enemy entered Paris, combined with continued economic distress among the common people to create an explosive situation. Formerly passive citizens, disenfranchised by tax requirements under the constitution, pressed into the National Guard and the sections. The sections where radicals won the struggle formed an insurrectionary commune or city government. Finally, the uprising of 10 August 1792, "the second Revolution," toppled the monarchy. The trinity of Nation, Law, and king, sanctified inside an equilateral triangle, broke into pieces. The fall of the monarchy meant that the plans of Davy de Chavigné, De Varenne, Du Morier, Prieur, and others that included figures of Louis XVI were hopelessly outdated. Some projects could be rescued by changing the names of boulevards or squares and by inserting different statues, if the designer was willing to adapt to new circumstances. In any case, a new, more radical symbolic order was called for. ▲

The first five of the six stations of the Festival of Unity and Indivisibility. (Figure 142)

V

THE REPUBLICANIZATION OF PARIS

THE IMMEDIATE IMPACT OF THE OVERTHROW of the monarchy on urban space was negative, the process that we have called delegitimization or desacralization. In Paris during the first few days following 10 August 1792 the populace focused its wrath on the statues of the Bourbons on the Place Royale, the Place des Victoires, the Place Louis-le-Grand, the Place Louis xv, and the Hôtel de Ville. On 11 August, as news reached the Legislative Assembly that Parisians were intent on destroying royal monuments, the deputy Sers demanded that the destruction be carried out by competent agents, engineers or architects. His colleagues Fauchet, Thuriot, and Albitte supported this proposal, the second arguing that some of the monuments might be useful to the arts and the third suggesting that a statue of Liberty be placed on each pedestal.[1] The Assembly then decreed that, since the people had shown their wish that no public monument should remain that recalled the reign of despotism, it was urgent to remove the statues in public squares, and "that monuments in honour of liberty be substituted for them."[2]

Even the statue of Henry iv, the most popular of French kings, next to the Pont Neuf did not escape the popular fury. On 14 August a spokesman arrived from the Section Pont Neuf to report to the Assembly that Henry's statue also had been toppled. "This king's virtues made us hold back for a time," the spokesman declared, "but we did not hesitate once we remembered that he had not ruled with the consent of the people."[3] Stirred by this report, the deputies Thuriot and Lacroix proposed that all royal monuments in bronze, those in churches and palaces as well as public places, be turned into cannon. The Assembly thereupon passed a more detailed decree than the one approved three days earlier.[4] It ordered the removal of all such statues, low-reliefs, inscriptions, and other monuments, in bronze or other material, from squares, churches, gardens, parks, and public buildings. In Paris municipal officials were to oversee the task of converting into cannon all the above articles, under supervision of the minister of the interior, two members of the Commission des Armes, and two members of the Commission des Monuments. Officials in other communes were to follow suit. The Commission des Monuments was to conserve articles useful to the arts and to present a list of them to the legislature.

The destruction of royal monuments was impressed on the minds of the citizenry by crude illustrations in the newspaper *Révolutions de Paris* and later engravings on separate sheets. Only fragments survived of sculptures that such artists as Desjardins, Coysevox, Girardon, and Bouchardon had created with great labour and expense. The manner in which one of these fragments was treated should delight any semiotician. The Section de la Place Vendôme, previously called the Place Louis-le-Grand, on which the colossal equestrian statue of Louis xiv by Girardon had stood, presented an address to delegates from Marseille some time after 10 August.[5] The address praised the contribution of the Marseillais to the Revolution. It then went on to say that they had no doubt seen the statue of Louis xiv on the Place Vendôme. Even if his name had not been on the pedestal, they would have recognized him by his arrogant pose, especially the gesture of his right hand, which suggested that he wanted to rule the universe. Although the citizens of the section had destroyed the statue, they had preserved the expressive finger of the audacious right hand in order to present it to the Marseillais, "not as a pleasing present, but a memento of tyranny which can serve, by recalling to their descendents the atrocities of this crowned brigand, to sustain their indignation against kings and against royalty."[6]

The conspicuous royal statues on public squares disappeared in a few days, but the concomitant removal of all the fleurs-de-lis, coats of arms, emblems, and monarchical inscriptions took much longer since there were so many of them. Especially after the victory of the Montagnards on 2 June 1793, the Convention reiterated several times the order to complete the eradication of all visual remains of the monarchical regime.[7] There are thick dossiers in the Archives Nationales containing accounts of artisans who were employed to remove such remains during the first three years of the Republic.[8] Unfortunately, even when symbols and inscriptions were removed, the outline of them still remained. Citizens proposed various methods for overcoming this problem. An artist by the name of Mailly, for example, wrote to the Convention to report that he had developed an easy way of eradicating inscriptions, coats of arms, dedications, and other signs on public buildings.[9] Instead of just wrenching off the copper plate bearing such signs, which often damaged the building and left tell-tale traces behind, he had discovered that melted copper could be used to fill in the engraving so that a new inscription or image could be superimposed. The Convention sent his proposal to the Committee of Public Instruction.

This iconoclasm sometimes destroyed valuable works of art, but there was a countervailing movement: the idea of putting works of art which were ideologically unacceptable, but judged to have artistic worth, in a museum.[10] A statue taken out of a public square or church and placed in a museum lost its political significance. This attempt to rescue certain works of art led to the creation of the Musée des monuments français in Paris, in the former convent of the Augustines, and of a number of provincial museums. There was also an attempt to modify certain statues and low-reliefs so as to change their meaning. On the fronton of the School of Surgery a figure of Louis XV, shown approving the plans of the building by a gesture of his right arm, was changed in 1794 by Pierre-François Berruer, the original sculptor, who was still living, by replacing the king with a figure of Beneficence while retaining the right arm. This relief can still be seen at 12 rue de l'Ecole de Médicine. Another example of such transformation can be seen on the fronton of a side entrance to the church of Saint-Nicolas du Chardonnet, where the sculptor Legendre changed the cross of Christ and that of Saint Nicholas, both carried by little angels, into revolutionary pikes. In other cases an image was simply given a new name: a low-relief at 6 rue Grégoire de Tours, dating from the seventeenth century, which showed an almost completely naked primitive man holding a club, was rebaptized "le sans-culotte."[11]

The negative process of delegitimization and desacralization was soon followed by its antithesis, the positive process of relegitimization and resacralization. Although the overthrow of the monarchy represented the failure of the Constituent and Legislative assemblies to stabilize the Revolution, it intensified the revolutionary faith of many Frenchmen, heightening once again their sense of a new beginning. The fact that the newly elected Convention declared France a republic on 21 September 1792, the date of the autumnal equinox, was seen by such revolutionaries as a good omen. On that date day and night were equal, suggesting that the heavens supported egalitarianism. On that day too the sun moved from one hemisphere to the other, illustrating how the Revolution would spread around the world. The symbolic significance of the date eventually gave birth to the new republican calendar, which numbered the new

era from the advent of the Republic rather than from the birth of Christ. It also got rid of the names of months derived from pagan deities and Roman emperors, which from a revolutionary viewpoint had sullied the old Gregorian calendar.[12]

The new calendar was only one product of a powerful psychological force at work. In normal times most humans are willing to tolerate numerous contradictions and imperfections in society. Revolution seems to offer the opportunity to eradicate these flaws and to establish a more perfect community. We have already seen this psychological drive at work earlier in the Revolution, but it intensified after the overthrow of the king, the traditional father-figure, and later his execution. Some Frenchmen shrank back from the violence involved in the insurrection of 10 August 1792, the September Massacres of suspected counter-revolutionaries, the later purge of the so-called Girondist deputies, and the advent of the Terror in the autumn of 1793, but others saw such radicalization as part of an on-going process of purification and rebirth. In their eyes such regeneration would justify the violence involved. Along with measures to create a democratic republic, there were projects to decimalize measurements, introduce a ten-hour day with a hundred minutes to the hour and a hundred seconds to the minute, transform national dress, cleanse the French language of words that recalled the *ancien régime*, create a more egalitarian etiquette, republicanize chess and playing cards, and rid people's minds of outdated religious beliefs.

Spurred by this psychological drive, the new civic cult that had been emerging during the first three years of the Revolution gradually developed in the minds of radical revolutionaries into a full-blown alternative to Christianity. The Altar of the Fatherland was already well established by 1792. When the king, the former sacred centre of the state, disappeared, the goddess Liberty was ready to take his place. As we have seen, at the very moment that the legislature legalized popular iconoclasm, some deputies proposed that Liberty should replace kings atop vacant pedestals.[13] Soon the expiring Legislative Assembly approved a new seal of state featuring Liberty holding the rudder of the Ship of State and fasces, the traditional symbol of state power. As the Revolution became even more radical, driven forward by the notion of popular sovereignty, the demands of war, the spectre of counter-revolution, continuing economic problems, and the mounting assertiveness of the lower classes, the civic cult developed further. By the autumn of 1793 it had all the ingredients of a religion – an altar, goddesses, symbols, rituals, hymns, dogmas, martyrs, even an eschatological vision. The republican calendar with its ten-day weeks was a direct challenge to the old Christian cycle of religious festivals. The new cult, however, like the old one, would need buildings to serve as focal points of devotion and to accommodate worshippers.

The link between the destructive process and the positive one can best be seen in the act of debaptizing the rebaptizing, which reached its crescendo as the Revolution moved forward. When feudal or monarchical, and later religious names of streets, quais, bridges, and squares were eradicated, republican names were imposed at the same time. Such renaming may seem of minor importance, but we should remember that when, according to the book of Genesis, God gave man the right to name all the creatures of the world, the right signified authority and superiority over them.[14] Similarly, in asserting their right to rechristen urban space, republicans were demonstrating their authority over it. Moreover, the new names were intended to give urban space a new significance and to engender in the citizens, who moved about in it, a new way of feeling about themselves and their place in the nascent political culture.

The rebaptism of space began at the local level. For example, a citizen named Jault, a member of the Commune of Paris, urged the Section de Bonne Nouvelle to get rid of all its obsolete names.[15] He pointed out that most of the names in the district carried the names of saints, which were offensive or ridiculous under popular government; therefore he proposed the names of men who had made outstanding contributions to philosophy, art, or agriculture – Descartes, Lesueur, Montaigne, Jouvenet, Mably, and others – or social virtues and ideals. Each name he proposed was followed by a brief justification. "In giving the rue Beauregard the name rue Populaire," he explained, "I intend to render homage to the zeal of citizens of that street, who acted together to return the revolution to its principles when the aristocracy wished to use its liberty-killing powers."[16]

Soon there were proposals to change all place-names in Paris systematically. The citizen Avril brought a report recommending such an initiative to the Commune a month after Jault's proposal to the Section de Bonne-Nouvelle. Avril complained that most of the street names in Paris were barbarous, ridiculous, or patronymic. "In general they are insignificant, and overall they present no motif," he argued. "It has been proposed to you to change them partially. We have put in front of you a project to change them all."[17] He proposed, like the Abbé Teisserenc in mid-century, to turn the city into a geographical picture of the country: the quais and boulevards were to be named after departments and the streets after communes. But there was also to be an ideological thrust: the squares and bridges were to commemorate the Revolution, and the streets were to be named after great men. Any streets remaining unnamed after all

worthy names had been exhausted were to receive numbers until virtuous patriots earned the honour of having their names used. The Committee of Public Instruction of the Convention ordered that this report be printed.

Avril's comprehensive scheme was never adopted, but so many names were changed that new guides to the capital were needed. One such guide, the *Almanach indicatif des rues de Paris, suivant leurs nouvelles dénominations*, published in Year III, explained that under the Republic, and especially under the leadership of the Mountain in the Convention, Paris had become the centre from that the light of Virtue and Reason radiated out.[18] The city itself had undergone a mutation in which names that recalled the old regime had given way to new ones that were genuinely patriotic and republican. The list of names of the sections alone confirmed this point: many bore the names of revolutionary ideals, such as la République, le Contrat Social, les Droits de l'Homme, l'Homme Armé, la Fraternité, l'Indivisibilité, or les Amis de la Patrie; some bore the names of heroes and martyrs such as Guillaume Tell, Brutus, Mutius Scevola, Lepelletier, or Marat; while others bore the names of revolutionary symbols, such as les Piques or le Bonnet Rouge. Similar changes had affected many squares, streets, quais, and bridges. The names of some places had been changed several times as the Revolution moved forward. The editor expected the process to continue "until its complete perfection."

In the atmosphere of destruction and renewal that followed the overthrow of the monarchy, many individuals were inspired with visions of urban space purified and transformed. Proposals for revolutionary gardens, bridges, monuments, squares, and temples proliferated, products not only of artists but of men of letters and even ordinary citizens. A visionary by the name of Verhelst sent a plan to the Committee of Public Safety to convert the whole centre of Paris into a vast allegorical garden that would convey an ideological message.[19] On the Place de la Révolution there would be a statue of Liberty erected on a model of a royal palace. Underneath there were to be four halls to display graphically the vices of the tyrannical monarchy to justify its overthrow. Leading from the square would be eight avenues, each illustrating some social virtue such as truthfulness, fidelity, fraternity, humanity, conjugal love, and devotion to the fatherland. Each of these avenues would be decorated with statues, low-reliefs, and inscriptions calculated to inspire the practice of those virtues. All the avenues would lead to Temples of the Supreme Being. If someone strayed from these avenues, he would find himself lost in a maze of pathways representing various vices. Leaving the temple he would enter the Champs-Elysées, where, beside a large basin and a waterfall, there would

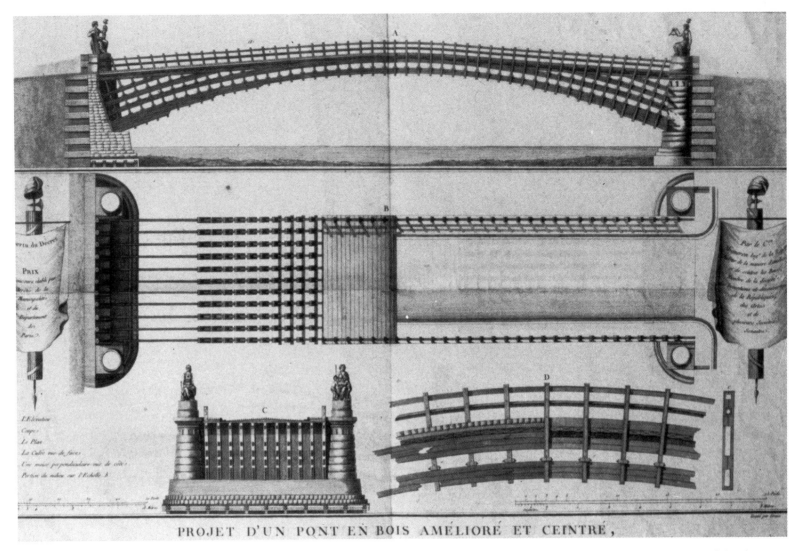

PROJET D'UN PONT EN BOIS AMÉLIORÉ ET CEINTRÉ,

130 Migneron. Project for a bridge to replace the Pont Rouge between the Ile de la Fraternité (Saint-Louis) and the Ile du Palais (Cité), elevation and details.

be monuments honouring Rousseau, Voltaire, and other benefactors of humanity.

An engineer by the name of Migneron submitted a project for a new bridge between the Ile de la Fraternité, formerly the Ile Saint-Louis, and the Ile du Palais, formerly the Ile de la Cité, a plan that combined a desire to improve the urban infrastructure, new ideas about improving wood for construction, and an ideological message (Figures 130–4).[20] The old bridge between the islands, the Pont Rouge, had deteriorated to the point where it had had to be removed. The inhabitants of the islands had demanded its replacement, complaining that houses were being deserted and commerce was languishing. The Conseil Général of Paris invited artists to submit proposals and set up a commission to choose the best one: the plan by Migneron was selected. He had developed a way of girding and strengthening wood, a process that won him an award from the Academy of Sciences.[21] He proposed to apply this process to create a wooden bridge between the islands, situated so as to extend the line of existing streets. This bridge was to be decorated at each end with large allegorical figures representing the ideals of the new Republic – Liberty, holding fasces and the tablet of the laws; Equality, holding a carpenter's level and a pike capped with a Phrygian bonnet; Fraternity, with two young boys clasping hands at her knee; and Force, clad in a lion's skin, holding a club, and exhibiting an all-seeing eye on her chest. The plan was approved by the Finance Committee of the Convention but derailed in a controversy over whether or not a stone bridge would be better.

Citoyenne Boulliaud, a war widow, submitted a plan to the Committee of Public Safety in October 1793 to transform the Place de la Révolution, the former Place Louis XV, into a vast monument to those who had died for the Republic or who had made outstanding contributions to the Revolution (Figure 135).[22] She began by pointing out that Barère, on behalf of the committee, had proposed to the Convention that the commissioners connected to the various units of the army should collect acts of heroism, and that the deputy Bourdon had proposed that such acts be published in a textbook. She suggested conversion of the vast *place* into "a picture that would speak to the hearts and eyes of all Frenchmen and foreigners by honouring the memory of heroes who had died for liberty and those who were still alive." She argued that, since the square was too large as it stood, its outer reaches should be divided into eight blocks of grass, creating an octagon, a shape with religious connotations.[23] These blocks would be bordered with trees. Between the trees she advocated placing thermae honouring heroes, with their names and accounts of their deeds inscribed on the casings. The inner edge of each of the eight verdant

blocks would be decorated with two statues of outstanding men of the Revolution, sixteen in all. On the outer sidewalks were to be eight little pavilions, each surmounted by another statue, making twenty-four statues altogether.

The widow Bouillard favoured leaving, in the centre of the octagon, the statue of Liberty erected for the Festival of Unity and Indivisibility on 10 August 1793, but she wanted an altar to be placed at its base, bearing an urn containing the remains of other citizens who had died in the defence of liberty. On each side of the urn were to be two figures on foot, one representing Immortality, the other Victory, together holding a civic crown over it. Around Liberty was to be a balustrade consisting of columns, each decorated with a medallion recounting the deeds of those still living. She declared: "This would be the first public museum to exist in the universe, one worthy of national gratitude. The people would be able to admire those virtuous citizens who have shed their blood in the defence of liberty, and founded a republic one and indivisible."[24] She argued that her plan would not be too expensive, since republican heroes needed monuments in stone rather than bronze. She enclosed a crude drawing of her scheme, remarking that the great David could refine it, if the committee approved the idea. For all its amateurishness and misspellings, the proposal was significant: it represented a revolutionary and democratic version of the *place d'émulation* conceived late in the Old Regime.

An even more visionary proposal for a *place d'émulation* was submitted to the government by the painter Maille Dussausoy, who before the Revolution had proposed a number of schemes for the embellishment of Paris that included statues of great men. He now proposed developing the area around the Pantheon, which still lacked a suitable architectural setting, into a vast memorial grove inside a square framed by a three-foot wall surmounted by a balustrade in the Doric style, the order of heroes.[25] This exterior wall was to be punctuated with socles, each containing an urn with a heroic deed inscribed on the pedestal. Inside the wall was to be the Field of Glory, where statues and tombs of outstanding legislators, generals, philosophers, republican martyrs, and young heroes such as Bara and Viala would be placed among trees lining the paths. Here citizens and their children would be inspired by the models presented to them. "Finally, if it should happen that a woman distinguishes herself sufficiently by the salient virtues of her sex to deserve the honour of having her sepulchre in this place of glory," he declared, "what a sublime lesson for her daughter and all persons of her sex." Two vast entrances, decorated with allegorical figures, would lead into this sacred enclosure. Adjacent streets would announce its proximity: rue des Grands Hommes, Chemin de la Gloire,

131 Migneron. Project for a bridge, detail of the statue of Liberty.

132 Migneron. Project for a bridge, detail of the statue of Equality.

133 Migneron. Project for a bridge, detail of the statue of Fraternity.

134 Migneron. Project for a bridge, detail of the statue of Force.

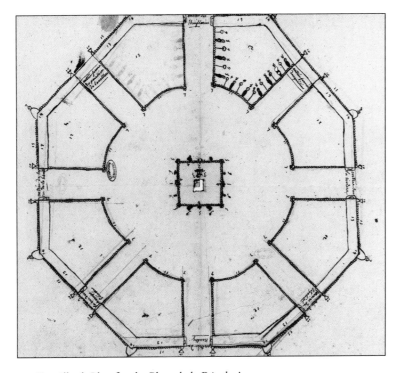

135 Brouillard. Plan for the Place de la Révolution.

Chemin de la Vertu, and Chemin d'Honneur. Dussausoy's vision of a memorial ground was very different from the traditional Christian cemetery.[26]

Despite all this fermentation, during the first two years of the Republic artists were confined to creating ephemeral architecture or to renovating existing buildings for revolutionary purposes. The ephemeral architecture was, however, extremely important because it provided focal points around which republicans could rally and give birth to projects for permanent structures. Soon after the collapse of the monarchy some temporary monuments were erected on vacant pedestals; for instance, an obelisk inscribed with the Rights of Man was placed atop the pedestal on the Place des Victoires.[27] A contemporary print imagined the obelisk rising out of the debris of the statue of Louis XIV (Figure 136).[28]

The principal temporary structures were created following the deaths of republican martyrs. The first such structure was a pyramid erected in the Tuileries Garden to serve as the centre of the funereal ceremony held on 26 August 1792 in honour of the citizens who had died in the recent overthrow of the monarchy (Figure 137).[29] The pyramid was a traditional shape used in monuments to the dead, the base representing the earth, the point suggesting the world beyond. Allegorical figures of Liberty and the Law, which had been pulled by oxen in the cortege from the city hall, were used to frame the site. Liberty sat in a majestic pose atop a square pedestal. She wore a civic crown, carried a Liberty Bonnet in her right hand, and leaned on a club in her left hand to show that she triumphed through force. One reporter called her a "Tutelary Divinity."[30] Law too sat atop a square pedestal, holding a sword in her right hand and a tablet representing the Rights of Man in the other.

All sides of the pyramid and all faces of the two pedestals were charged with low-reliefs and inscriptions. For example, on the east side of the pyramid an inscription promised mothers that their sons who had died would enjoy immortality, and imagined them passing on their patriotism to those whom they had left behind:

> MOTHERS SOOTHE YOUR SORROWS
> THEY SAVED LA PATRIE.
> If we have left this life,
> Our honours will be eternal.
> We leave you la Patrie,
> Who extends her arms to you.

According to the *Moniteur universal,* more than 350,000 participants massed around this monument in a ceremony that made an enduring impression on their minds.

Another ceremony for which temporary structures were erected occurred in Paris on 9 October. The fête had been ordered by the Commune three days previously to celebrate the "liberation" of Savoy.[31] The General Council called on all the sections of the city to assemble armed in front of the city hall, where they were to deposit flags and pennants that were now out of date. Although the festival was to celebrate a recent victory of the new Republic, it once again honoured citizens who had lost their lives on 10 August. Each section was asked to put the names of its dead on white standards, which were carried at the head of that section as it marched through the streets.[32] The names were read out at the city hall by the municipal officials representing each section; then the cortège marched to the Place de la Révolution. The standards were placed at intervals around the square for the duration of the ceremonies. A statue of Liberty had been placed atop the pedestal where an equestrian statue of

PLACE DES VICTOIRES

Louis le Grand renversé pour faire place a la Colonne de la Liberté et de l'Egalité

136 Monument on the Place des Victoires.

137 Ceremony in the Tuileries Garden on 26 August 1792 honouring the dead of 10 August.

138 Statue of Liberty erected on the former Place Louis XV for the festival on 9 October 1792 celebrating the "liberation" of Savoy.

Louis xv had stood until recently, anticipating the more permanent statue of the goddess erected for the Festival of Unity and Indivisibility eleven months later (Figure 138). She was shown holding a huge pike decorated with a Liberty Bonnet in one hand and a civic crown in the other.[33] Incense burners on the corners of the platform around the pedestal created a sacred aura about her. Crude benches, forming a sort of amphitheatre, completed the setting.

Other elaborate ceremonies centred on prominent individuals who died because of their devotion to the Revolution. The first of what became a trinity of outstanding martyrs was the deputy Lepelletier, assassinated on 20 January 1793 while he was dining in a restaurant in the former Palais Royal for having voted for the death of Louis xvi, whose execution was set for the following day. As a focal point for the mourners David, who was in charge of the funeral ceremonies, designed a structure that was built around the pedestal of the toppled statue of Louis xiv on the Place des Piques, formerly the Place Louis-le-Grand (Figure 139).[34] Once again the structure conveyed the idea of the new transcending the old. Again too it employed the form of a triangle, a modified version of the traditional pyramid. In this case the body of the martyr lay on public view on the apex, atop a wooden sarcophagus covered with canvas painted to look like granite, until he was transported to the Pantheon with great pomp.

The assassination of the radical publisher of the *Ami du peuple*, Jean-Paul Marat, by Charlotte Corday on 13 July 1793 provided radical revolutionaries with another martyr. His death was useful to the Montagnards in the Convention because it could be used to demonstrate the existence of plots against the Republic, justifying the purge of the so-called Girondists six weeks earlier, and to underline the danger of the Federalist revolt then under way. Robespierre and a number of other Montagnards, however, were wary of going too far in associating themselves with the martyred journalist because of his reputation as a bloodthirsty extremist.[35] It was significant that, although the Convention voted on 14 November 1793 to put his remains in the Pantheon,[36] this was not carried out until ten months later, after Robespierre had been overthrown.[37] The sans-culottes, however, identified strongly with the dead journalist, who in their opinion had been genuinely the friend of the people. Marat consequently became the centre of a popular cult in the sections, a cult that manifest itself in the inauguration of busts, eulogies, hymns, poetry, and monuments.

It was on the initiative of the Cordeliers Club,[38] with the support of sans-culottes and radical women,[39] that a tomb for the martyr, designed by the sculptor François Martin, was created in the garden adjacent to

139 Temporary monument in honour of Lepelletier.

140 Tomb of Marat in the Cordeliers' Garden.

the club (Figure 140).⁴⁰ The tomb formed a type of cave, built of stone and covered in grass, with the opening protected by an iron grille. Rising above the tomb was a four-sided pyramid surmounted by an urn bearing the inscription "Here rests Marat, the Friend of the People, assassinated by the enemies of the people, the 13th of July 1793."⁴¹ Also, an obelisk was erected on the Place de la Réunion, the present Place du Carrousel, site of one of the principal battles between the insurgents and the defenders of the Tuileries Palace on 10 August (Figure 141). As a contemporary engraving made clear, the monument was intended to inspire patriotism among the common people: "This little edifice, the same which contains the remains of the patriot Lazouwki [Lazowski], one of the leaders of the brave men who were triumphant on that memorable day, all inspiring in the true and good sans-culottes sorrowful and gratifying sensations that ought to nourish sublime thoughts that should prove valuable to liberty."⁴²

The most important ephemeral monuments erected early in the French Republic were constructed to serve as focal points in the Festival of Unity and Indivisibility on 10 August 1793. Just as the Festival of

Federation had attempted to consolidate the achievements of the first year of the Revolution, so this festival sought to rally the citizenry around the achievements of the Republic, especially the new democratic constitution framed by the triumphant Montagnards in the Convention and ratified by the voters. In the Old Regime kings had symbolized their control over the country by ostentatious entries into and processions through the capital and other cities, which were usually decorated with elaborate ephemeral architectural structures. Similarly, ecclesiastical authorities had organized processions that signified the authority of the church over society. In this great republican festival the procession moved through the streets of Paris, stopping for ceremonies and speeches at five stations, reminiscent of the Stations of the Cross, each representing a forward step in the Revolution, culminating in the proclamation of the constitution at the Altar of the Fatherland on the Champ de Mars.

Following the overall plans of Jacques-Louis David, the pageant-master of the great festivals of the Montagnard Republic, each station was decorated with sculpture or architecture designed to convey messages to the citizenry and to serve as ceremonial centres (Figure 142). The procession

INAUGURATION DU BUSTE DE MARAT AU TOMBEAU QUI A ÉTÉ ÉLEVÉ POUR SA GLOIRE ET CELLE DE LAZOWSKI, PLACE DE LA RÉUNION A PARIS, L'AN 2 DE LA RÉP. FRANC. UNE ET INDIVISIBLE.

Une main perfide
le ravit
à l'amour du peuple

A Paris chez l'Auteur, Rue P. du Place Maubert, N° 3.

Au fond
de son noir souterrain,
il fit trembler les traitres.

141 Monument to Lazowski and Marat in the Place du Carrousel.

142 The first five of the six stations of the Festival of Unity and Indivisibility.

The president then filled an antique cup with the regenerative water, drank a libation, and passed it to the oldest deputy of each department in alphabetical order, a sort of republican Eucharist.

Following the ceremony around the Fountain of Regeneration, the procession then followed the boulevards to a site near the market district from which the market women had marched to Versailles in 1789 to force the king and the royal family to take up residence in Paris among the citizenry, an important step in the radicalization of the Revolution. A very unusual triumphal arch had been erected there to remind the participants in the festival of that epochal event and to serve as a focal point for further ceremonies. Instead of the usual horses, women were shown atop the arch pulling cannon, and the façades were decorated with revolutionary symbols and inscriptions reminding onlookers of the heroism of the women:

LIKE A VILE PREY, THEY CHASED THE TYRANTS BEFORE THEM.
THE PEOPLE, LIKE A TORRENT INUNDATED THEIR PORTICOES;
THEY DISAPPEARED
ITS JUSTICE IS TERRIBLE
ITS CLEMENCY IS EXTREME

The reporter claimed that this triumphal arch surpassed those of antiquity. Once again the president of the Convention made a speech, addressing the women in the crowd. "The representatives of the common people come to offer you, instead of flowers which adorn beauty, the laurel which is the emblem of courage and victory," he announced; "you will transmit it to your children."[45]

The cortège then proceeded to the third station, on the Place de la Révolution, where a colossal figure of Liberty, created by the sculptor François-Frédéric Lemot, had been erected in the centre atop the pedestal of the former equestrian statue of Louis XV. Liberty was portrayed enthroned, like the kings on the former seals of state, wearing a Phrygian bonnet and carrying an orb in her left hand and a pike in her right hand, the symbol of popular power. Around her poplar trees had been planted, etymologically "trees of the people," their boughs bedecked with Phrygian bonnets, tricolour ribbons, bits of poetry, pictures of revolutionary events, and garlands of flowers. In front of the goddess a huge pile of feudal charters, coats of arms, and other emblems of the Old Regime had been amassed. The president of the Convention set this pile aflame in an expiatory gesture that the reporter called "une grande purification." A flock of doves was then set loose, each wearing a tricolour ribbon declaring "We

began at dawn, a time that itself suggested a new beginning, on the Place de la Bastille, in the centre of which stood a huge statue of Nature designed by Antoine-Léonard du Pasquier.[43] Nature was depicted as an Egyptian-like female reminiscent of the ancient goddess Isis, flanked on either side by lions, traditional symbols of the earth. On the base was inscribed WE ARE ALL HER CHILDREN. From her ample breasts, which she pressed with her hands, abundant water flowed into a large basin, signifying the inexhaustible fecundity of Nature. The president of the Convention, Hérault de Séchelles, made a speech in which he addressed the statue as though she were a living deity: "It is from your breasts, from your sacred sources," he declared, "that [the people] has recovered its rights and by which it is regenerated."[44] The reporter of the festival remarked that this was the first time in history that the representative of a nation had addressed Nature.

too are free." It was reported that one pair of doves returned to nest in the lap of Liberty, which was considered a good omen.

From the Place de la Révolution the parade proceeded to the fourth station, on the esplanade of the Invalides, where another unusual monument, this time designed by the sculptor Denis-Antoine Chaudet, had been erected to symbolize the victory over Federalism – somewhat prematurely, since the revolt had not yet been completely suppressed. A large figure of the People in the guise of Hercules stood atop a mountain, clearly representing the alliance of the radicals in Paris with *la Montagne* in the Convention, which had made possible the purge of the so-called Girondists at the beginning of the previous June. The figure of the People was shown about to strike the hydra of Federalism with the club in his right hand and holding up the fasces, symbol of state power and unity, in his left hand. The People had one foot on the neck of the counter-revolutionary hydra, a serpent with a female human head, which was trying desperately to unbind the fasces as it expired. In case the actual people at the festival did not recognize themselves in the role of Hercules, the president spelled it out for them: "French People! Here you are looking at yourself in the form of a emblem which is rich in instructive lessons," he explained. "The giant whose powerful hand reunites and reattaches in one bundle the departments which make up its grandeur and strength is you."[46]

The Mountain at the fourth station was one of the first conspicuous appearances of a symbol that was to be used repeatedly during the following year on engravings, in former churches, and on festival grounds. Although it originated as the nickname for the radicals who sat on the high benches of the Convention and who had won ascendancy in early June 1793, the name aroused profound connotations. A mountain is massive, dominates its surroundings, and seems to reach up into the heavens. Moreover, the name evoked deep memories, both Christian and pagan: Moses brought the Ten Commandments down from Mount Sinai; Christ preached a Sermon on the Mount; Zeus and other gods lived on Mount Olympus; and Apollo and his nine daughters, the Muses who preside over the various arts, dwelt on Mount Parnassus, to mention only some associations. During the Terror volcanic Mountains were used to represent the awesome power of the revolutionary government – for instance, in the background of the letterhead of the Committee of Public Safety.

Following the ceremony on the esplanade of the Invalides the procession moved westward to the Champ de Mars, on the edge of which a

143   Entranceway to the Champ de Mars erected for the Festival of Unity and Indivisibility.

special entrance had been created. Entrances have had great significance throughout history in announcing the meaning of a space set aside for important ceremonies – one thinks of the porticoes of classical temples, the portals of mediaeval churches, or the open gateway or *torii* under which one must pass to reach a Japanese shrine. For this festival two thermae had been erected, representing Liberty and Equality, designed by the sculptor Du Pasquier, between which a tricolour ribbon was stretched, from which hung a carpenter's level, the symbol that was increasingly used to signify equality (Figure 143). The entrance, the reporter stressed, announced a new social order in which men were equal under the law as they were by nature. It should be noted that women too passed under this level, although the new constitution denied them political equality. This entranceway, which was to survive throughout the Terror, thus reveals an important ambiguity or contradiction in the ideology of the Jacobins.

Having passed through the symbolic gateway, the procession then congregated around the fifth station, the Altar of the Fatherland in the centre of the Champ de Mars. The altar was much more elaborate than in previous festivals. A tall Doric column had been erected on the perron in front of the altar itself. Giant incense-burners stood in the four corners. From the highest point, "as though from a veritable sacred mountain," as the narrator described it,[47] the president of the Convention proclaimed the new constitution, which was then placed in an ark on the altar. The successive "stations," the symbolic entrance, the altar, the incense burners, the allusion to a sacred mountain, and the ark, all added to the sacred aura surrounding the event. Contemporary engravings reinforced this feature, one, for instance, showing the constitution emerging amid thunder and lightning from a Mountain, just like the tablets brought down from Mount Sinai by Moses.[48]

Some historians consider the fifth station the last one of the festival, but there was a further ceremony at the monument to dead republican soldiers that some contemporaries called a sixth station.[49] This monument took the form of a tholos open at the top. The circular architrave, a symbol of immortality, was decorated with a ring of stars. Later, in the Festival of Victories, an obelisk was added in the centre, its pyramidal apex serving as another sign of life beyond the earthly sphere. At this site Hérault made his sixth speech of the day, in which he asserted that the dead heroes had prepared the way for the new constitution, even though they had not lived to help draft it. Then he addressed them as though they could still hear him: "Sacred urn, I salute you with respect, I embrace you in the name of the French people," he exclaimed. "I lay on your protective remains the crown of laurels which the National Convention and the Fatherland present to you."[50] He then promised that, inspired by their example, their fellow citizens would carry on the struggle. Their work would thus outlive them. It was clear that for those who fought and died for the Republic the reward was to be a non-Christian, revolutionary immortality.

It has been argued that the stations of this festival represented stages of the Revolution, each superseding the previous one. From this point of view the fact that Hercules appears at the fourth station signifies that the brute power of the People had superseded the more moderate Liberty that had appeared at the previous station.[51] No doubt the stations do represent stages of the Revolution, but they should be viewed as *cumulative*, each of the successive steps producing a higher synthesis. Certainly the fact that Regeneration was symbolized at the first station on the Place de la Bastille was not meant to suggest that the process of regeneration was over: everything the revolutionary government did in the following year

makes it clear that regeneration was an ongoing process. David proposed that the medallion commemorating the festival should bear the image of the Fountain of Regeneration, not that of the People-Hercules.[52] Moreover, the great art contest of the Year II, which we shall discuss in the next chapter, included plans for a huge permanent figure of Liberty on the Place de la Révolution as well as a colossal one of the People for the point of the Ile de la Cité.

Besides ephemeral structures (some of which were repaired from time to time to make them last seven or eight years) erected for funeral ceremonies and civic festivals, the revolutionaries had to make do with existing buildings renovated so as to serve new purposes. One of the most important such conversions was the transformation of the Tuileries Palace into the meeting-place of the Convention.[53] Within a few days of the overthrow of the monarchy some patriots argued that it was imperative to make the symbolic gesture of moving the representatives of the people from the Manège, where they met in very cramped quarters, into the palace. When the deputy Broussonnet proposed this move in the Legislative Assembly on 13 August 1792, he was warmly applauded.[54] The proposal was made again on 8 September by a delegation from the Commune of Paris led by Pétion, which suggested using the part of the palace once occupied by the Théâtre-Français. "Previously palaces were for kings," declared Pétion. "It is time the people had one of their own."[55] This would not provide much more space than the Manège, but it would convey greater prestige than a former stable. Various architects submitted proposals outlining how to convert the former palace into a suitable meeting-place for the next assembly, whose main task was to be to draft a republican constitution – Guillaume-Edouard Allais, Perrard-Montreuil, Bernard Poyet, Pierre Vignon, and Pierre-Adrien Pâris, the architect of earlier assembly halls for the deputies of the Nation.[56]

A modified verson of a plan by Vignon eventually won out, although he did not implement it. He proposed creating an assembly hall on the second-floor level in the former theatre. It would be semicircular with a radius of sixty-two feet, decorated with a ring of Corinthian columns surmounted by a cupola. The benches would form a semicircular amphitheatre accommodating up to eight hundred deputies. Behind the columns there would be benches for 2,500 members of the public.[57] With the backing of Roland, the minister of the interior, Vignon's plan was approved on 13 September 1792;[58] however, during the next six weeks he was outmanoeuvred by Jacques-Pierre Gisors, originally a member of the panel appointed to choose the best design. Gisors offered a variation of Vignon's proposal, which he claimed would be cheaper.[59] The latter wrote

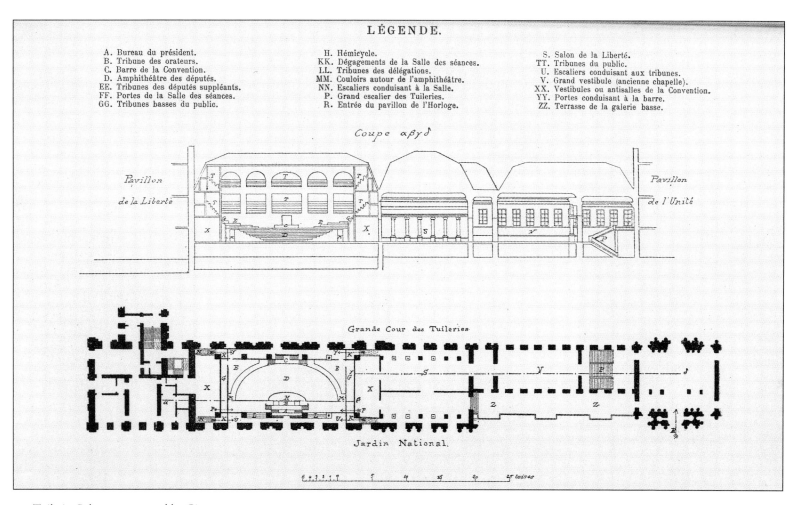

LÉGENDE.

A. Bureau du président.
B. Tribune des orateurs.
C. Barre de la Convention.
D. Amphithéâtre des députés.
EE. Tribunes des députés suppléants.
FF. Portes de la Salle des séances.
GG. Tribunes basses du public.

H. Hémicycle.
KK. Dégagements de la Salle des séances.
LL. Tribunes des délégations.
MM. Couloirs autour de l'amphithéâtre.
NN. Escaliers conduisant à la Salle.
P. Grand escalier des Tuileries.
R. Entrée du pavillon de l'Horloge.

S. Salon de la Liberté.
TT. Tribunes du public.
U. Escaliers conduisant aux tribunes.
V. Grand vestibule (ancienne chapelle).
XX. Vestibules ou antisalles de la Convention.
YY. Portes conduisant à la barre.
ZZ. Terrasse de la galerie basse.

144 Tuileries Palace as converted by Gisors.

a pamphlet complaining of plagiarism and defending his own version, but to no avail.[60] On 25 October the plan by Gisors was approved by the new Convention,[61] and work continued through the winter. On 24 April 1793, on a motion by Antoine-Louis-François Sergent (better known as Sergent-Marceau), the Convention rechristened the building the Palais National and set 10 May as the date when the deputies would move in.[62] The symbolic transference was complete: republican representatives took their places in the former royal residence.

The assembly hall was fitted into a parallelogram running north to south (Figure 144). The deputies sat on ten semicircular tiered rows of benches directed westward towards the Tuileries Gardens. Facing them were the elevated desks of the president and secretaries. In front of the president and slightly lower down was the podium for orators. Both the president and the orator could see the whole audience. This shape, which had been evolving since Pâris altered the Menus-Plaisirs in Versailles to accommodate the newly formed National Assembly, has prevailed ever since. The continuous rows of benches reflected the belief that the deputies were to unite in working for the national good. There was no idea of government and opposition as eventually evolved in Britain, nor of a member "crossing the floor" when he changed parties. Although factions did emerge – Girondists, Montagnards, the Plain, and so on – they were not part of revolutionary ideology and were not provided for in the architecture. Also significant in the new political culture were the galleries provided for journalists and members of the public behind the seats of the deputies, although for only 1,400 rather than the 2,500 Vignon had hoped for. Whereas in the Old Regime laws had been approved in secluded council chambers, the new regime called for them to be passed in full public view.

Another feature of the assembly hall that was related to the new political culture was provision of a bar at which members of the public could address the deputies of the nation. Pâris had already anticipated the need for such a facility when he redesigned the Menus-Plaisirs in Versailles for the National Assembly, and again when he converted the Manège in Paris to serve as its meeting-place. Gisors then integrated a similar arrangement into the new hall for the Convention. He provided a room underneath the upper benches, accessible by the corridor outside the hall, where delegations or individuals could wait. When their turn came, they could descend an aisle to reach a bar set amid the tiered benches. The public could therefore not only observe the deputies at work but could communicate with them. At any given session of the Convention a succession of groups or individuals usually appeared at the bar, speaking on behalf of local authorities, political clubs, or themselves. Some bore congratulations for something the deputies had done recently; many called for some new measure; while others brought patriotic gifts. When the Convention completed the new republican constitution in the summer of 1793, the right to petition public authorities was added to the Declaration of the Rights of Man and the Citizen.[63]

The decor of the hall was equally significant. Around the second level of the amphitheatre Jean-François Strasbaux, a pupil of Jean-Baptiste Regnault, painted eight figures eight feet high at intervals between the galleries after sketches approved by Gisors. These imitation bronze statues depicted Demothenes, Lycurgus, Solon, and Plato on the side of the president. On the opposite side towards the garden were Camillus, Publicola, Brutus, and Cincinnatus.[64] In the corners were fasces and Roman military ensigns. Thus, at first, the decor recalled classical antiquity, but as time went on the hall took on a more contemporary air as a number of works of art were added. This was especially true of works exalting certain martyrs of the Revolution. Felix Lepelletier, for example offered a bust of his assassinated brother by a young artist named Fleuriot, a work praised by David.[65] Later busts of Marat and Chalier were added to form a repub-

lican trinity.[66] More justly renowned were the canvases by David, the one of Lepelletier which was painted in the spring of 1793,[67] and that of Marat finished in the autumn of the same year,[68] both of which were hung in the hall behind the president's desk. The legislature took on the appearance of a Pantheon for eminent revolutionaries who had died for the Republic.

The antechamber of the Convention was also important. It consisted of a large room known as the Salon de la Liberté, which Gisors had created on the second level of the building, through which people passed on their way to the entrance at the northeast corner of the Convention. This vestibule got its name from a seated statue of the goddess Liberty ten feet high, holding a globe in her right hand and a Phrygian bonnet in the other, the work of the sculptor Du Pasquier. For the Festival of Unity and Indivisibility on 10 August 1793 Gisors ordered figures of Voltaire and Rousseau added to the decor. Sergent also accepted two paintings by a certain Bonnier, but no information about them has survived. On 10 Nivôse an 11 – 30 December 1793 – the citizen Duplain donated the *Battle of Jemappes*. Also exhibited was a ship atop a marble pedestal, probably the *Vengeur*, whose crew had fought defiantly until the end when surrounded and outnumbered by enemy ships. It was also for this vestibule that the Convention ordered a statue of Philosophy from Houdon, a statue that was not delivered before the fall of Robespierre.[69] Moreover, it was there that the projects for revolutionary paintings, monuments, and public buildings submitted to the contest of Year 11 were displayed in the early summer of 1794. As we shall see, this contest aimed at giving a new ideological appearance to the capital and the whole country.

Another dimension of the conversion of the former Tuileries Palace and the surrounding area deserves attention. We have already observed that the Revolution was a stage in the rise of the modern bureaucratic state. Gisors and his fellow architects had to abandon the idea of creating a huge new building or complex of buildings, as envisaged by Combes, Lahure, Mouillefarine, and other planners, to house the committees, offices, archives, and printing presses of the revolutionary government. Nevertheless, they managed to find space for over thirty such bodies. Quarters for guards were created on the ground level of the palace. The Committee of Public Safety occupied the former apartments of the queen on the same level. Later it expanded on to the second floor, where the apartments of the king had been. Almost all of the long building south of the central pavilion was taken up by offices. Despite its overall size, the former palace was not large enough; consequently, neighbouring mansions and monastic buildings were requisitioned for government use. The Committee of General Security occupied the Hôtel de Brionne, and printing facilities were installed in stables nearby. The Pavillon des Médicis and the Hôtels de la Vallière, Breteuil, and Noailles were likewise occupied. The archives moved into the library of a former monastery.[70] By improvisation planners thus succeeded in creating a political and administrative centre for the Republic.

On the outside of the former palace revolutionary authorities tried to give the building a new appearance. New names announced another trinity: the northern wing became the Pavillon de la Liberté; the central block became the Pavillon de l'Union; and the southern section became the Pavillon de l'Egalité. Over them all flew the tricolour flag. When on 24 April 1793 the Convention named the adjacent garden the Jardin National, this had more than a symbolic significance: it was also an extension of power over the area to the east and west of the building. Article 2 of the decree gave the minister of the interior control over the palace and authority to maintain and embellish the garden, the Place de la Révolution – the present Place de la Concorde – and the Champs-Elysées.[71] The architectural historian Ferdinand Boyer cites a letter by Sergent to Garat, the new minister of the interior, on the same day explaining that the objective was to embellish the garden with statues from former palaces. As Boyer remarks, a revolutionary artist-deputy urged the republican government to take up the work of kings and their ministers in planning the axis between the Louvre and Chaillot far to the west.[72]

Gisors had already begun to plan the approach to the National Palace. In the area in front of the palace (that is, towards the Louvre up to the Place de la Réunion, as the Carrousel was then called) the architect planned to create a courtyard enclosed by a wall, topped with fasces and shields bearing the names of all the departments. Inside this courtyard he planned to create a green area consisting of quinconces on either side of a path leading to the main entrance to the legislature. He hoped to decorate the entrance to this courtyard with pedestals supporting the famous horses from the Château de Marly. The Inspectors of the Convention, the commissioners in charge of the National Palace and its surroundings, favoured an entranceway flanked by Liberty and Equality, the goddesses who were frequently paired at this phase of the Revolution. Work progressed, clearing and levelling the area, during the summer and into the fall of 1793. There were delays, however, caused by problems of transporting the horses of Marly and other statuary from former palaces to their new destination at a time when most transport was needed for the war effort.[73]

Meanwhile the Convention envisaged developing the whole district adjacent to the new centre of government, the area up to the rue Saint-

Honoré to the north, the Carrousel to the east, the rue de la Révolution to the west, and the Tuileries Gardens. The nationalization of monastic property in the vicinity of the National Palace offered an unprecedented opportunity for planning the whole area. On 5 May 1793 Charles Delacroix won approval for a decree calling on artists to submit proposals.[74] On 12 June representatives of the Commune of the Arts (an organization formed in 1790 by artists opposed to the privileges of the Royal Academy of Painting and Sculpture) petitioned the Convention to have an overall plan, including completion of a north wing of the Louvre connecting it to the National Palace, opened to competition.[75] On 30 June the Convention approved a program calling for artists to submit their proposals by 15 September.[76] On 28 July another delegation from the Commune of the Arts complained about the short time allowed for preparation of plans. David and Sergent supported their complaint. On a motion by another deputy, the contest was put off until a joint committee of the Commune of the Arts and the Committee of Public Instruction could report.[77] In the autumn of 1793, however, the *gouvernement révolutionnaire*, headed by the Committee of Public Safety, emerged and took over planning the area around the National Palace and the whole city as part of a comprehensive cultural program, which we shall examine later.

Other significant developments following the overthrow of the monarchy involved the old Louvre and its wing along the quai. When the Louvre was abandoned in the seventeenth century as a royal residence, it had developed into a centre of artistic activity. Not only were privileged artists given space in it, but it served as the meeting-place of the Academy of Painting and Sculpture and the Academy of Architecture, both suppressed in 1793. Both the revolutionary organizations of artists, the Commune of the Arts and its successor formed in the autumn of 1793, the Popular and Republican Society for the Arts, likewise assembled there.[78] The palace had also been the site of the exhibitions of the works of members of the Academy of Painting and Sculpture held every two years after 1747, exhibitions that became known as *salons* because they took place in the Salon carré. These displays allowed the public to see and criticize the works produced by privileged artists. Public opinion had gradually become a factor to be reckoned with by officials and artists.[79] Cultured Frenchmen and Europeans regarded the *salons* with fascination, reading about them if they could not attend themselves.

Also in the last half of the eighteenth century the idea had emerged of turning the Louvre into a museum where the public could see the works of art collected by French kings since the Renaissance. The Comte d'Angiviller, who as superintendent of royal buildings after 1774 was a

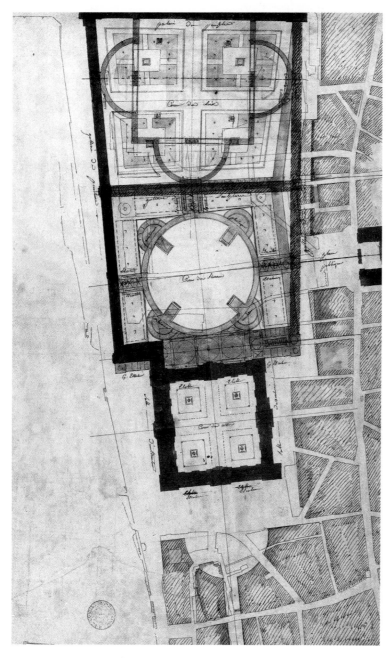

145 Anonymous. Plan for completion of the Louvre to form a political and cultural centre.

sort of minister of fine arts, had promoted this project, but the expense of creating skylights that would be fireproof retarded his plans.[80] Once again the revolutionaries took up a project from their royal predecessors: following a report by Sergent on 27 July 1793, the Convention declared that on the following 10 August – the choice of date was significant – the Louvre would become the Museum of the Republic, where works of art from former palaces and from collections of *émigrés* would be displayed. Moreover, a sum of 100,000 livres was allocated to the minister of the interior to purchase important works of art that might otherwise leave the country.[81] Some artists revived the idea of completing the Louvre by creating a northern wing, paralleling the one along the quais, to create a vast cultural centre. One example, in the Bibliothèque Historique de la Ville de Paris and dating from this period, is a crude sketch that shows how the completed Louvre could provide space for all the arts and sciences, including a library and teaching facilities (Figure 145).[82]

Like former royal buildings, ecclesiastical edifices were converted to serve the Republic. Churches, convents, and monasteries were transformed into sectional assemblies or meeting-places for political clubs. Above all, churches were transformed into revolutionary temples. The best-known example is that of Notre-Dame in Paris, transformed into a Temple of Reason in November 1793, one of the major steps in the coming of de-Christianization. For the festival in which the temple was inaugurated the former cathedral was decorated with a Mountain in the nave, on the top of which there was a little temple surrounded with busts of philosophers and benefactors of humanity (Figure 146).[83] On a pedestal atop a rock burned the flame of Truth. In the inaugural ceremony, after a procession through the streets, a choir of young women dressed in white sang a hymn to Reason; musicians from the opera and the National Guard provided musical accompaniment, and an actress, attired in a tricolour robe and carrying a pike, played the role of Liberty. Soon other Parisian churches were transformed into Temples of Reason – for example, the Eglise de la Sorbonne, Saint-Roch, and Notre-Dame-de-Bonne-Nouvelle.

Churches were also transformed into temples dedicated to revolutionary ideals, civic virtues, or useful activities: Saint-Antoine-des-Champs became the Temple of Liberty; Saint-André-des-Arts became the Temple of Revolution; the Eglise-des-Petits-Pères became the Temple of Morality; Saint-Germain-l'Auxerrois became the Temple of Beneficence; Saint-Sulpice became the Temple of Victory; Saint-Eustache became the Temple of Agriculture; and Saint-Médard became the Temple of Work. The process went on through the Terror into the Directory, when other chuches became Temples of Youth, Old Age, Filial Piety, Harmony, and so on. Religious

Décadi 20 Brumaire de l'an 2ᵉ de la République française une et indivisible, la Fête de la Raison été Célébrée dans la Cidevant Eglise de Notre Dame.

146 Notre-Dame in Paris converted
into a Temple of Reason.

imagery was torn out or covered over, and in its place were substituted tricolour fabrics, revolutionary allegorical figures, busts of republican martyrs, and political slogans or maxims. All this helped to give a new face to the old city.

The most important conversion of an existing building was the ongoing transformation of the church of Sainte-Geneviève into a Temple of Immortality under the direction of Quatremère de Quincy. His second report in November 1792,[84] and his third a year later,[85] show that he had worked out a complex iconographical program centred not on Christ or the Virgin but on the new goddess *la Patrie*. Fatherland, like Fraternity or Brotherhood, is feminine in French. On the outside of the temple, as he had promised in his initial report, Quatremère directed his team of artists to remove all the Christian imagery and substitute iconography related to the new fronton by Jean-Guillaume Moitte, which, as we have seen, showed an imposing female figure, accompanied by emblems that identified her as France, crowning Virtue and Genius. The large tablets under the peristyle, originally intended to be inscribed with the history of the church, were now to be inscribed with the Rights of Man and the

Constitution. Above them low-reliefs were to illustrate the same themes, as we see in the design for one relief by Guillaume Boichot (Figure 147). "One will see on the one hand what the Fatherland does for man," wrote Quatremère, "on the other hand what man owes to the Fatherland."[86] Atop the colonnade around the dome was to be a magnificent series of statues. In place of the lantern crowning the dome, a common feature of modern churches, was to be a giant figure of Renown by Claude Dejoux (Figure 148).

In his second report Quatremère predicted that most of the external changes would be completed in 1793. In the autumn of that year he predicted that the internal decoration would be ready for the second anniversary of the Republic the following year – that is, 10 August 1794 – a prediction borne out on the whole by the archival records.[87] As on the outside, new imagery was being created to illustrate the new world-view. The entrance nave was being decorated with allegories about History, Political Knowledge, Legislation, and Morality. The northern nave was being dedicated to Science, the southern nave to the various Arts, and the eastern nave to Patriotic Virtues. Pierre Cartellier was sculpting Force in

139

147 Boichot. Design for the low-relief illustrating the Rights of Man engraving by Moitte.

148 Dejoux. Design of the figure of la Renommée for the crown of the dome of the Pantheon.

the form of a warrior, a club in one hand, a figure of Victory on the other. Jean-Joseph Foucou was representing Good Faith and Fraternity, their hands joined symbolically. François Masson was illustrating patriotic devotion in the form of a dying Citizen at the moment when he glimpses a civic crown. Jean-Pierre Lorta was depicting disinterestedness by a scene showing Citizenesses, the wives of artists, offering their jewels to the Fatherland, a famous incident from the early history of the Revolution.

At the end of the eastern nave there was a sort of niche in which Quatremère proposed to place the goddess to whom all the iconography was related, *la Patrie*. "The idol of a free people," as he called her, was to sit on a throne, supported by two tutelary genii: on her right, Liberty with the usual pike and bonnet, presenting the goddess with a model of the Bastille, once an emblem of tyranny, now an emblem of its destruction; and on her left, the Genius of Equality, to whom the goddess is giving a level, symbol of the triumph over prejudice. With her right hand, supported by Liberty, she would hold up the palm reserved for her true friends. This group was to be raised up high on a perron decorated with low-reliefs and philosophical allusions. Altars in the form of candelabra would burn on either side, creating an aura of sanctity. Although Quatremère believed that the commission for the actual group should be the result of a contest, he published an engraving showing how he envisaged it, except that a baton was substituted for the palm in the goddess's right hand (Figure 149). Overhead were to be four more huge genii corresponding to the themes of the four naves: the Genius of Philosophy, the Genius of Virtue, the Genius of Science, and the Genius of the Arts.

As the artist with overall responsibility for the Pantheon, Quatremère was well aware that the Pantheon lacked a suitable setting. Apparently the departmental officials to whom he reported were also conscious of the problem, since in the spring of 1793 they asked him to make recommendations for a Place du Panthéon. Like Dussausoy, whose ideas we have discussed, Quatremère aspired to create an Elysian field around the site, although on a smaller scale so that the temple would dominate. In response to the officials' demand Quatremère submitted three maps, one showing the existing surroundings, a second showing an *enceinte* of the limited size he favoured, and a third showing a more vast plan, which he thought would dwarf the temple and would be more expensive.[88] The report on the surroundings was sent by the department to the Committee of Public Instruction, but there is no mention of it in their proceedings. Little was done about the site: for the festival in honour of the young Bara and Viala, planned for July 1794 but never held, David had to design emphemeral architecture for in front of the shrine (Figure 150),[89] and Lesueur designed a new door with panels illustrating various civic virtues (Figure 151).[90]

Other buildings besides churches were renovated so as to serve the Republic better. One of the most fascinating examples is the transformation of the Théâtre Français, now known as the Odéon, into a Théâtre du Peuple (Figure 152). The idea of a theatre offering revolutionary plays to the masses went back to the very beginning of the Revolution[91] and was taken up by the Committee of Public Safety as part of its plans in Year II to rally the people around the Republic. One of the original architects of the Odéon, Charles de Wailly, was directed to oversee its conversion into a popular revolutionary theatre.[92] The auditorium inside was redone in tri-colour decor and the foyer was decorated with allegorical figures (Figure 153). Colossal figures of Liberty and Equality flanked the stage. The surviving drawings also reveal that at every level the stalls were removed and benches installed in order to turn the theatre as much as possible into an

149 Quatremère. Group with la Patrie in the centre for the eastern nave of the Pantheon.

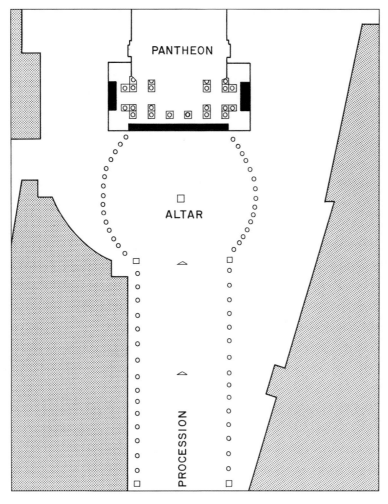

150 *Place* in front of the Pantheon, arranged for the abortive festival in honour of Bara and Viala.

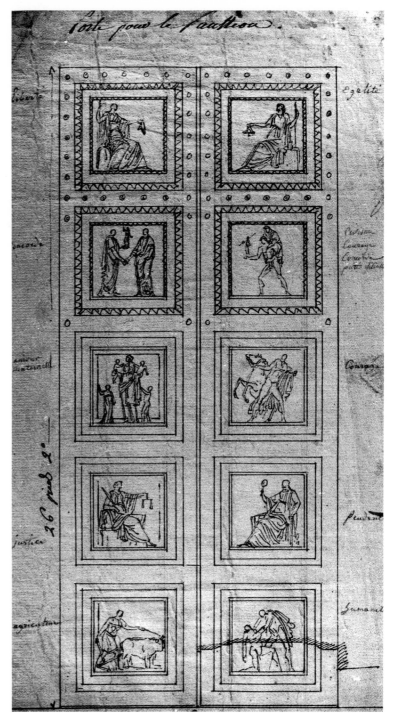

151 Lesueur. Door of the Pantheon decorated for the festival in honour of Bara and Viala.

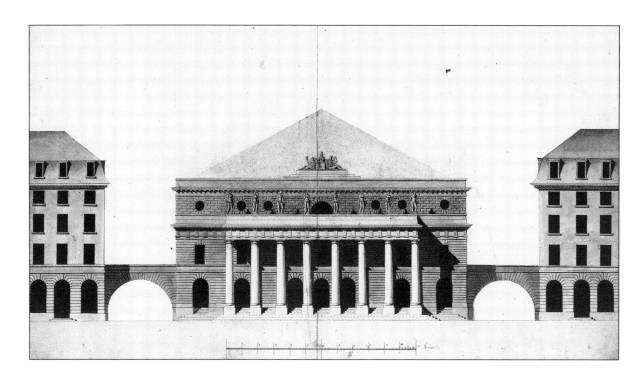

152 De Wailly and Peyre.
The Théâtre Français or
Odéon.

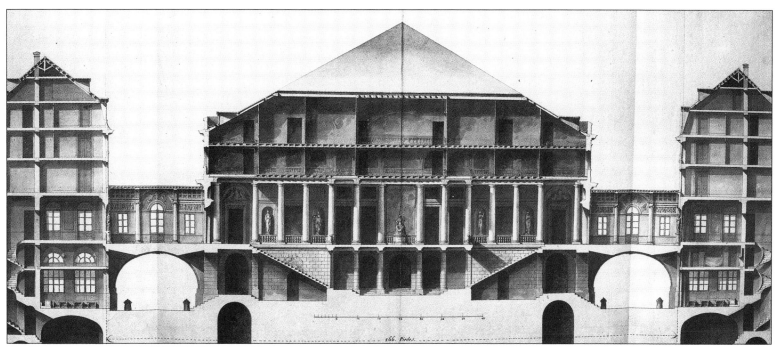

153 De Wailly. Plan to convert the Théâtre Français into a revolutionary theatre, cross-section.

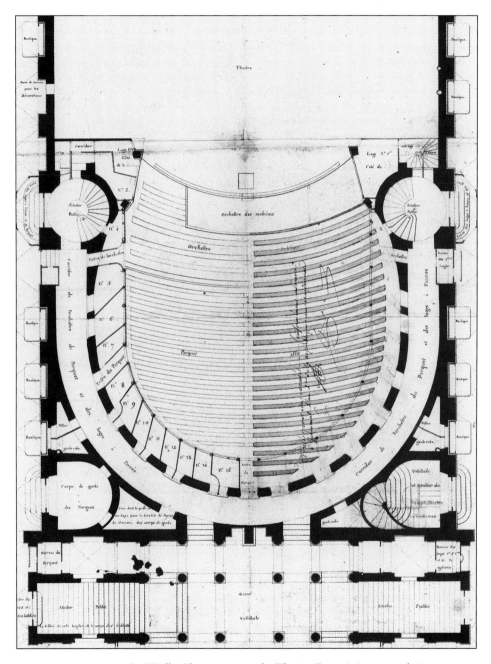

154 De Wailly. Plan to convert the Théâtre Français into a revolutionary theatre, ground level.

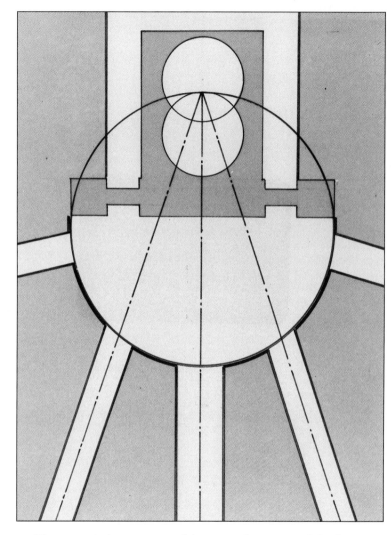

155 The geometrical arrangement of the streets, the square, and the theatre.

amphitheatre in which it was hoped that the citizens would merge and share emotions (Figure 154).[93] On the plans the old arrangement appears on the left, the democratic arrangement on the right.

As the internal renovations neared completion, the Committee of Public Safety changed the name of the theatre yet again, ordering that it be called the Théâtre de l'Egalité.[94] The reporter for the *Moniteur* understood very well the objective of the new seating arrangements. In his report on the opening night at the end of June 1794, he wrote: "It appears that this time they have had the aim of creating a more *popular* theatre, one in which the citizens will not be separated from each other in boxes but where they will join together and intermingle in the circular amphitheatres. This arrangement calls to mind equality, republican brotherhood, and justifies the name given to this new theatre."[95]

It is not clear to what extent the plans for the semicircular square in front of the theatre were realized, but they too offer a fascinating insight into revolutionary objectives. The semicircle had been designed to suggest the shape of the auditorium inside (Figure 155).[96] If we complete the circle, it transects the stage. Also, if we follow the lines of the three streets facing the theatre, they too converge on the stage. Following a suggestion by David, de Wailly redesigned this *place* so that it not only anticipated the auditorium but would itself become a covered outdoor amphitheatre with a stage in front of the entrance to the original theatre, of which the façade would now serve as a backdrop (Figure 156).[97] Moreover, the ground-plan shows the angle of the three streets facing the theatre changed so that they converge on the new stage like the two lateral streets. The square was to be enclosed by a colonnade punctuated by arches over the entrances from the adjacent streets. Benches were to be constructed around the edges. The whole space was to be covered with canvas to protect the audience from the elements (Figure 157). The poles supporting this cover were to be decorated with tricolour banners, Phrygian bonnets, and Levels of Equality.

Equally intriguing are the plans to convert tax offices and collection gates to a revolutionary purpose. The revolutionaries got a special satisfaction from the idea of changing the significance of buildings that had once served the hated tax farmers of the Old Regime. For example, the Archives Nationales contain records about a project to convert the building of the former tax authorities in the Section Halle aux Blés into a local assembly hall (Figures 158–160).[98] The Committee of Public Safety authorized use of the site for this purpose on 9 Messidor an 11 (27 June 1794) and the following month approved a plan. Drawings attached show the building decorated on the outside with a fasces, an amphitheatre inside

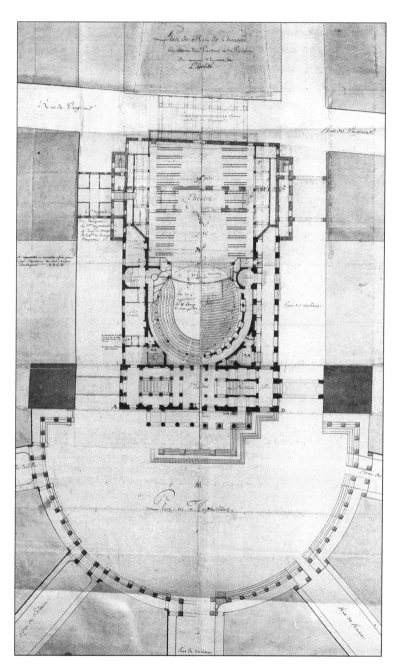

156 De Wailly. Project to convert the entrance to the theatre into a stage and the square into an outdoor amphitheatre, ground-plan.

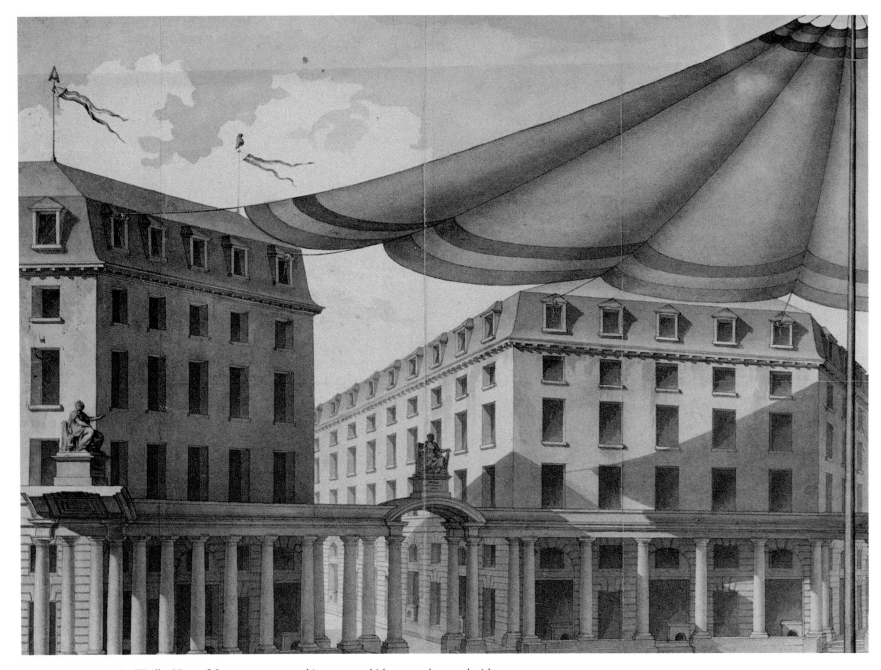

157 De Wailly. View of the square converted into an amphitheatre and covered with canvas.

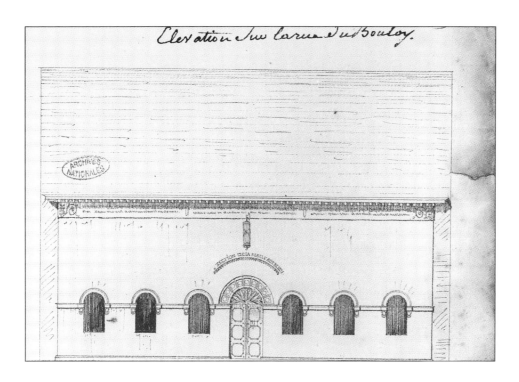

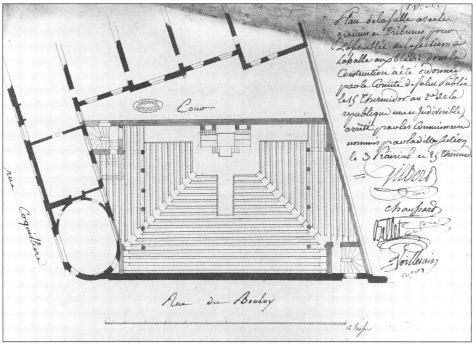

158, 159 Project to convert the former tax office in the section Halle aux Blés into a sectional assembly. *Above*: elevation; *below*: ground-plan.

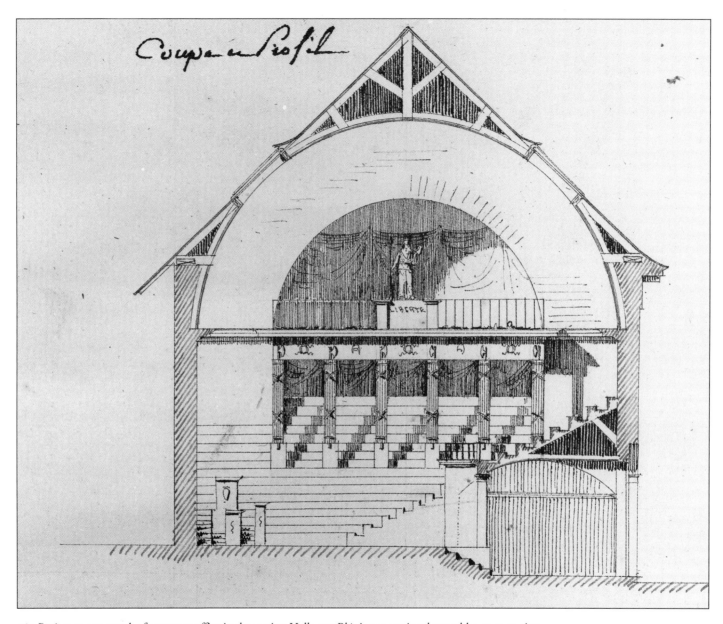

160 Project to convert the former tax office in the section Halle aux Blés into a sectional assembly, cross-section.

with more fasces serving as pillars, and a statue of Liberty at one end of the hall, watching over the auditorium like a tutelary divinity. A statue of Equality may have looked down from the other end.

A more ambitious scheme to reverse the meaning of structures used by the tax authorities of the Old Regime was that of Bertrand Barère to turn the tax gates of Paris, the *barrières* as they were called popularly, into triumphal revolutionary monuments. When a number of flags captured from the enemy at Ypres were presented to the Convention on 13 Messidor an II (1 July 1794), Barère reminded the assembly that in order to ransack passersby the tax farmers had turned the gates of the city into the haunts of vampires. Now citizens approaching those gates must be reminded of the successes of the people. The farmer, the traveller, or the foreigner coming to the city in future would have to pass through victory monuments. He told the cheering Convention: "The despots allied together at Pillnitz to destroy Paris; very well, Paris must display proofs of the destruction of despots. They did not want to leave one stone on top of the other; very well, we will engrave on those very stones, in ineffaceable letters, in letters of bronze, the victories over tyrants and the dates of the successful battles that consolidated the Republic. Paris henceforth will be the city of a hundred gates, each of which will point to a military victory or a revolutionary advance."[99]

The Convention approved Barère's proposal, and the authorities began collecting suitable inscriptions. The architect Ledoux, who had designed many of the gates in a progressive style, was in prison at the time as a suspected counter-revolutionary. Hoping to improve his fate, he wrote to the Committee of Public Safety, congratulating the Convention for having *défiscalisé* the gates of Paris, the propylæa as he called them, in order to turn them into monuments to republican victories.[100] He claimed that for twenty years he had been composing a work that would help to instruct young architects and had devoted himself to useful projects. He asked to be allowed to collect his plans so that he could continue his work. Released after the Terror, he later published his plans.[101]

By the spring of 1794, after twenty-odd months of republican rule, streets and squares had been rebaptized; a host of projects for monuments and buildings had been conceived; the city had been decorated with temporary monuments; the Tuileries Palace had been made over into the political centre of the republic; churches had been converted into revolutionary temples; the transformation of the church of Sainte-Geneviève into a Pantheon for French heroes was well advanced; the Théâtre Français had been remodelled into a Théâtre de l'Egalité; and work had begun to turn the gates of Paris into memorials to republican victories. But new names, ephemeral structures, and renovated buildings were not enough for revolutionaries who aspired to create a new Rome and impress the world. In the spring of Year II the revolutionary government launched projects for impressive monuments and public buildings, not just for Paris but for all of France. The contest for these projects was part of a broad cultural program, what Barère called "a vast plan for regeneration," to which we now turn.[102] ▲

Lequeu. Project for a triumphal arch, elevation and details. (Figure 168)

VI
A VAST PLAN
FOR REGENERATION

WHAT BARÈRE CALLED A "vast plan for regeneration" was the most highly developed program of integrational propaganda launched during the Revolution. We have seen that the constitutional monarchists had attempted to use festivals and other media to rally the masses around the institutions they had designed, but the program of the *gouvernement révolutionnaire* went much further, especially in the late winter and early spring of 1794. Although the government never established a single ministry of propaganda, the Committee of Public Safety and subordinate committees such as the Committee of Public Instruction (a committee of the Convention), and later the Commission of Public Instruction (an executive body), laid down plans for mass republican education, subsidized certain newspapers, exerted control over the theatre, encouraged the production of revolutionary songs and hymns, appealed to writers of all sorts to work for the new order, launched plans for a distinctive national costume, inaugurated a cycle of civic festivals, and announced a bold program for the arts, including a wide range of projects for monuments and public buildings.[1]

This cultural program was the result of the convergence of several powerful forces. Above all it was part of the effort of the revolutionary government to consolidate its power. Over the past half-century historians have emphasized how the popular forces in the sections or wards of the capital helped to push the Revolution to the left, contributing to the triumph of the Montagnards, the growth of the power of the Committee of Public Safety, and the creation of the machinery of the Terror. These historians have also shown that the leaders of the Convention not only responded to the pressures of the sans-culottes in the sections but attempted to bring them under control. The central government could not tolerate forty-eight rival republics in the capital. At the very moment that it yielded to the demand to make Terror the order of the day and to inaugurate economic controls, the revolutionary government limited the number and duration of the sectional assemblies and began to bureaucratize the local revolutionary committees. In the spring of 1794 Robespierre and his colleagues purged the radical Hébertists and closed the popular clubs that the sans-culottes had set up in the sections to bypass the restrictions on their assemblies. The government, however, realized that negative measures would not suffice: it was necessary to rally the masses around the ideals and institutions of the Montagnard Republic.

At the same time the revolutionary government was motivated by certain ideals. It justified its dictatorship and terroristic methods by holding up the goal of a democratic, egalitarian republic inhabited by a novel kind of citizenry imbued with a new morality. The government realized that such an ideal people did not exist: it would have to be created. "One must, so to speak, recreate the people whom one wishes to restore to liberty, because it is necessary to destroy ancient prejudices, change ingrained habits, perfect depraved affections, restrain superfluous needs, and extirpate inveterate vices," Billaud-Varenne explained to the Convention on behalf of the Committee of Public Safety.[2] The new republican constitution, proclaimed with great fanfare but never implemented, could only be made operative when the internal and external enemies of the regime had been crushed and the people made ready for it. This explains why the Committee of Public Safety paid careful attention to cultural matters, despite the fact that it was waging war on an unprecedented scale, trying to manage the economy, and dealing with various political crises. It explains too why the cultural decrees expressed a sense of urgency in such phrases as "within ten days," "as soon as possible," "without delay," or "at once."

The cultural program was also linked to the religious policies of the Committee of Public Safety. Robespierre and some others on the committee were concerned that extreme acts of de-Christianization, such as publicly destroying religious imagery, parodying traditional religious processions, or desecrating the Eucharist, would antagonize many of the common people, who still clung to traditional beliefs, and would also alarm neutral powers. The committee members suspected those who promoted the cult of Reason of being atheistic. Robespierre believed that such extremism masked counter-revolutionary intentions. In any case he was convinced that belief in God and the immortality of the soul, with some kind of reward or punishment in the hereafter, was the necessary foundation for republican morality. Throughout the winter of Year II,

1793–94, the committee tried to curb provocative acts by representatives on mission in the departments. Among the accusations against the Hébertists, who were executed in March, was the charge that they were atheists. Finally, on 7 May 1794 Robespierre made a great speech on religion and morality, followed by a decree affirming that the Republic supported belief in the Supreme Being and the immortality of the soul. The decree also inaugurated a cycle of festivals, four major ones commemorating the great days of the Revolution and lesser ones every "décadi" or tenth day, the republican Sunday. This deistic civic cult required sacred music, catechisms, statues, and places of worship.

The government also had to solve certain pressing practical problems. The toppling of royal statues had left many squares vacant, like frames without a picture. The ephemeral structures erected on some of these squares were fragile, composed of plaster painted to look like bronze, and canvas painted to create an illusion of marble, which deteriorated over time. Despite the renovation of certain buildings, many palaces and other buildings remained to be remodelled or replaced. If there were no resources to build an imposing meeting-place for the deputies of the nation, at least the Tuileries Palace, then housing the Convention, and its surroundings could be redecorated to symbolize its new use. In addition to the lack of suitable enclosures for republican liturgy every *décadi*, there were no buildings designed specifically for the primary assemblies of the citizens called for by the new constitution. Also there were no spacious indoor amphitheatres where festivals could be held in inclement weather.

Moreover, the government was bombarded by appeals from artists to put them to work. Since the patronage of the court, the aristocracy, and the traditional church had collapsed, only the Republic was left to commission great historical paintings, imposing monuments, and impressive buildings. Pressure on the government came from individual artists and the Popular and Republican Society for the Arts,[3] a sort of artistic Jacobin Club, to which at least 654 artists belonged in Year II of the Republic.[4] Furthermore, David, the outstanding artist of the period, a Montagnard deputy of the Convention, and a member of both the Committee of General Security and the Committee of Public Instruction, had the ear of the government. It was very sensitive to this pressure from artists because it was anxious to demonstrate that a republic could not only continue the patronage of the monarchy but far surpass it. It responded with a series of projects in April and May of 1794 that were eventually grouped together and later judged by a single jury in what has come to be known as the Concours de l'an II.[5]

The government called on painters to portray subjects of their own choice related to the Revolution. It appealed to sculptors to submit permanent versions of three of the temporary monuments erected for the Festival of Unity and Indivisibility the previous year: a figure of Nature Regenerated rising from the ruins of the old prison on the site of the Bastille; a huge figure of Liberty for the Place de la Révolution; and a figure of the French People trampling down Federalism for the esplanade of the Invalides. The statue of Philosophy by Houdon was to be purchased and placed on a simple pedestal in the antechamber of the Convention, where the statue would hold the Rights of Man and the Constitution. Sculptors were also called on to design a statue of Rousseau to be placed on the Champs-Elysées, a project that had been proposed several times. Finally, sculptors were asked to submit models of a monument first proposed by David the previous November for one of the most conspicuous sites in Paris, the promontory of the west end of the Ile de la Cité, near where the statue of Henry IV had once stood.[6]

David's proposed monument was to represent the triumph of the French People over tyranny and superstition. Once again the People was to be depicted as Hercules, fifteen metres high, one hand leaning on his club, which, David noted, had been a mere symbol in antiquity but now represented a real and terrible power. In the other hand he was to hold figures of Liberty and Equality, showing that they were dependent on the genius and virtues of the people. On his brow was to be inscribed the word LIGHT, the principal metaphor of the century for reason and knowledge dissipating ignorance. On his chest were to be two other key words of the age, NATURE and TRUTH, on his arms the word FORCE, and on his hands the word WORK. One might call it a proposal for *sculpture parlante*. This giant figure was to be raised up even higher on a mountain, no doubt to remind the onlooker that it was the Montagnards who led the people, made up of broken royal and religious statuary from Notre-Dame, all piled in confusion. "May the traveller who traverses this new territory carry back to his homeland lessons useful to the people," declared David; "may he say, I have seen kings in Paris, the objects of demeaning idolatry; I have passed by again, and they exist no more."

Architects were asked to design a permanent version of the monument that had marked the second station in the Festival of Unity and Indivisibility, a triumphal arch commemorating the march of Parisians to Versailles that had forced the royal family to take up residence in Paris on 6 October 1789. This had been situated on the boulevards, but artists were asked to propose better sites. Architects were asked as well to design a monument for the Place de la Victoire – the revolutionaries used the singular – honouring those citizens who had died on 10 August 1792, a column for the Pantheon commemorating those who had died in defence of the Fatherland, a Temple to Equality for the Beaujon Garden

172, 173 Durand and Thibault. Project for a column for the Pantheon.
Above: detail of the base; *left*: detail of the capital.

174 Anonymous. Project for a column for the Pantheon, elevation.

175 Anonymous. Project for a column for the Pantheon, detail of the pedestal.

Victories facing the column and holding out civic crowns. The column itself consisted of a massive fasces culminating in a palmiform capital. On the top was to be a statue of the Republic enthroned, holding Liberty in her right hand and Equality in her left hand, another example of the pairing of the two goddesses.

Two other designs for columns in the Pantheon survive in the Ecole des Beaux-Arts. One of them shows a perron with steps on all sides and decorated in the corners with trophies surmounted with Liberty Bonnets (Figures 174–6).[32] The faces of the pedestals bear lists of names, doubtless of those who had lost their lives.[33] Around the base of the column are four Renowns with their trumpets. The column itself is decorated with low-reliefs, not in a spiral but in a succession of bands showing a procession to the Pantheon, the heroism of young Bara, the assassination of Marat, and other revolutionary events.

The other surviving design for a column in the Pantheon has been attributed by one architectural historian to Jean-François Chevalier, but since there is no evidence that he submitted such a design, the attribution must remain uncertain.[34] It shows a shaft ringed with civic crowns

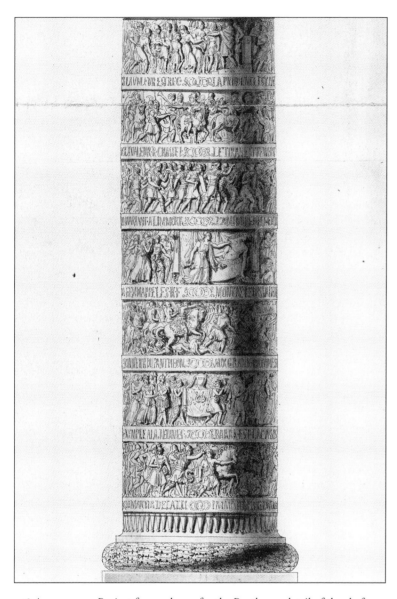

176 Anonymous. Project for a column for the Pantheon, detail of the shaft.

177 Anonymous. Project for a column for the Pantheon, elevation.

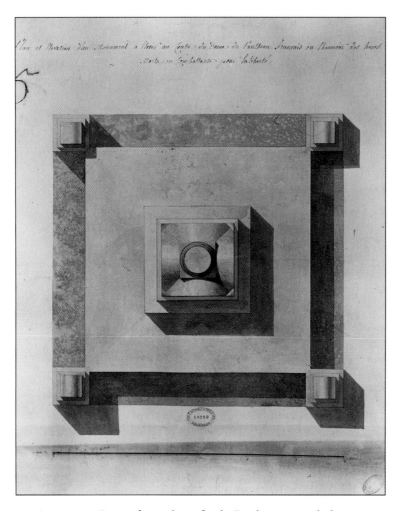

178 Anonymous. Project for a column for the Pantheon, ground-plan.

and capped with a figure of Renown holding more crowns in her right hand and a trumpet in her left hand (Figures 177, 178).[35] The faces of the pedestal and the perron bear bold inscriptions:

THE LIFE OF THE BRAVE IS FULL
THE FRENCH REPUBLIC
TO HEROES WHO HAVE DIED FOR LIBERTY AND EQUALITY
THEY LIVED. THEY CONQUERED.

Another very interesting project for a monument to the defenders of the Republic, which may be connected to the contest, is now in the Carnavalet Museum (Figures 179–81).[36] It may be by Charles Percier and Pierre-François-Léonard Fontaine, who won a prize in the category of embellishments for Paris for a project for a "monument to the glory of the defenders of the Fatherland." Since other artists, however, submitted projects with similar titles, the attribution must remain tentative. The design shows a stepped pyramid, a shape reminiscent of the mausoleum of Augustus in Rome 28 BC[37] and favoured by other architects of the period for memorials to the dead.[38] The faces of the monument were to be inscribed with the names of the honoured heroes, and the terraces were to be planted symmetrically with laurel trees, interspersed with benches at equal distances. The monument was designed so as to force visitors to pass along these terraces. "There citizens will come to pay tribute to virtues and courage," explains a note on the design. "Poets will find there heroes to sing about, and painters deeds to praise and reproduce." Crowning the pyramid was to be a little temple with baseless Doric columns, again a common feature of funerary monuments, sheltering a figure of Liberty triumphant, standing on a pedestal inscribed with republican victories. A figure of Renown holding civic wreaths was to crown the edifice.

The projects for a Temple to Equality, destined for the Beaujon Garden on the Champs-Elysées, are especially significant since they represent attempts to sacralize one of the ideals of the Montagnard Republic. Architects submitted twenty-seven designs for such a temple. The jury decided that the design by Durand and Thibault should be executed as a national monument, the only project so honoured (Figures 182–7). The original has been lost, but there is a copy of the elevation by Leo von Klenze in Munich,[39] as well as engravings of it, with the name changed and the radical inscriptions and symbols removed, published by Détournelle and his associates early in the nineteenth century.[40] Despite its classical look, it is quite unorthodox. Not only are the columns spaced in an unusual way, opening the interior to public view, but each of them stood for a public

Detail en grand du monument des deffenseurs de la patrie indiqué dans le plan g.t sous la meme divise

179 [Percier and Fontaine?] Project for a monument to the defenders of the Fatherland, elevation.

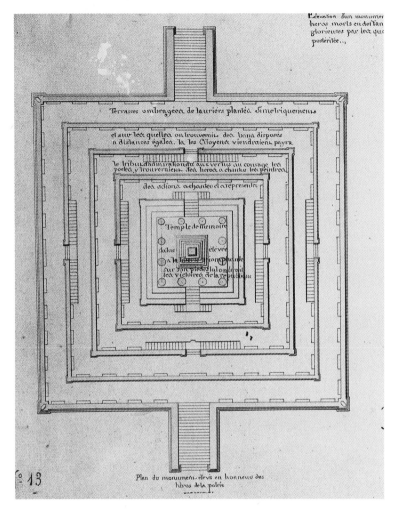

181 [Percier and Fontaine?] Project for a monument to the defenders of the Fatherland, cross-section.

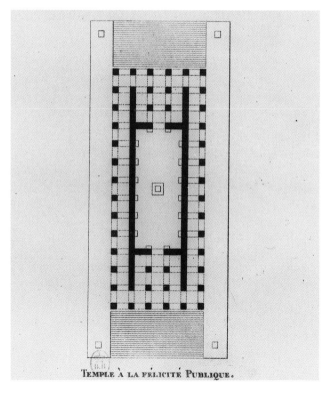

180 [Percier and Fontaine?] Project for a monument to the defenders of the Fatherland, ground-plan.

182 Durand and Thibault. Project for a Temple to Equality, ground-plan.

183 Durand and Thibault. Project for a Temple to Equality, elevation.

184, 185 Durand and Thibault. Project for a Temple to Equality. *Left*: detail of the columns on the left of the façade; *above*: detail of the tympanum.

186 Durand and Thibault. Project for a Temple to Equality, lateral section.

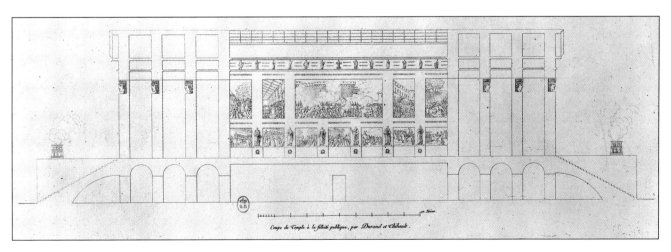

187 Durand and Thibault. Project for a Temple to Equality, longitudinal section.

171

188 Villers. Project for a Temple to Equality, elevation.

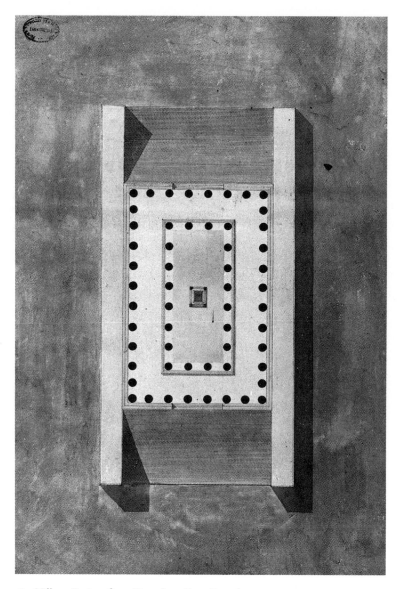

189 Villers. Project for a Temple to Equality, plan.

190 Duhameau. Project for a Temple to Equality, longitudinal section.

virtue, beginning with *civisme*, the cardinal virtue during the Terror. The nature of each virtue was outlined on the face of each column, turning the exterior into a civic manual.

Other features of the proposed temple by Durand and Thibault were also intended to speak to the citizen through words, symbols, and images. The copy in Munich shows an inscription along the entablature declaring that THE VIRTUES OF THE PEOPLE ARE THE MOST SOLID SUPPORT OF EQUALITY. The tympanum shows a figure of Liberty holding a *bonnet rouge*, and Equality holding a level, seated facing each other. In between is the radical declaration that THEY ARE INSEPARABLE. From the peak is suspended a line at the end of which hangs an equilateral triangle – a shape, as we have seen, often associated with equality and used to convey a sacred aura – inscribed with the word LAW. From the outside one can glimpse an allegorical statue representing the expected result of liberty and equality, Public Happiness. From the engravings published under Napoleon we see that the inner walls are decorated with scenes of the martyrdoms of Lepelletier and Marat (reverse images of the paintings by David), revolutionary festivals, popular uprisings, and battle scenes, creating a sort of museum of the Revolution. In these engravings, however, the civic virtues were changed, the allegorical figures on the pediment were given flowers to hold, the declaration that liberty and equality are inseparable was removed, and the triangle disappeared.

The design for a Temple to Equality by another prize-winner,

Maximilien Villers from Lyon, has recently been identified at the Ecole des Beaux-Arts (Figures 188, 189).[41] Like Durand and Thibault, he proposed a rectangular edifice with canalized Doric columns atop a massive foundation that would have made it more visible from the Champs-Elysées. It too is an example of *architecture parlante*, since the rights and duties of the citizen are engraved on the perron at either side of the staircases at both ends of the structure. In the centre of the entablature one reads in large letters TO EQUALITY. Inside on a pedestal, decorated with a level of Equality, sits an allegorical figure holding a horn of plenty on the left and what appears to be a nest full of chicks or hearts, a symbol of equality and fraternity common at the time. In the tympanum is the goddess Equality flanked by two smaller figures, probably representing equal citizens, who are holding a level over her lap. The metopes represent Nature, the scales of Justice, a level being placed on an altar, horns of plenty, and equilateral triangles superimposed to form a star.

The architect Duhameau also chose a rectangular plan (Figure 190). His design, also recently identified at the Ecole des Beaux-Arts, shows a temple with Corinthian columns set in a long Ionic colonnade.[42] To identify his project he chose the motto: "Mortals are equal; it is not birth, it is virtue alone that makes the difference."[43] In keeping with this motto, his temple shows Equality enthroned, holding the usual level, surrounded by other social virtues such as Modesty, Friendship, and Harmony. An oculus overhead illuminates the divinity and her entourage. Unfortunately,

173

191 Croizier. Project for a Temple to Equality, cross-section.

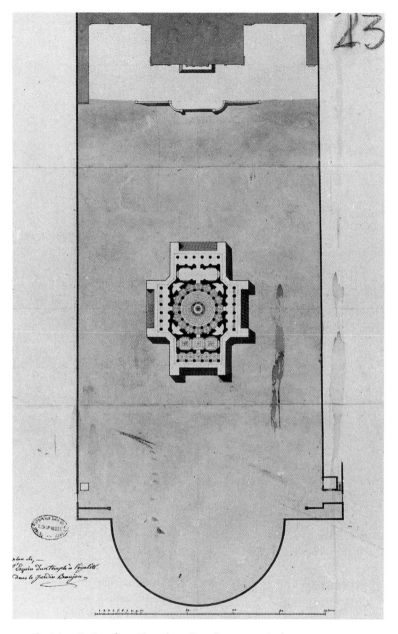

192 Croizier. Project for a Temple to Equality, ground-plan.

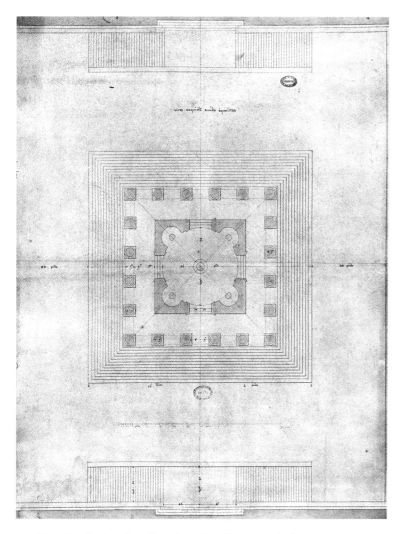

193 Chevalier. Project for a Temple to Equality, ground-plan.

194 Chevalier. Project for a Temple to Equality, cross-section.

the plan and elevation have not been found. Another obscure architect called Crozier chose to place a circular hall, ringed by Ionic columns with Equality in the centre, on a cruciform base with entrances on all four sides (Figures 191, 192).[44] Jean-François Chevalier set a circular hall on a square base (Figures 193, 194).[45] Inside we see a huge figure of Equality, flanked by lesser statues of two republican martyrs, Lepelletier and Marat, their deeds inscribed overhead.

Still other architects chose to make their temples circular inside and out. The circle, an endless line with no beginning or end, conveys a sense of perfection and timelessness. Alexis-François Bonnet proposed such a round temple atop a symbolic Mountain, suggesting that it was the Montagnards who had promoted Equality (Figures 195−7).[46] At the base of the Mountain is a cave in which the visitor would see Tyranny and Crime enchained. Over the cave at the base of the temple is Hercules, again symbolizing the People, resting after his labours, his left arm leaning on a fasces,

175

195 Bonnet. Project for a Temple to Equality, ground-plans, elevation, and section.

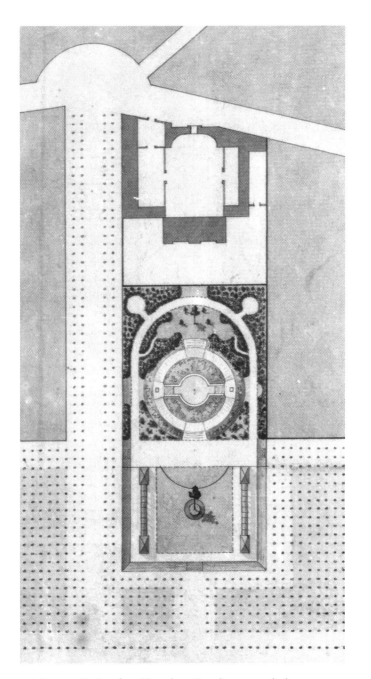

196 Bonnet. Project for a Temple to Equality, ground-plan.

A.F.⚜A.

Plan, et Coupe.

197 Bonnet. Project for a Temple to Equality, detailed ground-plan and cross-section.

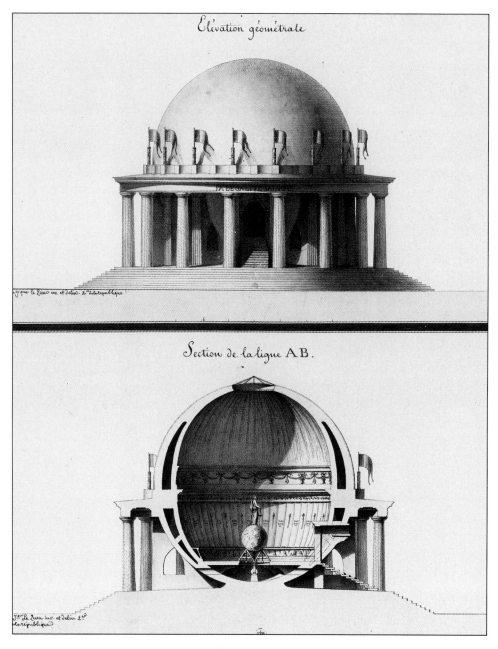

Élévation géométrale

Section de la ligne A.B.

198 Lequeu. Project for a Temple to Equality, elevation and section.

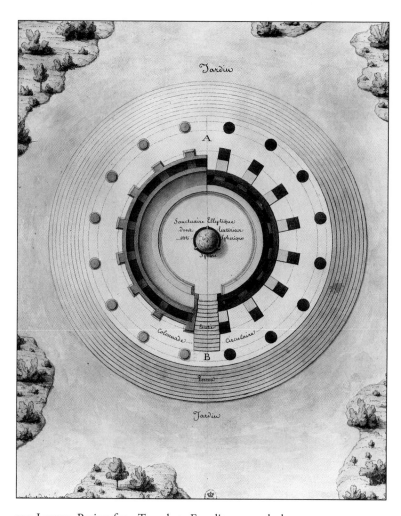

199 Lequeu. Project for a Temple to Equality, ground-plan.

the other holding a club. The way this figure was positioned suggests that the force of the People had prepared the way for the triumph of the goddess above. Both in front of the temple and behind are two semicircular paths leading up to entrances at the sides of the temple where they meet, completing a circle around the edifice. The paths pass by Virtue on one side and Reason on the other, signifying the two routes to equality. Levels suspended from garlands decorate the façade. There are inscriptions on the slopes of the mountain and on the temple on either side of Hercules. Inside the cylindrical building, lit by semicircular openings, is a circular hall with Equality in the centre. Bonnet wanted to group the cafés of the Champs-Elysées in the verdant esplanade so that citizens would always be attracted to the site.

Lequeu also chose to submit a project for a Temple to Equality circular in both shape and setting (Figures 198,199). Like other avant-garde architects such as Boullée, who had chosen a sphere for his visionary centotaph for Newton in 1784, Lequeu proposed to give the temple a spherical shape.[47] The sphere was to be supported by a ring of baseless Doric columns. On the entablature over the doorway is the dedication TO HOLY EQUALITY. The tympanum of the doorway takes the form of a giant level, barely visible in the elevation, announcing clearly to all who entered the significance of the space inside. Encircling the base of the dome are fasces atop pedestals, each containing a pole capped with a tricolour flag. Inside in the centre is a globe, held up by more levels, on which Equality stands erect, holding a scale or another level. The whole centrepiece seems designed to rotate. An oculus in the dome spotlights the goddess below. The circular perron with its continuous steps underscores the ring of columns and the spherical form of the temple.

Lequeu also designed another spherical building, Temple of the Earth,[48] which some historians have surmised is related to the program for a Temple to Equality (Figures 200–2).[49] A note on the back of the design in Lequeu's handwriting supports this conjecture: it states that the temple was aimed at re-establishing Eternal Equality; that it was destined for the Beaujon Garden, the site prescribed by the government program; and that it was sent on 10 Prairial an II – 29 May 1794 – for exhibition in the Salle de la Liberté, the antechamber to the Convention where other works submitted to the contest were displayed.[50] Over the entrance to the temple is a carpenter's level, creating a Doorway of Equality, as the artist calls it in his notes. The globe, inscribed with a map of the world, is supported by columns similar to the Temple to Equality designed by Durand and Thibault. Moreover, the inset on the upper right showing Lequeu's final resolution of the entablature shows a line "which indicates that day and night are equal when the sun passes over it." Also, the inscription

200 Lequeu. Project for a Temple of the Earth, note on the back.

TO THE SUPREME WISDOM employs a term for the divinity close to the one promoted by Robespierre just at the time when artists were preparing their projects.[51]

In this design the sphere is pierced with apertures, turning it into a kind of planetarium. A mobile globe in the centre of the interior adds further to the cosmic character of the project. This design may be the spherical temple mentioned at the end of the list of Temples to Equality in the catalogue of works exhibited in the Salle de la Liberté, with an explanation that it had arrived, along with a letter dated 29 Prairial – 16 June 1794 – after the Contest of Year II had closed.[52] This of course conflicts with the date Lequeu wrote on the back of the design, but he evidently added the note later when his memory may have been inexact.[53] In fact the date appears to have been altered. In any case the project is further linked to the program for a Temple to Equality by another poignant note by the artist on the back, disclosing that after the Revolution he had submitted it to the minister of the interior for erection as a chapel in the Père Lachaise Garden, known at the time as the Mont Louis Cemetery, "because [the temple] is truly useless to the French, enemies of equality, who never accommodate themselves to their fellows."

An entry by Favard, described in the register as a "tomb for the martyrs of liberty," was displayed among the projects for a Temple to Equality

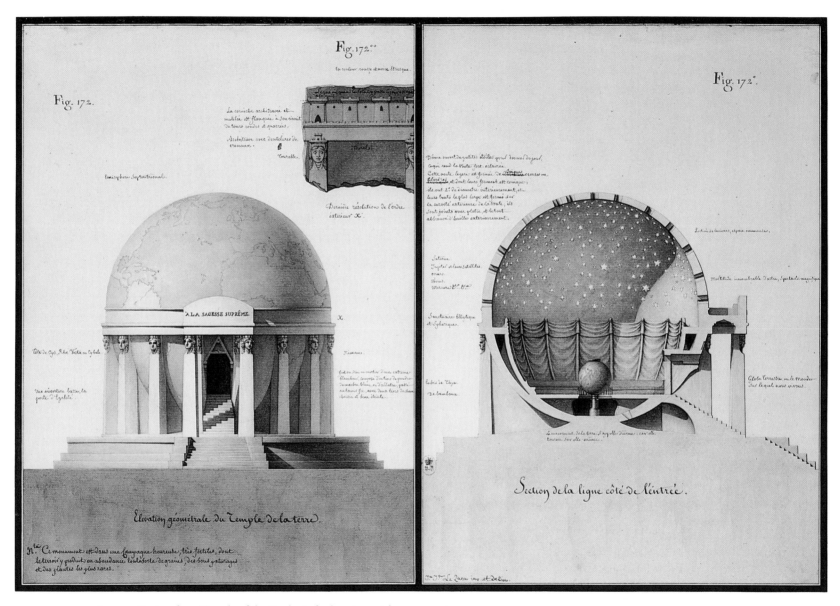

201, 202 Lequeu. Project for a Temple of the Earth. *Left*: elevation; *right*: cross-section.

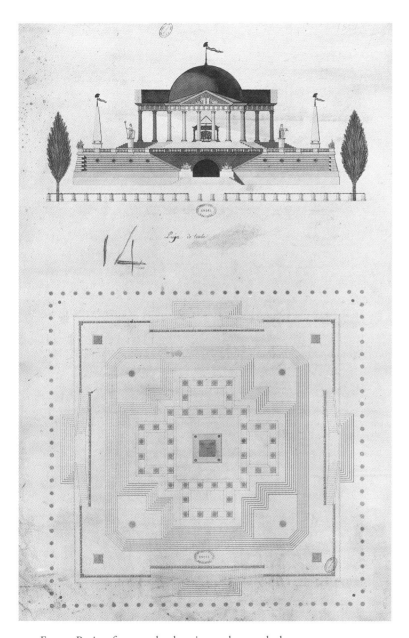

203 Favart. Project for a tomb, elevation and ground-plan.

(Figure 203).[54] This is understandable since the design, which is among those recently identified in the Ecole des Beaux-Arts, combines the symbolism of equality with a funerary monument.[55] The association of a revolutionary ideal with death is not surprising: despite the Revolution's promise of a better society on earth, there was a heightened consciousness of death. Many citizens had died in the series of insurrections that led to the Republic, in the effort to suppress revolutionary activity inside the country, in the war against the coalition of European powers, or in attacks by assassins. Favart proposed a sort of outdoor Pantheon raised up in a square enclosure marked by border stones. The first set of steps leads to the low entrance to a crypt in the rusticated foundation. Two lateral stairways lead to a terrace with four obelisks in the corners, perhaps one for each of the principal martyrs, crowned with tricolour flags and Liberty Bonnets. Raised up on a cross-shaped base is the shrine itself, in the form of a baldachin. In the corners formed by the arms of the cross are allegorical figures, including Liberty and Equality. The canopy is supported by Doric columns. Underneath is an altar covered with greenery and with a huge level over it, suggesting the ideal for which the martyrs died. This naïve design has a festive air about it, a suggestion of triumph over death.

The Temples to Equality were shrines to visit, not places to sit or stand for prolonged ceremonies. *Temples décadaires* were to provide such accommodation. All societies have set aside units of time and space for devotion to ideals that transcend the concerns of everyday life. Under the new calendar, the tenth day and certain anniversaries were designated for republican rituals around the Altar of the Fatherland, rituals that would include speeches, swearing of oaths in front of the altar, singing of revolutionary hymns, proclamations of recent laws, awards to outstanding citizens, recitations of the Rights of Man by students, and perhaps republican marriages. And just as other societies have created sacred spaces for rituals of transcendental importance, so the government leaders of Year II called for temples consecrated to the ideals of the Republic. Like the leaders of various world religions before them, the revolutionary planners hoped that, after involvement in the activities in these special portions of time and space, citizens would return to everyday life more deeply committed to the new order.

Again in the competition for *temples décadaires*, which inspired eleven submissions, Durand and Thibault were the winners. They won prizes for two different but similar designs. One is known by engravings published in the nineteenth century (Figures 204, 205),[56] the other by the original in the Carnavalet Museum as well as engravings (Figures 206, 207).[57] The second is clearly the larger of the two – whereas the first temple

204, 205 Durand and Thibault. Project for a small *temple décadaire.*
Above: elevation and cross-section; *right*: ground-plan.

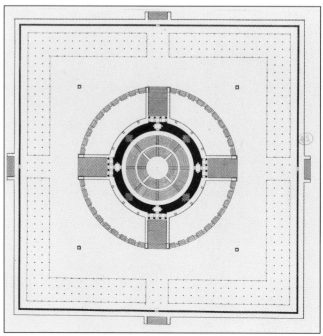

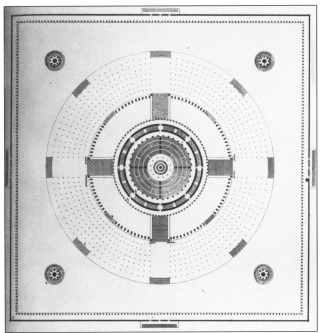

206, 207 Durand and Thibault. Original design for a large *temple décadaire*.
Above: cross-section and elevation; *left*: ground-plan.

183

208 Delalande. Project for a *temple décadaire*, elevation.

is only 130 metres wide (230 if we include the enclosure) and 45 metres high, the second is 200 metres wide (375 if we include the enclosure) and 70 metres high. These dimensions made them far larger than most of the other projects.

Both projects feature large square settings, sacred precincts distinct from the surrounding city, framing circular temples with entrances balancing each other on the four sides, raised up on round perrons. Outside, each shows a dome in the form of a half terrestial globe, and inside each has a circular auditorium with tiers of benches, exactly the sort of space that the revolutionaries thought would encourage citizens to merge together. They each have ceilings pierced with stars to give a cosmic significance to the space, as in Boullée's mausoleum for Newton and Lequeu's Temple of the Earth. Moreover, they each have braziers burning, the one around the outside of the perron and the temple, the other around the audito-

rium inside, heightening the aura of sanctity of these sacred buildings. The two, however, differ considerably in scale and richness of decor. Whereas the first has a simple setting, the second is surrounded by a high wall with an arcade along the inside. The first has statues flanking only the entrances; the second has also a ring of statues on top of the entablature and more on the free-standing columns in the four corners of the enclosure – nearly one hundred statues altogether.

We know more about the larger temple because of notes under the engraving of the ground-plan published by Détournelle in his *Recueil d'architecture nouvelle*, and because in the original elevation in the Carnavalet Museum the inscriptions are legible which in the engravings are omitted or reduced to mere hatching. The notes explain that the four porticoes are to represent the four corners of the world and are intended to house displays of minerals, plants, and animals from Europe, Asia, and Africa (America seems to have been omitted). The statues atop the colonnade are to honour those who in making themselves useful to their Fatherland and fellow men have the better honoured the divinity. Around the outer rim of the amphitheatre are thirty-six small altars dedicated to the themes of each *décadi*. In the centre of the temple is a large altar encircled by smaller ones devoted to the four seasons and the twelve months. The tiered hall has sections for women, children, youths, adults, and the elderly. Outside the inscriptions link the project to the religious policies of Robespierre and add to its pantheistic character:

THE FRENCH REPUBLIC

THE FRENCH PEOPLE RECOGNIZE THE SUPREME BEING
AND THE IMMORTALITY OF THE SOUL

THE UNIVERSE IS THE TEMPLE OF THE ETERNAL. THE
FRENCH REPUBLIC IS ITS SANCTUARY

In contrast to the avant-garde designs by Durand and Thibault is the more traditional one, now in the Ecole des Beaux-Arts, by Delalande, an architect from Rouen (Figures 208–10).[58] His project arrived too late to be considered in the competition, but it reveals the same desire to create a vast amphitheatre where citizens would be able to see each other and emote together. The basic plan was derived from the Roman Pantheon: a porch in front of a main circular building. It was, however, to be encircled by boundary stones and a Corinthian peristyle. Massive walls and pillars were to hold up a vault twenty-six *toises* in diameter, or about fifty

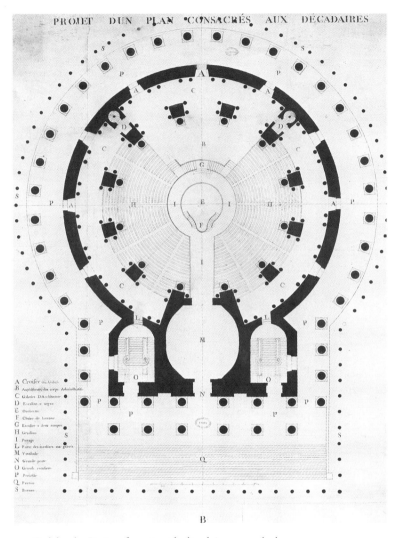

209 Delalande. Project for a *temple décadaire*, ground-plan.

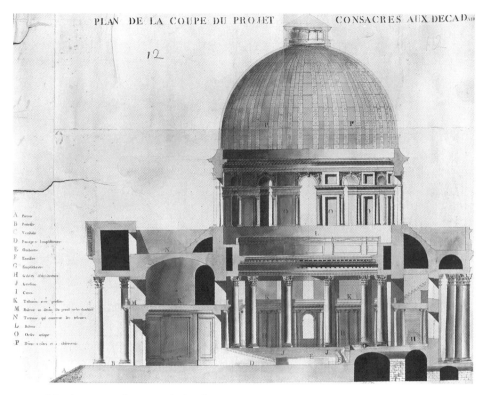

210 Delalande. Project for a *temple décadaire*, cross-section.

metres. This made possible the huge auditorium with tiered benches for the citizenry, a platform for officials, a space for an orchestra, and a podium slightly off centre. This interior was to be lit by windows in the drum holding up the dome. The plan lacks the cosmic symbolism, rich statuary, and bold inscriptions of the prize-winning projects.

Another project for a *temple décadaire* that has survived in the Ecole des Beaux-Arts is one destined for a large city by Charles-Etienne Durand, who described himself as an engineer of roads and bridges in the department of the Gard (Figure 211).[59] He proposed a rectangular edifice inspired by the Temple of Jupiter Olympian and the Temple of Hadrian at Athens. The edifice was to be raised up on a perron extending in front of and behind the peristyle of Corinthian columns. At one end of the hall inside were to be benches for elected officials, and along the sides sections for women, elderly citizens, and children. The centre appears open, presumably for

185

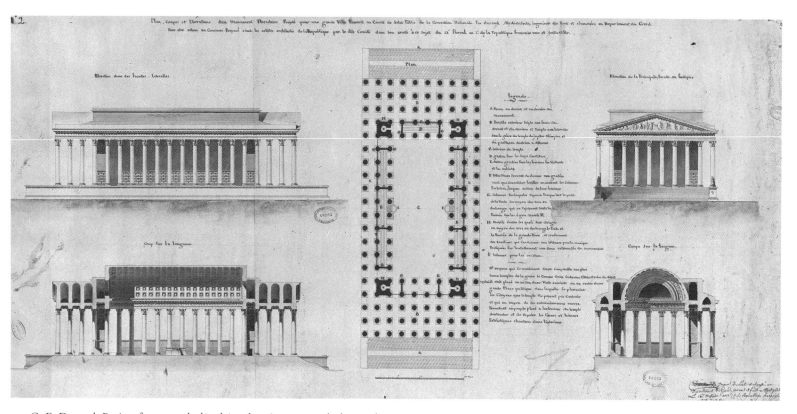

211 C.-E. Durand. Project for a *temple décadaire*, elevations, ground-plan, and sections.

men to congregate. Tribunes for orators jut out on either side. The architect claimed that his temple would rival the most beautiful in Greece. It was small in comparison with those proposed by J.-N.-L. Durand and Thibault, but the architect argued that, if it were placed in a spacious square, citizens who could not find a place inside would be able to gather outside to hear the patriotic music coming out through the columns.

The architect Nicolas Goulet, who worked in the assessment division of the Department of National Domains, submitted a plan, now in the Carnavalet Museum, for another temple that was not called for specifically by the government (Figures 212, 213).[60] He proposed an imposing Temple of the Laws, to be erected in the area of the National Palace of the Tuileries and the Louvre, with covered passages for pedestrians and wide streets linking it to these buildings and adjacent streets. It would, therefore, have become an integral part of the legislative and administrative

centre of the nation. The edifice was to be in the form of a giant cross with entrances at the four extremities, the arms consisting of long courtyards lined on all sides with galleries lit by skylights overhead. From the four courtyards porticoes were to lead to antechambers that would surround the heart of the temple, a rotunda spanned by a cupola with an oculus in the summit to illuminate the interior. The focal point of the rotunda was to be an area, enclosed by a grille, divided by different colours of marble to denote different departments of France. In the centre of this symbolic map was to stand a statue of Liberty. Overhead the dome was to exhibit a painting of the great Federation of 1790 on the Champ de Mars in Paris.

The objective of this temple was similar to that of Kersaint and his architect associates, Legrand and Molinos, earlier in the Revolution with their plans for *prytanées* in each neighbourhood: to propagate the laws and

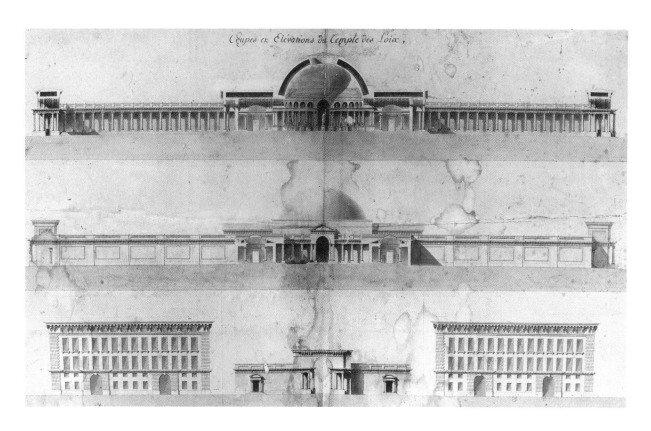

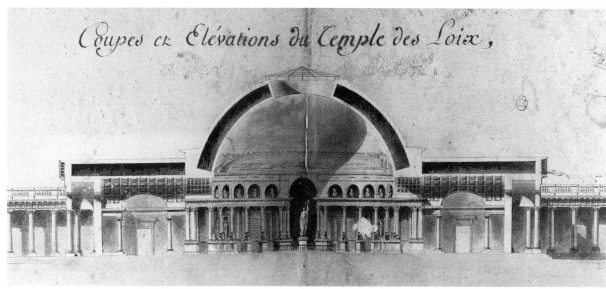

212, 213 Goulet. Project for a Temple of the Laws. *Above*: elevations and sections; *below*: detail of the section through the central rotunda.

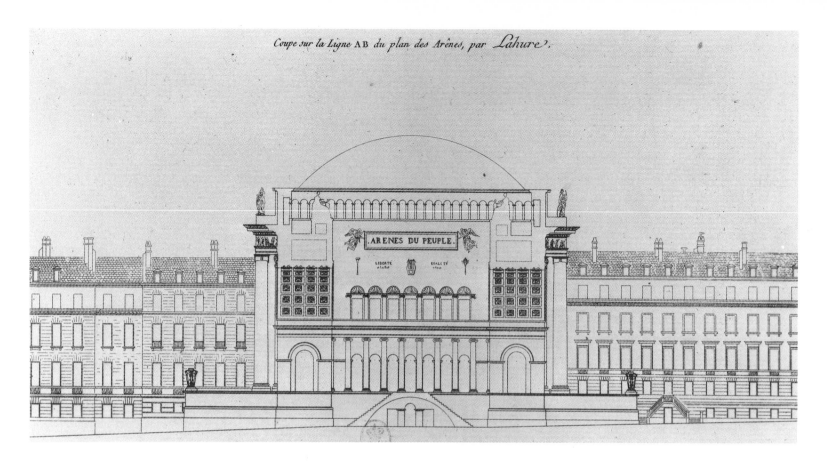

.AR ENES DU PEUPLE.

LIBERTÉ   ÉGALITÉ

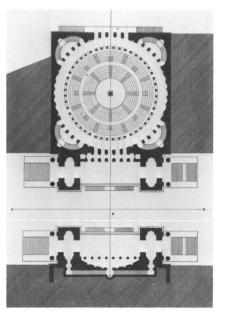

214, 215 Lahure. Project for a covered arena. *Above*: elevation; *left*: ground-plan.

arouse reverence for them. Goulet was especially concerned with reaching the common people. Laws posted on walls were ephemeral; those printed in newspapers were mixed with a lot of other information, and in any case newspapers were too soon discarded. Moreover, the poor could not afford either newspapers or bound collections of the laws. "It is, therefore, indispensable and imperative that the Law itself be always and perpetually exposed to public view in quiet, suitable, secure places," he argued in a pamphlet outlining his project.[61] The constitution was to be inscribed in gold on eight huge marble tablets around the rotunda. New laws were to be displayed in the galleries around the courtyards, which would provide 1,200 *toises* (about 2,400 metres) of surface, in gold letters on huge wooden panels painted to look like marble and placed in frames so they could be changed as need arose. The laws were to be accompanied by lessons in history: statues of Rousseau, Voltaire, Montesquieu, and Mably, who had written the most about the constitutions of great states,

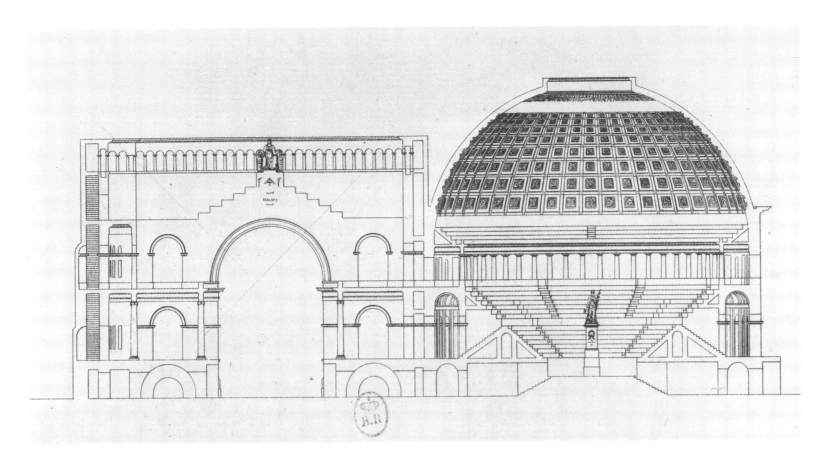

216, 217 Lahure. Project for a covered arena. *Above*: cross-section; *right*:
perspective view of the triumphal arch on the boulevard Saint Martin.

were to occupy niches between the tablets of the constitution in the rotunda,
and busts of the founders of liberty were to be displayed in front of the
columns around the central hall and in the arches above.

Besides buildings to accommodate republican rituals on the tenth
day or to display the laws, there was need for enclosures protected from
the elements in which to hold larger periodic festivals. Consequently the
government called for designs for a covered arena on the site of the old
Opera between the boulevard St Martin and the rue de Bondi. Architects
responded with nine projects, and Charles Percier and Pierre Fontaine submitted a project for a different site. The artists showed considerable
ingenuity in designing an arena for such a limited space. The winning
project by Jean-Baptiste Lahure features a building containing an
amphitheatre and linked to the boulevard by a triumphal arch decorated
with revolutionary symbols (Figures 214–17).[62] Another plan in the Ecole
des Beaux-Arts by the architect Riffault envisages an arena into which horses

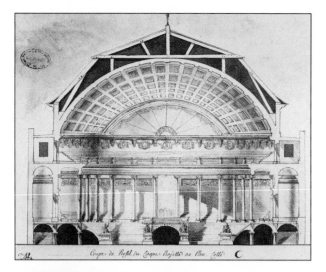

218 Riffault. Project for a covered arena, cross-section, elevation on boulevard Saint-Martin, and elevation on rue de Bondi.

and festival floats could enter from the street (Figures 218, 219).[63] Pierre Bernard entered an elevation and a section of a covered arena, which he called an Odeum National, both of which are also in the Ecole des Beaux-Arts (Figures 220, 221).[64] It shows a very plain exterior devoid of the usual low-reliefs, statues, and slogans. Inside is an amphitheatre with a level suspended overhead to remind citizens that they were now equal under the law. On the front wall tablets of the laws appear, and leaning against them on either side are clubs, the weapon of the People-Hercules.

Charles Percier and Pierre Fontaine rejected the site selected by the government as too confined for celebrations and festivals of the Republic, as they explained in copious notes on the design now in the Carnavalet Museum (Figures 222–6).[65] They advocated a huge development of the Left Bank of the Seine opposite the National Palace between the Pont National and the Pont de la Révolution, now the Pont Royal and the Pont de la Concorde, that is along what is now called the Quai Anatole France. They envisaged a vast amphitheatre along the river-bank, with a parade-ground extending down the middle, demarked by triumphal arches at each end, one dedicated to Victory, the other to Peace. This amphitheatre would enable a multitude of citizens to view processions on land and mock naval battles on the Seine. Above the stands there was to be a large edifice with three porticoes, forming three temples: the Temple of Good Faith to the left, the Temple of Liberty in the centre, and the Temple of Concord on the right. At the rear of the central temple was to be a large semicircular auditorium, with an Altar of the Fatherland as the focal point and an area for an orchestra around it, where civic ceremonies would reach their climax.

In addition to *temples décadaires* and arenas, the government's plan for regeneration required theatres different from traditional ones. The revolutionaries believed that, if properly directed, the theatre could be a school of civic virtue. In this category, however, the response was disappointing: just three designs, only one of which seems to have survived, that by Charles-Etienne Durand now in the Ecole des Beaux-Arts (Figures 227–9).[66] He envisaged a huge oval neoclassical structure capable of accommodating nine thousand to ten thousand spectators. The auditorium inside exhibits exactly those features that one would expect after seeing the changes de Wailly introduced into the Odeon in Paris. It is shaped so that the spectators would be able to see each other. There are no balconies or boxes to divide citizens from one another. On the ground level in the centre of the auditorium there is a large space with mobile benches that could be carried away to make room for dances and other popular festivities.

The government had also called for primary assembly halls where citizens would assemble at the grass-roots level. Six such designs were entered

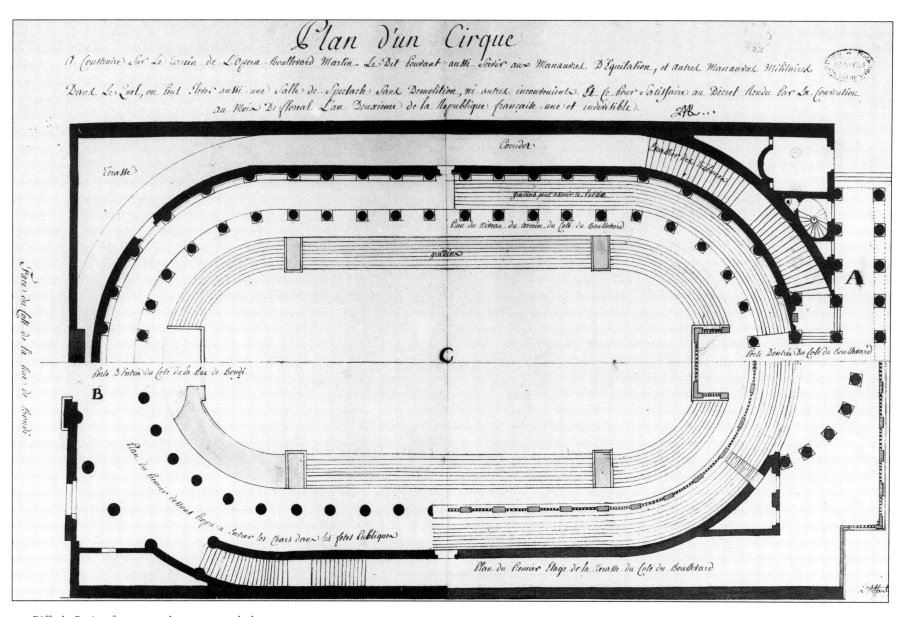

219 Riffault. Project for a covered arena, ground-plan.

220 Bernard. Project for an Odeum National, elevation.

221 Bernard. Project for an Odeum National, cross-section.

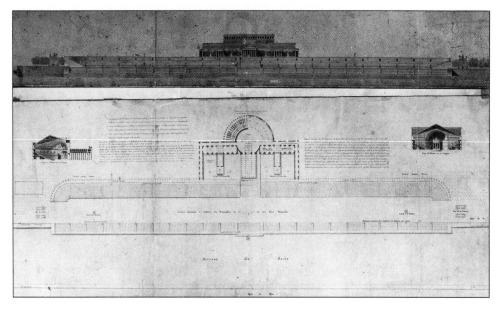

222 Percier and Fontaine. Project for an arena along the Left Bank of the Seine, ground-plan and details.

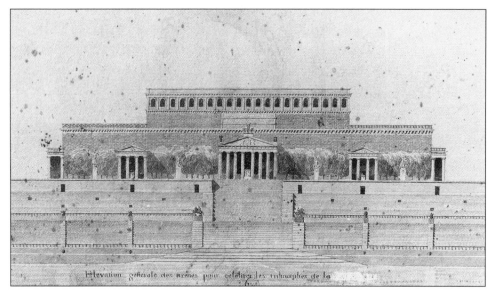

223 Percier and Fontaine. Project for an arena along the Left Bank of the Seine, elevation of the three Temples.

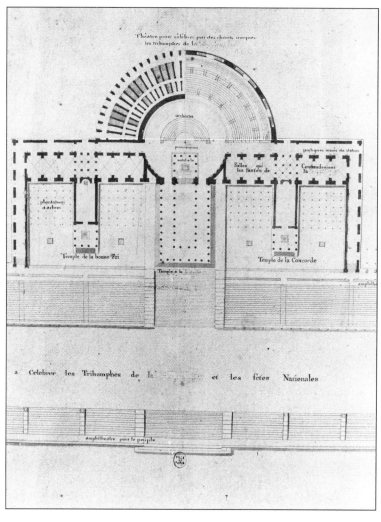

224 Percier and Fontaine. Project for an arena along the Left Bank of the Seine, ground-plan of the three Temples.

225 Percier and Fontaine. Project for an arena along the Left Bank of the Seine, cross-section of the amphitheatre at the rear of the Temple of Liberty.

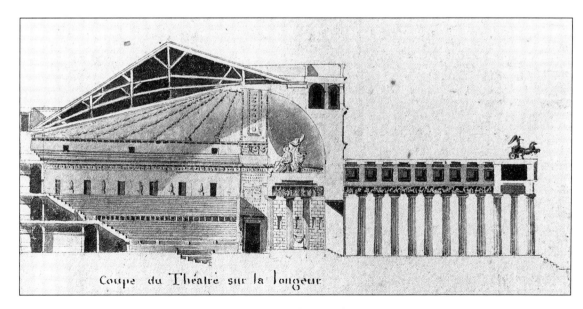

226 Percier and Fontaine. Project for an arena along the Left Bank of the Seine, longitudinal section of the amphitheatre at the rear of the Temple of Liberty.

227 C.-E. Durand. Project for a revolutionary theatre, elevation.

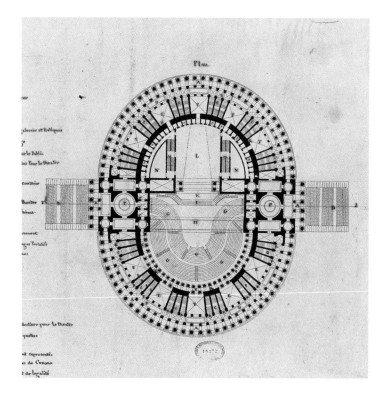

228 C.-E. Durand. Project for a revolutionary theatre, ground-plan.

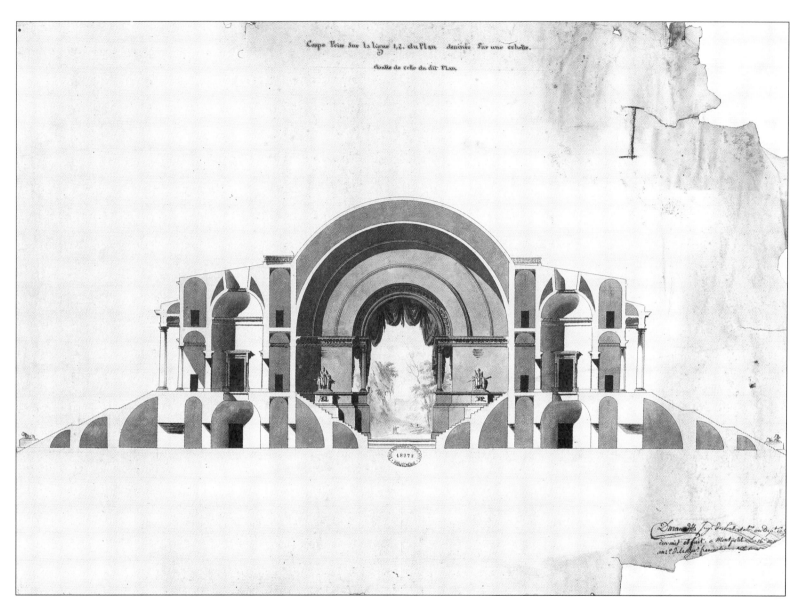

Coupe Prise sur la ligne 1,2, du Plan dessinée sur une echelle

double de celle du dit Plan

229 C.-E. Durand. Project for a revolutionary theatre, cross-section.

Assemblée de Section.

230, 231 Durand and Thibault. Project for a small primary assembly.
Above: elevation; *right*: ground-plan.

in the contest, including two by Durand and Thibault, each of which won a prize (Figures 230–3). Both are known through copies, now conserved in Weimar, by Clemens Wenzelaus Coudray.[67] The project for a small assembly hall shows a Doric porch with the wall behind covered with inscriptions, another example of *architecture parlante*. The fronton is decorated with allegorical figures, the scales of Justice, and the level of Equality. Inside is a semicircular amphitheatre. The plan for a larger meeting-place shows a massive building with three Doric porches, the one on the left dedicated to Courage, the one on the right to Virtue. In the monumental central porch incense burns on an altar, creating a religious aura. Low-reliefs on the fronton represent citizens gathering around an enthroned female figure, perhaps the Republic. On either side of the roof

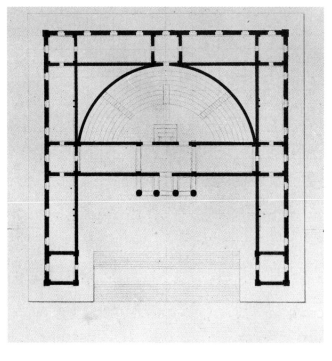

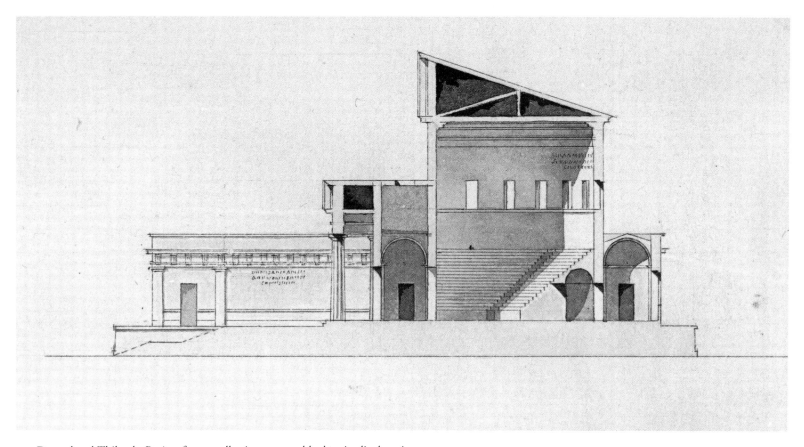

232 Durand and Thibault. Project for a small primary assembly, longitudinal section.

233 Durand and Thibault. Project for a large primary assembly, elevation.

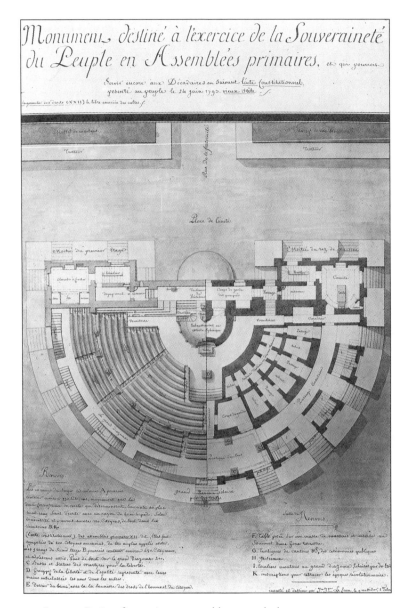

234 Lequeu. Project for a primary assembly, ground-plan.

235 Lequeu. Project for a primary assembly, elevation and cross-section.

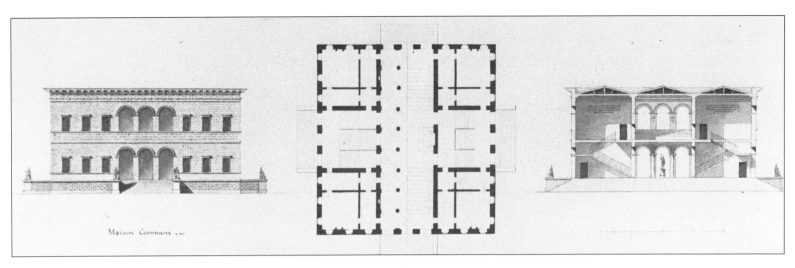

Maison Communale.

236 Durand and Thibault. Project for a small city hall, elevation, ground-plan, and cross-section.

are Liberty and Equality, while on the pinnacle two figures side by side portray Fraternity.

Lequeu also entered a project for a primary assembly, one charged with revolutionary symbolism. The design, now in the print collection of the Bibliothèque Nationale, consists of an elevation, cross-section, and ground plan (Figures 234, 235).[68] The elevation shows a semicircular building with a ring of entrances, each surmouted with a triangle the apex of which takes the form of a level, denoting the equality of the citizens who passed beneath it. In between the entrances are inscriptions above and stars beneath. On the dome a tricolour banner hangs from a pole capped with a *bonnet rouge*. The plan shows a vestibule decorated with busts and statues of revolutionary martyrs. The hall inside is organized in the way preferred by the revolutionaries, a semicircular amphitheatre to house the citizens of a section or canton. The section shows that the focal point was to be a pedestal upholding statues of Liberty and Equality, their hands intertwined. Just behind the pedestal is the platform surrounded by a ring of fasces. Still further back is a symbolic Mountain crowned by a temple. Rays of light radiate out from behind the Mountain, while Renowns blow trumpets on either side. On the walls are ensigns and Phrygian bonnets.

Like the *temples décadaires*, arenas, theatres, and primary assemblies, the administrative buildings were all interrelated. Thus the projects for city halls, or "maisons communales" as they were then called, that have survived feature the same sort of decor and provide for amphitheatres where

citizens could congregate. The team of Durand and Thibault again won prizes for their two designs (Figures 236–8). Both plans feature cubic buildings housing large halls.[69] The larger city hall shows an immense circular assembly hall, very like that inside the covered arena designed by Lahure, surrounded by other facilities. "Besides a great hall for municipal assemblies, besides different offices," Durand later explained in his *Précis d'architecture*, "an edifice of this sort, whatever its dimensions, requires porticoes to receive those whose business calls them there."[70] Other projects for city halls done around the same time show the same features.

Some designs grouped cultural and political facilities, again underlining the close connection between the two. The architect Claude-Ennemond-Balthazar Cochet from Lyon, the artist who had designed the ephemeral architecture for the Festival of Federation in that city, proposed to create a forum consisting of seven separate buildings arranged around a semicircle (Figure 239).[71] In the centre there was to be a temple, with a porch leading to a circular main building like the Roman Pantheon, to accommodate ceremonies on the tenth day. On the left end of the semicircle is a large building, raised up on a perron, at the end of a series of steps and surrounded by a peristyle, intended for national festivals. Balancing it on the right-hand side is an identical building for primary assemblies. The other four buildings in between are destined for mothers, young female citizens, young male citizens, and elderly citizens. As Monat Ozouf has pointed out, in republican festivals social distinctions gave way

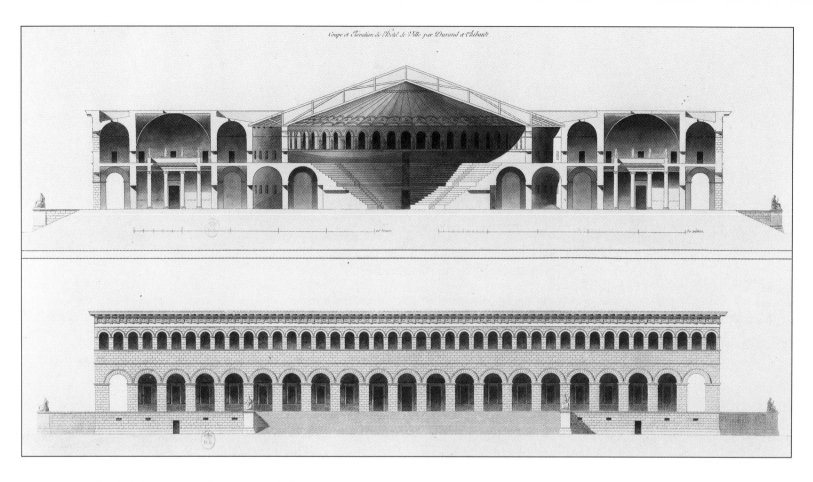

237, 238 Durand and Thibault. Project for a large city hall.
Above: cross-section and elevation; *right*: ground-plan.

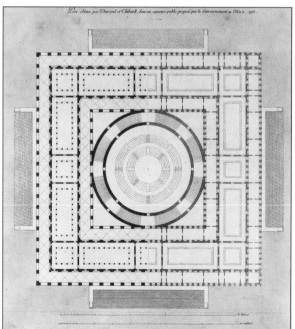

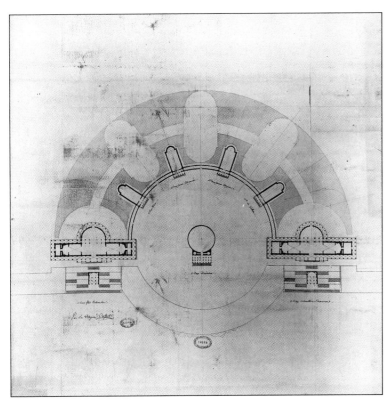

239 Cochet. Plan for a complex of a *temple décadaire*, festival hall, primary assembly, and facilities for different sex and age groups.

to natural ones, sex and age.[72] Despite the fact that his entry arrived late, Cochet was awarded a prize.

Even projects intended to show that the regime was concerned with the physical needs of the citizenry, such as baths, fountains, and latrines, could serve an ideological purpose. The designs for fountains and lavatories by Durand and Thibault, which won a prize in this category, make this clear, even though the engraver early in the nineteenth century may have moderated the decor (Figure 240).[73] One fountain is in the form of a giant fasces supporting a statue of Liberty enthroned, while the basin is ringed with other allegorical figures. A second fountain has a group featuring Nature in the centre crowning smaller figures of Liberty and Equality to her right and left, with the wall on either side covered with inscriptions. A third features a Liberty Tree flanked by allegorical figures. A plan

240 Durand and Thibault. Projects for fountains and lavatories, elevations and ground-plans.

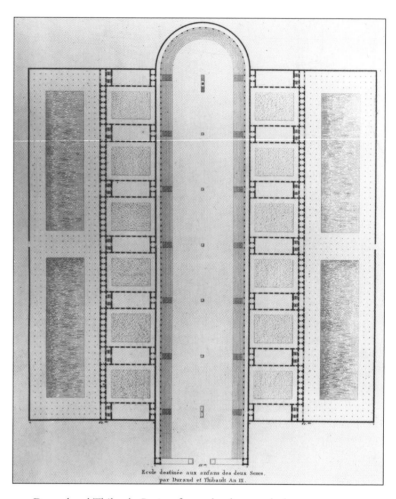

242 Durand and Thibault. Project for a school, ground-plan.

241 [Huet?] Project for a pool and bath-houses on the Champs-Elysées,
ground-plans, elevation, and cross-section.

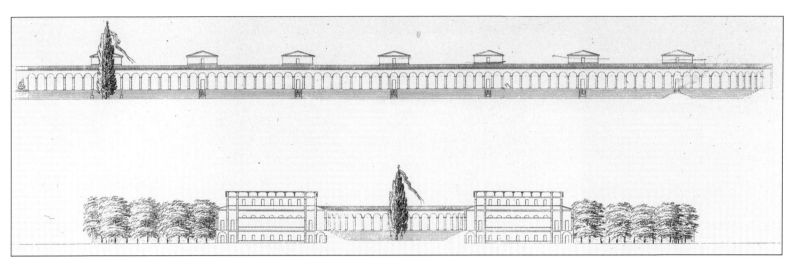

243 Durand and Thibault. Project for a school, elevation and section.

now in the Ecole des Beaux-Arts for a huge rectangular swimming pool and baths for the Champs-Elysées, possibly by Durand and his associate but more likely by J.-C. Huet, is especially interesting (Figure 241).[74] It shows a pool, with a filtration system and waterfall at one end, surrounded by grass and trees. Parallel to the pool on either side are bathhouses in the shape of atria, one for men and one for women. The galleries around those baths are punctuated by allegorical figures, with inscriptions overhead. The complex was thus to have combined utility, aesthetics, and education simultaneously.

The government did not specifically call for designs for schools, an omission noted earlier; nevertheless Durand and his associate submitted such a plan for a primary school for young citizens of both sexes under the rubric of embellishments for Paris (Figures 242, 243).[75] An arena or stadium, surrounded by tiered benches and an arcade, forms the central axis of the project. Around it are fourteen three-story pavillions to house classrooms and other facilities, separated from each other by grass but linked by arcades. The perfect symmetry reflects the clear division of the sexes that we have seen in the project for public baths. Near the entrance is a Liberty Tree, evidently a poplar, "the tree of the people." The stadium and the large open spaces behind the school buildings illustrate the emphasis on physical education in the later eighteenth century. Athletics were

considered essential for forming a healthy and productive citizenry and, for males at least, preparatory to military training in defence of the Republic.

Architects submitted seventeen projects for tribunals, court-houses, buildings for justices of the peace, detention centres (*maisons d'arrêt*), and prisons. This was the period of the Committee of General Security, the Revolutionary Tribunal, the network of revolutionary committees, and the Law of 22 Prairial against suspected counter-revolutionaries, very broadly defined. One architect accompanied his project with the slogan SECURITY AND NATIONAL VENGEANCE.[76] Like many of the projects we have already examined, some of the projects "speak" through their form, inscriptions, low-reliefs, and symbols. The message of some of the court-houses was less intimidating than others. For instance, the project for a court-house for a justice of the peace by Barthélémy Vignon, who won one of the more valuable prizes, conveyed the purpose of the building through inscriptions, figures of Concord and Abundance in the porch, and allegorical figures of civic virtues lining the hall inside (Figures 244–8).[77] A library at the rear was to be devoted to "Conciliations." The whole building was to be a lesson in social harmony, a commodity badly needed in France at the time.

Other projects did not speak so much in this direct fashion as convey an impression of their purpose through their *caractère*. During the delib-

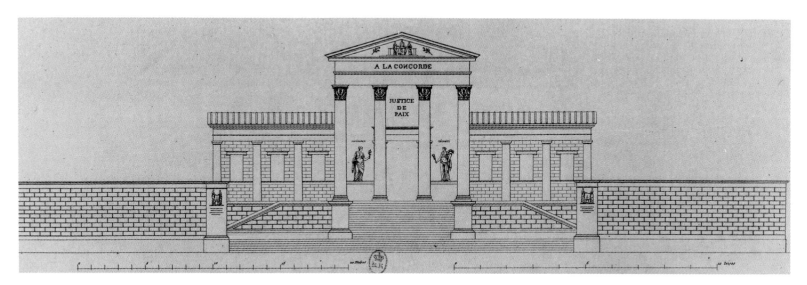

244 Vignon. Project for a courthouse, front elevation.

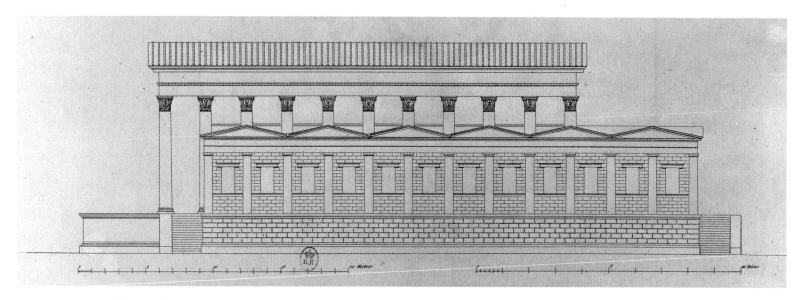

245 Vignon. Project for a courthouse, side elevation.

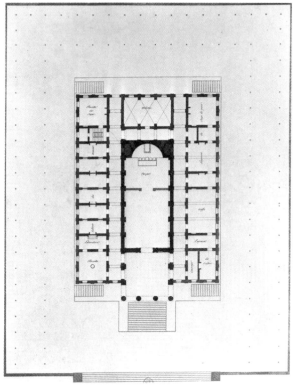
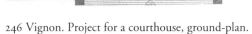

246 Vignon. Project for a courthouse, ground-plan.

247 Vignon. Project for a courthouse, cross-section.

248 Vignon. Project for a courthouse, longitudinal section.

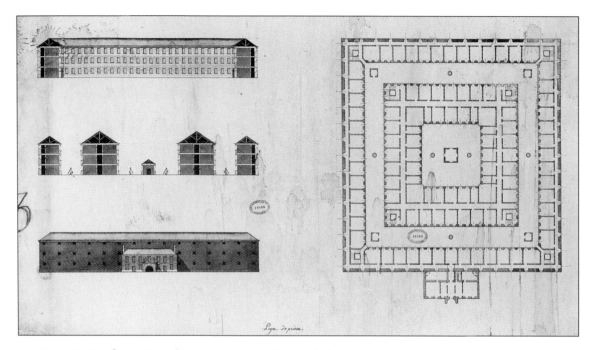

249 Favart. Project for a prison, elevation, sections, and ground-plan.

250 Favart. Project for a prison, detail of the entrance.

erations of a jury judging student architectural projects in January 1794, one of the jury members restated succinctly what this term meant. "The artist ought to take pains with the exterior," declared the painter François-Marie Neveu; "he must not confuse a hospital with a gymnasium, an arsenal or a prison with a temple to reason or to liberty."[78] It is the designs for prisons submitted to the contest of Year II that illustrate "character" best. For example, the project by Favart has allegorical figures of the Law and Justice over the doorway, but it is primarily the forbidding low entrance, the ragged bossages, the heaviness of the massive block, and the small windows that together warn the citizen of his fate should he contravene the laws of the Republic (Figures 249, 250).[79]

A number of submissions that were classified in the catalogue of the public exhibition as *embellissements* reveal a mix of beautification, utility, and revolutionary purpose. There were projects by Thierry for urban development of the land between the rue Saint-Honoré and the Tuileries,[80] by Chevalier and Butay for a construction of a cross-shaped temple of some sort on the Place des Piques (Figure 251),[81] by Capron for a commercial square on the site of the Bastille,[82] by Lemoyne for a canal from Dieppe to Paris,[83] and by Courteau for barracks.[84] Mangin took advantage of the contest to resubmit his plan for central Paris, which he had been promoting since 1791 – no doubt the republicanized version.[85] Another celebrated promoter, the self-styled "patriot" Palloy, used the contest once again to push his project for a column on the site of the Bastille and development of the area between it and the river.[86] And Percier and Fontaine submitted a project for an enclosure around the Pantheon as well as one for a northern wing of the Louvre to join it to the Tuileries Palace, recently rechristened the Palais National, one of a long series of such plans from the age of Louis XIV to the nineteenth century.[87]

After most other projects had been submitted, Lequeu submitted another proposal for a monument that fitted none of the government programs, unless it could be considered an embellishment (Figures 252, 253). Architectural historians have not connected the project to the Contest of Year II because a government official misdated it and Lequeu himself repeated the error. On the back an official has written that it was forwarded to the inspectors in charge of the hall of the Convention on 4 Vendémiaire an II, that is on 25 September 1793. This date is obviously wrong: the republican calendar was not approved until 5 October 1793, and we know from the register kept by the inspectors that the project reached them on 5 Vendémiaire an III, a year later than the official stated. The number 2445 written vertically on the upper left of the back is the registration number assigned to it in Year III. The first official evidently forgot, as many of

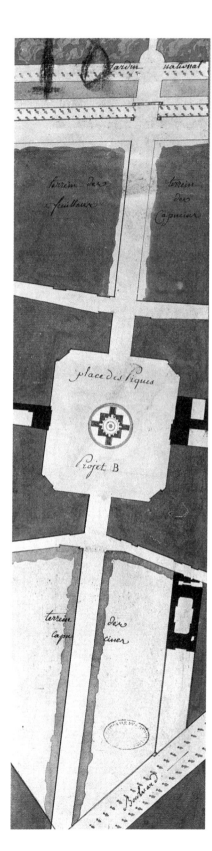

251 Chevalier and Butay. Plan for the Place des Piques.

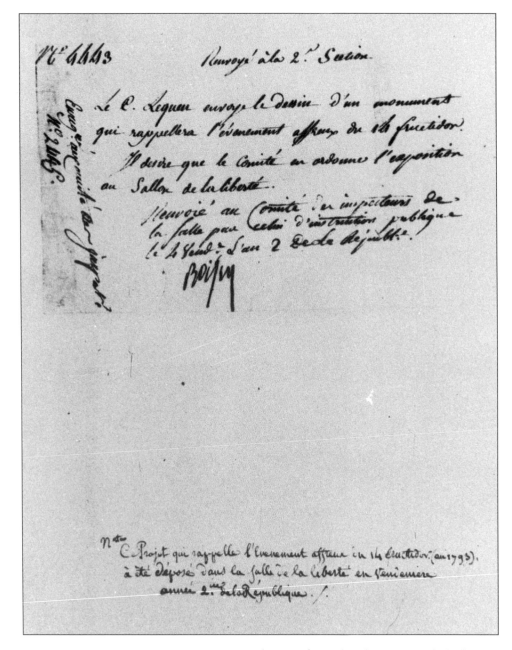

252 Lequeu. Monument in honour of arsenal workers, note on the back.

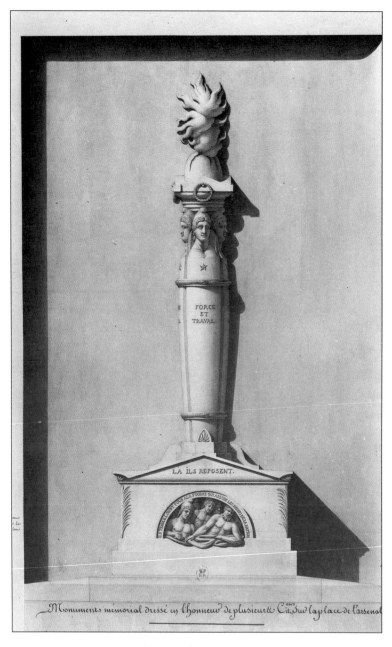

253 Lequeu. Monument in honour of arsenal workers, elevation.

254 View of the National Garden (Tuileries) decorated for the Festival of the Supreme Being.

255 View of the Champ de la Réunion (Champ de Mars) decorated for the Festival of the Supreme Being.

us do, that the new year had just begun. Lequeu later repeated the error in his own note, and some historians have perpetuated it.[88]

This project honoured workers killed in an explosion in the arsenal on 14 Fructidor an 11, 31 August 1794. A semicircular opening in the pedestal reveals a group of workers, which Lequeu explains in the margin was intended "to preserve the memory of their misfortunes." An inscription arches overhead, declaring: THEY WORKED ON THE LIGHTNING THAT PROTECTS THE RIGHTS OF THE NATION. Above this again is another inscription, stating THERE THEY REST. Halfway up the column is a third inscription, FORCE AND WORK. The column suggests four upright sarcophagi, tied together by two bands consisting of snakes biting their tails, an ancient emblem of eternity, an idea reinforced by stars. The sarcophagi terminate just below the capital with human heads, all wearing Phrygian bonnets. Over their heads hang civic crowns. Above the capital a sort of bomb explodes. Despite its strangeness, this projected monument was significant: it was to honour ordinary workers who died in the service of their country.

It was in the midst of the Contest of Year 11 that another aspect of the government program was launched: the program of an annual cycle of national festivals to commemorate the anniversaries of important landmarks of the Revolution – 14 July 1789, 10 August 1792, 21 January 1793, and 31 May 1793 – plus lesser festivals in honour of various social ideals and republican martyrs every tenth day. This cycle of festivals was inaugurated with the Festival of the Supreme Being on 8 June 1794, which was decorated with the most impressive architecture of the Revolution, again under the guidance of David. On the façade of the National Palace a balcony was built, from which Robespierre made a speech in two parts, between which a statue of Atheism with its evil attributes was burned, revealing a smoke-stained statue of Wisdom (Figure 254). The procession then moved to the Champ de Mars, where an immense symbolic Mountain had been erected, large enough to accommodate officials, a large corps of musicians, and 2,400 singers from the sections of Paris (Figure 255). On the peak of the Mountain was a Liberty Tree decked with revolutionary symbols. To one side was a huge Doric column topped with a figure of the People – Hercules holding an orb on which stood a figure of Liberty. Again we find the two ideals of the age expressed architecturally – nature represented by the Mountain, and culture or civilization by the column.

The festival at which Robespierre officiated as president of the Convention was his finest hour, but within less than two months he and his closest colleagues would be overthrown and executed on 9–10

Thermidor, 27–28 July 1794, by a coalition of extremists and moderates united by fear. This sudden turn of events profoundly affected the circumstances in which the jury was chosen, the atmosphere in which it made its decisions, and the context in which artists would work after the awards were handed out. However, before examining the *dénouement* of the bold program for the arts in Year 11, we must look at what was happening in the provinces, for the government program was not just for Paris but for the whole nation. Moreover, there were local initiatives that must be integrated into the overall picture, as they have not been done in the past. Overall there was an attempt to create what the Nazis in our own century (with very different ideological content) were to call a *Kulturlandschaft*, a new face for the country. ▲

Dutour. Project for a symbolic Mountain in Bordeaux, cross-section. (Figure 273)

VII

TOWARDS AN IDEOLOGICAL LANDSCAPE

FROM THE BEGINNING the French revolutionaries sought to achieve one of the principal goals of certain reform ministers before 1789: to standardize the administrative system throughout France and to treat Frenchmen in a similar way from the Atlantic to the Alps and from Flanders to the Pyrenees. The revolutionaries carried out this objective by creating uniform departments, abolishing local privileges, removing internal trade barriers, planning a national educational system, introducing standardized measurements, and attempting to suppress local dialects and foreign languages that survived within French borders. This obsession with uniformity reached its peak under the Republic, especially after the suppression of the so-called federalist revolts in the summer of 1793. The Republic was to be *une et indivisible*, symbolized by the fasces, the bundle of identical rods or pikes tied tightly together. It was natural, therefore, that in their plans for public space the republican leaders of Year II should seek the same uniformity throughout the country.

This thrust was first exemplified in a negative way, the determination to efface every sign, symbol, or inscription that would remind citizens of the old order. The decree passed by the Legislative Assembly in the wake of attacks on royal monuments in August 1792 called specifically for removal of such monuments throughout the country. Moreover, all "feudal" signs and symbols were to be eradicated systematically. Since such symbols were omnipresent, the Convention had to reiterate this demand several times, listing the objectionable relics more specifically. On 1 August 1793, for example, the Convention called on owners to remove within eight days all coats of arms in all parks, gardens, enclosures, houses, and buildings

or face confiscation of their property.[1] The following October a citizen named Vaudeuil complained that his house had been confiscated because he had failed to remove some *fleurs-de-lis* from a grille separating his land from a street and some weather-vanes in the form of lions on his roof. The Convention affirmed that it was important to uphold the penalty of confiscation for displaying such emblems.[2] Even old chimney-plates decorated with lilies were ordered removed until republican versions could be supplied.[3]

The drive to efface every trace of the old regime throughout France was accompanied by a resurgence of the mania, encouraged by the Convention, that ordered an inventory made of towns with undesirable names.[4] Some towns simply replaced a name recalling monarchy or feudalism with a geographic one – Nogent-le-Roi became Nogent de la Haute Marne, Bourgon-Lancy became Bellevue-les-Bains, and Bar-le-Duc was changed to Bar-sur-Ornain. In other cases the new names had an ideological significance – Fontenay-le-Comte became Fontenai-le-Peuple, Mont-Louis became Mont-Libre, Bucy-le-Roi became Bucy-la-République, Chapelle-la-Reine became Chapelle-l'Egalité, and Auxi-le-Château was changed to Auxi-la-Réunion. As de-Christianization got underway in the autumn of 1793, there were numerous moves to get rid of such words as "saint": for instance, Saint-Dizier became Désireville, Saint-Aubin became Aire-Libre, Pont-Saint-Esprit took the name Pont-sur-Rhône, and Saintes changed its name to Xantes.[5]

The movement to bring place-names into line with the republican regime extended to the streets, squares, quais, and entrances of towns and villages. Some towns went about the rebaptism of their urban space in a very systematic way, carrying to a logical conclusion under the Republic the trend exemplified by Toulouse under the constitutional monarchy. For example, the small town in the Gard that had changed its name from Pont-Saint-Esprit to Pont-sur-Rhône submitted plans to the government in March 1794 for a new quay and other urban improvements.[6] Down the right-hand side of one plan were listed the new names of the four quarters of the town – Quartier révolutionnaire, Quartier Sans-culottes, Quartier de l'Union, and Quartier de la Montagne. Inside each quarter the names indicated civic virtues, revolutionary symbols, or weapons of the common people. The streets dividing the quarters from each other were named after revolutionary heroes such as Favre, Lepelletier, or Marat. Also shown on the plans is a monument on one of the islands near the port and a new square on the edge of town for popular festivals.

To cite one more example, La Rochelle carried out such a thorough rebaptism that in a letter to the Committee of Public Instruction its town

256 Statue of the French People, "devourer of kings," proposed by the newspaper *Révolution de Paris*.

councillors claimed to have created a sort of *nouvelle ville*: "It would have meant little to substitute insignificant names in the place of ridiculous or puerile ones; on each corner one reads the name of a philosopher who has instructed the human race, of a hero who has fought for liberty, of a virtue which can be put into practice, or a duty to be fulfilled." [7] The city also reported that it had applied the metric division of the day in a new clock, which had struck the first hour of the Festival of the Supreme Being. Above the frame of the new clock was inscribed

THE HOUR OF THE AWAKENING OF PEOPLES IS
THE LAST OF THE OPPRESSORS OF THE WORLD

The desire for uniformity inspired efforts to systematize nomenclature. In November 1793 a delegation to the Convention from the section Les Arcis in Paris argued that morality was the indispensable foundation for republic.[8] "To achieve this goal," declared Chamoulaud, spokesman of the delegation, "I propose that a silent course in morality be provided for the people by giving squares, streets, etc. of all the communes of the Republic the names of all the virtues."[9] Public squares would be given the names of principal virtues, and the names of adjacent streets would be named after related virtues. The president of the Convention praised the objective of this proposal, arguing that at the moment when reason was attempting to efface superstition and error it was essential to imprint virtue everywhere. The following spring, in a report commissioned by the Committee of Public Instruction, Grégoire reviewed a number of such schemes, then called for a unified system of nomenclature for the whole country. In the effort to create a new order, he argued, one must republicanize everything.[10]

The call to use nomenclature to give an ideological stamp to the whole country was accompanied by proposals for republican monuments along highways, in every commune, and around the frontiers. In September 1793 the Convention decreed that Liberty Bonnets be substituted for fleurs-de-lis on milestones that bordered French highways.[11] In the last days of the monarchy the Legislative Assembly had already passed a law calling for an Altar of the Fatherland in every commune.[12] The Convention decreed that a Liberty Tree be planted in each town and placed under the care of good citizens.[13] It also sent to its Commission on Civic Deeds a proposal that a monument inscribed with the names of its citizens who had died for liberty be erected in the main square of every town.[14] Moreover, as part of a proposed decree banning the royal family from

France, the deputy Joseph Guiter proposed that the frontier of France be ringed with columns at fixed distances, bearing the inscription

KINGS ARE BANISHED FROM FRANCE
PEACE TO NATIONS. LIBERTY, EQUALITY[15]

The newspaper *Révolutions de Paris* published an engraving of the sort of statue it thought should be placed on the most prominent points along the frontier (Figure 256).[16] Instead of the idealized classical figure of the People-Hercules that had appeared at the fourth station in the Festival of Unity and Indivisibility and that David proposed for the tip of the Ile de la Cité, the newspaper suggested a colossal figure of an ordinary sansculotte with a club, whom it described as "The People devourer of kings." Not only was a commoner now atop the pedestal, but the idea of his devouring kings echoed a traditional component of the rituals surrounding the overthrow and killing of tyrants, of which there had been many cases during the Renaissance.[17] Chroniclers recounted how tyrants were killed like pigs, their bodies put on display and then dismembered. One chronicler used the word "boccanare," "to cut into bite-sized pieces." In numerous cases the crowd actually ate some of the bits. To turn the body of the tyrant into meat reduced him to the level of an animal. What was left of the body was thrown into a river or burned, as the king is about to be in the engraving. The body of another king is already in the flames. A third king appears on the face of the pedestal, upside down and stripped of most of his clothing, other traditional ways of inverting the coronation of a ruler.[18]

Meanwhile, throughout France there were numerous examples of destruction of monuments of the Old Regime followed by substitution of temporary replacements or projects for permanent monuments. In Troyes the statue of Louis XIV over the doorway of the city hall was torn down and later replaced by a statue of Liberty by Denis Glédu after drawings by Louis-Joseph Rondot.[19] At Arles the globe covered with fleurs-de-lis and crowned by a sun was replaced by a red Liberty bonnet atop the obelisk on the Place de l'Hôtel de Ville.[20] In Nantes the city council had already decided, following the abortive flight of the royal family to Varennes, to crown the new column with a statue of Liberty rather than one of Louis XVI.[21] Although the sculptor N. Lamarie did not finish the statue, the Colonne de la Liberté repeatedly served as the centre of republican ceremonies. In their *Voyage dans les départements* La Vallée and his fellow editors published an engraving of the unfinished column as it appeared in 1794 (Figure 257).[22] The column was ideally situated on the Place de la Liberté

257 View of the column in
Nantes as it appeared
in 1794.

at the middle of the tree-lined axis formed by the two promenades, now renamed Cours de la Liberté and Cours de la Fédération, running up from the Cours Cincînnatus on the bank of the Seine.[23]

In Nancy the statue of Louis XV on the Place Stanislas, which we discussed earlier, was toppled and interred at the base until its final fate was decided.[24] In the end citizens who were still attached to it could not save it from being sent to the cannon foundry.[25] It was around the vacant pedestal that a choir sang a revolutionary hymn following proclamation of the Republic from the balcony of the city hall on 7 October 1792.[26] Subsequently there were various proposals for the site, but in the meantime it was decorated to serve as the focal point of republican ceremonies. For the fête held on 11 November 1792 to celebrate the first victories of the Republic and the conquest of Savoy, a fasces was placed on the pedestal, from the middle of which rose a pike surmounted by a Liberty Bonnet. On each of the sides of the pedestal a key republican word was inscribed – Liberty, Equality, Property, Security. It was around this pedestal on the

Place du Peuple, as the square was now called, that officials, contingents of volunteers, troops of the line, and citizens gathered to acclaim General Wimpfen, who had just come from the heroic defence of Thionville.[27]

The case of Reims is of special interest because it had been the site of the consecration of French kings, during which ceremony they were anointed with oil from the Sainte-Ampoule said to have been brought down from heaven by a dove for the coronation of Clovis. Following the overthrow of the monarchy, the bronze statue of Louis XV by Pigalle on the Place Royale had been toppled, and later cut up to be sent to the cannon foundry in Metz. Since most revolutionaries had no objection to the figures representing the Gentleness of Government and the Citizen, these were left in place around the pedestal. It was at the base of the vacant pedestal that on 7 October 1792 the representative on mission, Philippe Rühl, performed one of the most dramatic acts of desacralization during the decade. He ordered the Sainte-Ampoule brought to the site, where he ceremoniously smashed it to smithereens.[28] He then bundled the pieces into a parcel that he sent to the Convention, explaining that everything had to disappear that led people to believe that heaven had favoured some mortals more than themselves, in order to put them in chains. The Convention greeted news of his deed with enthusiastic applause.[29]

As elsewhere, however, there was a need at Reims for focal points for revolutionary ceremonies. For the festival on 23 October 1792 celebrating recent victories over enemy troops, a figure of Liberty was placed atop the pedestal on the Place Royale, now renamed Place de la Liberté.[30] The figure was a statue of the Virgin from a nearby church, holding a pike in her right hand and a shield in the other inscribed with the word LAW. She wore a helmet interlaced with the national colours. After being transported through the streets on a chariot drawn by eight horses, she was put in place atop the vacant pedestal. As she was hoisted into place, a chain carried by a young citizen broke into pieces. Urns were then placed around her in which incense burned continuously, another sign that the religiosity of the Revolution was intensifying further. Finally the statue was dedicated, along with singing, instrumental music, and cannon fire. The planners hoped that around her citizens would unite, that they would "forget all the particular sentiments that might lead them astray and, struck with respect at the sight of a Liberty who subjects all wills to the general will, will conform to the just limits laid down for them."[31]

This makeshift Liberty, however, was not considered satisfactory. At the moment when destruction of the statue of Louis XV had been decided, it had already been proposed to replace it with a triangular obelisk bearing inscriptions related to the Revolution.[32] The following July a professor of philosophy at the local college renewed the proposal at the city's Jacobin Club, suggesting that the obelisk should bear inscriptions in honour of the Rémois who had died for the Fatherland. A subscription was opened to finance the project.[33] The obelisk was to be capped by a golden orb surmounted in turn by a bronze renown holding a scroll inscribed with the names of the fallen heroes. A design in the Carnavalet resembles this description, with Pigalle's statues around the base of the pedestal still in place (Figure 258).[34] Although it was not completely finished at the time,[35] it was inaugurated on 10 August 1793, the first anniversary of the overthrow of the monarchy. The festival began at the Altar of the Fatherland on the espalande on the outskirts of the city, then proceeded to the Place de la Liberté, where the obelisk had been erected.[36] After some revolutionary music, the mayor and the president of the Jacobin Club both made speeches. A child then took from an urn the names of the fallen, which the mayor read in a loud voice. Young girls tossed flowers, incense was

258 Obelisk in Reims erected atop the pedestal of the former statue of Louis XV.

259 Altar of the Fatherland in Reims.

burned, and the crowd intoned a hymn written for the occasion. Thus an act of desacralization by Rühl at the base of the pedestal was followed a year later by sacralization of a new monument on the same site.

There were proposals to purge the former Place Royale further of what were considered reminders of the old order. One citizen lauded the idea of erecting a monument to the war dead from Reims, but he called for removal of the statues by Pigalle around the base, arguing that the sculptor had been a courtesan of a despot. He contended that the female figure leading a lion suggested royal power and military alliances. He also disliked the male figure, which not only suggested commerce but had a melancholy air. The figure seemed to be mourning the emigration of gold from France.[37] The Jacobin Club complained that the barriers that encircled the pedestal suggested chains, but the city council replied that they did not resemble chains, that they never had been part of the monument itself, and that in any case the iron was of no use for anything else.[38] Surviving festival programs reveal that the monument served repeatedly as one of the focal points of republican rituals. In the Festival honouring Reason in December 1793, for example, the procession did not halt for long at the obelisk, but the participants saluted it in passing and left two incense-burners at its base.[39] Another focal point was the Altar of the Fatherland at the western edge of the city (Figure 259).

As we have seen, even before the Revolution Bordeaux had been the object of some ambitious plans, including a huge *place* on the site of the Château Trompette on the bank of the Garonne. This planning continued into the Revolution, spurred on by the confiscation of church property, the decision to raze the château, the activities of local architects, and the arrival of the Parisian architect Alexandre-Théodore Brongniart during the Terror. Before the overthrow of the monarchy Louis Combes had already exploited the opportunity offered by secularization of the convent of the Chartreux to draw up a plan for the whole area (Figure 260).[40] The plan included several features of eighteenth-century urban planning – green spaces, straightened streets, a radiating square, a hospital, public baths, and an area for public festivals. Combes also designed a meeting-place for the Jacobin Club in the former cloister adjoining the church Sainte-Dominique (Figures 261, 262).[41] It featured the amphitheatre favoured by revolutionaries for places where citizens would congregate, with a space for deputations in the centre. On the middle of the balcony on one side there was to be the inscription LIVE FREE OR DIE.

Following the overthrow of the monarchy, Combes and the other local architects responded to a call by the municipal council on how best to use the Jardin Public west of the château, which was already being used

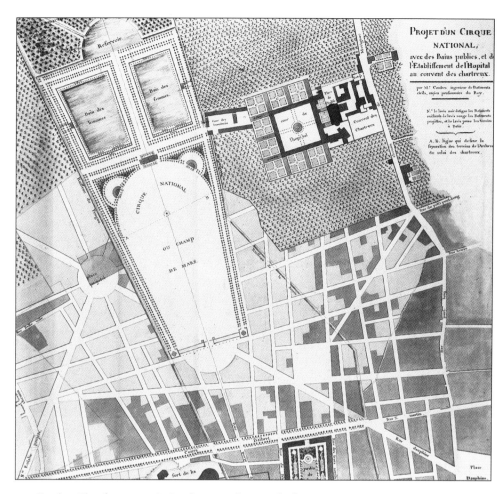

260 Combes. Plan for a *cirque* in Bordeaux on the site of a former convent.

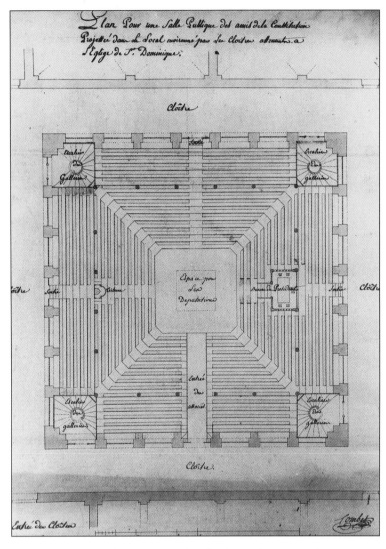

261 Combes. Project for a meeting-place for the Jacobins in Bordeaux, ground-plan.

for republican festivals.[42] Several architects proposed creating an immense amphitheatre capable of holding up to thirty-five thousand people. In this vast enclosure festivals lasting several days could be staged.[43] Combes believed that, if skilfully managed, such festivals could remove the divisions among the people and their sense of individual problems. Two other architects, Dufour and Bonfin, also emphasized the psychological advantages of such rallies for the regime: "For our new political life, for our new customs, for our new goals, we need an immense theatre where the actors and the spectators excite each other, where the presence and applause of some redoubles the enthusiasm of others, and where the imposing scene of a great city assembled together will stir the coldest spirit."[44] The citizen Lagarde, who prepared a report on the various plans, argued that this was not the only sort of utility that one could derive from this public land. Citizens would also benefit from having a green oasis in which to relax. In the end the city council decided to postpone a decision until it received guidelines from the central government.

Brongniart accepted an invitation from an actor friend in the spring of 1793 to work on completing the Théâtre de la Montagne in Bordeaux because the Revolution had stripped him of the wealthy clientèle in Paris who had commissioned him to design luxurious *hôtels*.[45] He never completed his work on the theatre and was not paid for what he did accomplish. During his stay he was also active in converting churches into revolutionary temples and in designing props for civic festivals. When the municipal council decided on 27 November 1793 to create a Temple of Reason in the city,[46] Brongniart led a team of artisans in transforming the church of Notre-Dame into such a temple for the Festival of Reason less than two weeks later. "At night I had the church illuminated in my own way," Brongniart wrote to his daughter back in Paris; "that is to say that on entering one found it perfectly lit without seeing a single light. Also the Mountain erected at the end of the church made a surprising impact."[47] It was on the peak of this symbolic Mountain that a young woman representing Liberty took her place at the climax of the festival. The program also reveals that the Christian imagery on the façade was masked by a portico bearing the inscription TEMPLE OF REASON.[48]

Brongniart's biographer, Jacques Silvestre de Sacy, thought that it was the cathedral Saint-André that Brongniart helped to transform into a Temple of Reason for the festival on 10 December 1793. François-Georges Pariset has pointed out that a number of designs in the Brongniart collection are unquestionably for the cathedral.[49] The confusion arises because there were plans for *two* Temples of Reason in Bordeaux, both with symbolic Mountains: because the original temple was overcrowded, the

Coupe d'une Salle publique pour la société des amis de la Constitution

Projettée dans le cloître joignant L'Eglise St. Dominique.

262 Combes. Project for a meeting-place for the Jacobins in Bordeaux, cross-section.

263, 264 Brongniart. Cathedral of Saint-André in Bordeaux converted into a revolutionary Temple.
Above: cross-section; *below*: longitudinal section.

representatives on mission in the area ordered the following spring that the cathedral also be transformed into a Temple of Reason according to designs by Brongniart.[50] These are undoubtedly the plans in the collection (Figures 263–5). The representatives on mission called for immediate action, but it is not clear to what extent these plans were carried out. They show a lot of greenery, grottoes on the slopes, serpentine paths, and a statue of Liberty on the summit. From a ground-plan of the nave, one can imagine the surprising effects that would have been created by processions following these paths, disappearing into grottoes, emerging to mount up to the statue of Liberty, expressing veneration for her, then descending by another route.[51]

Also in the Brongniart collection are the architect's plans for the area adjacent to the cathedral (Figure 266). He planned to open up the area by creating two symmetrical squares on either side of the cathedral and another behind the apse. New parallel streets would run off into the neighbourhood from these lateral squares. The cathedral was to be augmented by a portico flanked by towers. In front there was to be a large public square created by extending the line of the outer perimeters of the squares on each side of the cathedral. On both sides of this large square were to be identical buildings, each with three courtyards. One of these symmetrical buildings was to cut into the area around the old Fort du Hâ; the other was to lead into a garden with huge flowerbeds. After narrowing somewhat, the large square was to branch out into three tree-lined avenues. The scheme would have involved destruction of the mediaeval tower Pey Berland. As Pariset has observed, Brongniart's plan not only anticipated some of the changes made in the area during the nineteenth century, but also some of the ruthlessness of Haussmann in effacing historic buildings.[52]

This example of urbanism was related to another plan by Brongniart for a huge circular public *place* where four broad avenues would converge (Figures 267–9). Brongniart did ten drawings for this circus. One axis was to run from the river-bank through the square to the cathedral. The other axis was to run from Victor Louis" theatre to where the Place de la Victoire is now located, an axis corresponding approximately to the present rue Sainte-Cathérine. An obelisk was to be erected at the intersection of these axes. Each quarter of the circus was to consist of a curved building with a pavilion protruding at the end. A colonnade of eleven columns was to run between the two pavilions. In the most finished elevation among the drawings, the architect introduced an imposing central pavilion. This plan shows a mixture of styles: the roof is reminiscent of Mansart and the Place Vendôme in Paris; the segment between the pavilions has a classical rigour reminding one of Gabriel and the Ecole Militaire, and the portico echoes some aspects of Victor Louis' theatre, but most of the elements

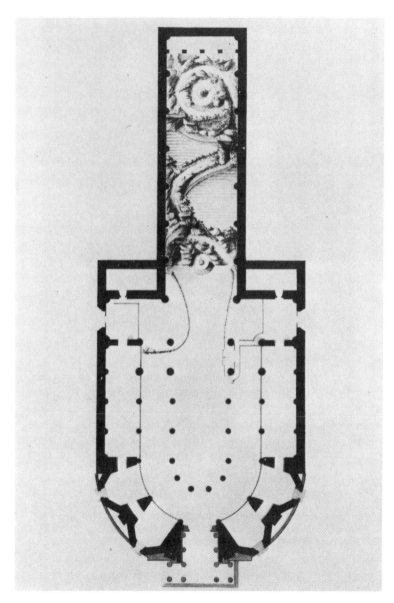

265 Brongniart. Cathedral of Saint-André in Bordeaux converted into a revolutionary Temple, ground-plan.

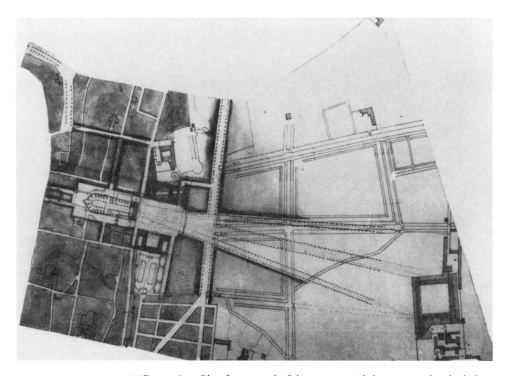

266 Brongniart. Plan for renewal of the area around the converted cathedral.

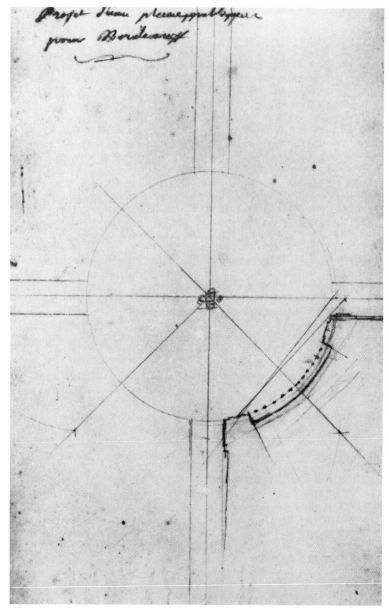

267 Brongniart. Project for a public square in Bordeaux, ground-plan.

268 Brongniart. Project for a public square in Bordeaux, elevation of a section of the surrounding buildings.

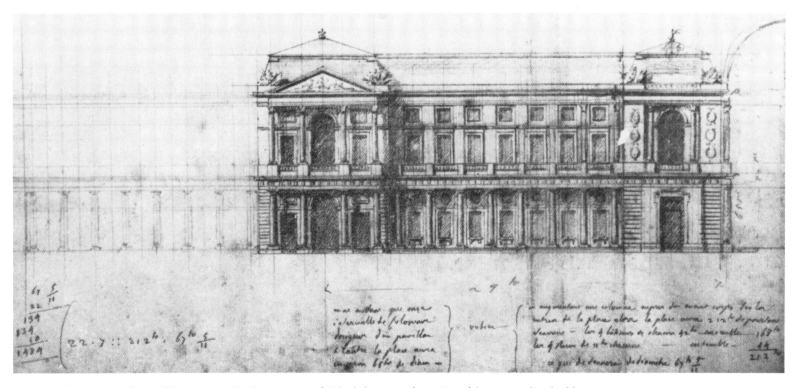

269 Brongniart. Project for a public square in Bordeaux, a more finished elevation of a section of the surrounding buildings.

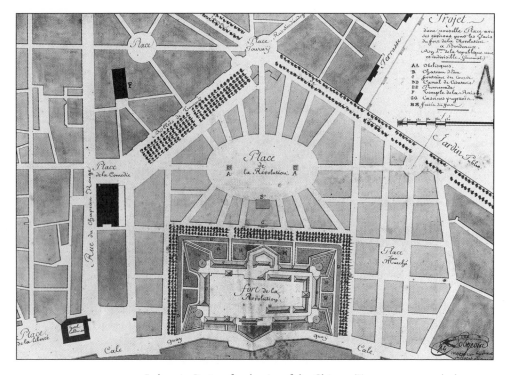

270 Lobgeois. Project for the site of the Château Trompette, ground-plan.

stem from the French classical tradition rather than from the stereometric forms of such avant-garde architects as Ledoux or Boullée.[53] Once again, however, Brongniart would have cut boldly through the existing maze of streets to create the circus and the broad avenues leading to it.

Much of the planning in Bordeaux centred on the Château Trompette. It was the local Bastille: the citizens remembered that royal troops had in the past made sorties from it to put down insurrections. Early in the Revolution it was decided to raze this symbol of the Old Regime, although the work proceeded much more slowly than in Paris and was not completed until the early nineteenth century. In the spring of 1794 an engineer by the name of Lobgeois proposed a plan that would have preserved the centre of the old fortress, now rechristened Fort de la Révolution, to accommodate barracks, while creating an oblong Place de la Révolution on its western slopes (Figures 270, 271).[54] The new square was to have obelisks near each end and a water tower on one side. Fifteen streets were to radiate from it. On either side of the fort the terrain was to be subdivided on a grid plan. Other characteristic features of eighteenth-century urbanism included blocks of trees, promenades, a new market, and a fountain. As we shall see, under the Directory the government launched a contest for development of the site that produced more than thirty projects. Lobgeois changed the date on his scheme in order to compete in this contest.

We have seen already that Bordeaux was the centre of construction of, or plans for, two huge symbolic Mountains, one erected in Notre Dame in the process of converting it into a Temple of Reason, the other proposed for the Cathedral Saint-André to transform it into a larger such temple. Invoices in the departmental archives from artists and craftsmen reveal that a third Mountain was erected on the Champs de Mars, as the Jardin Public was then called, to serve as the centrepiece of festivals in Year II.[55] Apparently on its slopes were a model of the Bastille, a waterfall, a windmill, and a globe, plus a statue of Liberty on the summit. Unfortunately there seems to be no drawing or engraving of this Mountain.

In the Archives Nationales there are designs for two more Mountains, both attributed to an engineer-architect from Bordeaux named Dutour but only one of them signed.[56] The unsigned one is an elevation showing a tomb in the side of the Mountain and a circular temple on the summit (Figure 272). The other is a cross-section of a different Mountain signed and dated 5 Fructidor an II, or 22 August 1794 (Figures 273–5). Again the Mountain is surmounted by a temple, this time with a statue of Liberty ringed by busts visible in the interior. On one slope is a small

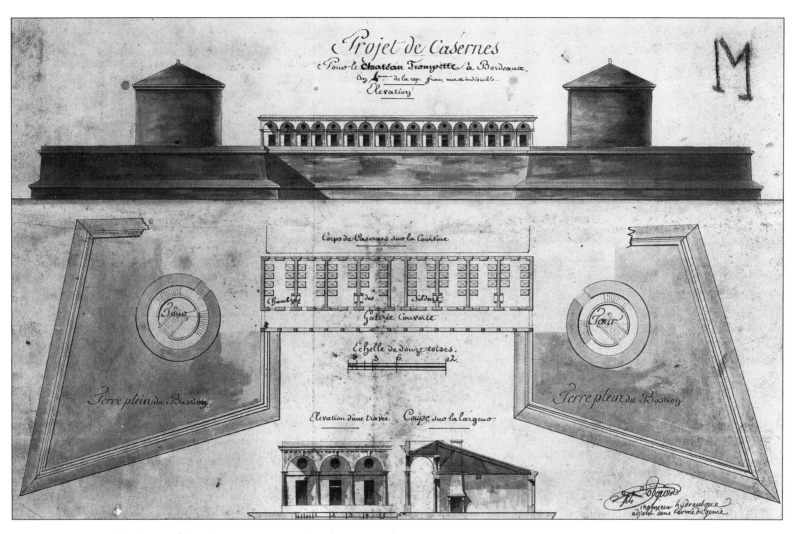

271 Lobgeois. Project for the site of the Château Trompette, plan, elevations, and section.

272 Anonymous. Project for a symbolic Mountain in Bordeaux, elevation.

273 Dutour. Project for a symbolic Mountain in Bordeaux, cross-section.

274 Dutour. Project for a symbolic Mountain in Bordeaux, detail of the Temple.

275 Dutour. Project for a symbolic Mountain in Bordeaux, detail of the crypt.

276 Verly. Church of Saint-Laurent in Lille converted into a revolutionary
Temple, view of the nave.

277 Verly. Church of Saint-Laurent in Lille converted into a revolutionary
Temple, view of the Mountain and statue of Liberty.

amphitheatre and a staircase to the summit. On the other side is a catafalque
with an obelisk on the top terminating in a fasces capped with a Liberty
Bonnet. Inside the Mountain are a pump feeding a waterfall, staircases
leading into large chambers, and a crypt containing funeral urns, doubtless for the remains of revolutionary heroes. There is no evidence about
the destination of these Mountains, but they may be connected to a plan
by the Club National to erect a permanent Mountain as a tribute to *la
Montagne* in the Convention.[57]

The most striking plans for urban space during the Revolution
occurred in Lille, the work of the local architect François Verly, who had
been responsible for the impressive ephemeral architecture erected for the
Festival of Federation among the northern departments.[58] Throughout
the Revolution he continued to design props for the revolutionary festivals in the city.[59] Like Brongniart in Bordeaux, he was also commissioned
to oversee transformation of a church into a Temple of Reason. Beginning

late in the autumn of 1793 and continuing into the following year, Verly and a team of artisans worked to convert the church of Saint-Laurent into such a temple.[60] Although historians of Lille usually refer to the converted church as the Temple of Reason,[61] the name predominated for only a short time. The members of the Committee of Public Safety, especially the Robespierrists, thought that the Cult of Reason was too extreme, smacked of atheism, and would alienate many citizens. The terminology used locally seems to have reflected the ideology of the revolutionary government. The municipal records show that the building was usually called "le Temple de la Morale," "le Temple de l'Eternel," or simply "le Temple."[62]

As in many churches converted into Temples, the centrepiece was a huge Mountain at the end of the nave, complete with caves, tombs of revolutionary martyrs, an Altar of the Fatherland, and the usual statue of Liberty (Figures 276–8). This statue was to be done by the local sculptor Corbet, first in plaster, then in white marble.[63] The background showed lightning striking down from heaven, symbolizing the awesome power of the revolutionary government. Apparently there was some sort of amphitheatre around the base of the Mountain.[64] The columns and the vaults were decorated with painted foliage, obscuring the original purpose of the building and bringing the outdoors inside. In this case we have watercolours of the new decor as it looked, or would look, when finished.[65] Also, an expert was hired to enlarge the organ so that martial music could be played at the desired volume.[66] Equally significant was the alteration of the entrance: fasces capped with Liberty Bonnets were placed on either side, supporting a huge Level of Equality overhead. An inscription underscored the significance of this symbol:

THE LEVEL OF EQUALITY ALONE ASSURES THE REVOLUTION
NO ONE WILL ENTER THE TEMPLE
EXCEPT THROUGH THIS SACRED ENTRANCE
WOE BETIDE ANYONE WHO IS TOO BIG FOR IT

Work on the transformation of the church continued through the summer of 1794, although it was used before it was finished. On 19 September the artists asked the municipal council to appoint inspectors to guarantee the solidity of the Mountain before the official opening.[67] The inauguration took place the following day. The temple was to provide a place for citizens to congregate for revolutionary rites. The municipal council ordered that "the bell in the tower of the Temple will be rung every tenth day at the break of day and at nine in the morning to announce the assembly at the Temple."[68] It was also used for festivals commemo-

278 Verly. Church of Saint-Laurent in Lille converted into a revolutionary Temple, design for the backdrop.

rating epochal events such as the execution of the king. For example, on 2 Pluviôse an III, 21 January 1795, the temple was the final destination of the cortège. There professional and amateur musicians gave a concert mixed with songs related to the occasion. Also, on a transparent screen a spectacle was presented in which the French People in the guise of Hercules used his club to destroy the throne and all the "baubles of royalty," as the program put it.[69]

It was Verly too who designed a whole new city centre for Lille in 1794. In the bombardment of the city by the Austrians back in 1792 much of the city had been destroyed, but the enemy had been repulsed. In the Convention there had been a proposal to present a tricolour banner to the city with the inscription TO THE CITY OF LILLE, THE GRATEFUL REPUBLIC. David had intervened to say that, however glorious such a banner might be, it would be too perishable to commemorate the heroism of the citizens of Lille, or those of Thionville, which had also resisted a siege. David called for erection of pyramids or obelisks constructed of granite like the great monuments of antiquity. He also suggested that marble and bronze from statues that had been torn down in Paris could be used to embellish the proposed monuments. Moreover, he reminded the other

279 Verly. View of the proposed Place de la Reconnaissance in Lille.

deputies that it was a fire that had made it possible to achieve openness, beauty, and regularity in London. David proposed, therefore, that a general plan be drawn up before reconstruction of the two cities was begun. In drawing up such a plan, one could select the most suitable site for the proposed monuments.[70]

Subsequently David wrote to the municipal officials in Lille to inform them of his motion, which he said had been favourably received by the Convention before it was sent to the Committee of Public Instruction.[71] He asked the officials for their advice and for a map of the city so that he would know what location would be best for the proposed monument in the likely event that the Convention gave it final approval. He asked whether they agreed that the area around Saint-Saveur was the most suit-

able site, since it had suffered the most devastation. He also called on any artists in the city to submit their ideas so that he could include them in his report and make their names known to the Convention. The municipal council ordered an extract of David's letter printed and sent to all artists and amateurs.[72] It seems likely that it was this appeal that inspired the designs Verly submitted to the council a year and a half later. The delay was probably the result of Verly's involvement in designing props for republican festivals in the city and in converting the church of Saint-Laurent into a revolutionary temple. The architect's designs were for the quarter Saint-Saveur, featured a Place de la Reconnaissance, and included a massive obelisk, all elements mentioned by David.

On 29 Thermidor an II, or 16 August 1794, Verly presented his plan to the municipal council in Lille in five parts, three elevations and two ground-plans.[73] Unfortunately, the ground-plans have disappeared since they were last displayed in an exhibition in the city commemorating the centenary of the Revolution. At the heart of the plan was a Place de la Reconnaissance, a view of which survives in the local Musée Hospice Comtesse (Figure 279).[74] It shows a spacious elliptical square with a monument in the centre in the form of a giant fasces atop a pedestal bearing an inscription, "To the inhabitants …," with the rest now illegible. The huge *place* contrasts in many ways with the customary squares constructed throughout France in the seventeenth and eighteenth centuries. It would have provided the sort of open-air space with a focal point envisaged by Rousseau in which the people could assemble for festivals.[75]

In the background of this square is a concave block of residences or offices three stories high. The ground level of this block features arcades providing shelter for pedestrians without breaking the continuity of lines. The second storey is pierced by plain rectangular windows, while the third has a gallery on all sides. In the middle of this severe block is a paramounting temple set on a platform atop a massive perron, a stairway leading to the top in three stages. At the top, slightly to the rear, is a second platform confined within a circular wall and planted with trees around the periphery, forming a sort of tumulus. The entrance to the temple is a portico composed of huge Doric columns, with an inscription on the entablature: TO THE LILLOIS. THE GRATEFUL REPUBLIC. ERECTED IN 1793. On the pediment are Scales of Justice, and on the semicircular façade above are two Renowns facing each other on either side of another fasces. The temple itself takes the form of a half-cylinder resting on a parallelepiped, completing an ensemble reminiscent of some designs by Ledoux. The end result would have been a sort of republican Capitol.

A watercolour in the Musée des Beaux-Arts in Lille shows the second elevation presented to the city council. It shows a belfry next to a prytaneum, replacing the destroyed church of St Etienne, on another new square (Figure 280). As we have seen in discussing the projects of Kersaint and his architect colleagues earlier in the Revolution, the word "prytaneum" recalled a hall in ancient Greece in which a sacred fire was kept burning and important ceremonies were performed. In Verly's plan the prytaneum takes the form of a circular building, reminiscent of the Halle au Blé by Le Camus de Mézières recently constructed in Paris, with an oculus on the top of the dome. There are a few openings at the ground level and in the gallery around the base of the dome. The decoration is confined to three simple bands, one tying together the doorways around the base, the second underscoring the gallery, the third underlining the dome. As

280 Verly. View of the proposed belfry adjoining a prytaneum in Lille.

Jean-Jacques Duthoy has noted, the architect sought large unadorned spaces, simple lines, and the effects of mass. The impression is strange and powerful.[76]

At one side of the prytaneum is a belfry rising up from a massive plinth, the top of which is obviously designed as a platform with a podium in centre, from which speeches could be made or on which ceremonies could be performed. The belfry itself consists of an enormous Doric column crowned by a lantern in which a flame was to burn, announcing the gospel of the Revolution. This column is almost twice the height of the adjoining building, unlike the one next to the Halle au Blé, which barely rose above the dome.[77] Once again the decoration is simple: a frieze around the plinth and another underneath the capital. The prytaneum and its belfry are set in an irregular square, again providing a space in which the people could congregate for republican rituals. The square is encompassed by three-storey buildings, with galleries at the street level and uniform openings on the other two levels. To the right one can glimpse the side of the Théâtre du Peuple in the third part of Verly's plan.

It is this third design, also in the Musée des Beaux-Arts in Lille, that is the most unconventional (Figure 281).[78] It shows another immense square, this one stretching between two poles, an obelisk at one end and the Theatre of the People at the other. Since Blondel and others reveal that eighteenth-century architects were aware of the sexual connotations of forms[79] – Freudian before Freud – the obelisk may suggest "masculine" thrust juxtaposed to the "feminine" orifices and rounded forms of the theatre. In any case, David had called for an obelisk to commemorate the resistance of the Lillois to the enemy, and the revolutionary government wanted theatres in every town to present inspirational plays to the common people. In between the two poles are twin sunken public baths, presumably one for each sex, showing the same concern for the needs of the population that we have seen in Combes's plan for Bordeaux and in the contest of Year II. The baths are framed by four equestrian statues high atop massive pedestals. In the foreground is a semicircular hedge on the edge of a canal, reflecting, as it were, the half-circles of the façade of the theatre. The idea of a new city centre, rising like a phoenix from the ashes, was emphasized by the projected structures contrasted with the ruins depicted in the foreground.

Verly's proposed new city centre combined a variety of ingredients. It drew on the repertory of antiquity – the sort of temple housing the beacon atop the belfry, the prytaneum, the fasces which appear several times, the obelisk rising out of a vast exedra, the cubical pedestals, the peristyles, the colonnades, and the architraves. Even the idea of public baths

goes back to antiquity. At the same time Verly's plan showed affinities with progressive contemporaries such as Boullée and Lequeu – the huge independent column aside the prytaneum, the asymmetry of the prytaneum-belfry complex, the grand masses, the clean lines, and the geometric shapes. If at times the effect was somewhat heavy and lugubrious, as in the case of the monument on the Place de la Reconnaissance, it was very much his own.

What is even more striking is how Verly used these ingredients as a symbolic language – the temple atop a giant staircase, representing a kind of ladder to heaven; the disproportionate entrance to the temple, emphasizing the invitation to all to enter the sanctuary; the semi-spherical prytaneum, lending a cosmic significance; the verdure surrounding the temple and the obelisk, suggesting nature and life-force; the water jetting and cascading from the sides of the sunken baths, the base of the obelisk, and the walls of the canal, signifying purification and regeneration; the gigantic tower and the massive obelisk thrusting upward, symbolizing aspiration and ascendancy. Above all there were the semicircles of the façade of the theatre, rising like the morning sun on the horizon, heralding a new era for mankind. Thus Verly was able to communicate his message without the excess of signs and inscriptions that cluttered some revolutionary projects.

At the other end of France, Montpellier was another centre of remarkable projects. The Colonne de la Liberté on the esplanade of the city was updated to continue to serve as a focal point for revolutionary rituals. The inscription THE NATION, THE LAW, THE KING on the shield held by Liberty atop the column was replaced with THE FRENCH REPUBLIC.[80] Then for the anniversary of the overthrow of the monarchy, all sides of the pedestal were redecorated with republican inscriptions and symbols, including medallions with the all-seeing Eye of Surveillance in the centre.[81] The column served as one of the main stations of the festival in honour of Marat staged on 1 November 1793. After traversing much of the city, the cortège halted at the foot of the column, where for a time the people regarded the image of Liberty, "the Divinity of the French."[82] A funeral urn was placed at the foot of the pedestal, after which the representative on mission in the area, Joseph-Antoine Boisset, and others eulogized the martyr. On the eve of the Festival of the Supreme Being in June 1794, to cite one more example, fireworks were launched from the foot of the column. "Rockets rising at short intervals … seemed to carry up to the clouds the tokens of gratitude of a free people," the program explained.[83]

Another focal point for republican ceremonies was the Place du Peyrou. Soon after the news of the overthrow of the monarchy, the depart-

281 Verly. View of the proposed public bath and theatre in Lille.

mental officials called for the removal of all external signs that might remind citizens of their former servitude, including the equestrian statue of Louis XIV on the square, but for preservation of the pedestal as the base for a future national monument.[84] Also, the inscription LUCIVICO MAGNO was effaced from the triumphal arch at the entrance to the site.[85] An invoice submitted to the city council much later reveals that an obelisk had been erected on the square, before which feudal documents had been burned.[86] The following September the local Jacobin Club agreed to remove from its meeting-place the flag of England, once considered another free nation, and to burn it along with a mannequin of Pitt on the square. In this fête a Liberty Tree was planted on the very spot where the statue of the king had once stood. The club also decided to petition the department to rechristen the square Place de la Révolution.[87] The department agreed a few days later. During Year II the site continued to serve as one of the stations in revolutionary festivals. It was from a podium near the pedestal that the mayor announced the motif of the Festival of the Supreme Being.[88]

A third ceremonial centre was the cathedral of Saint-Pierre. Following the conversion of Notre Dame in Paris into a Temple of Reason in November 1793, the departmental council of the Hérault declared that churches in different localities were to be turned over to the local authorities, to be used to celebrate the principles of universal morality. In Saint-Pierre the Christian decorations were covered up, removed if they had some artistic value, or smashed if they were thought to have none. The main altar was overthrown and replaced with a pike surmounted by the inscription THE EARTH DESTROYS HEAVEN. A procession of a new kind marched through the streets, displaying inscriptions from the former altar and remnants of sacramental objects. The pulpit was left standing to serve as a rostrum for patriotic orators. For example, on 20 Nivôse an II or 9 January 1794, a member of the Jacobin Club declaimed that the pulpit was now to serve truth rather than falsehood. "Liberty and Equality rise up today on the debris of dogmatic royal authority and barbarous fanaticism," he asserted.[89]

Soon this temple became one of the starting-points of civic processions, such as the one on 30 Nivôse an II or 19 December 1793 celebrating the recapture of Toulon from the British. It was organized by Boisset, the representative on mission. He declared that beautiful women had always graced the celebrations of free peoples; consequently the procession included forty women attired in Roman togas and a Goddess of Reason in "simple but majestic dress." They would have been attired even more simply had they conformed to the theories of Boisset: "the daughters of Sparta," he declared, "were never so chaste as when they presented themselves in cer-

emonies completely nude." The following spring, in conformity with an order of the Committee of Public Safety, the inscription THE FRENCH PEOPLE RECOGNIZE THE EXISTENCE OF THE SUPREME BEING AND THE IMMORTALITY OF THE SOUL was traced in huge letters over the doorway on the rue des Carmes. It endured into the nineteenth century until it was finally erased by the elements.[90]

This temple still recalled too much the superstition of the past; consequently, late in 1793 Boisset promoted the idea of erecting a new temple to Truth and Philosophy.[91] The local architect Moulinier and the celebrated Parisian sculptor Augustin Pajou, who had been in Montpellier since October 1792, were commissioned to draw up plans. These were submitted to the Commission for the Amelioration of Agriculture and the Arts, which had been created recently by the department to oversee repair and construction of ports, canals, bridges, public buildings, and monuments.[92] The municipality then petitioned Boisset for permission to demolish the water-tower on the former Place du Peyrou and the church of Notre-Dame des Tables, the materials for which were to be used to serve as the foundation of the temple.[93] Boisset sent a glowing report to the Convention that was reproduced in many newspapers:

> On the debris of the foolish figure of the fourteenth
> Capet, on the former Place du Peyrou, where travellers
> once saw the three Estates submit themselves to slavery,
> a Temple of Reason is rising up, round in shape, flanked
> by 160 columns. The statue of Philosophy, executed by
> the famous sculptor Pajou will unveil the Truth to the
> world … This monument will be one of the most
> beautiful that the work of Liberty has ever produced.[94]

The local Jacobin Club opened a public campaign to raise the 350,000 livres that the architect estimated would be needed for the project. Hundreds of copies of a letter were printed with a space left for the name of the citizen.[95] The letter condemned the old churches, not only for the bad taste they exhibited – "vast, but Gothic" – but because they had served the privileged rather than the weak. It reported that these edifices were now being converted into something useful, but a new temple was needed that by its very proportions would communicate the idea of equality. Although this appeal stressed that contributions were voluntary, it announced that they would be listed on a plaque in the club's meeting-place. The names of those who refused to donate would be conspicuously absent. In conclusion it contained an even less veiled threat directed at

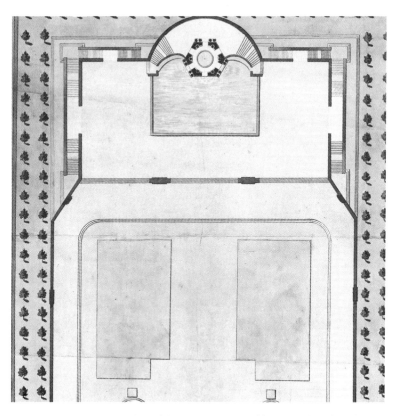

282 Moulinier. Ground-plan of the water-tower and basin on the Place du Peyrou in Montpellier.

283 Moulinier. Ground-plan of the revolutionary Temple to replace the water-tower on the Place du Peyrou.

the rich egoist who congratulated himself on having escaped making a contribution. "This man will soon fall prey to a belated regret; reproved by the opinion of all virtuous men, he will become an outsider in the Republic." And in case such threats did not work, an appeal to the Convention was printed asking for permission to impose a revolutionary tax on the rich in order to help finance the project.[96]

A local historian in Montpellier, Louis Grasset-Morel, has asserted that no designs were ever made for this projected temple, but the plans presented to the Commission for Amelioration of Agriculture and the Arts by Moulinier and Pajou must have been fairly advanced, since members made various suggestions that the artists incorporated into their project.[97] Also, the records show that demolition of the water-tower on the Place du Peyrou was begun to make way for the projected temple. Moreover,

the Archives Nationales has two ground-plans by Moulinier, one showing the outline of the foundation of the water-tower on the former Place du Peyrou, the other showing the foundation of a circular building with a statue in the centre surrounded by a colonnade (but not the 160 columns mentioned by Boisset) on the same site (Figures 282, 283).[98] The Caisse Nationale des Monuments Historiques also has an elevation of a temple attributed to Moulinier and Pajou (Figure 284).[99] Unfortunately, these fragments are not very revealing, but they do show that planning for the new building was well underway by the end of the Terror.

As well, the Archeological Society of Montpellier has two slightly different sets of projects for a temple for the same site by an architect-engineer called Dartain, about whom nothing is known (Figures 285–90). These alternative designs are both very obsolescent in style and share a similar

284 [Moulinier?] Fragment of a Temple for the Place du Peyrou in Montpellier.

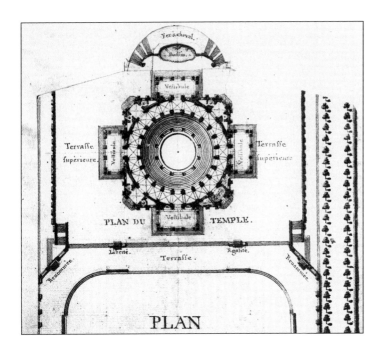

285, 286 Dartain. Project for a Temple of Reason for the Place du Peyrou.
Left: ground-plan of the site; *below*: elevation.

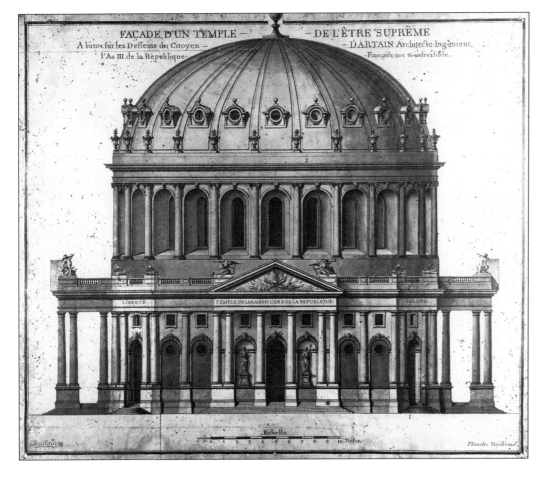

287, 288 Dartain. *Right*: project for a Temple of Reason for the Place du Peyrou, ground-plan; *below*: project for a Temple of Reason with an external portico for the Place du Peyrou, elevation.

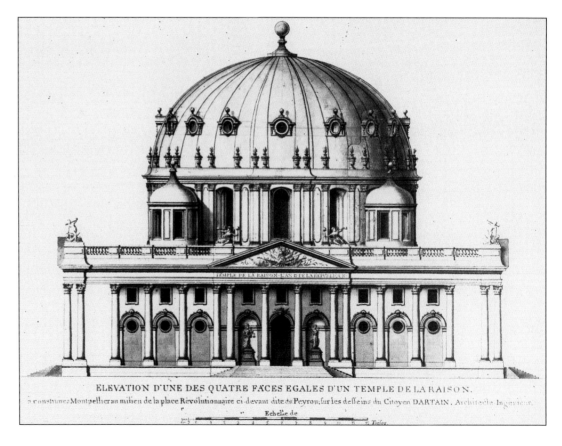

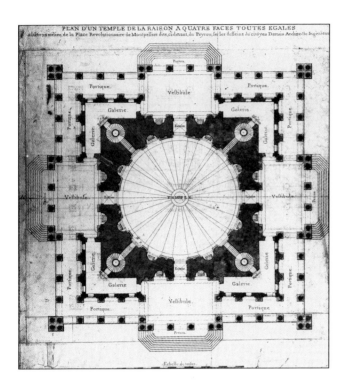

289, 290 Dartain. Project for a Temple of Reason with an external portico.
Left: ground-plan; *below*: cross-section.

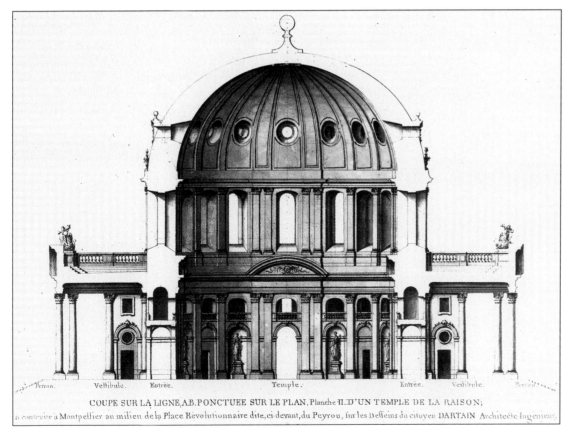

Plan et Elevation d'un Hotel de la Patrie. Par le Citoyen Dartain Architecte-Ingénieur

291 Dartain. Project for an Altar of the Fatherland in Montpellier, ground-plan and elevation.

structure. Both show a square ground floor with a terrace on the roof surrounded by a stone balustrade. In both cases the upper part of the building consists of a drum crowned by a spherical vault. Moreover, in both designs windows encircle the drum, illuminating the interior and lightening the effect, and dormers pierce the dome. In the first plan, however, the columns and pilasters are Doric at the ground level and Ionic around the drum. Also, in addition to the porticoes on all sides there are smaller entrances on the corners leading to vestibules inside. In the second plan the columns and pilasters are Corinthian at both levels, the vault is supported by twin pillars, and the drum is flanked by four lanterns enclosing staircases leading to the tribunes. There is also an external portico encircling the whole temple. Nevertheless, both plans share features common to most *temples décadaires* of the period: revolutionary inscriptions, statues of Liberty and Equality, and above all the circular auditorium where citizens would merge into a single entity.

Dartain's labels reflect some of the conflicting strains in the ideology of Year II. He mixes the terminology of the Cult of Reason of late 1793 with the Robespierrist terminology of the spring of 1794: on one elevation TEMPLE OF REASON appears on the entablature of one of the entrances, but the whole sheet is labeled TEMPLE OF THE SUPREME BEING. Two other designs by Dartain survive, one for a column standing by itself, the other for an Autel de la Patrie, with "autel" spelled phonetically as "hôtel" (Figure 291). This Altar of the Fatherland may have been intended for the centre of the former Place du Peyrou, at the end of which the temple was to be erected. It was to consist of an octagonal base raised up several degrees supporting a column, probably topped with a statue of Liberty, but the top of the design is missing. The ornate rococo base contrasts with the severity of the column. When compared with the plans of Verly in Lille, or those of Durand and Thibault for the Contest of Year II, these plans show that there was no single revolutionary style, although there were common objectives.

In Montereau near Paris another obscure architect-engineer by the name of Belu designed a Temple à l'Etre Suprême suitable for a public square in a small town in the country (Figures 292–5). The project bears a stamp revealing that it reached the Committee of Public Safety on 29 Thermidor an II, that is on 16 August 1794.[100] Although the design is on a much smaller scale and is more crudely drawn, it shares many of the features of more grandiose designs by accomplished architects. The building was to be rectangular in shape with very plain walls: only small panels bearing inscriptions and a heavy cornice were to relieve the severe surfaces. There were to be entrances at both ends, and on the sides too if it

Elevation vue de face

Elévation vue de Côté

292 Belu. Project for a Temple to the Supreme Being, front elevation.

293 Belu. Project for a Temple to the Supreme Being, side elevation.

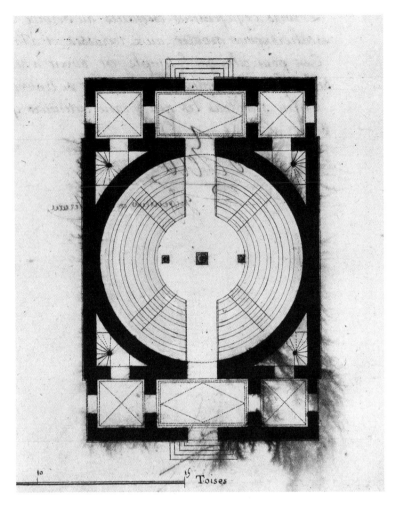

294 Belu. Project for a Temple to the Supreme Being, ground-plan.

295 Belu. Project for a Temple to the Supreme Being, cross-section.

were built on a larger scale, to emphasize that the temple was accessible to all citizens. Inside there were to be small antechambers leading to a circular amphitheatre similar to those we have seen in plans by Durand, Lahure, Dartain, and others. In the centre was to be a large figure of Justice holding in one hand an oak branch, a symbol of immortality, and in the other scales. Justice was to be flanked by figures of Liberty and Equality, "since there could be no justice without these traits." These figures accompanying Justice appear on the ground-plan but not in the cross-section.

Around the circular amphitheatre were to be four low-reliefs representing the four stages of human life. In between were to be busts of great men set into niches in the wall. The cupola was to be divided into twenty-four parts, twelve of which were to be glass to illuminate the interior. Low down on each of the opaque sections were to be painted emblems analogous to the various fêtes, thirty-six in all, so that the whole republican year was to be symbolized. As we have seen, Durand and Thibault expressed the same idea with a ring of thirty-six antique altars in the larger of their designs for *temples décadaires*. Higher up on the vault Belu proposed depictions of the various attributes of Nature so that all eyes would be lifted upward. On the outside the dome was no longer to be crowned with a tower or a spire but with a tricolour banner and a Liberty Bonnet atop a pike. Around the bottom of the pike was to be a great ring marking the time or season. Also, no longer would a "meaningless bell" call citizens to congregate; instead a crier with a megaphone would announce at fixed hours the object of the gathering.

Even Lyon, which rebelled against local extremists and the central government in the summer of 1793, produced some projects worth noting. In fact, during the siege by the armed forces of the Convention, the sculptor Joseph Chinard, who had done the statue of Liberty atop the hillock on the Plaine des Brotteaux for the Festival of Federation in the area back in 1790, completed a low-relief that gave the city hall a new appearance (Figure 296).[101] When the municipality decided to replace the statue of Louis xiv on the fronton of the main doorway, Chinard offered to do a group composed of colossal statues of Liberty and Equality at no cost, provided the municipality furnished the materials and scaffolding. The municipality agreed, and Chinard did a model that was put on display at the headquarters of the representatives on mission, Claude Basire, Joseph Rovère, and Louis Legendre. This model survives in the Musée des Beaux-Arts of the city. The design was approved before the break with the Convention, and Chinard continued to work on it during the siege. A medallion was struck to mark the inauguration in August 1793.[102] The new fronton survived until 1810. It can be seen in an engraving in an

296 Chinard. Low-relief for the city hall in Lyon.

247

297 Gay. View of the Mountain in the Church of Saint-Jean in Lyon.

almanac depicting the arrival of Napoleon as First Consul on 9 Nivôse an x, that is 30 December 1801, in which the city hall appears in the background illuminated for the occasion.[103]

The description of the fronton in the *Bulletin du Département du Rhône-et-Loire*, published by the Lyonnais during the siege, reveals how a journalist "read" the iconography. It also shows that he did not consider resistance to the Montagnards in Paris anti-republican:

> A fasces of rods, emblem of all the citizens of the Republic, represents the tight union that creates their power and must terrify the tyrants allied against them. Liberty plants a pike in the middle of the fasces; it is capped by a bonnet; Liberty fixes her attention on it while with her right hand she holds a civic crown for those who know how to earn it. On the other side Equality, her immortal companion, in an unpretentious but nevertheless imposing posture, arranges all Frenchmen under the same level before the law, to signify that they are all equal under it; it is the law that is represented by the tablets that form the background and on which it is proposed to engrave the Declaration of the Rights of Man and the Citizen and the laws of the Republic as indicated by the titles over the two figures.[104]

Not everyone interpreted Chinard's work so sympathetically. Some revolutionaries accused him of ridiculing Liberty by placing the civic crown in such a position that she seemed to be crowning her backside. They claimed too that they could find disguised fleurs-de-lis in the simulacrum of a funerary monument he had sculpted. They contended also that the lions with which he had crowned the Barrière Saint-Clair were too passive. Their tails were curled around their feet, which was interpreted as an insult to the bravery of the Lyonnais. In addition, they criticized the figures of Renown and Victory that he had done for the Pont Saint-Clair, contending that Renown faced Switzerland, as though she were inviting the *émigrés* to return. Moreover, they claimed that Chinard had supported the rebels in the revolt against local radicals and the central government. As a result of these charges he was incarcerated as a counter-revolutionary in October 1793, following the "liberation" of the city. The sculptor protested his innocence, pointing out that the model of the fronton had been displayed ahead of time at the headquarters of the envoys of the Convention and reminding his accusers of his patriotic works throughout the Revolution. He eventually won the support of the deputy Boisset, who wanted him to assist with the Temple to Truth and Philosophy in Montpellier.[105] He was acquitted in February and continued to sculpt figures for revolutionary festivals until the end of the decade.

Some of the architecture erected for these festivals in what was now called la Commune-Affranchie, "the Liberated Municipality," was among the most spectacular in France, promoted by the representatives on mission from the Convention. Following the pattern we have seen in other cities, in November 1793 the church of Saint-Jean was converted into a Temple of Reason under the direction of the painter Philippe-Auguste Hennequin.[106] As a contemporary sketch shows, a huge Mountain was created stretching from the crossing to the rear of the apse (Figure 297). In the transept on either side were tiered benches, creating a sort of amphitheatre. At the base of the Mountain was a half-globe on which stood a huge figure of Liberty sculpted by Blandin, a pupil of Chinard. On the peak was a little temple, perhaps dedicated to Reason.[107] This decor seems to have been enriched later: at the time of the Festival of the Supreme Being there was a giant figure in the choir representing the French People in the guise of Hercules crushing a hydra with a hundred heads, flanked by smaller figures of Liberty and Equality. The large figure was by Chinard, the smaller ones by Blandin.[108]

Another immense Mountain was erected on the Plaine des Brotteaux, rechristened Champ de l'Egalité, on which a huge figure of Equality was placed to serve as the focal point of the Festival of Equality on 10 March 1794.[109] A description of this festival, in the form of a letter to a deputy in the Convention, exulted in the fact that Equality had become the "idolized divinity" of the city that had once persecuted its champions.[110] On 25 March 1793 the municipal council decreed that the statue of Equality be done in marble by Chinard "since free men ought to consecrate to the symbols of regeneration the precious materials that slaves defiled by using them for monuments that only depicted despotism and slavery." The council said that it would have called for the statue to be done in bronze, but at that moment all the bronze available was needed for the struggle against the allies of tyrants.[111]

Again for the Festival of the Supreme Being impressive structures were erected, designed by Chinard and Hennequin. This time the main focus was on the former Place Bellecour, renamed Place de l'Egalité, where a statue of Louis XIV had once stood (Figure 298). In the centre of the square a huge amphitheatre had been constructed with a wide stairway in front. On either side of this stairway were pedestals supporting colossal statues,

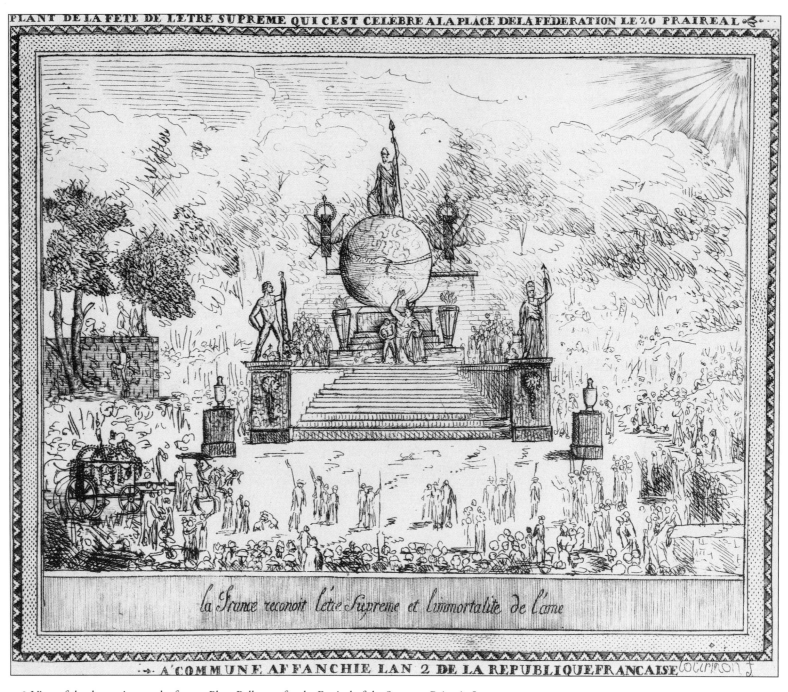

298 View of the decoration on the former Place Bellecour for the Festival of the Supreme Being in Lyon.

299 Granet. Decoration of the present-day Cour Mirabeau in Aix-en-Provence, prepared for acceptance of the republican constitution.

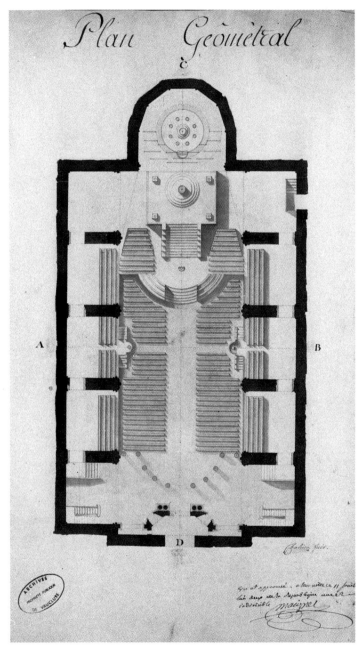

300 Chabrier. Project to convert the Eglise des Prêcheurs in Marseille into a Temple of Reason, ground-plan.

one representing Hercules trampling down the hydra of Federalism, the other representing Wisdom, both by Chinard. In the centre of this structure were two funerary monuments, one honouring the defenders of the Fatherland, the other honouring Chalier. On the summit was a globe with a group of figures personifying Atheism accompanied by Ambition, Discord, and Egotism. After a speech by the deputy Jean-Baptiste Dupuy, these figures were set on fire. As they disappeared, a figure of Wisdom emerged, "who alone ought to reign over the world."[112] In a contemporary engraving, marred by curious errors in spelling, this figure seems to resemble Minerva.[113] Young girls threw flowers towards heaven. The procession then marched across the Rhône to the Mountain, where musicians took their place on the summit and a citizen made another speech about the Supreme Being.

One could multiply examples of similar efforts to put a new ideological stamp on various cities, but a few others must suffice. In Aix-en-Provence the Cours Mirabeau continued to provide a site for rituals such as the celebration of the defeat of Federalism and the acceptance of the new republican constitution on 29 September 1793.[114] A watercolour by François-Marius Granet in the Musée Granet in Aix depicts the avenue decorated for festival (Figure 299). The watercolour shows a gateway formed by Ionic columns, framing in succession the Altar of the Fatherland, a statue of Liberty by Barthélémy-François Chardigny, and finally a symbolic Mountain with a Liberty Tree on the summit. In the Festival of the Supreme Being the procession again followed this axis from a Liberty Tree on the circle to the altar in the centre and finally to the statue of Liberty, with rituals at each of these focal points.[115] This statue of Liberty endured until 1804.[116]

As in many other cities, the cathedral Saint-Saveur in Aix was turned into a revolutionary temple that formed another meeting-place for revolutionary ceremonies. Also, like La Rochelle, Aix was the site of an effort to carry out publicly the Convention's decree calling for metrification of time. The municipal council approved a proposal by a citizen named Fregier to mount a large sundial, showing both the old and new times, on the walls of a house on the former Place des Prêcheurs. After an engineer reported that the idea was feasible, the sundial was put in place. Like the new nomenclature and the monuments, the novel sundial was a public expression of the idea of a new order superseding an old one. The municipality congratulated the citizen who had conceived the idea, the owner of the house for allowing his wall to be used, and itself for being one of the first to carry out the will of the Convention.[117]

As in Aix, there was an ambitious project in Marseille to convert a

301 Chabrier. Project to convert the Eglise des Prêcheurs in Marseille into a Temple of Reason, longitudinal section.

church, the ancient Eglise des Prêcheurs, into a Temple of Reason, a project prompted by the representative on mission, Etienne-Christophe Maignet. The inauguration of the temple took place at the climax of the Festival of Fraternity on 20 March 1794. "In these premises the worship of Philosophy will replace that of Imbecility," declared Maignet.[118] The transformation of the old church was still far from complete. The architect Chabrier made a series of plans stretching from the summer of 1794 into the following year. All these plans were variations on the same scheme: construction of benches across the nave and along the side aisles, an altar accompanied by a statue of Liberty at the end of the nave, and a temple in the form of a tholos encircling an obelisk in the apse (Figures 300, 301).[119] This temple was to be raised up on a platform or a symbolic Mountain. In one longitudinal section one can glimpse the space allotted along the walls to the huge friezes designed by Jacques Réattu. These friezes were among the most ambitious projects of the Revolution. There were to be

ten in all, illustrating allegorically the attainment of Liberty and Equality. The one entitled Liberty and Equality Chasing the Privileged Castes from Their Territory is typical of the whole series (Figure 302).[120]

As French armies drove the enemy back and spilled over the pre-1789 borders, plans to transform space accompanied them. Charles de Wailly has left us a plan to convert a former Jesuit church in Brussels into a hall for a Jacobin club (Figures 303, 304).[121] The plan is very revealing. It shows an interior turned into an amphitheatre, the favourite shape for popular gatherings where citizens were to unite. Overhead at the front the Spirit of France lifts a curtain to reveal a Temple of Liberty and Equality. In this case Equality is depicted holding the Scales of Justice rather than the usual carpenter's level. The podium is flanked by fasces, while over it are tablets inscribed with the Rights of Man. On either side the front wall is decorated with revolutionary inscriptions and symbols. The ceiling was to be decorated with the signs of the zodiac, each associated by means of inscrip-

302 Réattu. Frieze showing "Liberty and Equality Chasing the Privileged Castes from Their Territory."

tions to epochal events in the history of the French Revolution and the liberation of the Belgians. The design is signed by the club executive, which ordered that it be executed as shown.

In other cities, too, ambitious projects were in progress. In Amiens the architect Jacques-Pierre-Jean Rousseau proposed to turn the huge cathedral into a kind of cultural centre, anticipating in some ways the idea of Palaces of Culture in the twentieth century in the Soviet Union, and to convert the adjacent archbishop's palace into a library and art museum.[122] In Arras during the early summer of 1794 the sculptor César-Auguste Lapage was working on a colossal statue of Liberty commissioned by the representative on mission, Joseph Lebon, for a public square.[123] This statue was finished by the following December, when it was put in place on the Place de la Fédération (Grand-Place).[124] Likewise, in Nancy the sculptor Jérome Marlet was busy on a similar statue commissioned by the representatives on mission in the region, Marc-Antoine Baudot and Jean-Baptiste Lacoste, to be placed in the former cathedral recently converted into a revolutionary temple.[125]

There were also plans for monuments associated with private resi-

dences. For example, Lequeu designed a monument for the country home of Marie-Riche Prony in Asnières, evidently to be placed up against a wall, judging by the ground-plan (Figure 305).[126] This was probably done after Lequeu joined the Bureau du cadastre or Land Survey in 1793 under the direction of Prony.[127] The proposed monument was to take the form of an obelisk terminating in a fasces enclosing axes and a pike capped with a Liberty Bonnet, encircled with burning hearts to convey the idea of ardent patriotism. On the upper right of the design is an explanatory note, one of Lequeu's trademarks, describing the bonnet crowning the monument and giving his interpretation of the tricolour: "The Liberty Bonnet will be surrounded by a crown, one half of which will be composed of little sheafs of ears of corn, the other of an olive branch intertwined with laurels. The national colours are: blue, the emblem of the guardian heavens; white, the emblem of innocence; and red, the colour of ardour."

These initiatives in or for the departments were extremely uneven; consequently, they did not satisfy completely the objective of imposing a new ideological stamp on the whole country. The government's plans for urban renewal and public buildings therefore embraced all France. The

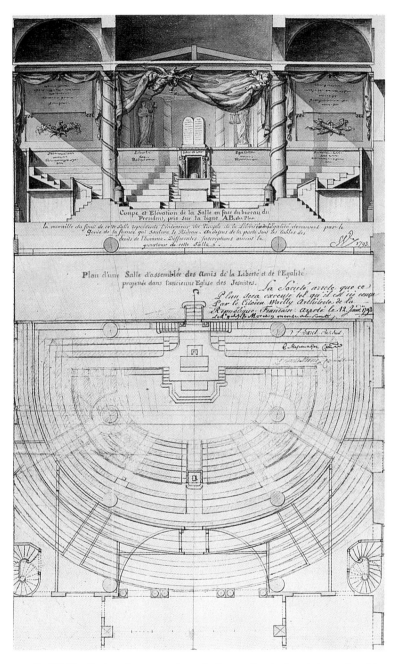

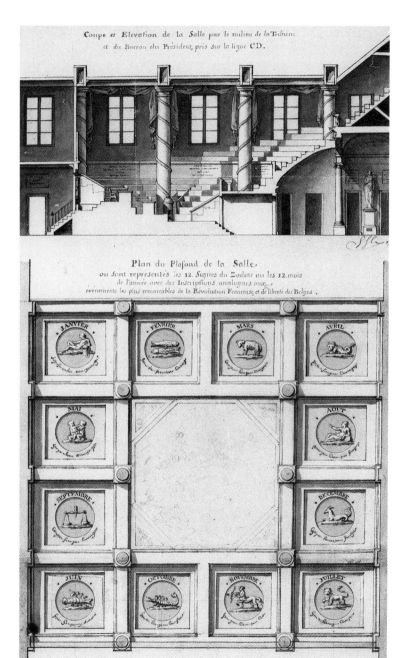

303 De Wailly. Project for conversion of a former Jesuit church into a Jacobin club, cross-section and ground-plan.

304 De Wailly. Project for conversion of a former Jesuit church into a Jacobin club, longitudinal section and ceiling.

305 Lequeu. Project for a revolutionary monument in the country, elevation and ground-plan.

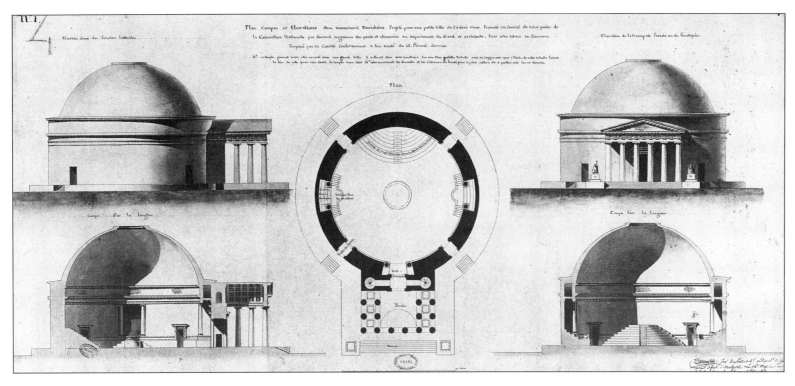

306 C.-E. Durand. Project for a *temple décadaire* for a small city, elevations, sections, and ground-plan.

decree of the Committee of Public Safety of 28 June 1794, calling on artists to submit plans for making the capital healthier and more beautiful, also appealed for similar plans for all other communes throughout the Republic. "For this purpose the artists of all departments are invited to send plans already completed to the Commission of Public Works within four *décades*," stated the fifth clause of the decree. This was emphasized in an appeal to artists published a week later by the Commission of Public Works.[128] At the same time the great Contest of Year II called not only for monuments and temples for Paris but also for *temples décadaires*, revolutionary theatres, primary assembly halls, administrative buildings, fountains, baths, and lavatories for other cities. For instance, we have the design by C.-E. Durand for a *temple décadaire* suitable for a small city (Figure 306).[129] And we must not forget that Goulet proposed a Temple of the Laws not just for the capital but in all departmental centres as well.[130]

Moreover, the Contest of Year II appealed to architects to design new farm buildings that would have changed the rural landscape and demon-strated the concern of the regime for the peasantry. "Watch Equality applaud the sight of the farm rejuvenated, showing off a useful luxury, a modest beauty, and revenged at last for the arrogant slate roofs of the châteaux," declared a pamphlet published by the Commission of Public Instruction to supplement the decree of the Committee of Public Safety.[131] Part of this "revenge" was to be that the very stones of demol-ished castles were to be used in the construction of the new buildings. The pamphlet also emphasized that the buildings were not only to make peasants healthier and more comfortable but were to help in turning them into citizens. This was to be done both by having special rooms honouring the elderly who had worked conscientiously all their lives and by short inscriptions on the walls. The Declaration of Rights was to be displayed in the most conspicuous spot. There the family would gather on the tenth day, led by the father, who would preside over a "fraternal tribunal" that would appraise deeds of domestic virtue and patriotic devotion.

Nine artists submitted eleven proposals for rural buildings in

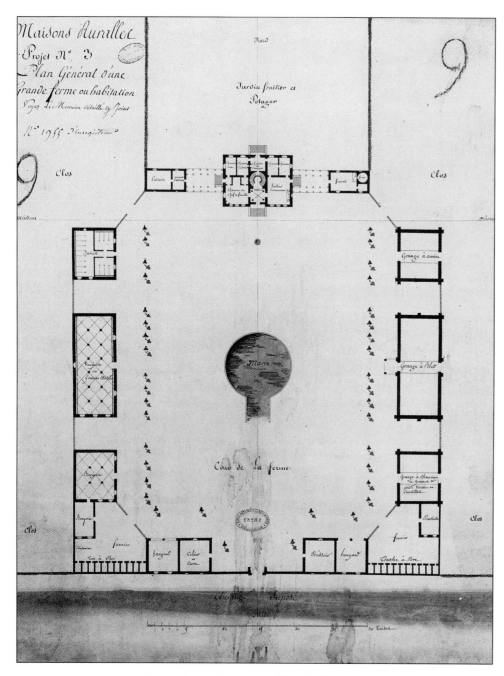

307 Benoît. Project for improved farm buildings, ground-plan.

response to the government appeal. Only parts of two proposals are known to have survived, both identified recently in the Ecole des Beaux-Arts. Only a ground-plan survives out of six drawings submitted by an artist named Benoît for three rural dwellings of different sizes (Figure 307).[132] Likewise, only a ground- plan survives out of a plan, section, and elevation that another artist named Perreau submitted for a "ferme, ditte Républicaine" (Figure 308).[133] Both surviving plans show a number of buildings organized around a courtyard, but that of Perreau is more interesting because the notes down the right-hand side reveal how carefully he tried to meet the objectives of the government. The large residence at the entrance to the complex is divided into special rooms for the farmer's office, for his bedroom, for young children, for his daughters, for his sons, for the elderly, and for the sick. Around the courtyard are facilities for baking, processing milk, pressing grapes, housing livestock, storage, equipment, and the laundry. There are four basins for storing water. The main focal point is the "cherished Liberty Tree."

All these plans were coming to fruition in July 1794, just as the *gouvernement révolutionnaire* was entering a critical period. After ten months of trying to stabilize the country, manage the economy, wage a war against a coalition of foreign powers, and deal with challenges from the left and right, the members of the Committee of Public Safety were becoming divided. Divisions were engendered by the specialized tasks which members were assigned within it, ideological differences, personal grudges, and sheer fatigue. Also, the Committee of Public Safety was superior to but had never completely subordinated the other major committee, the Committee of General Security, which was seething over several encroachments on its police powers. Meanwhile, the members of the Convention, who had repeatedly re-elected the same men to the Committee of Public Safety, were becoming afraid that the Terror might strike against them, as it had struck Danton and other deputies. By this time the success of the republican army in suppressing counter-revolution and pushing back the foreign powers seemed to have made dictatorial and terroristic government unnecessary. Moreover, the sansculottes in the sections of Paris, who the previous September had demanded "that terror be made the order of the day," had become disillusioned as the revolutionary machine struck down their leaders, suppressed their clubs, and enforced wage controls.

Although all members of the Committee of Public Safety bore responsibility for measures taken by the revolutionary government, fear and resentment focused on the Robespierrists – Robespierre himself, the young Saint-Just, and the crippled Couthon – because they had been the chief

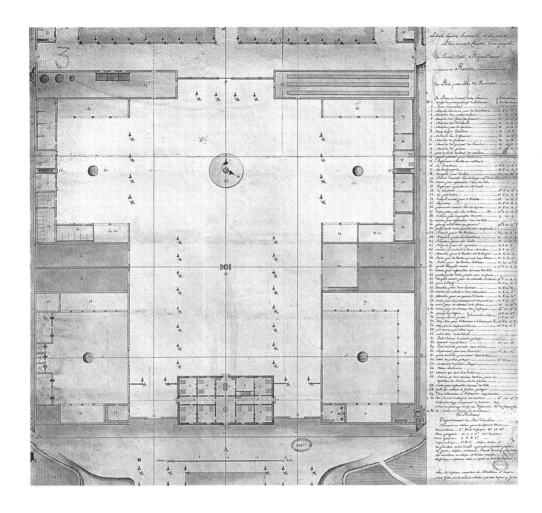

308 Perreau. Project for improved farm buildings, ground-plan.

theoreticians of the Terror and were the authors of some of the most dreaded police legislation. Above all Robespierre, advocate of the Republic of Virtue and pontiff of the Cult of the Supreme Being, seemed a threat to deputies whose records were tainted with extremism and corruption. On 9 Thermidor an II, that is 27 July 1794, the Convention indicted Robespierre. When he and his associates took refuge in the city hall and tried to arouse the sections to support them, they failed to muster sufficient support. On 10 Thermidor they were executed. This dramatic turn of events profoundly affected the outcome of the plans for central Paris, the Contest of Year II, and other projects for monuments and public buildings: politics had given birth to them; politics would decide their fate. ▲

Monument decreed for Bedouin by Jean de Bry. (Figure 310)

VIII
DERADICALIZATION AND MILITARIZATION

THE FULL SIGNIFICANCE OF THE DOWNFALL of Robespierre and his colleagues was not immediately evident. At first it seemed that what had happened was a repetition of what had occurred earlier as the Revolution moved forward: once again it appeared that patriots had excised a group that had conspired against the Revolution. The conspirators were denounced as monsters on whom all the blame for any abuses could be heaped. A contemporary engraving showed the People, once again in the guise of Hercules, lopping off the heads of a three-headed hydra, the three heads representing the triumvirate of Robespierre, Saint-Just, and Couthon.[1] Extremists believed that, with the Robespierrists out of the way, the Revolution could continue on its course; consequently the Terror was not immediately disavowed. In September 1794 pro-Jacobin deputies managed to persuade the Convention to decree that Marat, the advocate of mass executions, be translated to the Pantheon.[2]

But to the surprise of the extremists, 9 Thermidor opened the way for a swelling reaction that fundamentally altered the course of the Revolution. Soon the machinery of the revolutionary dictatorship of Year II was dismantled, many suspects were released from prison, and in November 1794 the Jacobin Club was closed. During the following winter the *jeunesse dorée* or "gilded youth," young reactionaries from the upper classes, attacked the busts of Marat that decorated many theatres. They also attacked the monument to his honour on the Place du Carrousel. Since such acts threatened to provoke a revival of the popular movement in the sections, the government was finally forced to act. On 8 February 1795 Mathieu, spokesman of the Committee of General Security,

reported that the radical Babeuf had been arrested, two popular clubs had been closed, and busts of Marat had been banned from public places. The Convention seized this moment to decree that Marat be de-Pantheonized.[3] This was done on 21 February: after only five months in the shrine for heroes, Marat's body was moved to the cemetery of St Etienne-du-Mont.[4]

As the reaction intensified, caricatures proliferated lampooning Jacobins, anti-terrorist plays appeared in the theatre, moderate songs such as "Le Reveil du Peuple" became popular, and fashions became more extravagant. During the peak of the Terror the simple dress of the sans-culottes, the common people whose men wore trousers rather than aristocratic breeches, had been symbolic of democratic ideals. Now more showy attire became permissible. In Clairville's play *Arlequin perruquier*, the wigmaker rejoices with his mistress Columbine that fashion has come back again:

> Since the ninth of Thermidor
> Brought joyous liberty,
> The golden things appear once more –
> Our jewels and finery.[5]

Some of the plans of Year II died soon after Thermidor, while the fate of others was not decided until the reaction was more developed. One of the first victims was the Committee for Embellishment, the body charged with implementing Hubert's plan for the area between the Place du Carrousel and the entrance to the Champs-Elysées. The minute-book shows that the committee survived the overthrow of the Robespierrists by just over one week.[6] It broke up following the resignation of Hubert, the arrest of David, and the dismissal of Granet and Fourcroy, the other deputies on the committee. Subsequently a government report dated 13 November 1794 argued that the planning the committee had done before Thermidor had been the result of a tyrannical regime that had frequently acted without approval of the Convention.[7] The report recommended that all work not ordered by a specific decree of the Convention should be halted. It called for new proposals, to be judged in a contest, for completion of the Louvre and embellishment of the National Garden, the Place de la Révolution, and the Champs-Elysées.

Next to come under attack were monuments that were too closely associated with the Montagnards. The *jeunesse dorée* not only attacked busts of Marat and the monument to his memory on Place du Carrousel but also assaulted the statue of the People crushing Federalism on the esplanade of the Invalides.[8] These monuments were eventually removed. Also the symbolic Mountains on the Champ de Mars, on similar festival grounds

Aux Malheureuses & Innocentes Victimes Immolées à Lyon après le Siége de leur Patrie

Monument élevé aux Broteaux en 1795 et abattu en 1796.

309 View of the Monument erected in Lyon to victims of the siege.

in other cities, and in churches that had been converted into revolutionary temples were denounced as reminders of the ascendancy of the Montagnards and the terror they inaugurated. On 20 February 1795 the Convention ordered the demolition of the Mountain on the Champ de Mars along with all others throughout the Republic.[9] In Lille, for example, the Mountain constructed with great care and expense in the former church of Saint-Laurent had to be dismantled after only six or seven months.[10]

Also in Lille, the bold plans by Verly for a new city centre came to

naught. His five designs had been submitted to the municipal council on 29 Thermidor an II – 16 August 1794 – just three weeks after the purge of Robespierre and his colleagues.[11] The municipal records do not reveal what happened to them after that: perhaps the fact that they had been inspired by a proposal by David, who barely escaped with his life after Thermidor, decided their fate. In Lyon the Mountain erected on the Plaine des Brotteaux, featuring a giant figure of Equality, had to be levelled following the decree of the Convention banning such symbols. A monument

262

to the victims of the repression of the rebellion in the city against local extremists and the government of Paris in 1793 took its place temporarily (Figure 309).[12] In Montpellier the ambitious project, promoted by the deputy Boisset, for a grandiose Temple to Philosophy on the former Place du Peyrou was halted. On 15 Floréal an III – 4 May 1795 – the deputy on mission in the region, Jean-Baptiste Girod-Pouzoul, ordered that the square be restored to its original state using funds collected for the temple.[13] On 19 Thermidor – 6 August – the municipal council ordered that the name Place de la Révolution be terminated and the old name restored.[14]

The signs of reaction were evident even in small centres. The little town of Bedouin had been burned down and many of its citizens executed on the orders of the representative on mission during the Terror, Etienne-Christophe Maignet, following the cutting down of a Liberty Tree and incidents in which decrees of the Convention had been dragged in the mud.[15] After Thermidor the town was rehabilitated by the Convention. On 15 Floréal an III – 4 May 1795 – the new representative on mission, Jean de Bry, ordered a monument erected on the very spot where sixty inhabitants had been massacred.[16] The monument consisted of an Altar of the Fatherland in the form of a pedestal supporting a shaft surmounted by a funerary urn (Figure 310).[17] An inscription on the pedestal announced the motif:

> AFTER A YEAR OF TEARS ON THESE FRIGHTFUL RUINS
> THE LAW BRINGS BACK JUSTICE.
> CONSOLE YOURSELVES UNFORTUNATE ONES
> FOR THE SCANDAL OF CRIME FORETELLS ITS PUNISHMENT

This simple monument, minus the urn, still stands today.

Most important of all, the Thermidorian reaction profoundly affected the outcome of the contest of Year II. As we saw earlier, the projects were pouring in just as the revolutionary government was entering its final crisis. In fact thirty sculptors and architects submitted their projects on 9 and 10 Thermidor, 27 and 28 July 1794.[18] The jury was not elected until 10–12 December by which time the reaction was well advanced.[19] Not only had the political climate shifted by the time the jury was chosen, but some of the twenty-seven jurors and thirteen substitutes had been imprisoned during the Terror – among them, Ledoux and Quatremère de Quincy. Other artists had proved moderate during the radical phase of the Revolution – Etienne-Louis Boullée, Jacques-Charles Bonnard, Antoine-François Peyre, and François Soufflot le Romain. Also, the radical politicians who had sat on the jury established to judge student works the previous year were now gone. Furthermore, it was while the

310 Monument decreed for Bedouin by Jean de Bry.

jury was beginning its deliberations that the Convention banned symbolic Mountains.

The deliberations of the jury stretched through the winter into the early summer of 1795. Artists complained of the delays and worried about whether the judging would be fair.[20] Only on 9 June did the secretary of the jury, Léon Dufourny, complete the report.[21] It was then relayed to the Committee of Public Instruction. Finally, on 31 August Louis Portiez read the definitive version of the report to the Convention, which then passed a decree confirming the jury's decisions.[22] Between the time of the election of the jury and the confirmation of its decisions the rightward drift of the Revolution continued. In February 1795 the government negotiated an armistice with the counter-revolutionaries in the Vendée and decreed separation of church and state. The last popular insurrections in April and May succeeded only in intensifying the determination of the legislators to prevent such uprisings in future. The army was given permission to enter the capital if it was necessary to suppress disturbances. Finally, just nine days before the Convention sanctioned the prize-list, it approved a conservative constitution featuring a five-man Executive Directory, a bicameral legislature, and electoral regulations intended to concentrate power in the hands of the well-to-do.

In its report the jury expressed disapproval of the specifications laid down by the government for many projects. It thought that they were impractical, badly conceived, or restricted artistic freedom. The jury was especially scathing in its comments on David's proposal for the colossal statue of the People, with inscriptions on various parts of his body, to stand on the promontory of the Ile de la Cité atop a huge pile of broken statuary from Notre Dame:

> After several members had brought out all the disparities which it [the program] contains, the gigantic puerility of most of the accessories, the incongruities of its pedestal, and above all the disadvantage that can result in general from dictating to artists conditions and specifications more likely to shackle the imagination than to guide its course: the jury decided that, in view of the vices in this program, it would take into account when judging this contest the difficulties and obstacles that may have impeded the genius of artists.[23]

The jury also denounced the program for the statue of Liberty to be erected on the Place de la Révolution. It agreed that the idea of showing Liberty rising up on the pedestal of the former equestrian statue of Louis XV was appealing symbolically, but charged that it was impractical in view of the paltry dimensions and half-ruined state of the pedestal, which made it completely unsuitable for a grand new work of art. It found such specifications "bizarre and extraordinary." As for the program for a statue of Nature Regenerated to be situated on the site of the Bastille, the jury found it "obscure and unintelligible." Once again it decided that in making its judgment it would take into account the faults of the program, in this case the fact that abstract and metaphysical entities were not suited to be rendered in sculpture.[24] The jury also contended that the requirement that the statue of Rousseau destined for the Champs-Elysées should show him as the author of both *Emile* and the *Social Contract* was impossible to realize. The jury felt that Jean-Guillaume Moitte had shown Rousseau well as an educator, but recommended another contest for a statue depicting him as an apostle of liberty, to be placed in the Pantheon.[25]

The jury also criticized the programs and the resulting designs for architecture. It argued that a column honouring those who had died for the Republic was ill suited to the Pantheon. It thought too that the monument to the citizens who had lost their lives on 10 August would be better situated on the very site of the battle, the Place du Carrousel, rather than the Place des Victoires. It contended as well that the site designated for covered arenas was far too limited to accommodate national festivals, thus implicitly agreeing with Percier and Fontaine, who chose an area along the Left Bank opposite the Tuileries.[26] In the end the jury decided that only the plan by Durand and Thibault for a Temple to Equality was worthy of execution, but it thought that it too should be erected on a site larger than the Beaujon Garden. In the opinion of the jury none of the projects for national theatres deserved a prize because architects had not risen above the confined auditoriums designed for avaricious capitalists. Neither did the jury think the proposals for fountains and other embellishments worthy of the *cité commune* of all the Republic. It suggested that the architects study classical prototypes. Nor did it think that architects had risen to the challenge of designing rural buildings, which it considered a new genre.[27]

Although some of these judgments were obviously aesthetic, the fact that the jury was elected and made its decisions in a period of reaction makes it probable that some of its decisions were influenced by political considerations. It could scarcely have awarded a prize to Bonnet, whose Temple to Equality was to sit atop a symbolic Mountain. When it criticized the accessories and feasibility of the colossal statue of the People for the promontory of the Ile de la Cité, it may have been influenced by the fact that the statue was to stand atop a sort of Mountain, was to represent popular power, and had been promoted by David, who had been a

311 De Wailly. Plan for completion of the Louvre with a basin in the centre.

member of the revolutionary government of Year II and author of a painting glorifying Marat, who was now discredited. It was probably with relief that the jurors were able to rule out the other figure of the People, again atop a Mountain, crushing Federalism, for the esplanade of the Invalides on the grounds that all representations of Federalism had been outlawed.[28] Also it seems unlikely that they could have approved Brongniart's triumphal arch glorifying sans-culottes and extremists such as Marat and Chalier.

In the end the jury awarded prizes to 108 out of 480 works of painting, sculpture, and architecture. The prizes totaled 442,800 livres, 205,000 for painting, 128,800 for sculpture, and 109,000 for architecture.[28] The top prize was commitment by the government to finance execution of a project. In sculpture only Moitte's Rousseau was judged worthy of such an award, but the bronze version was never completed. In architecture only the temple to Equality was considered deserving of execution. Before the temple was built, however, the two architects were required to do a model on a scale quadruple that of the cross-section, for which they would be paid 7,000 livres as their work progressed. The model was displayed in the Salon of 1799, but soon political conditions ruled out any chance

265

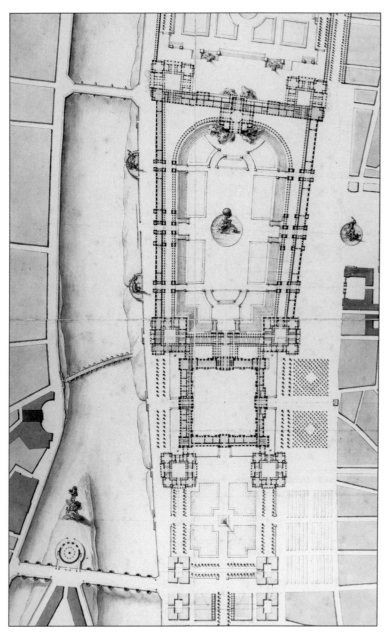

312 De Wailly. Plan for completion of the Louvre with a huge amphitheatre in the centre.

of such a temple being built. Durand and Thibault along with several other major prize-winners were asked to do models of their projects. Lesser prize-winners were given pecuniary awards of various values (see the complete lists in Appendix C).

The awards for sculpture averaged nearly 5,000 livres per prize-winning project, while those in architecture averaged over 2,700. Such awards seemed to constitute an important government stimulant for the arts at a time when private patronage had dwindled. Payments, however, dragged out over years. The jury met again on 18 Vendémiaire an IV – 9 October 1795 – in an effort to speed up payments,[30] but they continued to be delayed by lack of funds and the unstable value of money. Originally payment was to be in *assignats*, which lost much of their value. When payment in metallic currency was substituted, the amount was reduced by a third to a half, depending on the genre of the project.[31] Even then payments were not forthcoming: the first third of the reduced payments was not made until April 1798, almost four years after the contest began.[32] Artists continued to demand payment. It is not clear if and when the other thirds were paid. Moreover, the contest failed utterly to produce the works of propaganda for which the government of Year II had hoped: no major monument and no public building.

Just as the Contest of Year II was being judged, there were some projects that showed continuities with the earlier phases of the Revolution. For example, in the very year when the Constitution of Year III was completed, De Wailly made several designs for the Louvre and the surrounding area (Figures 311–14).[33] His plans included completion of a north wing linking the Louvre to the former Tuileries Palace, a huge outdoor amphitheatre between the wings, a colonnade encircling the inside of the Cour Carrée, expanded facilities for the government, and large squares to the east and west of the complex. The designs show features reminiscent of the radical phase of the Revolution, such as monuments featuring Hercules atop Mountains. In fact, on one design the demigod appears four or five times. On the same design a note reveals that the legislature was to sit on the outline of a Mountain. "The palace is set within the mountain of which our representations form the summit," explains de Wailly; "The red dotted line indicates the base of the mountain." In their bold restructuring of the political centre of Paris these designs remind us of the scope of de Wailly's planning on the eve of the Revolution.

In the four years of the Directory one can trace other continuities. The ideas of an amphitheatre on the Champ de Mars[34] and of a column on the Place de la Bastille surfaced again.[35] The Pantheon continued to be the subject of further planning because of the inadequacy of the walls

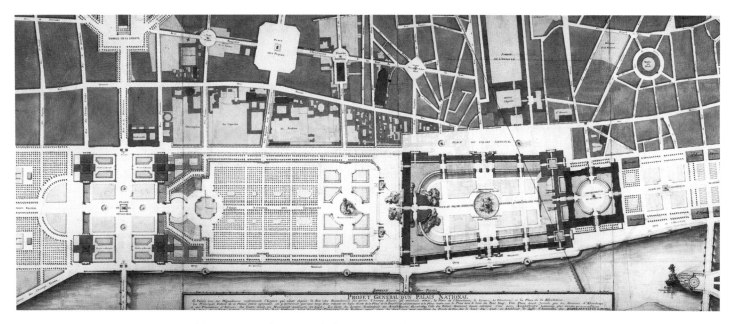

313 De Wailly. Plan for completion of the Louvre with two amphitheatres, ground-plan.

314 De Wailly. View of the Cour Carrée of the Louvre encircled with a colonnade and an amphitheatre.

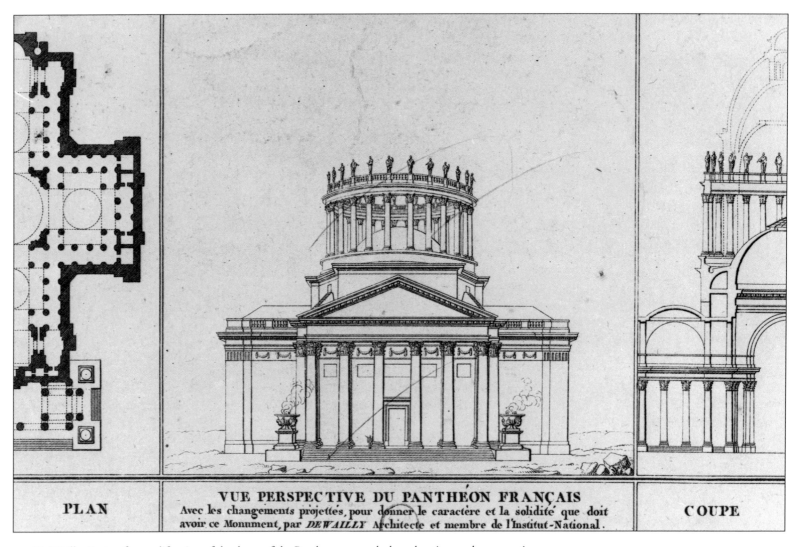

PLAN

VUE PERSPECTIVE DU PANTHÉON FRANÇAIS
Avec les changements projettés, pour donner le caractère et la solidité que doit
avoir ce Monument, par *DEWAILLY* Architecte et membre de l'Institut-National.

COUPE

315 De Wailly. Project for modification of the dome of the Pantheon, ground-plan, elevation, and cross-section.

to support the huge dome. De Wailly proposed a solution that would have replaced the traditional dome with a sort of tholos, which would have enabled the onlooker to glimpse the statues on all sides (Figure 315).[36] For the interior Brongniart envisaged an obelisk under the dome reminiscent of the column proposed for the same site in Year II (Figure 316).[37] There were reports in the press of statues of Liberty being placed in front of *temples décadaires* or the city halls of provincial towns and cities.[38] There were also reports of monuments being erected in other places in honour of soldiers who had died for the Republic.[39] And there were appeals to architects for proposals to turn churches into more suitable enclosures for republican ceremonies on the tenth day.[40] One such plan survives that shows how the chief engineer in Orléans proposed to create a circular amphitheatre

316 Brongniart. Project for reinforcing the dome of the Pantheon, cross-section.

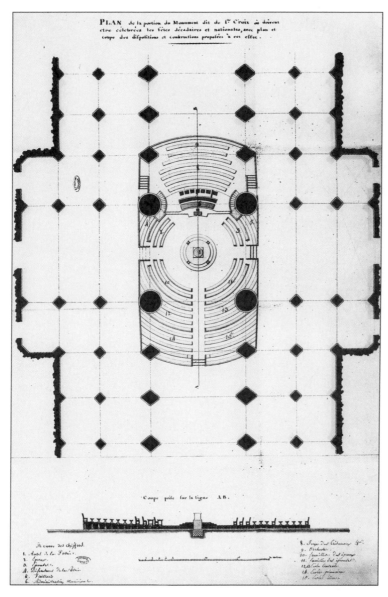

PLAN de la portion du Monument dit de St Croix ù doivent
être célebrées les fêtes décadaires et nationales, avec plan et
coupe des dispositions et constructions proposées à cet effet.

Coupe prise sur la ligne A B.

317 Project to convert the cathedral in Orléans into a *temple décadaire*,
ground-plan and cross-section.

around the Altar of the Fatherland in the crossing of the former cathedral of the Ste-Croix, in complete contradiction to the cruciform shape
of the building (Figure 317). In this case the government decided that the
plan would involve too much expense.[41]

Despite such continuities after Thermidor, there were major shifts
in emphasis revealed in two conspicuous trends: deradicalization and militarization. Deradicalization is very evident in a project by the civil engineer
in Versailles, Eustache Saint-Far, presented to the local authorities at the
beginning of Year III – September 1794 (Figures 318–21).[42] His plan concerned the Jeu de Paume, where the representatives of the Third Estate
had defied the king on 20 June 1789 and had sworn not to disband until
they had completed a constitution. There had been various proposals to
use the building for some worthy purpose that would mark its historic
significance – for instance, to use it for public instruction – but nothing
had come of them. Saint-Far revived the idea of turning the building into
a shrine to the Revolution. The interior was to be restored to its condi-
tion at the time of the famous oath. The scene as it had been depicted
by David was to be engraved in bronze on the wall. A dignified portico
was to be constructed providing access to the building from a new square
at the end of a large avenue. The plan is a minor example of late eighteenth-century urbanism, but what is remarkable is the lack of revolutionary
fervour in the project. The female figure in the portico is very demure,
and although she holds a Liberty Bonnet, there are no pikes or Levels of
Equality. The new street is labelled "rue de la Stabilité."

A few months before its end, on 28 Floréal an III – 17 May 1795 –
the Convention approved a project that typified the repudiation of the
radicalism of Year II. It approved a decree, proposed by the deputy Delecloy
in the name of the Committee of General Security, to efface every trace
of the meeting-place of the Jacobins, from which so much had spread that
was now considered evil, and to replace it with a marketplace. Delecloy
declared: "Hercules had only to clean out the Augean stables; by a metamorphosis more worthy of you, representatives of the people, you will
convert this contaminated den, fouled from the start by monsters whose
name recalls the idea of the disastrous inquisition that they inaugurated,
… into a genuinely popular monument, consecrated to abundance and
public happiness."[43] Originally called the Marché Public du Neuf
Thermidor, it became known as the Marché Saint-Honoré. Not surpris-
ingly, the elevation attached to the decree showed not a trace of the symbols
of Year II (Figure 322).[44] At its very last session on 4 Brumaire an IV –
26 October 1795 – with the conservative constitution completed, the
Convention made a final symbolic gesture. The great square, once ded-

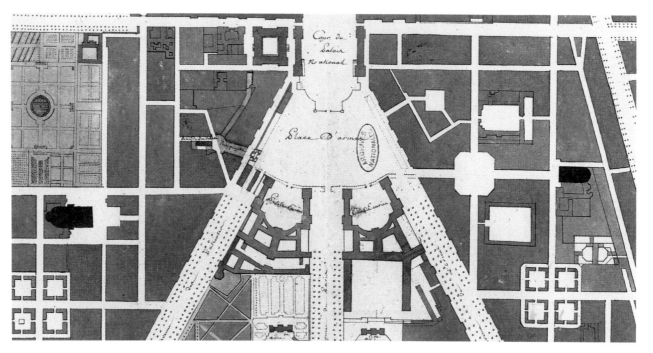

318 Saint-Far. Plan of the area around the projected Temple of the Oath.

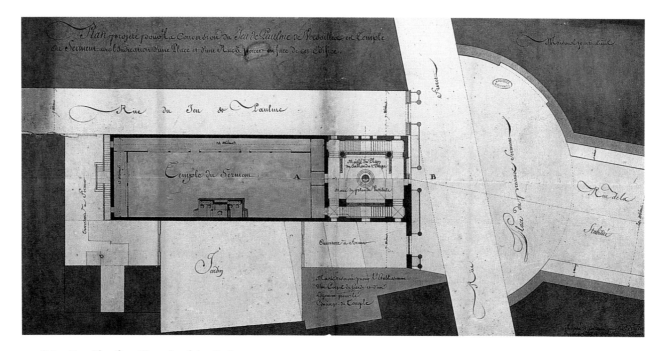

319 Saint-Far. Plan for a Temple of the Oath.

320 Saint-Far. Project for a Temple of the Oath, elevation of the façade.

321 Saint-Far. Project for a Temple of the Oath, cross-section.

Marché Public du Neuf thermidor, décrété dans L'Emplacement des Ci-devant Jacobins
Commission des Revenus Nationaux le 13 Prairial suivant par le Comité de sûreté générale et Certifié véritable par les Représentants du Peuple

322 Anonymous. Project for a Public Market of 9 Thermidor decreed for the site of the former Jacobin Club, elevation.

icated to Louis XV and later renamed Place de la Révolution, was rechristened Place de la Concorde. Harmony was to replace insurrection.[45]

Despite the dramatic shift in political climate, the Directory did not abandon the idea of using architecture for ideological goals, or of showing concern for the citizenry in promoting urban improvement. In the early spring of Year IV – 1796 – the Executive Directory asked the minister of the interior to launch a contest for an Altar of the Fatherland, presumably for the Champ de Mars, a monument for the Place de la Concorde, and another for the Place des Victoires.[46] In Floréal an IV – April 1796 – the minister, Pierre Benezech, then issued an appeal in the press and on posters to artists calling for proposals for these and other sites, reiterating the idea that monuments should convey a message. "May they rise up simple and majestic, may they present great examples, may they provide great lessons, may their image evoke great memories," he declared.[47] It was significant that he did not consider resurrecting any of the nearly three hundred designs for monuments submitted to the great Contest of Year II.

Not many of the projects submitted to the Contest of Year IV have survived or can be identified with certainty, but those that can be associated with it are very different from those conceived two years earlier. In his *Recueil d'architecture nouvelle*, which appeared nine years later under the Empire, Athanase Détournelle published several projects related to the contest. One is a triumphal arch dedicated to Concord by the editor himself and his colleague Armand-Charles Caraffe (Figure 323).[48] Along the top is a bold inscription:

> YEAR V OF THE REPUBLIC THE GOVERNMENT GAVE THE FORMER
> LOUIS XV SQUARE THE NAME OF CONCORD AND PROPOSED TO
> ARTISTS TO DESIGN PROJECTS FOR ITS EMBELLISHMENT WHILE
> NOTING THAT THE MONUMENTS SHOULD REPRESENT
> ALLEGORIES OF UNION AND CONCORD.
> THE ARTS RESPONDED WITH NUMEROUS PROJECTS

This inscription creates two false impressions. As we have seen, it was in Year IV that the former Place Louis XV, later the Place de la Révolution, was rechristened Place de la Concorde. Also, the contest to redecorate it and other squares was launched in the same year, although it was not judged until the following year.

What is significant, however, is the contrast between this arch and the ones proposed for the earlier contest. On the left-hand side male figures embrace a giant fasces, while on the right female figures play a similar role. Underfoot these figures trample down other figures representing Discord.

323 Détournelle and Caraffe. Project for a triumphal arch dedicated to Concord, elevation and ground-plan.

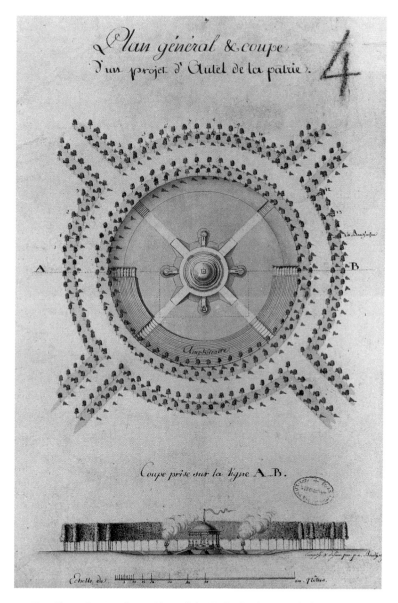

324 Boudhors. Project for an Altar of the Fatherland, ground-plan and cross-section.

Among its other uses, the fasces was traditionally associated with the goddess Concord. There are no likenesses of revolutionary martyrs or of the People in the guise of Hercules. One of the female figures on the right holds a Level of Equality, but it is barely visible.

Another design connected to the contest, a plan and cross-section in the Ecole des Beaux-Arts of an Altar of the Fatherland by Alexandre Boudhors, shows the same moderation (Figure 324).[49] The altar consists of a sort of temple set in the centre of an amphitheatre, which is in turn encircled by rows of trees. The focal point inside the temple is a conventional statue of Liberty. The elevation of this temple shown at the bottom of the design is very small, but there seem to be no other allegorical figures or symbols.

Particularly revealing are the projects for the huge square successively dedicated to Louis XV, then to the Revolution, and subsequently to Concord. One of the prizes in this category went to Jean-Jacques Tardieu, winner of the *grand prix* for architecture in 1788. This artist envisaged for the centre of the square a sort of temple, possibly dedicated to the goddess Concord, raised upon an enormous sub-basement pierced with arches that would have opened up long vistas along the two axes that intersected at right angles on the site, one running from the Tuileries to the Champs-Elysées, the other from the Madeleine across the bridge to the Left Bank (Figures 325, 326).[50] This temple, which evoked to some extent the Mausoleum of Halicarnassus, was to be surmounted by a column crowned by a large winged figure. Encompassing the square and framing the monument was to be an impressive colonnade, probably inspired by that of St Peter's in Rome, which turned the square into an amphitheatre. Two immense fountains on the terraces of the Tuileries, both with columns in the centre, completed the plan. Although the project manifested the megalomania of the period and provided space in which festivals could have been staged, it was conspicuously lacking in revolutionary imagery.

A design for a monument on the same site by Carlo Lucca Pozzi, now in the Carnavalet Museum, is even more revealing (Figure 327).[51] All three allegorical figures express moderation. Minerva on the left has a shield in her hand, but she uses it in a way that traditionally signified her support for the figure above, in this case the ancient goddess Concord. Minerva has thrown her helmet back and is armed only with a book labelled WISDOM. Hercules on the right has laid down the club that earlier in the Revolution had represented the power of the people. At the apex of the pyramid formed by the three figures is Concord herself, shown tying together the bands of the fasces, signifying the unity of the nation.

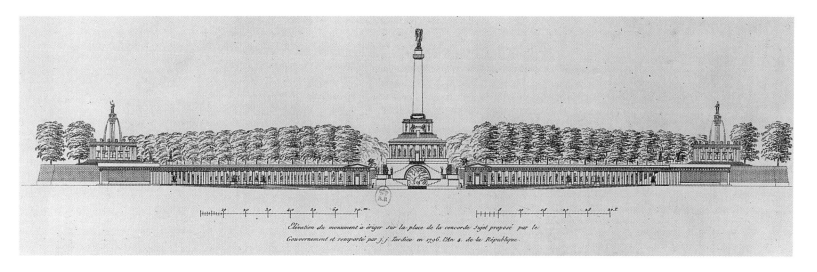

Élevation du monument à ériger sur la place de la concorde sujet proposé par le
Gouvernement et remporté par j.j. Tardieu en 1796. l'An 4. de la République.

325, 326 Tardieu. Project for the Place de la Concorde.
Above: elevation; *left*: ground-plan.

327 Pozzi. Design for a monument for the Place de la Concorde.

Coupe du Monument a la Concorde par Détournelle et Caraffe An V.

Il est vu du Jardin des Tuileries. en tems de guerre la Statue serait ainsi Voilée deux portes grillées laissent voir au peuple le piedestal de Louis XV.
Mutilé et brisé, allégorie qui signifie que la Concorde s'élève triomphante, sur les ruines Causées par la division des Citoyens. les deux piedestaux, sont ceux qui donnent
entrée, aux Champs elysées, dans le profil général on ajoutoit a la suite, des promenoirs et des Salles de rafraichissemens. le Monument a de Hauteur 60. pieds et 18. a sa base.

Normand S.

328 Détournelle and Caraffe. Project for a monument to Concorde, elevation seen from the Tuileries Garden.

Significantly, the usual axe in the centre of the fasces is absent. Another monument to Concord by the team of Détournelle and Caraffe for the same square shows her seated, embracing two children who represent fraternity, within a little shrine, the base of which houses the pedestal of the former statue of Louis XV, an idea carried over from the Contest of Year II (Figures 328, 329).[52] The idea of the new transcending the debris of the old was a familiar one, but now it was a figure representing harmony rather than revolution that replaced the king.

Another project for the Contest of Year IV was a monument for the former Place Royale, then known as the Place de l'Indivisibilité and now called the Place des Vosges, where a statue of Louis XIII had once stood. The entry by Détournelle and Caraffe was even less revolutionary than their triumphal arch or their monument honouring Concord (Figure 330).[53] To represent Indivisibility they did not use the fasces, not even one without an axe. Instead they used Hymen, the personification of marriage in classical Greece. He had become well known mainly because his name was used frequently as a refrain in poems celebrating marriage. The design features a young couple in classical attire linked by a yoke and a garland

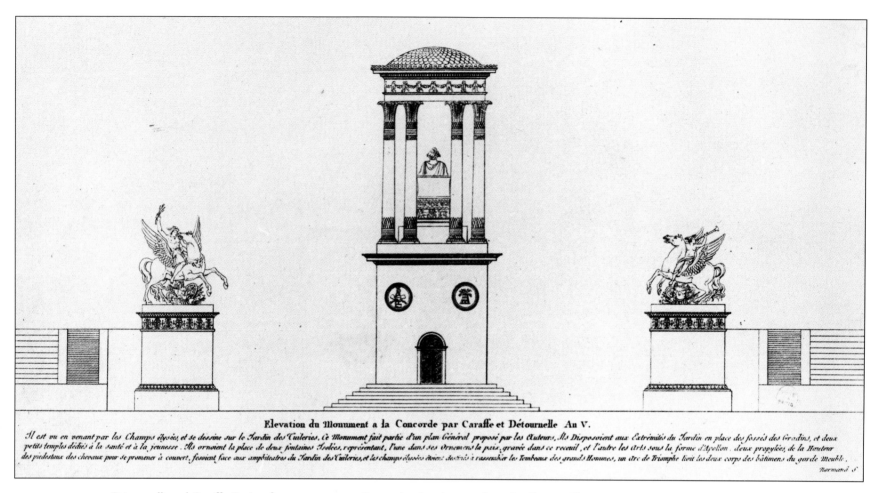

Elevation du Monument a la Concorde par Caraffe et Détournelle An V.

Il est vu en venant par les Champs élysées, et se dessine sur le Jardin des Tuileries. Ce Monument fait partie d'un plan Général proposé par les Auteurs, Ils Disposoient aux Extrémités du Jardin en place des fossés des Gradins, et deux petits temples dédiés à la santé et à la jeunesse. Ils ornoient la place de deux fontaines Isolées, représentant, l'une dans ses Ornemens la paix, gravée dans ce recueil, et l'autre les arts sous la forme d'Apollon. deux propylées, de la Hauteur des piedestaux des chevaux pour se promener à couvert, fessoient face aux amphitestros du Jardin des Tuileries, et les champs élysées étoient destinés à rassembler les Tombeaux des grands Hommes, un Arc de Triomphe lioit les deux corps des bâtimens du garde Meuble.

Normand S.

329 Détournelle and Caraffe. Project for a monument to Concorde, elevation seen from the Champs-Elysées.

of flowers. The young man has his arm around the young woman, again suggesting union. This idea is reinforced by the figures of Cupid and Hymen, their arms resting fraternally on each other's shoulders. The pedestal is decorated with torches, one of the traditional emblems of Hymen. Again the radical symbols of the Terror have disappeared.

While some of the projects for Year IV display moderation, others show the nascent militarism that was to become increasingly conspicuous in the last half of the decade. One would expect a militaristic character to projects for the Place des Victoires, but one would not expect all rev-

olutionary figures and symbols to have vanished, as they have in the case of Jean-Baptiste Faivre's prize-winning project for this site (Figure 331).[54] Atop the pedestal stands a huge figure of Athena with what appear to be shields in a testudo formation on her chest, a cover of overlapping shields resembling a tortoise shell, used by attacking forces in classical antiquity. She carries two shields decorated with medallions, one with an image showing Hercules with a submissive lion, the other a female figure with a tamed two-headed eagle. These medallions seem to celebrate the defeat of England and Austria. Lower down a winged figure of Victory or Renown

330 Détournelle and Caraffe. Project for a monument to Hymen, Allegory of Indivisibility, for the Place des Vosges, elevation and ground-plan.

331 Faivre. Project for a monument for the Place des Victoires, elevation.

crowns two warriors. On each face of the pedestal the word VICTORY! is superimposed over Italy and other parts of Europe. Above, another inscription asserts that French youth know how to establish such victory. Underneath a third inscription conveys the dedication of the monument:

TO THE SHADES

OF THE CONQUERORS

YEAR IV

The Contest of Year IV, like its predecessor two years earlier, failed to fulfil the expectations aroused by Benezech's rhetoric. Information about the contest is scanty, but we know that numerous works were exhibited in the Salle du Laocoon in the Palais du Museum, as the Louvre was then called, in the middle of 1796.[55] This time the works were judged by the Class of Literature and the Fine Arts of the Institut National, the umbrella organization that included all the recently restored academies, rather than by a jury elected by the competitors themselves. The prizes were distributed at a general meeting of the institute on 5 Messidor an V – 23 June 1797.[56] Unfortunately the prize list does not indicate the works that won awards, but one can identify them from the minutes of the class.[57]

The architect Jean-Baptiste Faivre won the highest level of encouragement for his design for the Place des Victoires. The architect Etienne-François Levasseur won an encouragement of the second level for his proposal for the Place Vendôme, as did the sculptor Jean-Baptiste Stouf for his proposal for the Place des Victoires. The sculptor Charles-Louis Balzac won an encouragement of the third level for his project for an Altar of the Fatherland, as did the sculptor Robert-Guillaume Dardel for his project for the Place des Victoires, and the architect Lemercier for his project for the same site. As well, the architect Jean-Jacques Tardieu won two encouragements of the third degree for his plans for the Place de la Bastille and the Place de la Concorde. The decline in the scope and seriousness of the contest since the one in Year II is underlined by the fact that the prize-winners, who included some accomplished artists, were presented with books – like schoolboys, as Détournelle pointed out later in an essay on contests.[58]

There were complaints that the government program for the contest was poorly thought out. The sculptor Charles-Louis Corbet wrote to Lagarde, secretary-general of the Executive Directory, that the projects for monuments that he had seen in the Salle du Laocoon were worse than bad.[59] He complained that the guidelines were too vague. He also thought that it would have been better to restrict the competition to artists who

had already demonstrated their ability and to reimburse them for the cost of making models. Moreover, he criticized the composition of the jury, which had been made up of literary people, physicists, geometers, painters, astronomers, actors, chemists, and musicians, along with some sculptors and architects. Corbet thought that each science should be judged by specialists in the field.

Another critic, the writer Pierre Chaussard, complained that the government had no overall plan for the area between the Louvre and the Etoile, including the Champs-Elysées, "this stately avenue which announces to the visitor and the foreigner the city of the sciences and arts, the new Athens."[60] His own suggestions reveal the growing tendency to celebrate French military prowess. He wanted the Pont de Neuilly transformed into a triumphal bridge, all the radiating streets of the Etoile decorated with triumphal arches, and in the centre of the Etoile a vast rock pierced in the middle. On the summit he wanted a huge statue representing French Heroism, standing upright in a chariot drawn by winged horses. He proposed too that the whole route along the Champs-Elysées be decorated with trophies of arms inscribed with the prodigious feats that had brought national glory. Altars to the "unknown virtues" would also punctuate the avenue. The whole route would be known as "Sacred Way".

The militarism we have noted in the project by Faivre and the proposals by Chaussard had begun to emerge at least as early as Year III. It is already conspicuous in the project by Antoine Voinier for a colossal triumphal arch to serve as a gateway to Paris at Neuilly (Figure 332).[61] This project has been included among those for the Contest of Year II because Voinier submitted a plan for an arch at that time.[62] Furthermore, the inscription over the arch reads:

TO THE VICTORIOUS ARMIES THE GRATEFUL FATHERLAND

YEAR II OF THE REPUBLIC

These facts, however, do not prove beyond question that this design is identical to the one done for that contest. The mention of Year II does not prove when it was done because it could have been a later tribute to the decisive victories in that year. There is no mention of the events of 5–6 October which had been specified as the motif of the arch called for by the government in the spring of 1794. The very polished nature of the design suggests that it was not done hurriedly for the contest. We also know that the artist submitted this design to the Committee of Public Instruction on 8 Frimaire an III – 28 November 1794 – when the projects for the contest were still on exhibit in the antechamber of

332 Voinier. Project for a triumphal arch for the entrance to the western end of the Champs-Elysées, elevation.

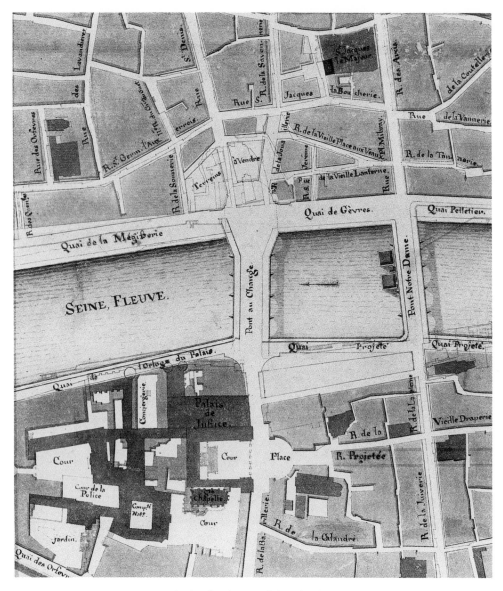

333 Giraud. Plan for the site of the Châtelet.

Convention and the jury had not yet been chosen.[63] Moreover, the design bears figures of Liberty and Equality but none of the other radical emblems or figures of the Terror. Finally, Voinier's pamphlet about the arch was not published until Year III. In any case, whether it was done for the Contest of Year II, was modified for later use, or was a new design, it is pervaded by a militaristic ethos.

In his pamphlet Voinier argued that in addition to monuments celebrating particular French victories there should be one to all of them together, "the fasces of our victories, so to speak." The triumphal arch was therefore to honour all fourteen French armies. The opening was to be sixty-four feet wide, flanked by vast galleries on either side to protect travellers when the weather was bad. Around the arch standards were to be placed that had been captured from the enemy, joined together in pairs by civic crowns honouring the heroes who had captured them. Medallions depicting these heroes were to be placed between the flags. At each end of the principal inscription there were to be Renowns, each holding a French flag in one hand. In the other hand one would hold a statue of Liberty, while the other would hold a statue of Equality. Fourteen crowns and the names of each unit would decorate the façade. On either side of the arch would be low-reliefs representing important battles. Above there were to be stylobates forming a circle decorated with prows of ships, signifying naval victories. These stylobates were to support huge figures of Victory sitting on the spoils captured from the enemy and crowning the warriors of each army. The whole pyramidal structure was to be surmounted by a Temple of Immortality with an obelisk in the centre inscribed with the names of those who had died for the Fatherland. A winged figure, holding a crown of stars signifying Immortality, would crown the edifice.

In Voinier's proposed triumphal arch the figures of Liberty and Equality were still present, but overshadowed by those of Victory and Immortality. Liberty and Equality were again pushed from the centre of the stage in a plan for the site of the Châtelet by Pierre Giraud, architect of the Palace of Justice and of prisons for the Department of the Seine, presented to the minister of the interior on Vendémiaire an V, September 1796 (Figures 333, 334).[64] The proposal was typical of the urbanism of the period in that it combined improvement of the circulation of traffic, embellishment of a section of the city, and creation of saleable property. It involved creating a semicircular square facing the Seine, piercing two wide avenues leading to this square, straightening and widening existing quays, constructing a new quay along the Left Bank, enlarging the entrance from the Pont au Change to the rue de la Barillerie, which led to the Palace of Justice, and forming another *place* in front of the palace. The decor,

334 Giraud. Project for the site of the Châtelet, perspective view.

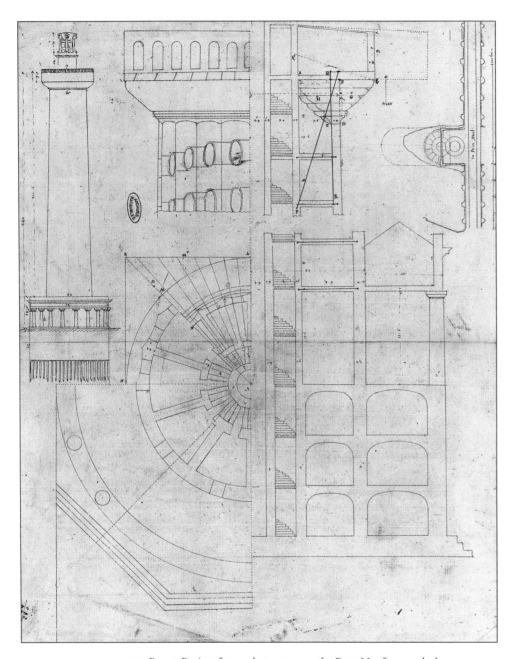

335 Poyet. Project for a column next to the Pont Neuf, ground-plan.

336 Poyet. Project for a column next to the Pont Neuf, engraved elevation.

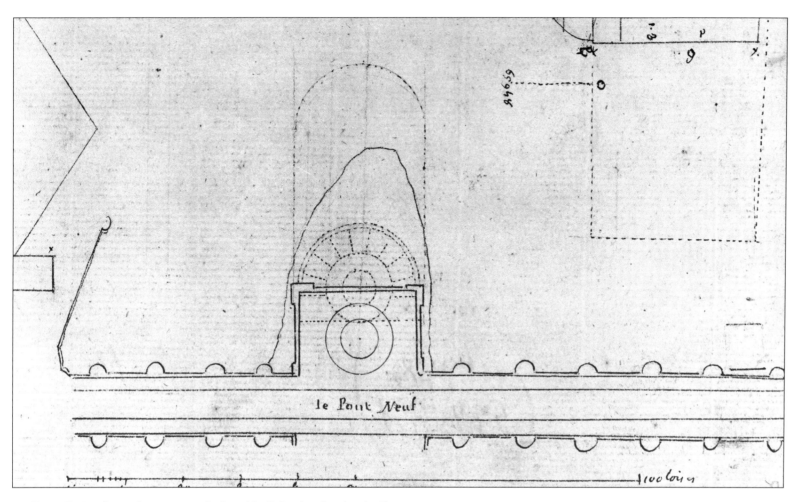

le Pont Neuf

337 Poyet. Project for a column next to the Pont Neuf, sketches showing details.

however, revealed a shift in ideology: Liberty and Equality are still visible on the pavilions around the new square on the riverbank, but Victory is now the central figure.

Another striking example of growing militarization under the Directory was the proposal by Bernard Poyet in Year IV for a giant column for the site where the statue of Henry IV had once stood (Figures 335–7).[65] The base was to be a circular colonnade, forming a Temple of Victory whose columns would bear the names of different armies of the Republic until trophies of their conquests could be placed there. The shaft was to be seventy-eight metres (two hundred forty feet) in height and thirteen and two-thirds metres (forty-two feet) in diameter. It was to be decorated with five hundred shields, each inscribed with the name of an important French victory and paired with a laurel crown. The column was to be surmounted by a tripod whose summit would be ninety metres (two hundred eight feet) above the ground. Its capital would be crowned with statues of four generals who had died on the field of honour. The architect said that this idea came from the victor of Arcole – Bonaparte – who had proposed statues of Hoche, Marceau, Dugommier, and Laharpe.

Poyet emphasized that his column would be higher than all previous columns and would surpass the Tower of London by eighty feet. He contended that his monument, placed on the point of the junction of the two branches of the Seine, would be visible from great distances. On days of public festivals it could be illuminated, making it visible from an even greater distance. Reflected on the river, it would provide a unique and ravishing sight. Inside were to be twin staircases, one ascending and one descending, punctuated with little rooms where visitors could rest and take refreshment. Poyet hoped to finance the project by charging an admission fee, which he called "a civic gift of three francs." Also to bolster his scheme he proposed putting a pump in the base to increase the water supply, and using the summit to make astrological observations. Finally, he stressed that his proposal could be linked to beautification of the whole area. This part of his scheme also had a military character: he suggested mounting trophies along the Pont Neuf on the model of the Capitol in Rome, each dedicated to one of the French armies.

The most ambitious project under the Directory was a scheme designed by Charles de Wailly, in conjunction with a consortium of Belgian real-estate promoters, to develop the land north of the Place Vendôme that had once belonged to the Capuchins (Figures 338–40).[66] There had been many proposals for a new opera house for Paris on various sites – in the area between the Louvre and the Tuileries Palace, in the garden of the Palais Royal, in the area north of the rue Saint-Honoré, and so on. The Belgian consortium offered to construct a huge new opera house on the Capuchin lands in return for the right to develop the rest of the area. De Wailly, who had designed various theatres including the Odeon, designed a huge Théâtre des Arts that was to contain two auditoriums, one for opera accommodating three thousand spectators and another smaller one for rehearsals and training young actors. The two auditoriums were designed to be merged in order to accommodate civic festivals.

De Wailly shared the conviction that architecture should have a clear "caractère" legible to the public. He also shared with Boullée and Ledoux a taste for grandiose projects, but tempered this with a stronger sense of what was possible. Moreover, as he had shown in his plan for the quarter around the Odeon, his proposal for remodelling the Place Louis XV before the Revolution, his bold plan for central Paris in 1789, and his plans for the area around the Louvre in Year III, he desired to link proposals for important public buildings with urban renewal.[67] In this case his plan proposed placing the new theatre in a large oblong square into which eight large streets and four smaller ones would lead. One axis would join the district of Saint-Honoré to the boulevards to the north; another running through the ground level of the theatre would join the quarters to the east and west. Galleries along the fronts of the buildings on the main arter-

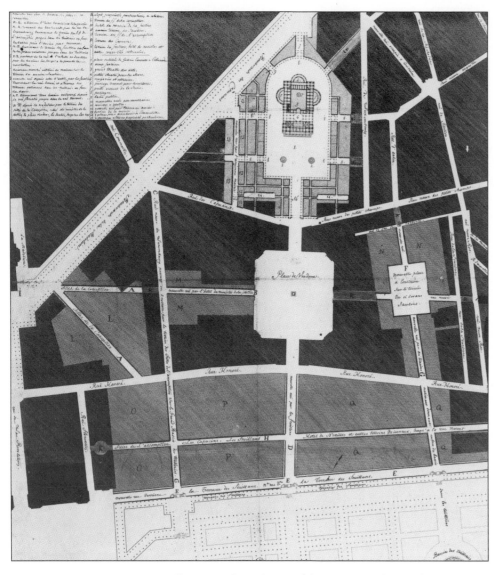

338 De Wailly. Project for a Theatre of the Arts, ground-plan of the site.

339 De Wailly. Project for a Theatre of the Arts, elevation of the triumphal arch at the entrance to the site.

ies and around the square were to protect pedestrians from rain and sun. Nine little temples in honour of great men, reminiscent of the Temple of Immortality in the Festival of Unity and Indivisibility, would decorate the galleries around the square. Rows of trees and allegorical fountains were to complete the decor.

The character conveyed by the overall plan was militaristic. "The principal building and the ancillary structures," reported the *Décade philosophique*, "would everywhere recall the victories of the French."[68] The

street leading northward from the Place Vendôme was to be called the rue des Conquêtes; a huge triumphal arch was to mark the entrance to the new square, and passages were to be named after victorious battles – passage des Alpes, passage du Rhin, passage de la Meuse, passage du Pô, passage du Lodi, and so on. The report on the project by a committee of the Institute praised many of its features but revealed uneasiness about the growing militarism.[69] It criticized the names of the passages and that of the main street leading to the square. And in what proved to be a pre-

289

340 De Wailly. Project for a Theatre of the Arts, view of the theatre and the shrines to great men.

scient remark in view of what happened later, the report observed that the Athenians would not have tolerated a triumphal arch in their city, and the Romans only erected them in honour of emperors.

Festivals and their decor under the Directory show the same growth of a militaristic spirit. Like earlier governments during the Revolution, the Directory tried to use festivals as a means of rallying the people around the institutions and ideals of the day. The evidence in national and local archives shows that this was an uphill battle.[70] Gone was the enthusiasm displayed by the masses at the time of the Festival of Federation in 1790, the Festival of Unity and Indivisibility in 1793, or even the Festival of the

Supreme Being in 1794. Local authorities complained repeatedly about lack of participation. There were attempts to arouse greater interest by introducing sporting events into the ceremonies. The only festivals that seem to have excited considerable enthusiasm were those celebrating victories, displaying the spoils of war, or mourning the deaths of popular generals such as Hoche (Figure 341).[71] The most spectacular festival was the one celebrating the triumphal entry of works of art, rare plants, and exotic animals on 9 and 10 Thermidor an VI – 27 and 28 July 1798 (Figure 342).[72] The booty was paraded through the streets to the Champ de Mars, where an impressive semicircular pavilion had been erected for the occa-

341 View of the funeral ceremony on the Champ de Mars in honour of General Hoche.

342 Festival celebrating the arrival of artistic and scientific objects acquired by the French army.

sion. There was still a statue of Liberty in the centre, but she was no longer the motif of the celebration. Also, the carpenter's level once suspended between the two thermae at the entrance had disappeared.

Despite the overall deradicalization and militarization, some projects show that elements of the radical phase of the Revolution survived until late in the Directory. An important example is the plan for urban renewal that François Cointeraux published in 1798 (Figures 343, 344).[73] Cointeraux said that he had already been working on the plan when he was spurred into finishing it by a contest announced by the minister of

the interior for development of the Champs-Elysées.[74] The plan exemplifies some of the major features of eighteenth-century urbanism: public promenades, more squares, wider streets, sidewalks, and more greenery. There were to be more and bigger hospitals, a much larger botanical garden, and new quays along the Seine. Moreover, he advocated extending certain streets to create powerful axes cutting through the ancient city, preparing for the day when the capital would house two million people. Above all he called for development of the area that had concerned so many planners from the seventeenth century through the Revolution, the area between

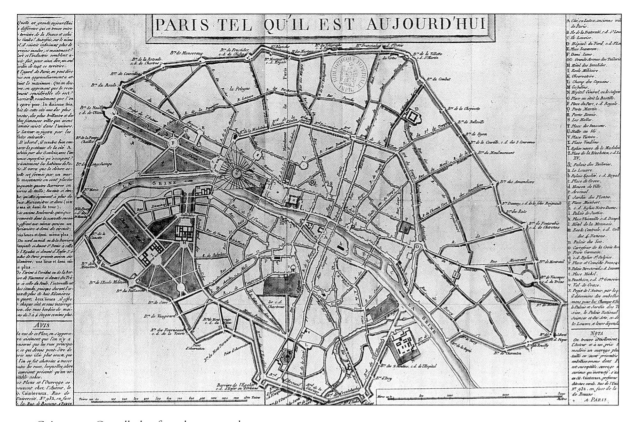

343 Cointeraux. Overall plan for urban renewal.

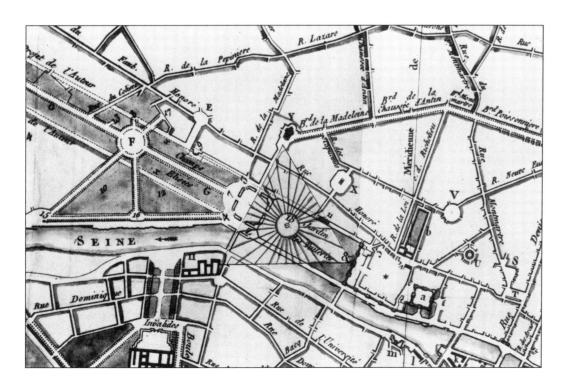

344 Cointeraux. Detail of his plan showing the Metric Centre and the Triangle formed by the Council of Five Hundred, the Council of Elders, and the Executive Directory.

345 Houël. Design for a public monument for one of the main squares in Paris.

the Louvre and the Tuileries, to create the most impressive governmental centre in the world.

Like such earlier planners as Bernard Poyet, Charles Mangin, and Charles de Wailly, Cointeraux called for construction of a northern gallery linking the Louvre to the former Tuileries Palace to match the one along the river. At the same time he proposed clearing away all the houses, shops, alleys, and intersections that cluttered the area between the two palaces to create the most beautiful *place* in the world. In a sense the city would be refounded: "I will say first of all that everything ought to take on a new appearance in a new empire such as that of the French Republic; that Paris above all ought so to speak be founded a second time along with this Republic so that everything will announce to foreigners that the city is worthy of being its capital."[75]

The centre of government was to be at the western end of the Louvre-Tuileries complex. Here Cointeraux applied the mystique of the equilateral triangle that the revolutionaries had exploited so often, pointing out that among all nations this shape had always been regarded as a symbol of perfection.[76] He advocated leaving the Council of Five Hundred where it was in the Bourbon Palace, putting the Council of Elders in the uncompleted church of the Madeleine, and accommodating the Directors in the former Tuileries Palace. When these three buildings were connected by straight lines, an equilateral triangle would result. Appropriately, the two representative assemblies would form the base, while the executive branch would form the apex. The whole would point towards the rising sun. He proposed calling the centre of the triangle the Centre Métrique, which he showed in his plan radiating light. In future all distances in France would be measured from his point, instead of the traditional point of the cathedral Notre-Dame. This shift of the centre of reverence from Notre-Dame to the locus of secular government signified one result of the Revolution.

The three branches of government at the centre of the Republic did not constitute the only trinity in Cointeraux's plan. The former Tuileries Palace, known as the National Palace during the Terror, was to become the Directorial Palace. The three sections of the palace were to retain the names given to them earlier, which represented revolutionary ideals: the central Dome de l'Unité, the northern Pavillon de la Liberté, and the southern Pavillon de l'Egalité. This repeated use of the mystical triangle and trinities represented an ongoing effort to legitimize and sacralize the ideals and institutions of the day. The effort, however, was becoming somewhat strained after so many trinities: the three good kings; the unity of the three Estates; the alliance of Nation, Law, and King; and the three principal martyrs, Lepelletier, Chalier, and Marat had all proved ephemeral. The sanctity of the trinity is diminished further when we find the three Directors who orchestrated the coup of 18 Fructidor an v – Barras, Rewbell, and Revellière-Lépaux – hailed as a "republican Trinity," saviours of the Republic.[77]

The nomenclature of streets and squares proposed or continued by Cointeraux was significant. As we have seen, the sections of the building housing the executive branch of the government were to continue to bear the names of revolutionary ideals. Other names were to signify republican aspirations and concern for the welfare of the population. The Place de la Révolution was to become the Place de la Constitution, and the western entrance to the city from Neuilly was to become the Barrière Constitutionnelle. The Ile Saint-Louis was to be known as the Ile de la Fraternité and the Barrière d'Orléans was to be called the Barrière de l'Egalité. One of the new *cours* on the Champs-Elysées was to become the Cours de la Prosperité, and another the Cours de la Félicité. Other names, however, revealed the impact of the war: the Allée d'Autun was to become the Allée des Orphelins, and the parallel walkway was to become the Allée des Veuves. The entrance to the city on the east from Vincennes was to become the Barrière Triomphale. What is most striking is the disappearance of the word "revolution."

Another project designed at the end of the Directory and the beginning of the Consulate in which some revolutionary content survived was that proposed for one of the principal squares of Paris by Jean-Pierre-Louis-Laurent Houël (Figure 345).[78] The monument was to consist of a globe, representing the earth, a dozen metres high, raised up six metres above the level of the square on sculptured clouds, creating the illusion that it floated in the air as it does in nature.[79] The clouds would seem to be formed out of the vapours rising from a huge basin. The various continents were to be outlined on the globe, providing citizens with a lesson in geography. Atop the globe was to be a figure of Liberty, with wings to suggest that she could fly wherever she wanted to go, as was appropriate for a divinity. She was to be shown releasing a bird from her left hand, and at her feet a flock of birds was to appear escaping through the open door of a cage. At Liberty's side was to be a figure of the Republic in the act of crowning her companion. If this group of figures was judged too complex, he suggested an alternative in which Liberty would be shown on horseback, again accompanied by the Republic. Houël argued that the globe was the ideal symbol to represent equality since it appeared always the same regardless of the side from which it was viewed, an idea he expressed in verse:

Un globe, en tous les temps, n'est égal qu'à lui-même;
C'est de l'égalité le plus parfait emblême;
Nul corps n'a, comme lui, ce titre capital,
Qu'un seul de ses aspects, à tout autre est égal.[80]

Despite the figure of Liberty, her companion the Republic, the symbolism of birds liberated from captivity, and the idea of equality implicit in the globe, this proposal too expressed the militarism of the period. The

chariot on the summit was to be shown making a victorious passage around the world. "One sees by the disposition of this chariot that it comes from Germany, Italy, and Egypt, that it has passed through Holland, and that it continues its victorious course," Houël explained in the pamphlet he published to promote the project. The fruits of conquest would be illustrated by the fact that the horses pulling the chariot were to be the four taken from the church of St Mark in Venice by the French army. On the part of the globe representing Europe the sites of French victories were to be marked with brilliant gold stars. Striking signs would call attention to the most important of these sites. Underneath would be the name of the victorious general in large letters. Bonaparte's name would appear in Italy and at the mouth of the Nile; that of Brune would appear on Holland, and so on. One curious feature of this unusual proposal was that the wheels of the chariot were to form the faces of a clock hidden inside it, with the old hours indicated along with the new metric ones. It is significant that in spite of the idea of equality represented by the globe, the carpenter's level, which had been the principal symbol of equality at the peak of the Revolution, is conspicuously absent.

One could adduce much more evidence of deradicalization and militarization under the Directory, but one government program deserves special attention: that for the development and decoration of the site of the Château Trompette in Bordeaux. We have seen earlier that the Château was that city's Bastille. As in the case of its counterpart in Paris, there had been many proposals to raze it completely, fill in its moats, and use the terrain for some impressive monument, but well into the Directory nothing had been constructed, although demolition had begun. On 21 Fructidor an V – 7 September 1797 – the Directory opened a contest calling for complete suppression of the château and erection of a monument to "these brave armies that have assured the conquest of liberty."[81] Since the government was dissatisfied with the initial results of the contest, it was extended several times, and the nature of the monument was more clearly defined. It was to celebrate Victory and Peace.[82] One competitor pointed out that there was a tension between these two ideals.[83] The contest was finally judged in Year IX. Thirty individuals competed, including some of the best-known architects of the period – Baltard, Clochar, Combes, Détournelle, Durand, Louis, etc – as well as some amateurs.[84] Together the plans provide a rich source of evidence of architectural planning at the end of the Revolution.

A project by Pietro Clochar, of which he submitted two versions, provides a good example of the sort of proposals that were entered in the contest, not only because it was among the prize-winners but also because it is particularly well documented (Figures 346–52).[85] The first version

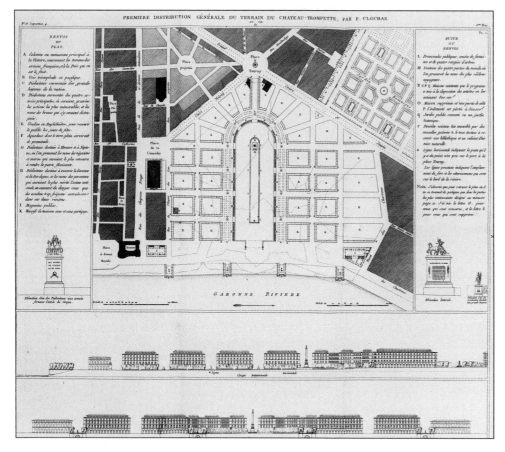

346 Clochar. Project for the site of the Château Trompette, ground-plan and elevations.

347 Clochar. Project for a column to Victory and to Peace, elevation.

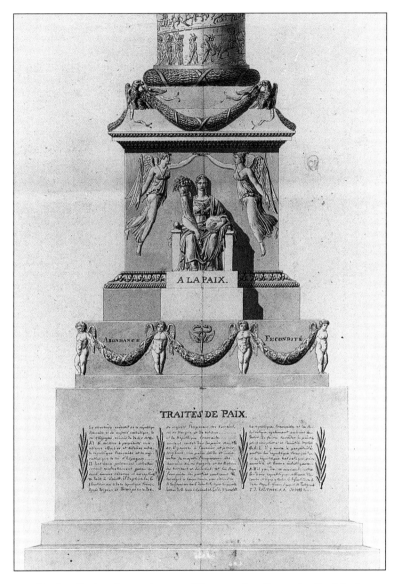

AUX ARMÉES DE TERRE

AUX ARMÉES DE MER

348 Clochar. Project for a column to Victory and to Peace, detail of the base.

349, 350 Clochar. Project for a column to Victory and to Peace.
Above right: detail of the statue honouring the French army;
right: detail of the statue honouring the French navy.

351 Clochar. Project for a column to Victory and to Peace, detail of the shaft.

352 Clochar. Project for a column to Victory and to Peace, detail of the figure of Victory.

shows an amphitheatre for festivals with streets leading into it from all sides.[86] In the centre of the amphitheatre are statues of heroes with their deeds inscribed on the pedestals. On either side of the entrance next to the river are monuments to the four main armies, with their most memorable feats recorded underneath. Along the river are aqueducts embellished with statues, the two in the centre representing the Garonne and the Dordogne, with accounts of rescues on those rivers, and the two on the flanks representing Mercury and Neptune, with the contribution of seafaring merchants related below. Around the amphitheatre are tree-lined promenades punctuated with fountains. The rest of the site is divided into blocks of houses with or without porticoes. Stores are located on either side near the river.

The militaristic character is even clearer in the principal monument, a huge column to be erected at the west end of the amphitheatre towards the Place Tourny. Admittedly the base features *la Paix* being crowned by two Renowns, but she is flanked by male figures on separate pedestals, one representing the land army and the other the navy, both standing amid cannon, rifles, and military standards. To give these figures a historic quality, they were to be made of bronze from captured enemy weapons. On the four corners of the socle were to be eagles holding garlands of laurel branches. The shaft, like that of Trajan's column, shows battle scenes spiralling upward. Finally, the capital is surmounted by a huge bronze figure of Victory crowning the successes of the French armies. Although the monument was supposed to show how the victories of the Republic had assured the survival of liberty, there are no republican or democratic symbols of any sort.

Another well-documented project for the site of the Château Trompette was the one by Louis-Pierre Baltard, who won an indemnity for the work he put into his project (Figures 353, 354).[87] He proposed a long rectangular *place* in the centre of the site stretching up from the banks of the Garonne, with a triumphal arch at the river end and a "Portique à la Paix" at the other end in the centre of a semicircular amphitheatre. On both sides of the central axis there were to be groves containing monuments consecrated to the French armies, seven on each side. The rest of the site was to be divided into rectangular blocks for residential and commercial development. Like most of the other planners, he included facilities useful to the citizenry – a public market, a school of botany, and shopping galleries along the river-front. The Musée d'Aquitaine has a perspective showing how Baltard envisaged the project if it were realized.[88] Baltard submitted an alternative scheme in which the central axis would be occupied by a huge circus or hippodrome for public festivals (Figures

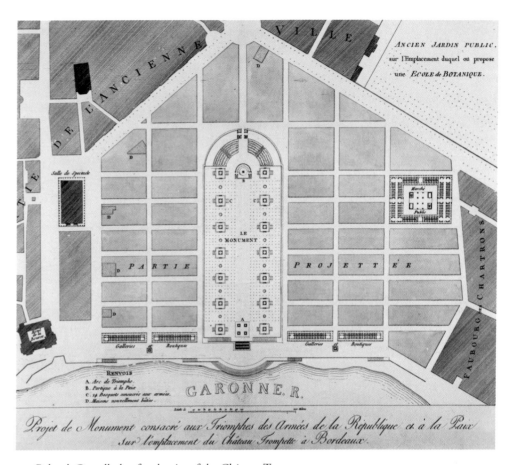

353 Baltard. Overall plan for the site of the Château Trompette.

PROJET DE MONUMENT CONSACRÉ AUX TRIOMPHES DES ARMÉES DE LA R.F. ET A LA PAIX

354 Baltard. View of the site from the Garonne as it would appear if his plan were adopted.

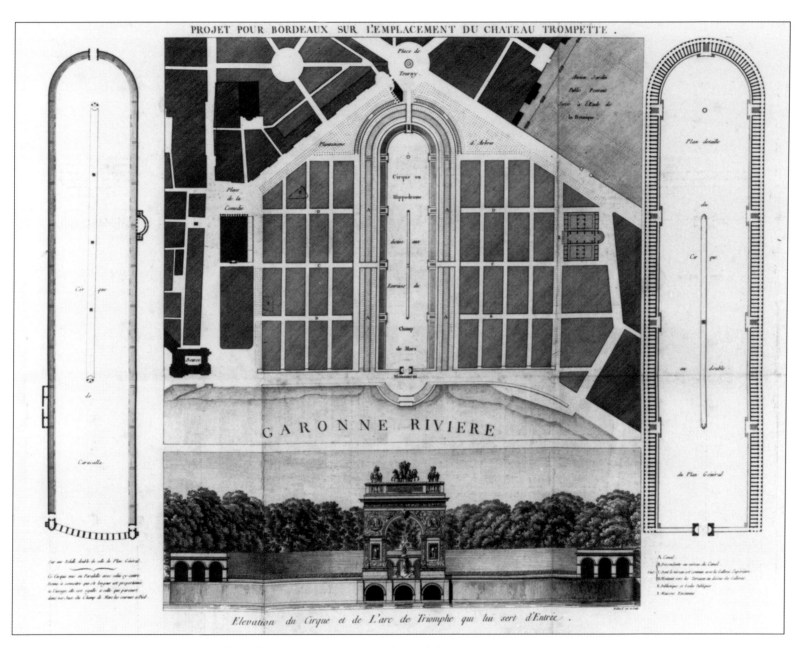

PROJET POUR BORDEAUX SUR L'EMPLACEMENT DU CHATEAU TROMPETTE.

GARONNE RIVIERE

Elevation du Cirque et de L'arc de Triomphe qui lui sert d'Entrée.

355 Baltard. Alternative project for the site of the Château Trompette, ground-plans and elevation.

356 Baltard. Alternative project for the site of the Château Trompette, detail of the triumphal arch.

355, 356).[89] Again a triumphal arch was to serve as the gateway on the riverside.

Another plan for the site by an architect named Jean Ramelet deserves our attention (Figure 357).[90] Repeatedly from the late Old Regime through the Revolution we have encountered examples of the idea of conveying a certain message by imposing a series of names on a piece of urban space. Ramelet's plan shows how this idea had become transformed after seven years of war. His plan involved creating a whole commune on the edge of the old city. It shows several *places publiques*, each devoted to an ideal. There was to be a Place de l'Egalité with a triangular obelisk in the centre dedicated to philosophers, warriors, and republican martyrs. Also there was to be a Place de la Paix, the focal point of streets named after various arts and sciences that flourish during peace. But the main square, a semi-circular one facing the river, was to be the Place des Victoires, ringed with triumphal arches leading to the streets radiating out. The main street was to be called rue des Conquêtes, and the others were to be named after French victories and satellite republics. The plans by other artists reveal the same militaristic tone.

The idea of creating a new commune bearing an ideological stamp also inspired a project by a land surveyor named Aubry.[91] Spurred on by a proposal in the legislature for a monument to the defenders of the Fatherland, he argued that such a tribute should not resemble those raised up to pride and charlatanry. For this reason he called for an entirely pure site where a new city could be created named "La Liberté." Despite its leading role in the Revolution, Paris was not suitable because it had been sullied by despotism and hypocrisy and later by the excesses of the Terror. Aubry proposed an unspoiled site in the centre of the Republic in a wooded National Park. The focal point of the city would be a colossal obelisk with as many faces as there were victorious French armies. The principal streets of the city were all to abut on one of these faces and were each to be named after one of the armies – rue d'Italie, rue du Rhin, and so on. Connecting streets would be named after generals and outstanding soldiers. Despite its name, the city was obviously to glorify French military prowess.

Like the host of projects under the Constituent and Legislative Assemblies, as well as those promoted by the Convention, all these designs were "paper architecture" destined never to be realized in stone. The competition for projects for the site of the Château Trompette was as fruitless as previous ones: the project that won first prize by a slim margin, the submission of Labarre of Paris, was judged impractical for several reasons, especially the fact that it included a circular *place* that would have

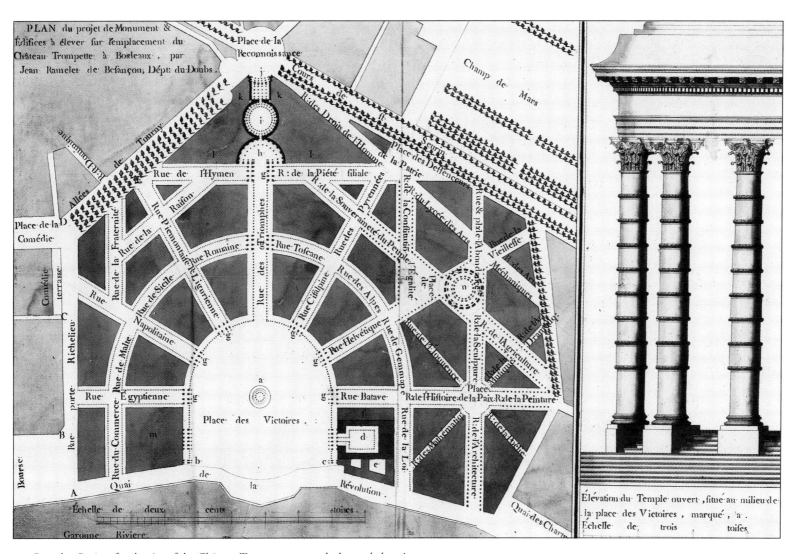

357 Ramelet. Project for the site of the Château Trompette, ground-plan and elevation.

358 Labarre. Project for the site of the Château Trompette, ground-plan.

protruded into a navigable part of the river (Figure 358).[92] Throughout the decade successive regimes were too unstable, money was too scarce, and ideology shifted too rapidly for ambitious urban projects. These plans are, however, historically significant. They reveal a continuation of the urbanism of the eighteenth century, with buildings serving a social purpose, spacious squares, tree-lined avenues, green oases, and improved lines of communication. Moreover, the projects under the Directory, revealing a progressive deradicalization and militarization, were the necessary transition from the projects of the Committee of Public Safety to the Napoleonic era, with its Napoléonvilles, obelisks, columns, triumphal arches, and the avenue de la Grande Armée. ▲

UNITE INDIVISIBILITE
DE LA REPUBLIQUE
FRANCAISE.

approuvé par la
commission des travaux
publics, pour être executé
conformement a l'arreté
du Comité de salut public
en datte du 13 messidor
a Paris le 21 messidor
de l'an 3e de la rep. fran—
Rondelet

359 Delannoy. Project for one of the bases for the horses of Marly, at the entrance to the Champs-Elysées.

IX

THE DREAM AND
THE MEMORY

DESPITE THE FACT THAT THE REVOLUTION inspired hundreds of designs for revolutionary monuments, squares, and public buildings, it produced very few permanent structures, unlike the monarchy of the Old Regime that preceded it or the First Empire that followed it. The monuments that were built were mostly torn down or completed with very different symbols and figures. The Column of Liberty on the esplanade in Montpellier was razed during the Restoration; the similar column in Nantes was later completed with a statue of Louis XVI instead of Liberty; the paired allegorical figures of Liberty and Equality by Chinard on the façade of the city hall in Lyon were replaced with a statue of Henry IV; and the statue of Liberty in front of the city hall in Toulon erected near the end of the Directory was toppled on the orders of the First Consul and then thrown in the Mediterranean near the Grosse Tour,[1] to cite only a few examples.

Only a few monuments survive, their origins largely forgotten, such as the figure of the Republic on the façade of the city hall in Troyes, the column on the Place Blair in Saintes, an Altar of the Fatherland in Thionville, and the strange Monument Sec in Aix-en-Provence. All that remains in Paris of the comprehensive plan by Hubert to redecorate the whole area around the Tuileries Palace are the pedestals supporting the horses from the Château de Marly at the entrance to the Champs-Elysées (Figure 359). In Suresnes, once a village on the outskirts of Paris but now one of its suburbs, the obelisk in honour of the defenders of the Fatherland erected in Brumaire Year II survived for a number of years before being replaced by a cross.[2] Only a crude sketch of the original monument survives in the local archives, signed by a group of citizens in the nineteenth

century to attest to what it had looked like. The fate of many projects of the Revolution is typified by the plinth that now supports a cross in the town of Saint-Lucien in the Eure-et-Loire: on it one can see the inscription A° 1789 LIB I (Anno 1789 Libertas Primo, "1789 Year I of Liberty"), referring to some revolutionary monument now vanished.[3]

The reason for the failure to turn hundreds of projects into permanent structures is clear: the inability of any one of the succession of revolutionary regimes to stabilize itself and endure for any length of time. We speak of *the* French Revolution, using the singular for the sake of convenience. The title Crane Brinton used, *A Decade of Revolution*, is closer to the truth. The decade saw not one sudden transformation of the Old Regime, rather a succession of interrelated but distinct uprisings, purges, coups, and reactions. The Revolution moved from so-called absolute monarchy through constitutional monarchy, moderate republic, Montagnard ascendancy, the revolutionary dictatorship of the Committee of Public Safety, the Thermidorian Reaction, and the shaky Directory to the Consulate, created after the fourth coup in three years. This instability is symptomized by the three Declarations of Rights and four constitutions in ten and one-half years. Since the planning and realization of a monument, square, or public building may take a decade or more, the instability of the Revolution frustrated any ambitious projects.[4] We are left with a paradox: the projects to "immortalize" the Revolution were negated by the very forces they were supposed to counteract.

Despite the failure of the revolutionaries to accomplish their plans, those plans are an important part of the history of the period and the history of art. The architects of the time denied forcefully that construction was the essential act in architecure. Boullée, for example, declared: "What is architecture? Shall I define it like Vitruvius as the art of building? No. There is a gross error in this definition. Vitruvius mistook the result for the cause. One must conceive before executing. Our ancestors only built their huts after having an image of them. It is this generation by the mind, it is this creation that constitutes architecture."[5] Boullée's conviction was shared by his contemporaries: "Architecture is the art of designing [projeter] and of constructing ... according to predetermined principles and proportions," asserted Louis-Pierre Baltard, the first to hold the chair in architecture at the Ecole Polytechnique.[6] Such a definition, making design the essential act of the architect, means that in examining the architectural projects of the period we are dealing with its creative imagination just as much as when we study its music, its painting, or its decorative arts.

Moreover, the ephemeral structures erected for the festivals and the proposals for permanent ones were part of the revolutionary dream: the hope of regenerating France and its citizens. The decorations and enclosures created for revolutionary ceremonies gave the impression that the old cities and towns were actually being transformed. This impression was reinforced by rechristening the old streets, squares, bridges, and quays, and in many cases the cities and towns themselves. The illusion of national renewal was further strengthened by the publicity surrounding proposals for permanent monuments, squares, and public buildings. They were publicized by pamphlets, newspaper reports, and very often by engravings showing what they would be like when completed. Many designs were exhibited at the *salons* in the Louvre.[7] Also, successive governments publicized their projects widely and called on artists throughout the country to compete in designing them. Moreover, the hundreds of proposals submitted in response to the government programs in the spring of Year II were displayed in the Hall of Liberty, the antechamber to the Convention. Likewise, the lesser number of designs submitted in response to the rhetorical appeal of the minister of the interior in Year IV were exhibited in the Louvre.[8]

The impression that the country was actually being permanently transformed helped to sustain revolutionary fervour until it waned or was redirected into military ambition. By analysing this dream we can gain further insight into what the revolutionaries were trying to do. The projects to transform public space cast new light on the extent to which the Revolution was over *status*. Over the last generation revisionists, intent on refuting the Marxist contention that the Revolution was the result of a clash between an ambitious aristocracy and a rising bourgeoisie, have argued that at the top of society in the final decades of the Old Regime there was an elite composed of high nobles and the upper level of the Third Estate.[9] They have emphasized that the juridical line that separated nobles and commoners was less important than the many factors that tied together high nobles and well-to-do commoners – substantial real property, investment in bonds, office-holding, tax exemptions, involvement in the seigneurial system, lifestyle, education, and intermarriage. In the opinion of revisionists the rift that occurred between nobles and commoners was almost accidental, largely the result of the decision of the Parlement of Paris that the Estates General should be constituted as it had been in 1614, with each order having one vote, a decision that seemed designed to allow the first and second orders to outvote the Third Estate.

A good case can be made that the juridical line between nobles and commoners was much more important than the revisionists have made out.[10] Nobility did bring social and judicial privileges that even the wealthy members of the Third Estate did not enjoy. A well-to-do family of com-

moners might cross the line, but this usually involved purchasing successively higher offices over a lengthy period. Moreover, the vast majority of commoners stood no chance of crossing the line. Originally the revolutionaries may not have intended to abolish nobility, but the Declaration of Rights of August 1789 already affirmed that all men were born equal and that "social distinctions may be based only on general utility." In any case, the possibility that an elite of wealthy commoners might share power in the new regime vanished quickly. Some nobles refused to accept the loss of their privileges and emigrated abroad, where they tried to incite foreign powers to intervene in France to suppress the Revolution. Some bourgeois leaders found it expedient to attack nobles in order to rally support among the lower classes. On 19 June 1790, one day short of a year since the Tennis Court Oath, the Constituent Assembly abolished titles of hereditary nobility. It also ordered the removal of all public signs of former noble status.

The plans for public space in the early years of the Revolution reinforce the argument that from the beginning one of the principal objectives was to eradicate the special status of the nobles and other legalized social distinctions. This egalitarian thrust of the Revolution is evident in both the temporary enclosures and projects for permanent arenas early in the decade. The designers of the huge improvised amphitheatre created on the Champ de Mars and smaller but similar ones in the provinces repeatedly emphasized that such enclosures were aimed at obliterating social divisions of all sorts and creating a unified citizenry. The same objective lay behind the permanent amphitheatre that Kersaint and his architect associates, Legrand and Molinos, proposed two years later. The objective of suppressing social differences and private interests was restated by Combes and the others who advocated creating a huge amphitheatre in the Public Garden in Bordeaux in which to stage civic festivals. Significantly, Boullée incorporated a circular amphitheatre into his plan for a massive city hall designed to be like a beehive where citizens would congregate.

The egalitarian thrust of the Revolution could not be complete so long as the monarchy survived. The monarch as the head of state, even a monarch with limited powers, was still a remnant of the former hierarchical social structure of which he constituted the apex. The king was a reminder of the time when the ruler had been the chieftain of the nobility of the sword. With the overthrow of the monarchy and the later execution of the king the legalized hierarchical social structure was finally completely eradicated. Also, the distinction between active and passive citizens based on taxation was finally abolished, and the *sans-culottes*, with their disdain for superiors and advocacy of direct democracy, enjoyed temporary power. The goddess Equality became increasingly conspicuous. The gateway consisting of the twin figures of Liberty and Equality, with a carpenter's level suspended between them, erected at the entrance to the Champ de Mars for the Festival of Unity and Indivisibility on the first anniversary of the overthrow of the monarchy, announced to all who passed through it the new emphasis on equality. The idea of such an entrance, with a level over it, recurred in the transformation by Verly in Lille of the church of Saint-Laurent into a revolutionary temple and in the plans for primary assemblies and revolutionary temples by Lequeu.

The same egalitarian thrust lay behind the removal of all the boxes in the Théâtre Français to transform it into a Théâtre de l'Egalité and the replacement of boxes with rows of benches in the plans for new theatres in the Contest of Year II. It lay too behind the amphitheatres proposed for primary assembly halls, covered arenas, and *temples décadaires*. Moreover, it was significant that only the goddess Equality was to have a temple dedicated to her in the government program. It was very significant too that on the façade of the Temple to Equality designed by Durand and Thibault figures of Liberty and Equality were to be shown facing each other with the inscription in between THEY ARE INSEPARABLE. The idea that one cannot have liberty without equality and vice versa was one of the most radical affirmations of the Revolution at its peak. The same linkage of the two goddesses occurred in David's proposal for a colossal statue of the People in the guise of Hercules for the tip of the Ile de la Cité, where the giant was to uphold the two goddesses in his right hand. The pairing of the two goddesses occurred again in the gateway to the legislature from the Carrousel side planned by the Committee for Embellishment in the spring of 1794, in the weeks just preceding the overthrow of Robespierre.

The objective of uniting citizens around revolutionary ideals expressed in the great Festival of Federation and similar festivals throughout France persisted throughout the Revolution, although the ideals changed in the succession of different governments that followed. The Revolution destroyed the corporate bodies that had enjoyed distinctive privileges in the Old Regime – the *parlements* controlled by the nobility of the robe, town corporations enjoying special rights, guilds of craftsmen with exclusive privileges – but the Revolution did not want to leave citizens as free-floating atoms; rather, it sought to create a nation-wide community. It was to engender such a community that the government in Year II called on artists to design various kinds of buildings in which citizens could congregate. Leaders envisaged citizens throughout France

meeting on the tenth day in similar *temples décadaires* to participate in the same kinds of ceremonies and to sing the same civic hymns. On the other nine days of the week fraternal union was to be encouraged by gatherings in primary assembly halls, revolutionary theatres, and arenas especially designed for civic festivals. Meanwhile, impressive monuments would remind citizens of the ideals of the Republic.

We should understand clearly the objective of this architectural planning. To commemorate the bicentenary of the Revolution, the Ecole des Beaux-Arts in Paris mounted an exhibition of revolutionary designs under the title "The Architecture of Liberty," which is quite valid for some of the projects but glosses over the elements of conformity, exclusion, and coercion in others. The aim of the projects in Year II was not to accommodate a variegated and pluralistic citizenry but to create a homogeneous one. Those who could not accept the ideals of the Montagnard Republic – refractory priests, many nobles, moderate bourgeois, and large numbers of peasants – were excluded from the new corporate body. Moreover, those who were suspected of opposing the revolutionary ideals of the day were to be purged because they endangered the community of good citizens. We should not forget that five programs in the great Contest of Year II called for courthouses, detention centres, and prisons. The physical basis for the homogenized and purified national corporation was never built, but the intention is important to our understanding of what the revolutionaries were trying to do.

At the same time the representatives of the nation were to unite in striving to embody the general will of the community in legislation. This too was to be encouraged by the seating arrangements in the legislature. As we have seen, an amphitheatre with continuous rows of seats was created by Pâris as soon as the Estates General was metamorphosed into a Constituent Assembly. This shape was subsequently transported to Paris when the Assembly followed the royal family there in the autumn of 1789. It was used successively in the Archbishopric, the Manège, the Tuileries Palace, and in the assembly halls used by the two legislatures of the Directory. This shape reflected the rejection of the idea of parties and the legitimacy of opposition, which was part of the revolutionary ideology. It has been argued that the Revolution saw the birth of a modern republican political culture, in fact that this was its principal legacy.[11] The Revolution did create some of the elements of such a political culture – abolition of the monarchy, elections at all levels, representative bodies, highly politicized newspapers, and political caricatures – but because its political culture was *revolutionary*, it did not countenance rival parties or what the English call "loyal opposition." These features of normal demo-

360 Baltard. Painting of a project for a monument to the French plenipotentiaries assassinated at Rastadt.

cratic politics did not emerge until the nineteenth century. The Revolution did bequeath the semicircular rows of benches, which originally expressed a very different political ideal.

The projects that the Revolution produced also deepen our understanding of the intense religiosity it produced, another feature that distinguishes it from most modern democratic politics. More than a decade before the Second World War Aulard had already described how in the first four years of the Revolution a civic cult had grown up that offered substitutes for most of the ingredients of the Catholic faith – civic altars, sacred symbols, martyrs, hymns, commandments, even an eschatological vision and a non-Christian form of immortality.[12] The conversion of churches into temples dedicated to various revolutionary ideals beginning in the autumn of 1793 is a familiar story; however, the hope of creating new temples specifically designed for republican ceremonies has not yet been integrated into the religious history of the Revolution. In this regard the *temples décadaires* designed for the Contest of Year 11 are especially revealing. The award-winning plans by Durand and Thibault, with their sacred precincts, their Robespierrist inscriptions, their antique altars for each month and each ten-day week, and their links to natural phenomena, were ideally designed to facilitate the new cult. The designs for Temples to Equality and the Laws also provide striking examples of the application of the process of sacralization, the attempt to surround revolutionary ideals and laws with an aura of sanctity such as had formerly surrounded the king.

This revolutionary religiosity reveals a paradox: a movement that promised happiness on earth often seems preoccupied with death, just like Christianity before it. "Happiness is a new idea in Europe," declared Saint-Just, but the Revolution brought death to many of its supporters as well as to its opponents. As we have seen, for the Festival of Federation in 1792 a pyramid was erected near the Ecole Militaire in honour of the war dead, the harbinger of many war memorials in the future. Another pyramid was constructed for the ceremony honouring those who had died in the overthrow of the monarchy. The following year saw monuments raised to the martyrs Lepelletier and Marat. Then the great Contest of Year 11 called for several monuments to those who had paid the supreme sacrifice. Following Thermidor there were monuments to the victims of the Terror. Such erection of monuments and proposals for others continued under the Directory–for instance, the monument designed by Louis Pierre Baltard in memory of the French plenipotentiaries assassinated at Rastadt in April 1799 (Figure 360).[13] It was therefore fitting that the decade end with a design by Jean-Nicolas Sobre for a temple dedicated not to terrestrial happiness but to the secular substitute for the Christian after-life, Immortality (Figure 361).[14]

The plans for public space also add another dimension to the upsurge of nationalism during the Revolution and the desire for uniformity throughout France that have been emphasized by most historians. In addition to describing how the revolutionaries created uniform political institutions throughout France and tried to create a national system of education, historians have called attention to the plans to impose linguistic uniformity on those who spoke Breton, Flemish, Basque, Italian, German, or some other tongue than French. What has not been recognized is the attempt to impose an ideological stamp on the rural and urban landscape – milestones bearing revolutionary symbols, better farm buildings announcing a new order in the countryside, Liberty Trees and Altars of the Fatherland in every commune, Temples of the Laws in major centres, obelisks honouring the republican war dead everywhere, similar administrative buildings throughout the country such as were planned in Year II, and revolutionary monuments along the frontier announcing that France led the world in breaking from the past. Once again the revolutionaries were unable to achieve their goal, but their objective needs to be recognized in any future comprehensive account of the Revolution.

The dream of meeting-places where citizens would merge together, of a legislature in which the deputies would express a single will, and of a network of monuments and buildings that would put a revolutionary stamp on the whole country vanished as the Revolution failed to stabilize itself and created bitter divisions, some of which endure still. But the bold plans for monuments, squares, and public buildings left certain memories that have also endured. The mania for the rechristening of space subsided, and gradually Frenchmen learned to tolerate names that survive from various regimes. Nevertheless, under the Third Republic most French cities got a Place de la République, an avenue de la Liberté, or a boulevard de la Nation. Paris has a rue de l'Egalité and nearby a rue de la Fraternité. And in 1833 Paris got the Colonne de Juillet on the Place de la Bastille, crowned with the Spirit of Liberty, realizing to a large extent the dream of Davy de Chavigny, Cathala, Gatteaux, and Palloy. Also, perhaps we can see in the construction of the Opéra de la Bastille an echo of the plans by Brullée and Palloy to introduce cultural facilities into one of the less fashionable districts of the capital.

Although the Pantheon was restored for a time as a church, it emerged finally as the shrine to great Frenchmen planned by the revolutionaries. Even more significant, the idea of honouring great men, which had emerged in the last decades of the Old Regime and was taken up enthusiastically

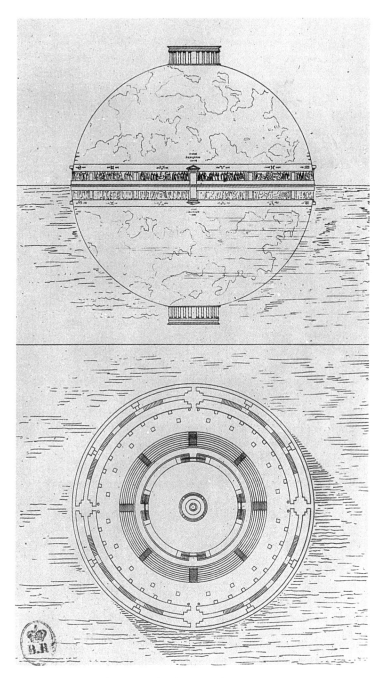

361 Sobre. Project for a Temple of Immortality.

by the revolutionaries, was expanded far beyond the walls of the Pantheon, punctuating urban space with statues honouring statesmen, scientists, artists, philosophers, and literary figures, creating "an outdoor Pantheon," as one art historian has described it.[15] In some cities such as Dijon whole districts have been turned into textbooks, teaching the public by means of street signs. Along with the name of the famous man or woman are the dates when he or she lived and a short description of his or her work. In Bordeaux, to cite just one other example, one district known as the *quartier des grands hommes* honours the philosophes and Encyclopedists of the eighteenth century.

Moreover, the Revolution was clearly an important stage in the development of modern urbanism, despite the fact that it constructed very little. The flood of projects shows that architects continued and expanded the eighteenth-century idea of planning urban space to make it more beautiful, healthier, and better suited for economic activity. Entirely apart from the revolutionary objective of a monument, square, or building, the plans we have examined provide for wider streets, avenues that tie the city together, tree-lined boulevards, green oases, port facilities, public baths, and fountains. In some cases, such as the planning for the area around the Bastille, the completion of the Louvre, the development of the site of the old Châtelet prison, or bridges across the Seine, the projects anticipate the developments of the nineteenth century. The "Plan des artistes," drawn up at the very peak of the Revolution, provided a starting point for future planners.[16] Even the idea of the Grand Louvre, a comprehensive cultural centre instead of a palace where paintings have been hung, was anticipated by several plans during the Revolution.

Mention of the Louvre reminds us too of how various revolutionary architects envisaged a sort of museum of the Revolution. The massive pedestal of the column that Gatteaux proposed for the Place de la Bastille was to house rooms in which landmark revolutionary legislation could be displayed. The huge *prytanée* which Kersaint and his architect associates proposed for the same site was to accommodate similar display space. This idea was repeated both by ordinary citizens and by outstanding architects – for instance, the widow Bouillard, who wanted to turn the Place de la Révolution into a public museum, and Durand and Thibault, who envisaged scenes of the Revolution covering the internal walls of their project for a Temple à l'Egalité. This dream has recently been realized by the creation of a Museum of the Revolution in the former château of Vizille. This metamorphosis of a symbol of privilege into a revolutionary monument, of the old superseded by the new, would also have pleased revolutionary planners.

After two hundred years there is little chance of reviving other aspects of the revolutionary dream. No one is likely to propose creation of a network of *temples décadaires*, Temples to Equality, Temples of the Laws, or Altars of the Fatherland. Even avid admirers of David are unlikely to resurrect his proposal for a colossal statue of the People in the guise of Hercules with slogans on his body, not even as a tribute to the artist's role in the Revolution to mark the bicentenary of 1789. Nor would anyone want nowadays to ring the French frontier with colossal republican monuments. Such projects were the product of a particular historical moment now long past. This study of how the revolutionaries tried to replan space in order to educate, inspire, and serve the citizenry may, however, provoke some urban planners and architects to devote themselves anew to what Helen Rosenau called "social purpose in architecture." ▲

Appendix A

PROJECTS FOR REVOLUTIONARY MONUMENTS AND PUBLIC BUILDINGS EXHIBITED AT THE SALONS 1789–99

These projects have been extracted from the guidebooks to the *salons* edited by Jules J. Guiffrey, *Collection des livrets des anciennes expositions de 1673 jusqu'en 1800*, 42 vols. (Paris 1869–72). The numbers are those given in each *livret*. We have followed the numerical rather than the alphabetical order.

Although most of the projects exhibited at the *salons* for monuments, squares, and public buildings have disappeared, the list is revealing in several ways. It shows that a large number of projects related to the Revolution were displayed – in fact, a larger proportion of these genres than in the case of engravings and paintings.[1] The list also shows that planning for an impressive legislative building or buildings continued longer than is usually recognized. Finally, it shows the transition from monuments and temples devoted to Liberty and Equality to ones devoted to generals and Victory.

Salon of 1789

De Wailly, [Charles]. Two plans of Paris; on the one are traced the old and new enclosures; on the others are indicated by a red wash projects for the utility and embellishment of this Capital. 57.[2]

Salon of 1791

Sobre, the younger [Jean-Nicolas]. Huge monument to be erected on the Champ de la Fédération. 390.[3]

Varin. Perspective view of a project for a public square in Bordeaux, engraved after the design by Louis. Engraving, 414.

Four[r]eau, sculptor. Bronzed low-relief, a monument in honour of the citizens who died in the storming of the Bastille. 426.

Duret, sculptor. Low-relief in clay. Triumph of Liberty. 427.

M****. Project for an allegorical monument to the Revolution. 456.

Milandre. Plan in relief of the Champ de la Fédération. 477.

De Seine, deaf and dumb. Allegory of Liberty accompanied by a figure of M d'Orléans. Sculpture, 514.

Beauval[l]et, [Pierre-Nicolas]. Liberty on the ruins of the Bastille. 515.

M****. Project for a monument to Liberty to be erected on the ruins of the Bastille. 516.

Boulanger, [Michel-Victor], architect. Plan projected for a hall to accommodate the National Assembly. 519.

Mauré, sculptor. Plan projected for a monument in memory of several deputies to the National Assembly. 553.

Fourreau, sculptor. Project for a tomb for Mirabeau. 557.

Pil[l]on, sculptor. A group in plaster. An allegory about Washington and Liberty. 560.

Marin, [Joseph-Charles]. A group in plaster. Allegory about M de la Fayette. 562.

Beauval[l]et, [Pierre-Nicolas], sculptor. Project for a funerary monument to Mirabeau. 611.

Salon of 1793

Gois, [Etienne-Pierre]. Model of a monument in honour of Voltaire. He protects Innocence and tramples down Fanaticism. Sculpture, 1.

De Wailly, [Charles]. Assembly hall for a patriotic club that had been constructed in the Jesuit church in Brussels. Painting, 341.[4]

Desfonds [Desfonts in the index], citizenness, sculptor. Project for a triumphal column to be placed on the ruins of the Bastille. Sculpture, 18. [There follows a detailed description.]

Lesueur, [Jacques-Philippe], sculptor. Rough plan of a low-relief executed in stone under the peristyle of the French Pantheon. It represents Public Education. Sculpture, 39.

Suzanne, [François-Marie]. Liberty accompanied by Union and Equality [a note says that this is the model of a work that the artist was doing on a large scale]. Sculpture, 64.

Jacob, sculptor. Project of a monument in gratitude to the Supreme Being and to Liberty. Sculpture, 110.

Lorta, [Jean-Pierre], sculptor. Sketch of one of the pendentives of the eastern nave of the Pantheon. It represents Disinterestedness expressed by two Women who deposit their jewels on the Altar of the Fatherland. Sculpture, 128.

Radel, [Petit-Radel, Louis-François], architect. A model in porphyry, granite, and bronze of a column to be erected to Concord and projected for one of the National Square. Architecture, 1, 2. Model and perspective view.

Migneron, engineer. Plan, section, and elevation of a project for a wooden bridge, which was to be constructed across the branches of the River Seine that separate the Islands of Fraternity and of the Palace [of Justice]. The bridge has an opening of two hundred feet and a single arch. It won the designer the prize in the contest and the highest compensation … Architecture, 3.

Prieur, architect. Model of a monument projected for the site of the Bastille. Architecture, 6.

Levasseur, architect. Project for a monument to the National Assembly. Architecture, 15. Ground-plan, elevation, and section.

Vignon, Pierre. Ground-plan and section of the National Palace, the former Tuileries Palace, containing a hall for the Convention as had been decreed by the Legislative Assembly on 15 September 1792. Architecture, 17.

Balzac, [Louis-Charles], architect. Plan for a public square on the site of the Bastille. Elevation of a monument in the centre of this square. Second edition of the *livret*, 556.

Chaudet, [Denis-Antoine], sculptor. Devotion to the Fatherland. Model of a low-relief under the peristyle of the Pantheon. Supplement, 631.

Boulanger, V. [Michel-Victor]. Part of a project for a French Pantheon to be erected in memory of the great men who won fame in the Revolution. Supplement, 638.

Boulanger, V. [Michel-Victor]. Lateral and geometrical elevation of a hall for the National Assembly. Supplement, 639.

Boulanger, [Michel-Victor]. Perspective elevation of a triumphal arch destined for the entrance to a city. Supplement, 640.

Dupasquier, sculptor. Legislation giving Laws to the French Republic. This is the model of a pendentive destined for the Pantheon. Supplement, 886.

Salon of 1795

Boichot [Guillaume]. Model of Hercules, representing Force. This figure has been executed fifteen feet in size under the porch of the French Pantheon; she [*la figure*] forms a pendant to that of the Law, who, although she appears seated, seems to be on guard against malevolence. 1006.

Daiteg, sculptor. Temple of Liberty of which the model in relief is in one of the rooms in the National Archives and was presented by the author to the Constituent Assembly. Drawing. 1025.

Dejoux, [Claude]. Colossal figure of Renown, which is to be cast in bronze and placed atop three cupola of the French Pantheon. 1028.[5] [The *livret* says that this figure was twenty-seven feet in proportion. The plaster model could be seen in the workshops of the city of Paris in the Faubourg du Roulle.]

Suzanne, [François-Marie]. Rough plan in plaster for a pendentive to be executed in stone in the northern nave of the Pantheon. The subject is Geometry and Practical Theory demarking the departments on the part of a terrestial globe belonging to France. 1088.

Bienaimé, [Pierre-Théodore]. General plan for an Elysium to be constructed ... on a terrain in which the bodies of the victims of tyranny have been interred. Architecture, 2001, 2002, 2003, are the ground-plan, elevation, and a section of the same project.

Boulanger, [Michel-Victor]. Project for the establishment of a new quarter in the vicinity of the Tuileries. Architecture, 2007, 2008.

Brongniart, A.-T. [Alexandre-Théodore]. A model of a square on the former terrain of the Bastille. Architecture, 2009.

Brongniart, A.-T. [Alexandre-Théodore]. Bridge planned for the Seine River between the Arsenal and the Jardin des Plantes. Architecture, 2010, 2011, 2012. [A note says that 2012 is an overall plan of the two preceding projects.]

Détournelle, [Athanase]. Plan. Geometric elevation of a triumphal bridge projected between the Arsenal and the Museum of Natural History. Frame enclosing a drawing of the triumphal entrance to the bridge ... 2021.

De Wailly, [Charles]. Various designs for subdivision of the Salon; for completion of three sides of the courtyard of the Louvre; and for the Place de la Révolution. Architecture, 2022bis.

Anonymous. Liberty rests on Virtue alone. Project for a monument to Legislative Power. It is designed to accommodate the two Councils and the Committees. Architecture, 2023. Ground-plan and elevation, 2024.

Levasseur, [Etienne-François]. Project for a National Palace on the site of the former Capuchins of the Place Vendôme for the sessions of the Council of Elders. Ground-plan, elevation, and section. Architecture, 2026.

Levasseur, [Etienne François]. Project for a Triumphal Bridge to be erected facing the Champ-de-Mars. Architecture, 2027.

Levasseur, [Etienne François]. Project for a public library. Plan, section, and elevation. Architecture, 2028.

Levasseur, [Etienne-François]. Project for a monument to the arts of architecture, painting, and sculpture. Architecture, 2029.

Levasseur, [Etienne-François]. Palace of Justice for a department. Plan, section, and elevation. Architecture, 2030.

Levasseur, [Etienne-François]. General and detailed plan for an extensive market for a large city in a department. Architecture, 2031.

Levasseur, [Etienne-François]. Temple to the Supreme Being. Ground-plan, section, and elevation. Architecture, 2032.

Levasseur, [Etienne-François]. Temple to Liberty and Equality. Plan. Elevation. Architecture, 2033.

Peyre, [Antoine-François]. Ground-plans, sections, and elevation of the project for a National Palace placed in the centre of the Monuments to the Sciences and the Arts between the Louvre and the Tuileries. Architecture, 2049.

Peyre, nephew, [Marie-Joseph]. Project for a Museum of Antiquities in the old building of the Quatre-Nations. Plan, section, and elevation. Architecture, 2054.

Peyre, nephew, [Marie-Joseph]. Project for a Museum of Natural History on the site of the Jardin des Plantes. Plan, section, and elevation. Architecture, 2055.

Peyre, nephew, [Marie-Joseph]. Project for a National Library in the Luxembourg Palace. Plan, section, and elevation. Architecture, 2056.

Silvestre. Plan for an Educational House [Maison]. Plan, section, and elevation. Architecture, 2057.

Sobre, Jean-Nicolas. Ground-plan, section, and elevation of a triumphal arch recalling the events of 6 October [1789]. This monument is to be placed facing the Pont de la Révolution. Architecture, 2058.[6]

Thierry, Ch.-S. Interior of the Pantheon with the column called for in honour of great men. Drawing. Architecture, 2059.

Thierry, Ch.-S. Ground-plan, elevation, and section of a Temple to Liberty. Architecture, 2061.

Voinier, [Antoine]. Project for a monument in honour of the fourteen armies of the Republic. This edifice will form the entry to Paris next to Neuilly, facing the National Palace. Architecture, 2062.[7]

Voinier, [Antoine]. Project for the monument erected in honour of the spirits of the victims immolated by Tyranny. This edifice should be placed in the vacant part of the Champs-Elysées. Architecture, 2063.

Salon of 1796

Attiret, M.-L. Plans, sections, and elevations of a Palace for the French Government as prescribed by the Constitution of Year III. Architecture, 700.

Baltard, L.-P. [Louis-Pierre]. Geometrical elevation with the ground-plan and section of a project for a meeting-place for the Council of Five Hundred. Architecture, 701.

Baltard, L.-P. [Louis-Pierre]. Coloured perspective view of a public monument destined to receive and preserve the tablets of republican laws ... Architecture, 702.

Baltard, L.-P. [Louis-Pierre]. On a single sheet, in the form of sketches, three plans for cities in different locations, an overall elevation of the main plan, and two monuments useful to the public. Architecture, 703.

Brullée, engineer and architect. Plan for square to be created on the ruins of the Bastille. Architecture, 706.[8]

Brullée, engineer and architect. Project for a bridge to be constructed in front of the Museum of Natural History. Architecture, 707.

Brullée, engineer and architect. Project for embellishment of the interior of Paris. Architecture, 708.

Brullée, engineer and architect. Model of a monument on the ruins of the Bastille. The group is by Citizen Chardin, the trophies by Citizen Compereau. Architecture, 713.

De Wailly, Charles. Six designs, of which four are for joining the Islands of Saint-Louis and Louvier and the establishment of a dock; the two others are for a national palace, one for completion of the courtyard of the Museum, and the other for the Place de la Concorde. Architecture, 717.[9]

Oudinet, G. Project for a correctional prison. Architecture, 718.

Topin, Silvestre. Plans, section and elevation of a Central School planned for Paris. Architecture, 719.

Glize, André. Joining of the two colonnades of the Place de la Révolution by a triumphal arch. Column to erect on this square, in honour of republican victories. Perspective sketch. Architecture, 720.

Espercieux, Jean-Joseph. Liberty. [A description says that she held a little statue of Public Happiness in one hand and a sword and the torch of Philosophy in the other, while at her feet lay a broken yoke. A note says that this design won a prize in a national contest.] Sculpture, 523.

Salon of 1798

Lorta, [Jean-François]. Peace. [A note says that this design won a prize in a national contest.] Sculpture, 530.

Baltard, Louis-Pierre. Geometrical design of a triumphal monument in honour of the armies of the Republic, forming part of a project for Bordeaux on the site of the Château Trompette. Architecture, 601.

Brogniard [Brogniart, Alexandre-Théodore]. Perspective view of the interior of the French Pantheon with obelisks and tablets bearing inscriptions to reinforce the four pillars of the dome without detracting from the existing decoration of this monument. Architecture, 603.

Brogniard [Brongniart, Alexandre-Théodore]. Model in painted wood of one of the four pillars of the Pantheon showing the additions necessary to reinforcce it. Architecture, 606.

Sobre, [Jean-Nicolas], architect. Project for an obelisk to be placed at the upper end of the Champs-Elysées. Architecture, 610.

A Citizen of Brest. Two plans for a maritime hospice planned for Brest in 1793. Architecture, 611.

Salon of 1799

Baltard, Louis-Pierre. Picture showing the project for a monument consecrated to recalling the memory of the assassination at Rastadt. Drawing, 11.

Boquet, [Simon-Louis]. Sketch representing the Spirit of Liberty marking victories of the French on tablets. Sculpture, 400.

Suzanne, [François-Marie], sculptor. Liberty, a model in plaster two metres in proportion, leaning with her right arm on a fasces, while holding in her hand the symbols of agriculture and of force; with her left hand she supports the tablet of the laws, placed on a cube symbolizing stability; on her head she wears the symbol of the Spirit of Arts and Commerce. Sculpture, 443.

Anonymous. Seven designs of a project to turn the Place de la Revolution into an amphitheatre [cirque] (1) to be used for public games on days of national festivals, and (2) to serve as place of assembly for the citizens of Paris, providing for the largest commune in France a site comparable to the ancient forum in Rome. Architecture, 500.

Durand, J.-N.-L. [Jean-Nicolas-Louis]. Models of a Temple to Equality and a temple décadaire that won prizes in the Contest of Year III [actually the contest held in Year II with prizes awarded the following year]. These models were executed by J.-P. Fouquet and belong to the Republic. Architecture, 504.[10]

Giot [Guyot?]. Architectural model. It represents a Temple of Victory dedicated to the glory of General Bonaparte; one sees there, represented on low-reliefs, the four initial deeds of this great man, from the time of his departure from Paris up to his debarking in Egypt where he was immortalized. Architecture, 506.

Gisors, [Alexandre-Jean-Baptiste-Guy]. Project for a National Library in the edifice begun by the parish of the Madeleine. Ground-plan, section, and elevation together. Architecture, 506.

Sobre, J.-N. [Jean-Nicolas]. Project for a Temple of Immortality, consecrated to great men, to be erected on the Champs-Elysées. Two plans, 516; the overall plan, 517; a model of the monument from a board, 518.[11]

Thierry, Ch.-S. Monuments to be erected in honour of the French Republic on the site allocated to construction of the former Church of the Madeleine. Architecture, 519.

Vignon, B. [Barthélémy]. Tribunal of the peace for various communes of the Republic. Architecture, 520.[12]

Voinier, [Antoine]. Triumphal arch to the glory of the defenders of the fatherland. This monument projected to be erected on the terrain called the Etoile, on the height of the Champs-Elysées, will form the entrance to Paris on arriving by the Neuilly, facing the National Palace. Architecture, 522.

APPENDIX B

MEMBERS OF THE POPULAR AND REPUBLICAN SOCIETY FOR THE ARTS[1]

This list is based on a document, found in the Archives Nationales, apparently compiled in response to a request by the Committee of Public Instruction.[2] The order, which is not quite alphabetical, has been retained along with the original spelling.

To the Committee of Public Instruction in response to the request that it made to the Free Society of the Arts by its letter of the *décadi* of Brumaire Year II of the French Republic one and indivisible.

Copy of the register containing the names of artists, painters, sculptors, architects, and engravers admitted to the former Commune of the Arts, at present known as the Republican Society of the Arts.

Painters

Ansiaux	Boilly	Boissieu Fils
Aubée	Bauzit	Baudot Cne
Augustin	Bonvoisin	Chaize
Alpique	Bouton	Callier J. Joseph
Baudard	Belle Fils	Chancourtois
Bertaux Fils	Bachelier	Chevin
Bertin	Bouillon	Colson
Bertin (J. Victor)	Bosio	Colibert
Bioche (J.B.)	Boze	Cazin
Boizot Fils	Baudoin	Cotibert
Bertrand	Berton	Chasselart
Bonneville	Boquet	Courteille
Bruandet	Bouche	Chéry
Bazin	Beaurain	Chaudepie
Balzac	Bidauld	Cazin Cne
Belle Père	Boucher	Chauvin
Bigand	Brion	Chateau
Belier	Bilcoq	Christophle
Bréat	Baltazard Fr Xavier	Capet Cne
Broceros	Budetot	Corot
Berthélemy	Berthier	Casenave
Bertaux Père	Beaurepaire Cne	Coutuly Cne

Chatelain	Elie	Isabey
Changarnier	Forty	Imbault
Cossard	Fribourg (Denis)	Jollain
Cassat	Fleury	Jouette
Duchateau Cne	Fache	Jeaurat
Defrance	Fouquet	Jault
Dupolir	Fragonard	Jeanteau
Duval L'Ainé	François	Leclerc
Dussouy	Fournier	Lambert
Dejivet	Fougea	Lepeintre (Charles)
Dubourg (Augustin)	Forestier	Lepeintre (François)
Duvivier	Frossard Cne	Lassare
Desfour	Franque Joseph	Leroy (Joseph)
Damame	Franque Pierre	Lagrenée L'Ainé
Désoria	Génillon	Lebrun (Père)
Dumont (F...)	Godefroy	Lorimier
Durand	Giraud Joseph	Lafond
Duplessis	Garnerey	Landon
Dabos	Gauthier	Lagrenée Jeune
Dupaty	Gautherot	Lemonier
Denouget	Garriguet	Laneuville
Dubois	Gaindat	Langlois
Demarne	Galliev	Lélu
Desfontaines (Swebach)	Garnier	Lesueur (Jean-François)
Drabot	Guénot	Lefebvre
Durameau	Gasgnier	Lespinasse
Ducreux	Guibert	Le Barbier
Delorme Père	Guilliardon	Lethière
Doucet Cne	Gérard (François)	Lenoir Cne
Desormery	Guyard Cne	Laberie
Desmarquais Cne	Georget J...	Landragin Cne
Delafontaine	Greuze	Lionnoir
Dardel Cne	Grégoire	Lesueur (Etienne)
Desrais	Garnier (Michel)	Landry
Debourger Fils	Guérin (François)	Lejeunne
Dubois (Auguste)	Hubert (J...)	Lafontaine
Desperreux	Huguenot	Lucas
Ducrey	Houzeau	Lenoir
Descat	Haumont	Lassaux
Drabonet	Houël	Lejeune
Desaint Jean	Hubert	Leriche (...)
Didot	Hué	Lefebvre (Etienne)
David	Holain	Letellier
Duplessis (Michel)	Hoin	Laborey (Sophie)
Desfosser	Horet	Laborey (Felicité)
Dutally	Jouy Cne	Laplace
Drolling Martin	Judelin	Lavalée Poussin

Letourneur
Laurent (J ... Antoine)
Marin Cne
Nonniot
Moreau (J.C.A.)
Moulin Neuf
Milbert
Machy
Messier
Mezières
Mouricaut
Molenchon
Métoyen
Mozillon
Marin
Moreau l'Ainé
Mozin
Mounet
Marchais
Martin Cne
Menjaud
Morel (Darleux)
Merlot
Mauperrin
Masson (Ambroise)
Magnier
Munié
Moufle
Mansuy
Michel
Naigeon
Nassau
Naigeon (Jean-Claude)
Naudet
Oyon Cne
Olivier
Potain
Patel
Provot

Pourcelly
Prudhon
Petit (Louis)
Petit (Pierre)
Petit Coupray
Poutrel
Pajou Fils
Parceval
Perrin
Perrin L ...
Parfait Cne
Pietre Cne
Patron
Pallier
Pinson
Rabillon
Royer
Romany Cne
Raimond
Reynault
Redouté
Roland
Royer P...
Renou
Robin
Robert Nicolas
Renault
Robert
Segaux
Schmidt
Savier (Antoine)
Schell
Schall
Serangeli
Strabaux
Suvée
Simon
St Martin
Swagert

Sauvage
Sablet
Sevin
Sénave
Trinquesse
Tavernier
Taurel
Tonesse
Taunay
Thibeault
Tarre (François Denis)
Thiboust
Taillasson
Thévenin
Thouvenin
Thiénon
Vapereau
Vieillard
Vauthier
Vien
Vandenburg Cne
Vanspandonk Corneille
Villers
Vanloo (Amedée)
Vincent
Vandael
Vanpol
Vaudzon
Vincent (François)
Vautier (Michel)
Vincent (...)
Vaujour
Weber Cne
Vatin
Wille Fils
Vernet
Veyrenc
Vanspandonk l'Ainé
Wanloo Fils

Charpentier (C...)
Castaix
Cardon
Canchy
Cartelier
Chaudet
Chardin
Chenu
Delaistre
Dumont Jacques
Desfond Cne
Dumont (P...)
Desenne sourd & muet
Dardet
Dejoux
Dutry
Duret
Desmur
Daiteg
Demontreuil
Espercieux
Francin
Foucou
Fortin
Fourreaux
Faillard
Forestier (Père Augustin)

Georgerie
Guillois
Gois
Girardière
Houdon
Julien
Jadouille Père
Jacob
Lestrade
Leconte
Larmier
Lesueur l'Ainé
Lucat
Lorta
Lenoir
Lemaut
Michalon
Moitte
Marin
Monnot
Milot
Masson
Mosmann
Morgan
Milot Cne
Moreau
Martincour

Moutony
Mérard
Mouchy
Monpellier
Martin (Jean-François)
Nicolet (J...)
Péquignot
Pigale
Pasquier
Rochard
Roland
Ramey
Riffard
Ricourt
Renier
Roger
Rosset
Sellier
Stouf
Sigisbert
Suzanne
Thiérard
Taunay
Thomire
Verbelst

Architects

Allard
Allais
Archangé
Bouvet
Boular
Bernard (Père)
Boulanger
Bénard (Nicolas)
Bienvenu
Boucher
Bernier
Bonnet
Barbier
Coutuly
Colir
Chabouillet
Cuillier
Cherrier

Croissant
Chevalier
Chassagnole
Clochard
Clavareau
Cherpitet
Coustdeple
Dubois
Debourge
Dwally
Ducampbussy
Delannoy
Dabos
Demoulin
Dubus
Duchêne
Deboeuf
Dauvergne

Durand
Destournelle
Delépine
D'Herbelot
Deletre
Dedieu
Eynard
Florence
Fontaine
Gizorn
Guignet
Gilbert
Goust
Gaucher
Gondoin (Jacques)
Garret
Galimard (Père)
Heurtaux

Sculptors

Auger
Boizot
Blaise
Boichot
Budulot
Beruée

Babovot
Boëyler
Bouri
Beauvallet
Bacarit
Boquet

Brunet
Berthélemy
Bouillet
Bruyère
Bridan
Choisy

Haron (Romain)	Molinot	Pertinchamp
Hubert	Moreau	Rondelet
Huot [Huet?]	Mandard	Riffaut
Jardin	Moitte	Radet
Jomard	Muly	Rieux
Jadouille Fils	Moithey	Rousset
Lussault	Montison	Raimond
Lequeu	Normand	Soufflot
Legrand	Norry	Sobre
Lemoine	Normand (Nicolas)	Tardieu (Jacques)
Labarre	Persier	Thierry
Leroy (David)	Peyre (Le Jeune)	Toutain
Lemaître	Poyet	Taraval
Leconte	Podevin	Thierry (Le Jeune)
Lemit	Petuand	Vignon (Barthélemy)
Lemaître (François)	Parent	Veny
Leroy (J. François)	Pirrot	Valot
Lecuyer	Pretret	Vaugel
Miche	Plon	Vestier Fils
Mignerot	Peyre (Oncle)	Bartholomée

Engravers

Anselin	Duvivier	Joubert
Andrieu	Dumarais	Lépine
Avril Père	David François	Lemire
Avril Fils	Duret	Laurent
Aubry	Delaunay	Lempereur
Beljambe	Deyhandt	Levasseur
Bervic	Demarteau	Lorieux
Bouquet	Duval	Letellier
Boutroy	Deletre	Meyer
Barbier	Droz	Masquelier (l'Aîné)
Charpentier Cne	Empereur	Masquelier (Jeune)
Cathelin	Gaucher	Moreau Jeune
Chrétien	Gattaux	Michon
Coincy	Guyot	Morel
Cernet Cne	Galle	Michau
Caron	Gauthier	Moisy
Choffard	Clairant-Mondet	Malbete
Clement	Gérard (Henry)	Marchand
Carré	Godefroy (François)	Monsaldy
Coquet	Helman	Maradan
Carpantier	Hubert Jean Jacques	Marcenay
Chaillou Cne	Halbou	Massard
Couche (Jacques)	Hubert (J...)	Nicolet
Desmel	Joui	Pillement
Dupré	Ingouf (François Robert)	Poisson

Pierron	Sergent	Tiolier
Ponce	Simon	Varin (Charles Nicolas)
Patas	Sellier	Varin (Joseph)
Ribault	Simon J.H.	Vidal (N. Etienne)
Romanet	Tardieu (Alexandre)	Wille Père
Roy	Tardieu Cne	Wilmin
Ruotte	Tourcaty	Viel
Ridé	Thillard	

Artists [who are] former academicians and others in the Republic who reside in Paris who have not yet presented themselves to the association since the decree of last 4 July, which had ordered the general reunion of all artists, (are not included in this list), as well as the competitors in the three contests and young artists under eighteen years; the committee will understand the reason.

Exact copy of the register and delivered by us the president and secretary of the Republican Society for the Arts, the fourth day of the second *décade* of the second month of the Republic one and indivisible.

Boizot, president
Bienaimé, adjunct secretary
Weber, secretary

Twenty-one names of artists were listed on the covers of Détournelle's *Aux armes et aux arts … Journal de la Société républicaine des arts*, February-June 1794, which did not appear on the manuscript list submitted earlier to the Committee of Public Instruction:

Painters	Huet	*Musicians*
Basille le jeune	Levasseur	Chemin
Phelippeaux	Stouf, Médard	Claretton
Riffault	Vilmorin	
Vandestein		*Men of Letters*
	Engravers	Bousquet
Architects	Baer, Valentin	Chamoulaud
Balzac	Beauvarlet	
Bienaimé	Fillhol	*Porcelain Workers*
Guyot	Petit	Chevalier
		Cosette

The combined lists show that, at one time or another, 654 artists belonged to the [Popular and] Republican Society for the Arts, 328 painters, 104 sculptors, 114 architects, 102 engravers, 2 musicians, 2 men of letters, and 2 workers in porcelain.

Appendix C

DECREES OF THE COMMITTEE OF PUBLIC SAFETY
RELATIVE TO PUBLIC MONUMENTS
AND THE ARTS AND LETTERS

Extracts from the register of the decrees of the Committee of Public Safety of the National Convention.

Palais-national

Place, Pont, and Temple de la Révolution
The twenty-fifth day of Floréal, the second year of the French Republic, one and indivisible.
The Committee of Public Safety, taking definitive measures on the embellishment of the Palais-national and its accessories, having taken into account the recommendations of the jury of arts charged with examining the various plans presented by artists in fulfilment of several previous decrees, decrees that:

1 The Palais-national, where the Convention holds its meetings, and the accompanying garden will be beautified according to the following guidelines contained in the plan presented to it by Citizen Hubert, architect, whose works were judged best by the jury of arts.

2 The courtyard of the Palais-national will be enclosed on the side of the Carrouzel [*sic*] by a circular stylobate. Figures representing the republican virtues will be placed on pedestals resting on a single base, symbolic of the unity of the Republic. On the face of each of the pedestals, on the courtyard side, will be placed a blazing star that will light the Palais-national at night. The Declaration of Rights and the Constitution will be inscribed on the stylobate in gilded bronze letters.

On the top of the national dome will be placed a bronze statue representing Liberty standing holding the tricolour flag in one hand and the Declaration of Rights in the other.

3 At the entrance of the courtyard statues of Justice and Public Happiness, raised on large pedestals, will hold the level of equality. The printing-house and buildings situated on the enclosure of the courtyard will be screened by groups of trees.

4 The two arcades located on both sides of the Pavilion of Unity will be joined by demolishing the obstructing walls on the garden side. These arcades will be decorated with statues of great men.

5 The terrace in front of the Palais-national will be enlarged as far as the flowerbed in order to place several rows of orange trees, statues, vases, and busts there.

6 This terrace will be bounded on the side of the bridge and the riding school by two forty-foot wide entrances composed of pedestals decorated with groups and with bas-reliefs analogous to the Revolution. These entrances will be closed during the night by levers, constructed so that they will not be seen when lowered.

7 On the side of the riding school, a large passage will be opened leading into the rue de la Convention.

8 Orange trees from Rincy, Isle-Adam, Meudon, and Saint-Cloud will be transported to the Jardin-national. An orangerie will be built in the courtyard of the former Feuillants to enclose the trees during the winter.

9 The so-called terrace of the Feuillants will be enlarged. The part of the garden situated below the terrace will be converted into a gymnasium to be used for young people's gymnastic exercises. A portico will be constructed across the length of the terrace, open on the south for the full length of the gymnasium. The interior of the portico will be decorated with paintings capable of developing and guiding the generous passions of adolescence.

10 The so-called terrace of the Feuillants will be provided with orange trees, pomegranate trees, and vases. It will be bounded by a grove opening on to a gentle slope on the side of the Place de la Révolution. This grove, as well as a similar one situated at the end of the other terrace beside the water, will be decorated with a monument analogous to the Revolution; on the waterside the terrace will be decorated with statues and vases.

11 The present flower garden will be changed into groups of shrubs and sculptures taken from national houses.

12 In front of the terrace of the orange trees will be built a vast esplanade intended for the assembling of the people on days of public festivals.

13 The large circular ornamental lake will be converted into a fountain composed of the principal rivers of France. The two side ornamental lakes will be changed into two fountains, one dedicated to Liberty, the other to Equality.

14 Several walkways will be opened among the large trees to facilitate the circulation of air. The squares placed among the trees will be decorated with marble monuments taken from the national houses. Hexahedrals will be built similar to those where the Greek philosophers taught.

15 The large octagonal ornamental lake situated in front of the Pont-tournant will be done away with. On both sides of the site of this lake will be planted groves with gushing fountains in front.

16 At the bottom of the grove ending the terrace on the waterside will be built an ornamental lake receiving water from the Seine and intended as a swimming school.

17 The entrance to the Jardin-national on the side of the Pont-tournant will be enlarged as far as the pedestals supporting the Renommées. On the sides of this entrance two porticoes will be constructed, back to back with the parapets of the Jardin-national. These porticoes will retrace the most memorable feats of the Revolution.

18 The statue of Liberty, erected on the pedestal of the second-to-last tyrant of the French, will be replaced by another statue, standing, of larger proportions; and around the present pedestal another pedestal of larger proportions will be constructed so as to allow the first to be seen.

19 The two colonnades forming the furniture repository will be joined by a trumphal arch in honour of the victories won by the people over tyranny. This arch will allow the former church of the Madeleine, which is to be converted into a Temple of the Revolution, to be seen.

20 Opposite this arch of triumph, and in front of the Pont de la Révolution, will be placed another arch that is to form part of the monuments of the Festival of 10 August and that is offered for competition by the decree of 5 Floréal.

21 Two gushing fountains, intended for the public use, will be erected, one on each side of the statue of Liberty, between the two triumphal arches; they will bear the emblems of the French Revolution.

22 On the Pont de la Révolution will be permanently placed ancient bronze statues taken from the national houses and originating from the former civil list or from *émigrés*.

23 The entrance to the Champs-Elysées will be enlarged. The Horses of Marli [*sic*] will be placed there opposite those of the Pont-tournant, as was stated by another decree of the said day 5 Floréal.

24 These horses will be flanked by two porticoes corresponding to those placed on both sides of the entrance of the Jardin-national, near the Pont-tournant. These four porticoes are destined to be decorated with revolutionary subjects in painting and sculpture.

25 The Place de la Révolution will be converted into a circus by means of gently sloped banks, which will allow all an unobstructed view (by means of banks whose gentle slopes will favour access from all parts) and which will be used for national festivals.

26 All designs for any vases, statues, fountains, and monuments that are not indicated in the present decree will be presented to the committee, which will decree definitively on the execution and placing.

27 The People's Representatives David, Granet, and Fourcroy are charged with supervising the execution of the present decree, with removing all obstacles opposed to its success, and with presenting to the committee suggestions for accelerating the progress of the work.

28 Since the overall plan that has just been described calls for a succession of monuments and projects necessitating a great deal of work, and since its execution has become essential for the enjoyment of the people, citizen Hubert is charged with obtaining the assistance of citizens Moreau, Bernard, and Lannoy in this work. The monuments that form part of this plan will be entrusted to each of these artists by the Representatives of the People named in the preceding article.

29 To ensure the prompt execution of the present decree, the Commission of Public Works is charged with furnishing all the men, materials, and funds necessary for the rapid construction of the works that it calls for.

30 The Commission of Transport and Cartage will give the necessary orders to transport the statues and materials that the artists designate.

Register signed by Robespierre, Carnot, C.A. Prieur, B. Barère, A. Couthon, R. Lindet, Billaud-Varenne, and Collot d'Herbois.

Monument to the Defenders of the Republic

10 August 1792 (old style). The twelfth day of the month of Floréal, the second year of the French Republic, one and indivisible.

The Committee of Public Safety calls upon the artists of the Republic to compete for the design of a monument, dedicated to the memory of the citizens who died for the Fatherland on the glorious [memorable] day of 10 August 1792 (old style), which is to be erected on Place de la Victoire.

Works will be displayed for competition in the Hall of Liberty from now until 15 Prairial. They will be judged before the twentieth of this month by the jury of arts.

The Commission of Public Works will supply the funds necessary for the execution of this monument, as soon as the contest has been judged.

Monument on the Pont-Neuf

The fifth day of the month of Floréal, the second year of the French Republic, one and indivisible.

The Committee of Public Safety decrees that the Commission of Public Works will consult with David, deputy, on the quickest possible execution of the bronze monument that is to be erected on the west point of the Isle de Paris, according to a decree of 27 Brumaire, and which is to represent the French people crushing fanaticism, royalism, and federalism.

The commission will report to the committee in ten days on the measures it has taken for the execution of the present decree, which will be inserted in the bulletin of the National Convention.

Monuments of the Reunion of 10 August 1793 (old style)

The fifth day of the month of Floréal, the second year of the French Republic, one and indivisible.

The Committee of Public Safety, in execution of the decree of the National Convention of the — of last August (old style), calls on all the artists of the Republic to compete in the execution of bronze and marble monuments that are to retrace for posterity the glorious epochs of the French Revolution, represented in the festival of the Reunion of last 10 August (old style).

The contest will be open for three months, reckoning from 10 Floréal or from the day of the reception of the present decree for artists who are in the departments; after this space of time the sketches will be exhibited for a complete *décade* in the Hall of Liberty, in the meeting-place of the National Convention; they will be transferred to the Hall of Laocoon to be displayed and judged the following *décade* by the jury of arts.

The three artists who are runners-up for the prize will be given priority in the execution of other monuments or other national works, which they will execute at the same time as the artists who obtain the prize in the competition; the committee reserves the right to designate the works to be done.

The present decree will be inserted in the bulletin of the National Convention.

Notice about the Subjects for Competition
The subjects for competition are:
1 The figure of Regenerated Nature on the ruins of the Bastille.
2 The triumphal arch of 6 October on the so-called boulevard des Italiens, with an invitation to the architects to position it better.
3 The figure of Liberty for [on] the Place de la Révolution.
4 The figure of the French People crushing Federalism.

Competition for Painters

The fifth day of the month of Floréal, the second year of the French Republic, one and indivisible.

The Committee of Public Safety calls on all the artists of the Republic to represent on canvas their choice of the most glorious epochs of the French Revolution.

The competition will be open for one month, reckoning from 10 Floréal or from the reception of the present decree for the artists who are in the departments. After this space of time the sketches will be exhibited for half a *décade* in the Hall of Liberty. They will then be transferred to the Hall of Laocoon to be displayed and judged the following *décade* by the jury of arts.

The present decree will be inserted in the bulletin of the National Convention.

The Column for the Panthéon

The fifth day of the month of Floréal, the second year of the French Republic, one and indivisible.

The Committee of Public Safety calls on the artists of the Republic to compete in the execution of a column to be erected in the Panthéon, by virtue of a decree of the National Convention, in honour of the warriors who died for the Fatherland.

The competition will be open for two *décades*, reckoning from 10 Floréal or from the day of reception of the present decree for the artists who are in the departments. After this space of time, the sketches will be exhibited for five days in the Hall of Liberty, in the meeting-place of the National Convention.

They will be transferred to the Hall of Laocoon to be judged in the following five days by the jury of arts.

The present decree will be inserted in the bulletin of the National Convention.

Statue of J.-J. Rousseau on the Champs-Elysées

The fifth day of Floréal, the second year of the French Republic, one and indivisible.

The Committee of Public Safety, in execution of the decree of the Constituent Assembly for a bronze statue in honour of J.-J. Rousseau, calls on all the artists of the Republic to compete for this monument, which will be placed in the Champs-Elysées.

The competition will end 10 Prairial. The contest entries will be displayed for five days in the Hall of Liberty, in the meeting-place of the National Convention, and transferred afterwards to the Hall of Laocoon to be judged by the jury of arts the following *décade*.

Covered Arenas to Accommodate the Concerts for the People

The fifth day of the month of Floréal, the second year of the French Republic, one and indivisible.

The Committee of Public Safety calls upon the artists of the Republic to compete in transforming the premises used by the Théâtre de l'Opéra, between rue de Bondy and the boulevard, into covered arenas. These arenas are intended for the celebration by civic and martial songs about the triumphs of the Republic and of national festivals during the winter.

The contest will be open for one month, reckoning from 10 Floréal or from the day of reception of the present decree for artists in the departments.

After this space of time, the sketches will be exhibited for five days in the Hall of Liberty, in the meeting-place of the National Convention.

They will then be transferred to the Hall of Laocoon to be judged by the jury of arts.

The present decree will be inserted in the bulletin of the National Convention.

Champs-Elysées

The fifth day of the month of Floréal, the second year of the French Republic, one and indivisible.

The Committee of Public Safety decrees that:

The two Horses of Marly be placed at the entrance of the Champs-Elysées opposite the two figures of Coysevox next to the Pont-tournant, on pedestals that David will design in collaboration with citizen Hubert, Inspector of National Works.

The Commission of Public Works will supervise the execution of, and furnish the funds necessary for, the creation of these works.

Temple to Equality

The twelfth day of the month of Floréal, of the second year of the French Republic, one and indivisible.

The Committee of Public Safety decrees that:
1 The garden of the national house known by the name of Beaujon House will be made public, and will be part and continuation of the Champs-Elysées.
2 The ditches and parapets will be demolished and filled in.
3 A Temple to Equality will be erected in the garden.
4 Artists are called upon to compete for the simple architecture and republican decorations most suitable for this monument.
5 The competition is open during the third *décade* of Floréal. The plans will be set

out in the Hall of Liberty on 25 Floréal. This competition will be judged on 30 Floréal by the jury of arts.

The Commission of Public Works will take the measures necessary for the prompt execution of this decree; it will furnish the necessary funds.

Statue of Philosophy

The twelfth day of the month of Floréal, the second year of the French Republic, one and indivisible.

The Committee of Public Safety decrees that:

1 There will be placed in the first hall of the meeting-place of the National Convention a simple pedestal to receive the statue of Philosophy holding the Rights of Man and the constitutional act.

2 The statue that was made by Houdon, representing Philosophy, will be evaluated and bought by the Commission of Public Works.

3 This commission will have the pedestal erected immediately from the marbles in the storehouse of the Petits-Augustins or in the national houses. It will furnish the necessary funds.

Rural Architecture

The thirteenth day of the month of Floréal, the second year of the French Republic, one and indivisible.

The Committee of Public Safety calls upon the artists of the Republic to compete in the improvement of the lot of the rural inhabitants by proposing simple and economical means of constructing more comfortable and healthier farms and houses, taking into consideration the localities of the different departments, and making use of the demolition of fortified castles, feudal buildings, and national houses whose conservation is judged unprofitable. The artists will attach detailed plans to their entries. The jury of arts will judge the contest, which will be open for three months.

The Commission of Public Instruction and Public Works are charged with supervising the execution of this decree.

Museum of Natural History

The twenty-seventh day of the month of Floréal, the second year of the French Republic, one and indivisible.

The Committee of Public Safety decrees that:

In order to succeed in implementing the decree for the improvement of the Museum of Natural History, issued 16 Germinal by the National Convention, citizen Molinos will examine:

1 Which national possessions and neighbouring territories could be joined to this national establishment.

2 How the Bièvre River – the so-called Rivière des Gobelins – could be incorporated, and how this useful monument could be extended as far as the boulevard and the horse market on one side, and rue Saint Bernard on the other. Citizen

Molinos will have a rough appraisal made of the houses or property of citizens within this enclave.

The Committee of National Property is requested to have suspended the estimation and sale of the national properties called Saint-Victor's and of other national properties that might be included in the enlargement projects of the Museum of Natural History.

The Museum of Arts in the Palais-National

Paris, 13 Floréal, Year II of the French Republic, one and indivisible.

The Committee of Public Safety decrees that:

Citizen Lannoi [Delannoy], architect, and curator of the museum, is charged with having the Museum of the Republic built immediately, in conformity with the plan (classification numbers 1 and 2) that he presented to the committee, and under the supervision of David and Granet, Representatives of the People.

He will begin with the side back to back with the Tuileries, Pavilion of Equality.

He will have it lit from the top and the reinforcements of the casement windows, which are destined to receive statues.

The Committee of Public Works is charged with accelerating the execution of the present decree and with furnishing the necessary funds.

The fourteenth Floréal, the second year of the French Republic, one and indivisible.

The Committee of Public Safety decrees:

That citizen Hubert, Inspector of National Buildings, will present in the course of the next *décade* an estimate of the expense that the execution of the preceding decrees for the embellishment of the Palais, Jardin-national, and Place de la Révolution, Museum of Painting, Museum of Natural History, and other public monuments may cause the Republic; to be presented for the approval of the National Convention in the report that is to be made to it on the arts and monuments of the entire Republic and the sums to be assigned to this end.

Improvement of National Dress

The twenty-fifty day of Floréal, the second year of the French Republic, one and indivisible.

The Committee of Public Safety requests David, Representative of the People, to present to it his views and projects on the means of improving the present national dress and of making it appropriate to the republican way of life and to the character of the Revolution; so that it can present the results to the National Convention to obtain the wish of public opinion.

Poets and Citizens Interested in Literature

27 Floréal, second year of the French Republic, one and indivisible.

The Committee of Public Safety calls on the poets to celebrate the principal events of the French Revolution; to compose patriotic hymns and poems, and republican plays; to publicize the heroic actions of the soldiers of liberty, the courageous deeds and the devotedness of Republicans, and the victories won by the French armies.

It likewise calls on citizens interested in literature to transmit to posterity the most significant events and greatest epochs in the regeneration of the French people; to give to history the firm, severe character appropriate to the annals of a great people conquering its liberty under attack by all the tyrants of Europe; it calls on them to compose school-books, and to incorporate republican principles in the works intended for public instruction. Meanwhile, the committee will propose to the Convention the form of national reward to be accorded their works, and the dates and forms of the competition.

The Teaching of Foreign Languages

Paris, 27 Floréal, Year II of the French Republic, one and indivisible.

The Committee of Public Safety decrees that public instruction in the languages of all countries other than those with whom the Republic is at war will be established for the use of sailors, naturalists, foreign agents of the Republic, and citizens interested in the sciences.

In this national establishment there will be a printing office in which all the foreign typographical characters that the Republic possesses will be gathered.

The Commission of Public Instruction is charged with searching out citizens most suited to this part of teaching.

The Committee of National Property is requested to designate the national house most suitable for this type of establishment.

National Institute of Music

28 Floréal, second year of the French Republic, one and indivisible.

The Committee of Public Safety decrees that the national house formerly called les Menus, located on rue Bergère, will hereafter serve as the National Institute of Music, established by the decrees of the National Convention.

The Committee of National Property will provide for the Section du Faubourg Montmartre to establish itself, along with its committees, in another national house.

The National Institute of Music cannot establish itself in rue Bergère until all the furniture and national possessions deposited there have been transported elsewhere, and the Section du Faubourg Montmartre has been established in another national house.

The Committee of National Property will give the necessary orders to have this national house evacuated.

The committee calls on all musicians or professors of music to compete, in the form to be prescribed by a decree of the Convention, in the composition of civic songs, of music for national festivals and for the theatre, of martial music and in whatever form their art is best suited to reminding Republicans of the sentiments and memories most dear to the Revolution.

National Civic Architecture

28 Floréal, second year of the French Republic, one and indivisible.

The Committee of Public Safety calls on all architects to compose and develop projects and civic architectural plans, appropriate for a Republic, for the various public monuments that are to be executed in the Communes of the Republic.

They will take particular care to give each type of monument the character suited to it.

The projects up for competition during the months of Prairial and Messidor are the places destined for the exercise of the sovereignty of the people in primary assemblies, the places consecrated to *décadi* celebrations, municipal buildings, tribunals, justices of the peace, prisons, jails, national theatres, public baths, and fountains.

The works will be displayed in competition in the Hall of Liberty until 30 Messidor. They will be judged before the following 10 Thermidor by the jury of arts.

Appendix D

Here we have listed the projects submitted by sculptors whether or not they were specifically called for by the government. A table of all the architectural projects has already been published by Szambien, *Les Projets de l'an II*, 198–208. The numbers are those under which works were registered, sometimes several under the same number. Asterisks indicate prize-winning works.

Antoine, [Etienne d'?]
- Figure of the French People trampling Federalism. 1978[bis].
- Sketch of Liberty. 1988.
- Two sketches of the People crushing Federalism. 1988.

Auger, [Louis]
- Pyramid in terra cotta on a marble base. "Justice opens the way for impartiality." 1383.

Bac[c]ari, [Antoine]
- A carton full of studies for public monuments (but a note in the register says he later withdrew them). 1361.
- A carton full of forty-two pieces consisting of studies for public monuments.(A note says he also removed these to take them to the Commission on Monuments.) 1848.

Batard
- A statue of Rousseau. 1351.

Bervet [Bervic, Jean-Guillaume?]
- A figure representing the People trampling Federalism. 2294.
- A statue of Liberty for the Place de la Révolution. 2294.
- Liberty announcing herself to all peoples. 2294.

Blaise, Barthélémy
- A statue of Rousseau. 1358.

Boichot, Guillaume
- A Colossus for the Pont Neuf. 1557.*

Boizot, [Simon-Louis]
- A terra cotta model of Rousseau unveiling natural laws to mankind. 1449.
- In the name of the sculptors of Sèvres [porcelain works], a project representing the People trampling fanaticism, royalism, and Federalism. 1536.*

Boquet, [Simon-Louis]
- A model in plaster in two pieces representing the French People. 1532.

Bouillet, [Jacques-Antoine]
- A statue showing Rousseau guiding Emile along the paths of virtue. 1424.

Bourreiff, [Louis-Jérôme]
- A statue of Liberty twenty inches [*pouces*] tall. 1977.

Bouvet, [Claude]
- A model in terra cotta representing the French People standing upright. 1520.
- A model in terra cotta of a monument in honour of the heroes who died fighting for Liberty. 1526.

Budelot, [Jean-Baptiste]
- A terra cotta statue of Rousseau. 1326.
- A terra cotta project for the Place des Victoires. "Liberty, Equality." 1503.

Cardon, [Nicolas-Vincent?], sculptor
- An addition to the former cathedral of Paris. 1913.

Cartellier, [Pierre]
- Sketch of a Colossus for the Pont Neuf. "Union." 1568.
- A figure of Liberty. 1986.
- A figure of Nature. 1986.*

Castel, [Jean-Jacques]
- A model of a Liberty. 1992.*

Chapelier
- The triumphant Mountain serving as a fountain and as a public clock. 1962.

Chaudet [Antoine-Denis]
- A sketch representing Rousseau. 1390.*
- A project for a Colossus for the Pont Neuf. "Force and Courage." 1565.*

Delorme
- A project for a Colossus for the Pont-Neuf, a Hercules carrying a statue of Liberty and Equality. "The weakest talents must be devoted to the Fatherland." 1554.

Desfond [Desfonts], Citizenness
- A Colossus representing the French People overturning Federalism. 1987.

Dumont, [Jacques-Edme]
- A Colossus representing the French People. 1561.*
- A group representing the People trampling down Federalism. 2004.*
- A figure of Liberty. 2004.*

Espercieux, [Jean-Joseph]
- A model of a statue of Rousseau. 1444.
- A sketch for a figure of Liberty. 1994.*

Foinon and Fouchon, sculptors
- A column for the Pantheon. 1465.

Foucaud [Foucou, Jean-Joseph]
- A statue representing the French People. 1575.

Four[r]eau, [Jacques-François]
- A project for the Place des Victoires. 1504.
- A project for a Colossus representing the French People trampling down Federalism. 1590.

Francin, [Guillaume]
- A figure representing Regeneration. 1957.
- Two figures of Liberty. 1957.
- A figure of Equality. 1957.

Gois, [Etienne-Pierre-Andrien?]
- A figure of Liberty. 1959.

Houdon, [Jean-Antoine]
- A statue of Rousseau. 1433.
- Busts of Rousseau. 1447.
- Project for a monument to the statue ("de monument à la statue"). 1447.

Lecomte, [Felix]
- Model of a statue representing the People in the guise of Hercules. "To the Republic." 1571.

Le Maux [Lemot, François-Frédéric]
- A figure of the French People. 1552.*

Le Sueur, [Jacques-Philippe]
- A figure in plaster representing Rousseau. "By unveiling Nature he founded our liberty." 1432.
- A figure representing the French people for the Pont Neuf. "Liberty, Equality." 1555.*
- A figure of Liberty. 1984.

Lorta, [Jean-François]
- A statue of Rousseau with the number 229. 1408.
- A sketch of a Colossus of the French People. "A free people is the friend of the virtues." 1564.*
- The French People crushing Federalism. 1981.
- A statue of Liberty. 1981.

Lucas, [Jean-Robert-Nicolas]
- A model representing the French People. 1570.

Maçon, [Masson, François]
- A model of a figure of Nature. 1990.
- The People trampling down Federalism. 1990.

Marin, [Joseph-Charles]
- A clay model of a statue of Rousseau. 1327.
- A clay figure of Liberty. 1964.
- A group representing Nature Regenerated. 1980.

Martin, François
- A sketch of Liberty.
- [An image of Rousseau uncovering Nature]¹

Michalon, [Claude]
- A statue of Rousseau. "Vitam impudere viro" (The life does not dishonour the man). 1315.
- A statue of the French People. 1560.*
- A figure of the French People overthrowing Federalism. 1960.*

Moitte, [Jean-Guillaume]
- A design 6 feet tall with the slogan, "Liberty, Equality." 1325.*
- A statue of Rousseau meditating on early childhood. 1412.*

Monot, [Martin-Claude]
- A figure of Rousseau. 1392.*
- A sketch representing the Colossus. "Everything for the Republic." 1622.

Morgan, [Jean-Jacques]
- A sketch of the figure of Rousseau. 1400.
- A plaster figure representing Liberty leaning on a fasces while holding in one hand a spade and a javelin and in the other hand two wings from which a flame emerges. 2057.*

Moutoni, [Antoine]
- A figure of Rousseau. 1365.

Pequignot, [Jean-Pierre]
- A sketch of Liberty. 1991.

Pouchou, [?], and Martin, [François]
- Rousseau. A model showing Rousseau unveiling Nature and showing the Eternal to a child. 1406.

Ramey, [Claude]
- A figure of Rousseau. 1355.
- A Colossus for the Pont Neuf. 1556.*

Riffaud, [L?]
- A figure representing Liberty seated. 1439.
- Another figure of Liberty standing on the ruins of the Bastille. 1439.

Roland, [Philippe-Laurent]
- Project for a Colossus representing the French People trampling down Federalism. 1591.*

Rousselot
- Clay model of the Republic uncovering truth in the eyes of Nature. 1478.

Siger, [?]
- Project for a triumphal entrance for the Barrière des Gobelins. 1847.

Sigisbert, [François-Michel]
- A statue of Liberty. 1982bis.

Somon, [? illegible. Could be read as "Foucou"]
- A model of Rousseau. 1466.

Stouf, [Jean-Baptiste]
- A design of the apotheosis of Marat "on his bed of honour." 1456.

Suzanne, [François-Marie]
- Two figures representing Rousseau. "Fraternity." 1450.
- Terra cotta, model of a monument for the Place des Victoires. "Perseverance." 1506.*
- Colossus of the French People for the Pont Neuf. Number only. 1550.
- Same description as the one above. 1613.
- A figure of Liberty. 1978.
- The statue of Nature [Regenerated]. 1978.*
- The French People crushing Federalism. 1978.*

Taunay, [August]
- A statue of Rousseau. 1385.

Thiérard [Jean-Baptiste]
- A statue of Rousseau in an allegorical group. 1425.
- A sketch representing the People. 1989.
- Another sketch representing Nature [Regenerated]. 1989.

Appendix E

PRIZES AWARDED BY THE ART JURY IN THE CONTEST OF YEAR II

This list is based on the report delivered by Portiez and approved by the Convention on 14 Fructidor an III (31 August 1795).[1] The numbers on the left are the numbers given to each work in the catalogue of the submissions as they were displayed for the public and the jurors in the Salle de la Liberté, the antechamber of the Convention.[2]

Awards to the Rough Designs for Sculpture

Contest for the colossal figure of the People to be erected on the promontory of the Pont Neuf

1	Lemot from Lyon	The model of his rough design	10,000
19	Ramey from the Côte d'Or	The model of his rough design	10,000
22	Michallon from Lyon	The model of his rough design	10,000
3	Lorta from Paris	The model of a figure of his choice	6,000
8	Baccarit from Paris	The model of a figure of his choice	6,000
9	Dumont from Paris	The model of a figure of his choice	6,000
11	Boichot from Chalons-sur-Marne	The model of a figure of his choice	6,000
5	Chaudet from Paris	A monetary award	1,500
6	Lesueur from Paris	A monetary award	1,500
12	Boizot from the Louvre	A monetary award	1,500

Contest for the statue of Nature Regenerated on the ruins of the Bastille

28	Suzanne from Paris	A monetary award	1,000
33	Cartelier from Paris	A monetary award	1,000

Contest for the statue of the People trampling down Federalism

40	Michallon from Lyon	The model of his rough design*	10,000
44	Dumont from Paris	The model of his rough design*	10,000
41	Suzanne from Paris	The model of a figure of his choice	6,000
36	Roland from Lille	The model of a figure of his choice	6,000

*Converted to a figure of their choice because of the ban on symbols of Federalism.

Contest for the statue of J.-J. Rousseau projected for the Champs-Elysées

54	Moitte from Paris	Execution in bronze of his rough design	no final value set

59	Chaudet from Paris	The model of a figure of his choice	6,000
68	Monot from Paris	A monetary award	1,800

Contest for the figure of Liberty on the Place de la Révolution

88	Morgan from Abbeville	The model of his rough design	7,000
103	Dumont from Paris	The model of his rough design	7,000
106	Espercieux from Marseille	The model of a figure of his choice	6,000
110	Castex from Toulouse	A monetary award	2,500

Contest for the clock (pendule) for the Hall of the Convention
The jury decided that no prize would be awarded.

Engravings and Medals

103	Duvivier from Paris	The medal made from his design would be purchased by the nation.	
No no.	Dumarest	The medal made from his design for a head of Rousseau would be purchased by the nation.	
No no.	Dumarest	A head of Brutus. Execution of a medal of his choice	6,000

Total (for sculpture)		128,800

Awards to Projects for Architecture

Contest for the triumphal arch in memory of the journée of 6 October

2	Moitte from Paris	The model in relief of his project	6,000
27	Sobre from Paris	The medium monetary award	2,000
11	Rousseau from Nantes	The minimum monetary award	1,000
18	Voinier from Paris	The minimum monetary award	1,000

Contest for the column to be erected in the Pantheon

4	Percier from Rome and Fontaine from Pontoise	The maximum monetary award	4,000
11	Meunier from Paris, resident in Nimes	The maximum monetary award	3,000
2	Durand from Paris and Thibault from Montierender	The medium monetary award	2,000
9	Vignon from Lyon	The medium monetary award	2,000
3	Lefebvre from Paris	The minimum monetary award	1,000

Contest for covered arenas on the site of the old Opéra rue de Bondi

6	La Hure from Paris	The medium monetary award	2,000

Contest for the monument to be erected on the Place des Victoires

23	Sobre from Paris	The maximum monetary award	2,000
6	Allais from Rouen	The minimum monetary award	1,000
7	Vignon from Lyon	The minimum monetary award	1,000
22	Suzanne from Paris	The minimum monetary award[3]	1,500

Contest for the Temple to Equality on the site of the Beaujon Garden

1 Durand from Paris and Thibault from Montierender	Execution of their project as a national monument	7,000
2 Lemercier from Paris	The medium monetary award	2,000
8 Villers from Lyon	The medium monetary award	2,000

Contest for rural architecture

6 Damesme from Magny near Mantes	The minimum monetary award	1,000
7, 8, 9 Benoit	The minimum monetary award	1,000

Contest for primary assemblies

3 Durand from Paris and Thibault from Montierender	The model in relief of their project	5,000
6c Durand from Paris and Thibault from Montierender	The model in relief of their project	4,000

Contest for temples décadaires

1 Durand from Paris and Thibault from Montierender	The model in relief of their project	6,000
2 Durand from Paris and Thibault from Montierender	The model in relief of their project	4,000
9 Lafosse from Rouen	The maximum monetary award	3,000
11 Cochet from Lyon	The maximum monetary award	4,000

Contest for city halls (maisons communes)

4 Durand from Paris and Thibault from Montierender	The model in relief of their project	5,000
5b Durand from Paris and Thibault from Montierender	The model in relief of their project	4,000
3 Protain from Paris	The model in relief of his project	2,000

Contest for court houses (tribunaux)

1 Durand from Paris and Thibault from Montierender	The maximum monetary award	3,000
3a Bienaimé from Amiens	The maximum monetary award	3,000

Contest for justices of the peace

3 Bienaimé from Amiens	The model in relief of his project	4,000
5 Vignon from Lyon	The model in relief of his project	4,000
6a Durand from Paris and Thibault from Montierender	The minimum monetary award	1,000

Contest for prisons and detention centres (maisons d'arrêt)

1 Destournelles [sic] from St Denis	The minimum monetary award	1,000
4 Florence from Paris	The minimum monetary award	1,000

Contest for national theatres

The jury has declared unanimously that there were no grounds for awarding prizes to the submissions in this category.

Contest for public baths

5 Durand from Paris and Thibault from Montierender	The minimum monetary award	1,000

Contest for public fountains

2 Durand from Paris and Thibault from Montierender	The minimum monetary award	1,000

Projects for the embellishment of Paris

2 Percier from Paris and Fontaine from Ponthoise	The maximum monetary award	3,000
4 Percier from Paris and Fontaine from Ponthoise	The maximum monetary award	4,000
18 Bienaimé from Amiens	The medium monetary award	2,500
1 Gisors from Paris	The minimum monetary award	1,000

Various objects

The jury declared unanimously that there were no grounds for awarding prizes in this category.

Total (for architecture)	109,000

[Signed] Quatremère, President

Dufourny, Secretary

Notes

I THE LEGACY

1 Werner Szambien, *Les Projets de l'an II. Concours d'architecture de la période révolutionaire* (Paris 1986), is a valuable study of one important event in the realm of architecture at the time, but it does not relate the projects to the overall policies of the revolutionary government. The little book by Annie Jacques and Jean-Pierre Mouilleseaux, *Les Architectes de la Liberté* (Paris 1988), is beautifully and profusely illustrated, but does provide much space for an in-depth analysis of the relationship between architecture and politics. Also useful is the article by Daniel Rabreau, "Architecture et la fête," in Philippe Bordes and Régis Michel, eds., *Aux armes et aux arts. Les Arts de la Révolution 1789–1799* (Paris 1989), 233–79, which contains some perceptive comments, despite several incorrect dates, wrong locations, and curious omissions in the bibliography. See too the article "Architecture" by J. Tulard, J.-F. Fayard, and A. Fierro, *Histoire et dictionnaire de la Révolution française* (Paris 1987).

2 Anatole Kopp, *Ville et révolution. Architecture et urbanisme soviétique des années vingt* (Paris 1967).

3 Barbara Miller Lane, *Architecture and Politics in Germany, 1918–1945* (Cambridge, Mass., 1968).

4 Robert R. Taylor, *The Word in Stone: The World of Architecture in National Socialist Ideology* (Berkeley 1974).

5 Gary Kates, "Propaganda," *Historical Dictionary of the French Revolution*, 2 vols. (Westport, Conn. 1985), 2: 785, argues that the philosophes were not propagandists because they tried to foster independent critical thinking, but this does not seem to be true in the case of their attacks on Catholicism. Gates contends that "it was not until the Revolution that propaganda emerged as a potent force," an assertion that seems to ignore many precedents.

6 Athanase Détournelle, *Aux armes et aux arts! Peinture, sculpture, architecture, gravure. Journal de la Société républicaine des arts séant au Louvre* (Paris, n.d.), 71.

7 There are a number of examples in Institut Français d'architecture, *Places et monuments* (Liège and Bruxelles 1984). In this collection Maurice Culot and others argue that to isolate a cathedral and treat it as a monument violates history.

8 Pierre Patte, *Monumens érigés en France à la gloire de Louis XV* (Paris 1765), pl. 39.

9 Voltaire, *Le Siècle de Louis XIV*, in *Oeuvres complètes*, ed. Louis Moland, 52 vols. (Paris 1877–83), XIV, chap. xxvii, 494.

10 Jean-Joseph Expilly, *Dictionnaire géographique, historique et politique des Gaules et de la France*, 6 vols. (Paris 1762–70), v: 410.

11 I am indebted to June Hargrove of the University of Maryland for the ideas she developed about the public monument in the late Enlightenment in a paper delivered in Pisa in 1980 to the Fifth International Congress on the Enlightenment. A brief outline appeared in *Studies on Voltaire and the Eighteenth Century* 193 (1980): 1752.

12 Bib. Nat., Estampes, Va 54, vol. 5.

13 *De la place Louis XV à la place de la Concorde*, Musée Carnavalet, 17 mai–14 août 1982, 42–57.

14 "Monument érigé par la ville de Reims en 1765," engraving drawn by C.-N. Cochin and engraved by P.E. Moitte, Bib. Nat., Estampes, Coll. Hennin, no. 9237.

15 On the growth and impact of nationalism see James A. Leith, "Nationalism and the Fine Arts in France, 1750–1789," *Studies on Voltaire and the Eighteenth Century* 89 (1972): 919–37, plus 8 plates; and "The Idea of the Inculcation of National Patriotism in French Educational Thought," ed. J.D. Browning, *Education in the 18th Century*, Publications of the McMaster Association for Eighteenth-Century Studies (New York 1979), VI: 59–77.

16 Patte, *Monuments érigés en France*, 210–12. There is no large engraving of Servandoni's plan, but a small view of it appears above the key to Patte's map, fig. 1.

17 On the idea of a "space of emulation" see Richard A. Etlin, *The Architecture of Death* (Cambridge, Mass., and London, England, 1984), 59–63.

18 Abbé Marc-Antoine Laugier, *Observations sur l'architecture* (The Hague and Paris 1765), 233–5.

19 Bib. Nat., Estampes, Pd 3, pl. 92, and Ha 59 fol., not paginated.

20 Etlin, *The Architecture of Death*, passim.

21 Ecole des Beaux-Arts, PR 1778.

22 *Projets et dessins pour la Place Royale du Peyrou à Montpellier*, Inventaire général des monuments et des richesses artistiques du Languedoc-Roussillon (Caisse nationale des monuments historiques et des sites 1983), 63.

23 Arch. Dép., Hérault, C 7960.

24 Ibid.

25 *Projets et dessins pour la Place Royale du Peyrou*, 65–6.

26 Leith, "Nationalism and the Fine Arts," Table F: Statues of Famous Frenchmen Commissioned by the Government from 1775 to the Revolution.

27 Bib. Nat., Estampes, Ha 56, pl. 47.

28 Bib. Nat., Estampes, Ha 56, pls. 26–31.

29 *Encyclopédie*, VII, col. 51.

30 See the Index des Programmes in Jean-Marie Pérouse de Montclos, *Les Prix de Rome. Concours de l'académie d'architecture* (Paris 1984), 251–2.

31 Anthony Vidler, *The Writing of the Walls. Architectural Theory in the Late Enlightenment* (Princeton 1986), 35 ff.

32 Yvan Christ and Ionel Schein, *L'Oeuvre et les rêves de Claude-Nicolas Ledoux* (Paris 1971) 41–130. See especially the plan on p 45 and the perspective view on p 51.

33 Helen Rosenau, *Social Purpose in Architecture* (London 1970), does not deal specifically with amphitheatres despite the intention of planners to use them for social manipulation and control. More recently Anthony Vidler, *The Writing of the Walls* (Princeton 1986), does not discuss them in his otherwise very revealing discussion of other forms of "architecture of association."

34 Pérouse de Montclos, *Les Prix de Rome*, 102–3; *Procès-verbaux de l'Académie royale d'architecture*, ed. H. Lemonnier (Paris 1911–29), VIII: 47–9, 59–60.

35 Pérouse de Montclos, *Les Prix de Rome*, 171–2. This design was published in Allais, Détournelle, and Vaudoyer, *Grands prix d'architecture*, with the date 1784, but there was no program for such a design in that year, whereas in 1781 there was a program for "une fête publique à l'occasion de la paix. Cette fête s'exécutera sur 300 toises de longeur sur 200 de largeur tant sur terre que sur l'eau. On indiquera dans la partie du pourtour des amphithéâtres commodes et agréables pour les spectateurs": *Procès-verbaux de l'Académie royale d'architecture*, IX: 55. There was no peace treaty in 1781, but there was anticipation of the end of the War of American Independence, which came in 1783. The original of Sobre's design is in the Bibliothèque Doucet, OA 577.

36 Pérouse de Montclos, *Les Prix de Rome*, 173–5; *Procès-verbaux de l'Académie royale d'architecture*, IX: 65. A future dauphin had been born to Louis XVI and Marie Antoinette on 22 October 1781.

37 Pérouse de Montclos, *Les Prix de Rome*, 183–5; *Procès-verbaux de l'Académie royale d'architecture*, IX, 100–2.

38 Pérouse de Montclos, *Les Prix de Rome*, 201–2; *Procès-verbaux de l'Académie royale d'architecture*, IX, 203.

39 Pérouse de Montclos, *Les Prix de Rome*, 67–71, 142–5, 199–201.

40 Bib. Nat., Estampes, Ha 55, 15–24.

41 Jean-Marie Pérouse de Montclos, *Etienne-Louis Boullée 1728–1799: de l'architecture classique à l'architecture révolutionnaire* (Paris 1969), 182, concludes that the designs were done in 1783.

42 Bib. Nat., ms français 9153, 111ᵛ. There are two editions of this text in English and one in French: Etienne-Louis Boullée, *Treatise on Architecture: A Complete Presentation of the "Architecture · Essai sur l'art,"* ed. Helen Rosenau (London 1953); Helen Rosenau, *Boullée and Visionary Architecture: Including Boullée's "Architecture, Essay on Art,"* (London and New York 1976); and Etienne-Louis Boullée, *Architecture. Essai sur l'art*, with an introduction and notes by Jean-Marie Pérouse de Montclos (Paris 1968).

43 Abbé Brotier, "Premier mémoire sur les jeux du cirque, considérés dans les vues politiques des Romains. Lû janvier 1781," *Histoire de l'Académie des inscriptions et belles-lettres 1780–1784*, vol. 45, (Paris 1793), 478–694; "Second mémoire", 495–508; and "Troisième mémoire," 509–24.

44 Bib. Nat., ms français 9153, 112r–112v.

45 Marc-Antoine Laugier, *Essai sur l'architecture*, 2nd ed. (Paris 1755), 10.

46 Jean-Louis Viel de Saint-Maux, *Lettres sur l'architecture des anciens, et celle des modernes, dans lesquelles se trouve développé le génie symbolique qui présida aux monuments de l'antiquité* (Paris 1787).

47 Vidler, *The Writing of the Walls*, 49.

48 Martin Couret de Villeneuve, *L'Ecole des Francs Maçons* ("Jerusalem" 1748), 13.

49 On the terminology of architectural discourse in the sixteenth, seventeenth, and eighteenth centuries see the excellent study by Werner Szambien, *Symétrie, goût, caractère: théorie et terminologie de l'architecture à l'âge classique 1550–1800* (Paris 1986).

50 Bib. Nat., ms français 9153, 70r–70v.

51 Ibid., 84r.

52 Ibid., 107v.

53 Marie-Joseph Peyre, *Oeuvres d'architecture* (Paris 1765), intro.

54 Hugh Honour, *Neo-classicism* (Harmondsworth, England, 1968), 29.

55 Allan Braham, *The Architecture of the French Enlightenment* (Berkeley and Los Angeles 1980), 83–5.

56 Peyre, *Oeuvres d'architecture*, intro.

57 Honour, *Neo-classicism*, 51–7.

58 These can be seen in Braham, *Architecture of the French Enlightenment*, 73–82.

59 Henri Lemonnier, "La mégalomanie dans l'architecture," *L'Architecte* 4 (1910): 92–7.

60 Emile Kaufmann, "Three Revolutionary Architects, Boullée, Ledoux, and Lequeu," *Transactions of the American Philosophical Society*, n.s. 42, pt 3 (1952): 431–564. Among those who have adopted the term is Jean-Marie Pérouse de Montclos, who entitled his lengthy study of Boullée *Etienne-Louis Boullée (1728–1799): de l'architecture classique à l'architecture révolutionnaire* (Paris 1969), and his shorter book in English on Boullée *Etienne-Louis Boullée, Theoretician of Revolutionary Architecture* (New York 1974).

61 There is a copy of a placard attacking him along with Ledoux, Le Roy, and the sculptor Dardel in Bib. Nat., Estampes, Ha 80.

62 This is on the back of his design for a "Porte de Parisis qu'on peut appeler l'arc du peuple," Bib. Nat., Estampes, Ha 80, fig. 174.

63 *Courrier du Bas-Rhin*, no. 1, 1ᵉʳ janvier 1783, 1–3.

64 Simon-Nicolas-Henri Linguet, *Mémoires sur la Bastille et sur la détention de M Linguet dans ce Château-Royal depuis le 27 septembre 1780 jusqu'en mai 1782* (Londres 1783).

65 *Projet d'une place publique à la gloire de Louis XVI sur l'emplacement de la Bastille, ses fosses et dépendances, avec la continuation du rampart jusqu'à la rivière, sur partie des fosses de la Bastille, par le Sʳ Corbet architecte inspecteur des bâtiments de la ville de Paris en 1784*. Bib. Nat., Estampes, Va 250 a.

66 Arch. Nat., Cartes et Plans, F¹⁴ 10253, Paris no. 1, plans 1a and 1b.

67 Maille Dussausoy, *Le Citoyen désintéressé, ou diverses idées patriotiques, concernant quelques établissemens et embellissemens utiles à la ville de Paris*, 2 vols. (Paris 1767).

68 Ibid., I: 131.

69 This is discussed at length in James A. Leith, *The Idea of Art as Propaganda in France 1750–1799: A Study in the History of Ideas* (Toronto 1965; repr. 1969), esp. chaps. 3, 4, 5.

70 John Arthur Passmore, *The Perfectibility of Man* (New York 1970), 159–64.

71 C.-A. Helvétius, *De l'homme, de ses facultés intellectuelles et de son éducation*, 2 vols. (London 1771), in *Oeuvres complètes* (Paris 1795), XII: 71 (sect. 10, chap. 1).

72 Roland Grimsley, "Rousseau's Paris," *City and Society in the Eighteenth Century*, eds. Paul Fritz and David Williams, Publications of the McMaster University Association for Eighteenth-Century Studies, 3 (Toronto 1973): 3–18.

73 The works of Laugier, Patte, and Dussausoy have already been cited in nn 8, 18, and 67. Voltaire repeatedly called for urban improvements: *Oeuvres Complètes*, IV: 499–500; VIII: 597; XXI: 4; XXIII: 297–304, 473–8; XLVI: 102.

74 Viel de Saint-Maux, *Lettres sur l'architecture*, septième lettre, 34.

75 Laugier, *Essai sur l'architecture*, 209–32.

76 The plans were nos. 56 and 57 in the Salon of 1789, *Collection des livrets des anciens depuis 1673 jusqu'en 1800*, ed. Jules J. Guiffrey, 42 vols. (Paris 1869–72), vol. 35. One plan is now in the Bib. Nat., Cartes et Plans, Ge c 4384. The whole title is worth noting: "Projet d'utilité et d'embellissement pour la ville de Paris qui s'accorde avec les projets déjà arrêtés par le gouvernement dans lequel on a rassemblé de nouveaux monuments, des places publiques, des percés nécessaires pour donner des communications, augmenter les courants d'air, et où l'on propose la réunion des trois îles en une seule, les moyens de diriger le courant du bras septentrional de la rivière de la manière à le rendre plus navigable, et de l'autre à en former un port ou gare au centre de la capital."

77 Bib. Nat., Estampes, Va 33 fol., vol. III. There is another engraving in Arch. Mun. Bordeaux, XXI M/29 Rec. 26.

78 The royal *lettres patentes* and other documents are in Arch. Mun. Bordeaux, ms 546, 3–5.

79 François-Joseph Bélanger, "Nouveau plan de la Ville des Adelphes à bâtir au fief d'Artois" and "Plan de la Nouvelle Amérique à construire dans une partie du fief d'Artois," both in the Bib. Nat., Estampes, Ha 58 c, fol.

80 James A. Leith, "Le Culte de Franklin avant et pendant la Révolution française," *Annales historiques de la Révolution française*, no. 4 (1976): 543–71.

81 Abbé Etienne Teisserenc, *Géographie parisienne, en forme de dictionnaire, contenant l'explication de Paris, ou de son plan, mise en carte géographique du royaume de France, pour servir d'introduction à la géographie générale. Méthode nouvelle pour apprendre d'une manière pratique et locale, toutes les principales parties du Royaume* (Paris 1754).

82 Ibid., xix.

83 Leith, "The Idea of the Inculcation of Nationalism," passim. The first coupling of the words "education" and "national" seems to have been L.-R. Caradeuc de La Charlotais, *Essai d'éducation nationale, ou plan d'études pour la jeunesse* (n.p., 1763).

84 Leith, "Nationalism and the Fine Arts," 924–31.

85 James Leo Connolly Jr, *The Movement to Create a National Gallery of Art in Eighteenth-Century France*, PhD diss., University of Kansas 1962, available from University Microfilms.

86 Keith Baker, *The French Revolution and the Creation of Modern Political Culture* (Oxford and New York 1987), vol. I. This volume, the first of three on the birth of modern political

culture, deals with the Old Regime. Part VI, "The Evolution of Concepts," deals with the evolution of political terms.

87 Thomas E. Crow, *Painters and Public Life in Eighteenth-Century Paris* (New Haven and London 1985). For a very impressive critique of Crow, see Warren Roberts, "David's *Horatii* and *Brutus* Revisited: Are they Prerevolutionary Paintings?" *Consortium on Revolutionary Europe Proceedings 1986*, 510–18.

II A NEW SYMBOLIC ORDER

1 Emile Durkheim, *Elementary Forms of Religious Life*, trans. J.W. Swain (London 1915).

2 Mary Douglas, *Natural Symbols. Explorations in Cosmology* (London 1970). See too Edward Shils, *Center and Periphery: Essays in Macrosociology* (Chicago and London 1975), and Clifford Geertz, "Centers, Kings, and Charisma: Reflections on the Symbolics of Power," *Culture and Its Creation: Essays in Honour of Edward Shils*, ed. Joseph Ben-David and Terry Nichols Clark (Chicago 1977), 150–71.

3 Douët d'Arcq, *Inventaire de la collection des sceaux des Archives Nationales*, 3 vols. (Paris 1863), no. 133, shows the "sceau de majesté" the year Louis XVI ascended to the throne. In the Arch. Nat., Salle des Inventaires, there are photographs matching all the seals in the inventory.

4 Arch. Nat., AD XXᶜ 90–3, contain a collection of vignettes on official acts in the seventeenth and eighteenth centuries.

5 Jean-Louis Soulavie, *Mémoires historiques et politiques du règne de Louis XVI*, 6 vols. (Paris an x 1801). The quotation is in 4: 153.

6 James H. Billington, *Fire in the Minds of Men: Origins of the Revolutionary Faith* (New York 1980).

7 For example, the engraving "Droits de l'homme. L'homme enfin satisfait d'avoir recouvré ses droits, en rend graces à l'Etre Suprême" shows a naked man holding a pike, standing amid the debris of the tree of Feudalism, which has been struck by a bolt of lightning. Bib. Nat., Estampes Coll. de Vinck, vol. 25, no. 4199.

8 For example, the engraving entitled "Le Grand Pas de fait, ou l'Aurore d'un beau jour" shows a Frenchman striding over engravings of some of the sites of 14 July 1789 and some severed heads. Louis XVI takes his hand and points to a book on which is inscribed "La loi dès le 14 juillet." The sun is shown rising in the background. Bib. Nat., Estampes, Coll. de Vinck, vol. 10, no. 1609.

9 For example, the engraving entitled "Nuit du 4 au 5 août 1789, ou le Délire patriotique," which shows commoners smashing insignia of nobles and ecclesiastics. Bib. Nat., Estampes, Coll. de Vinck, vol. 17, no. 2770.

10 Camus objected to the old seal at the 16 February session of the Constituent Assembly. The Abbé Maury protested that a new seal would be expensive, but the Assembly decreed that the king be asked to have a new seal made in conformity with the laws. *Réimpression de l'Ancien Moniteur* (hereafter cited as *Moniteur*) 3, no. 49 (18 février 1790): 397.

11 Douët d'Arcq, *Inventaire*, no. 134, shows the royal seal as changed in 1790.

12 *Décret concernant les statues de la Place des Victoires*, 19 juin [1790], in *Collections générale des décrets* (Collection Baudouin), juin-juillet 1790, pp 103, 107. The decree was passed on 19 June, then approved in its final version on 20 June.

13 On Roman origins of the fasces see Anthony J. Marshall, "Symbols and Showmanship in Roman Public Life: The Fasces," *Phoenix* 38, no. 2 (1984): 120–41, with numerous references.

14 Early examples occur on the standards of the new National Guard in 1790: Bib. Nat., Estampes, Coll. de Vinck, vol. 12, nos. 2027, 2028.

15 See James A. Leith, "Symbols in Revolution: The Strange Metamorphoses of the Triangle during the French Revolution," in J.A. Leith, ed., *Symbols in Life and Art* (Royal Society of Canada 1987), 105–18.

16 The Masonic triangle appears on the Great Seal of the United States, where it forms the apex of a pyramid with thirteen rows of blocks, each row representing one of the new states. The pyramid was incomplete because other states would be formed, so it was completed with an equilateral triangle, an all-seeing Eye in the centre, radiating light. The seal is reproduced on the back of American one-dollar bills.

17 Bib. Nat., Estampes, Coll. de Vinck, vol. 12, no. 2027, 8.

18 Bib. Nat., Estampes, Coll. Hennin, vol. CXXIII, no. 10832.

19 Arch. Nat., AD IX 541.

20 The most important emblem-book was Cesare Ripa, *Iconologia, overo descrittione dell'imagini universali* (Roma 1593), of which there were several French translations. Others included Jean Baudoin, *Recueil d'emblèmes divers* (Paris 1638–39); Honoré Lacombe de Prezel, *Dictionnaire iconologique* (Paris 1756); J.-B. Boudard, *Iconologie tirée de divers auteurs* (Parma and Paris 1759); Jean-Charles Delafosse, *Nouvelle iconologie historique* (Paris 1768); and Charles-Etienne Gaucher, *Iconologie, ou traité de la science des allégories*, a multi-volumed work, the appearance of which stretched into the Revolution.

21 Lacombe de Prezel, *Dictionnaire*, x.

22 Ibid., under the entry "Liberté."

23 For several examples see James A. Leith, "Reflections on Allegory in the French Revolution," *Consortium on Revolutionary Europe 1987*, 631–45, esp. pls. 2 and 3.

24 Cesare Ripa, *Iconology; or a Collection of Emblematical Figures*, English version by George Richardson, 2 vols. (London 1779), 2: 46.

25 J.M. Moreau and N. Delannoy, "La Sagesse soutient le bras de Louis XVI qui porte pour sceptre la Massue d'Hercule," Bib. Nat., Estampes, Qb¹ 1771–74.

26 Leith, "Reflections on Allegory," 636–7, and pl. 13–19.

27 *Alliance de la Société des amis de la constitution de Montpellier, avec la Garde Nationale de cette ville et la troupe de ligne y étant en garnison* (Montpellier 1790), 19–23.

28 Alain-Charles Gruber, *Les Grandes Fêtes et leurs décors à l'époque de Louis XVI* (Genève 1972).

29 J.-J. Rousseau, *Oeuvres*, ed. Mussay Pathay, 20 vols. (Paris 1826), XI: 169–70.

30 *Fédération des François, 14 juillet 1790. Extrait des délibérations du Conseil Général de la Commune de Montpellier* (Montpellier, n.d.), 6.

31 "Fédération des Départements du Haut et bas Rhin et partie des Départements voisins, exécutée près de Strasbourg sur la Plaine dite des Bouchers," Bib. Nat., Estampes, Qb¹ 13 juin 1790, and Coll. de Vinck, vol. 22, no. 3849.

32 Marcel Provence, *Le Cours Mirabeau: trois siècles d'histoire* (Aix-en-Provence 1973).

33 *Fédération de la Garde Nationale, et des troupes de la ligne de la Ville d'Aix, en présence de Messieurs les Maire et Officiers Municipaux* (1790). Arch. Mun. Aix-en-Provence, LL 248.

34 Ibid.

35 Bib. Mun. Amiens, ms. Bernard 846. Baron Albéric de Calonne, *Histoire de la ville d'Amiens* (Amiens 1899–1900), II: 439.

36 Arch. Mun. Amiens 3H2, no. 1. The municipal archives, previously in la Marie, are now in the municipal library.

37 H. Dusevel, *Histoire d'Amiens*, 2ᵉ éd. (Amiens 1848). The lithograph is between 451 and 452.

38 *Chronique de Paris*, no. 193, 13 juillet 1790, 774–5.

39 *Procès-verbal de la fête civique que la municipalité et les citoyens d'Orléans ont célébrée le 14 juillet 1790*, (n.p., n.d.).

40 A view of the altar, signed by Lebrun, is in the Bib. Nat., Estampes, Qb¹ 4–14 juillet 1790.

41 *Procès-verbal de la fête civique*, 4.

42 A print drawn and engraved by Albane, entitled "Fédération des Départements du Nord, du Pas de Calais et de la Somme qui a eu lieu à Lille de 16 juin 1790, entre les Gardes Nationales et les troupes de lignes," shows the scene: Bib. Nat., Estampes, Qb¹ 6 juin 1790, and Coll. Hennin, vol. CXXII, no. 10714. Apparently the same site was used again on 14 July of the same year. See the print drawn by L. Watteau and engraved by Helman: Bib. Nat., Estampes, Coll. de Vinck, vol. 22, no. 3851.

43 An anonymous engraving, "Camp Fédératif de Lyon tenu le 30 mai 1790," Bib. Nat., Estampes, Coll. Qb¹ mai 1790, and Coll. Hennin, vol. CXXI, no. 10711, shows the decor. See also Salomon de la Chapelle, "Joseph Chinard, sculpteur: sa vie et son œuvre," *Revue de Lyonnais* XXII, 90.

44 "Fédération de Lyon," *Annales patriotiques et littéraires*, no. CCLV, du lundi 14 juin 1790, 14. Signed "C."

45 *Moniteur*, vol. 3, no. 52, 21 février 1790, 424.

46 The ground plan is in the Bib. Nat., Estampes, Coll. Destailleurs, Ve 53 c-h, no. 575. There is a photograph of it in the Musée Carnavalet, Top. PC 78 c, taken from G. Lenotre, *Les Quartiers de Paris pendant la Révolution 1789–1804* (Paris 1896). In all these cases the plan is classified as anonymous, but the plan resembles those of Pierre-Andrien Pâris for renovating the Menus-Plaisirs in Versailles for the Estates-General and the National Assembly, and later the Manège in Paris when the National Assembly moved there.

47 Bernard Poyet, *Idées générales ... sur le projet de la Fête du 14 juillet à l'occasion du Pacte-Fédératif* (Paris 1790), 6.

48 I am very much indebted to the penetrating study by Richard A. Etlin, "Architecture and the Festival of Federation, Paris 1790," *Architectural History* XVIII (1975): 23–42. A French version appeared in J. Ehrard and P. Viallaneix, eds., *Les Fêtes de la Révolution*, Colloque de Clermont-Ferrand (Paris 1977), 131–54.

49 *Fédération des français dans la capitale le 14 juillet 1790 ... enrichi de toutes les inscriptions et allégories qui étaient autour de l'Autel de la Patrie, l'arc de triomphe, de l'Hôtel de Ville, la Place Henri IV, les Champs-Elysées, la Bastille, etc.* (Paris, s.d.), 5.

50 "Première frise de l'Arc de Triomphe élevé au Champ de Mars pour la Fédération du XIV juillet MDCCXC du côté de la Seine," Bib. Nat., Estampes, Qb¹ 14 juillet 1790, and Coll. Hennin, vol. CXX, no. 10771. Massard's engraving of the second frieze is also in the Qb series and Hennin no. 10772.

51 The print showing the left-hand side of the frieze, "L'Aristocratie et ses agens sont enterrés sous les ruines de la Bastille," Bib. Nat., Estampes, Coll. de Vinck, vol. 10, no. 1707, says that it was designed and drawn by Moitte, but the engraver is not mentioned. The print showing the centre of the frieze, "Les Dames françaises à l'imitation des Romains, viennent faire le sacrifice de leurs bijoux," ibid., vol. 17, no. 2854, is also anonymous. The print showing the right-hand side of the frieze, "Le Roi vient à Paris faire sa residence. A la suite de sa famille sont les Députés de l'Assemblée Nationale. La Milice Parisienne fait ranger le peuple pour indiquer que sa mission est de maintenir l'ordre et de protéger d'exécution des lois," ibid., vol. 18, no. 3003, indicates that it was drawn by [Jean-Louis-Charles] Pauquet and engraved by [Jean-Baptiste] Lucien, suggesting that they did the others in the series. The publisher Joubert announced three prints of the other frieze in 1792, but they never appeared.

52 *Description fidelle de tout ce qui a précédé, accompagné et suivi la cérémonie de la confédération nationale du 14 juillet*, 2nd ed. (Paris, s.d.).

53 *Fédération des français*, 2–3.

54 *Fête nationale qui sera célébrée aujourd'hui au Champ-de-Mars, aux Champs-Elysées, à la Halle et sur la Place de la Bastille et feu d'artifice au Pont Neuf* (Paris, n.d.), 8.

55 *Serment fédératif du 14 juillet 1790*, Mus. Carnavalet, Est., Histoire, 11C.

56 *Fête nationale*, 6–7.

57 *Fédération des français*, 7.

58 Ibid., 8.

59 Ibid., 7.

60 *Fête nationale*, 7.

61 *Révolutions de Paris*, no. 105, p. 31. A copy is in the Bib. Nat., Estampes, Coll. de Vinck, vol. 22, no. 3867.

62 Bib. Nat., Estampes, Qb¹ under the wrong date, 14 July 1790, instead of 1791.

63 "Fête commémoratif du 14 juillet 1792," Bib. Nat., Estampes, Coll. de Vinck, vol. 10, no. 1719, from the *Révolutions de Paris*. Nicholas Penny, "Ampor Publicus Prosuit: Monuments for the People and of the People," *Burlington Magazine* CXXIX, no. 1017 (December 1987): 793–800, reports that the first war memorial was erected in 1793 by the king of Prussia in Frankfurt and was dedicated to the Hessian troops who fell in reconquering the city from the French revolutionary army. The dead are listed by rank from colonel to private. Penny may be right that this was the first *permanent* monument, since the French one was temporary.

64 Mona Ozouf, *La Fête révolutionnaire, 1789–1799* (Paris 1976), esp. chap. 6.

65 Lynn Hunt, in the introduction to the English translation of Ozouf's book *Festivals and the French Revolution* (Cambridge, Mass. 1988).

66 *Songe patriotique, ou le monument et la fête* (Paris 1790).

67 Ibid., 41 n 3, is a long defence of using competitions to spur creativity, provided that they are run very differently from those of the Old Regime.

III PLANS TO IMMORTALIZE THE REVOLUTION

1 Armand-Guy Kersaint, *Discours sur les monuments publics, prononcé au conseil du département de Paris le 15 décembre 1791* (Paris 1792), vi-vii. For Speer's concept of the "ruin value of architecture," see his *Inside the Third Reich: Memoirs* (New York and Toronto 1970), 56 and 154.

2 *Annales patriotiques et littéraires*, no. XC, 31 December 1789, 1.

3 Ibid., CXLI, 20 February 1790, 3.

4 Ibid., CCCXXX, 6 December 1790.

5 For some other examples in Louans, Longwy, and Lille, ibid., DXXXVIII, 24 March 1791, 1208–9; DCCXXXIII, 5 October 1791, 2033; and *Révolutions de Paris*, vol. XII, no. 152, 9–16 June 1792, 498–500.

6 *Annales patriotiques et littéraires* CCCXVIII, 5 October 1790, 496.

7 *Lettres patentes du Roi, sur un décret de l'Assemblée nationale [19 juin] qui abolit la Noblesse héréditaire, et porte que les titres de Prince, de Duc, de Comte, de Marquis et autres titres semblables, ne seront pris par qui que soit, ni donnés à personne*, données à Paris, le 23 juin 1790, in *Collection générale des lois, proclamations* ("Collection du Louvre"), April-August 1790, 950.

8 "Bel exemple à suivre," *Annales patriotiques et littéraires* CCCCXCVIII, 12 February 1791, 1039–40.

9 *Lettres patentes du roi sur le décret de l'Assemblée Nationale qui autorisent les villes, bourgs, villages, et paroisses auxquels les ci-devant seigneurs ont donnés leurs noms de famille à reprendre leurs noms anciens*, données à Paris, le 20 juin 1790, in *Collection générale des lois; proclamations* ("Collection du Louvre"), April-August 1790, 950. This was the result of a decree of the Assembly the day after the one above.

10 J.-C. Renoul, *Colonne de la Place Louis XVI* (Nantes 1858).

11 Arch. Mun. Nantes, FF 104.

12 Renoul, *Colonne*, 10–11.

13 Ibid., 15–16.

14 Arch. Mun. Nantes, D¹⁻², Conseil Municipal 1790–, 11 mai [1790].

15 Arch. Mun. Nantes, 11 158*, no. 72. On the design it says it was approved on 10 May, but the records indicate it was approved a day later.

16 Renoul, *Colonne*, 18–20.

17 Arch. Mun. Nantes, D¹⁻², Conseil Municipal, 11 juillet [1791].

18 There have been several brief studies of this column: Louis Grasset-Morel, *Le Temple de la Raison et les Colonnes de la Liberté à Montpellier* (Montpellier 1901); Théophile Schmidt, *La Colonne de la Liberté de Montpellier élevée en 1791 et détruite en 1814* (Montpellier 1925); and

Louis-H. Escuret, *La Colonne de la Liberté de Montpellier* (Montpellier 1955). All of these have drawn on a manuscript consisting of copies of documents, with no location given, on Montpellier 1789–1815: Vincent Soulier, *Chronique de Montpellier*, 2 vols., n.d., Bib. Mun. Montpellier, mss 245.

19 *Alliance de la Société des amis de la Constitution et de l'égalité de Montpellier, avec la Garde Nationale de cette ville et la troupe de la ligne y étant en garnison* (Montpellier 1790), 19–23.

20 Ibid.

21 Arch. Dép. Hérault, L 5498, under 5 December.

22 Ibid., under 24 December. The professor was M. Danizy, a member of the Société Royale des Sciences.

23 Arch. Mun. Montpellier, dossier M 1/4.

24 "Procès verbal de la cérémonie civique qui a eu lieu à l'occasion du placement de la première pierre de la colonne à élever sur l'esplanade," dated January 1791, in Soulier, *Chronique*, 204–7.

25 Schmidt, *La Colonne de la Liberté*, 19.

26 Arch. Dép. Hérault, 1 Fi 119: *Plan par la masse de la Ville de Montpellier avec des environs sur lequel on a designé en couleur rouge les boulevards projettés d'après les alignements déterminés par Messieurs les Commissaires du Directoire de l'Hérault*, signed by city officials and dated 10 March 1792.

27 Grasset-Morel, *Le Temple de la Raison*, 17: "La colonne était encore inachevée, puisque le 27 brumaire an III il fallait 3,000 francs pour la terminer."

28 Arch. Dép. Hérault, L 5499, entry for 2 December 1791.

29 Arch. Mun. Montpellier, Registre du Conseil Municipal, vol. III, 18.

30 Arch. Dép. Hérault, L 5499, entry for 1 January 1792.

31 *Annales patriotiques et littéraires*, DCLX, 24 juillet 1791, 1723.

32 Bib. Nat., Estampes, Coll. de Vinck, vol. 46, no. 6283. At the bottom on the right the design is signed "A Saintes le 7 avril 1791 N????." Despite the date, it is entered in the collection, along with material concerning the Cult of the Supreme Being, in the early summer of 1794. The term "Etre Suprême" was sometimes used early in the Revolution.

33 Michel Vovelle, *L'Irrésistible Ascension de Joseph Sec, bourgeois d'Aix, suivi de quelques clefs pour la lecture des "naïfs"* (Aix-en-Provence 1975). The jacket has a different title: *A Aix-en-Provence une énigme architecturale: le monument Sec.*

34 The view reproduced here is a watercolour done under the First Empire, at present in the collection Fauris de Saint-Vincent in the Bibliothèque Méjanes in Aix.

35 De Varenne (huissier de l'Assemblée Nationale), *Projet d'un monument à ériger pour le Roi et Nosseigneurs des Etats Généraux* (1789).

36 *Arch. Parl.*, vol. 9, 197, reporting the session of 28 September 1789. De Varenne's project was drawn by J.-M. Moreau, junior, and engraved by Janinet. There are copies in the Bib. Nat., Estampes, Ef 105 Res., t 3; Coll. Hennin, nos. 10131 and 10132; and Qb¹, mars 1790.

37 Antoine-François Sergent[-Marceau], *District de Saint-Jacques-l'Hôpital. Assemblée ordinaire du mercredi 10 février 1790. Monument à la gloire de Louis XVI* ([Paris] 1790), with a plate.

38 *Projet d'un monument à la gloire de Henri IV* (n.p., n.d.).

39 [Jean-Nicolas] Sobre le jeune, architecte, *Projet d'un monument à élever dans le Champ de la Fédération* (n.p., n.d.).

40 [François-Antoine] Davy de Chavigné, "Colonne de la Liberté. Monument projetté [*sic*] sur l'emplacement de la Bastille à la Gloire de Louis XVI restaurateur de la liberté française," an engraving, under which it says on the left "Dessiné par Davy de Chavigné en mai 1789," followed by a description. Mus. Carnavalet, Top. GC 21 C. He presented his project to the Académie d'architecture on 8 June 1789: *Procès-verbaux*, IX, 249–50.

41 *Moniteur*, vol. 4, no. 143, 23 May 1790, 436.

42 Joseph-Pierre Du Morier, *Projet de cahiers lu au district assemblé en l'église Notre-Dame, précédé d'observations proposées à cette assemblée sur ses droits et sur sa convocation, et suivi

d'une note relative à la réforme des moeurs, à l'éducation publique, à l'honneur (n.p., n.d. [note in the Bib. Nat. Catalogue says 1789]).

43 Ibid., 28–9.

44 *Arch. Nat.*, Cartes et Plans, N III Seine 762, 1–3. No. 1 is the pamphlet; nos. 2 and 3 are the two variants of his plan.

45 [Etienne-Louis-Denis] Cathala, *Projet d'une place sur l'emplacement de la Bastille, avec une colonne au milieu, semblable à celle de Trajan à Rome* (n.p., [1791]), 2.

46 N.M. Gatteaux (Graveur du Roi et Membre de plusieurs Académies), *Projet d'un monument pour consacrer la Révolution* (Paris, n.d.), with plates.

47 Besides the engraving appended to the pamphlet there was a larger one published separately, copies of which are in the Bib. Nat., Cabinet des Estampes, Coll. de Vinck, no. 1715, and the Coll. Hennin no. 10878; and the Musée Carnavalet, Top. GC 21C. These have detailed notes along the bottom. This engraving was reprinted in the *Moniteur*, vol. 1, 336, with an incorrect date. (The engravings are grouped in two separate volumes.)

48 Prieur, "Temple dédié à la Liberté projetté sur les ruines de la Bastille; proposé par souscription, l'auteur rénonçant à toute espèce d'honoraires et contribuant par sa part de la somme de 300#." Mus. Carnavalet, Top. GC 21C.

49 *Arch. Parl.*, vol. 39, 564–6, and Annex 2, 572–89, giving the text of his plan. Palloy's letter asking to appear at the bar of the Assembly and his address are in the Bib. Nat. Imprimés, Lb³⁹ 5813.

50 Pierre-François Palloy, *Adresse et projet général … présenté à l'Assemblée Nationale et au roi des François* (Paris 1792).

51 Ibid., the frontispiece showing the monument in the centre of the *place* with a section of the surrounding buildings visible in the background.

52 Ibid., the fourth plate showing the ground-plan according to his proposal.

53 *Arch. Parl.*, vol. 39, 578–9.

54 Palloy, *Adresse et projet*, the third plate showing a plan, elevation, and section of the aqueduct.

55 *Arch. Parl.*, vol. 39, 573–4.

IV TEMPLES FOR THE NATION AND ITS HEROES

1 Fernand Boyer, "Projets de salles pour les assemblées révolutionnaires," *Bulletin de la Société de l'histoire de l'art français* (1933): 170–83. Boyer deals with a number of plans in the Archives Nationales, but misses some in other collections.

2 *Procès-verbaux de l'Académie royale d'architecture 1671–1793*, ed. Henry-Lemonnier, 10 vols. (Paris 1911–29), IX: 243.

3 Arch. de l'Institut, B 19. On the reverse of the drawing it says "Lelong élève du président de Cote." The drawing is marked with the letter C, which is not mentioned in the minutes.

4 *Procès-verbaux de l'Académie d'architecture*, IX: 276. The prize was awarded to Vergognon.

5 Armand Brette, *Histoire des édifices où ont siégé les assemblées parlementaires de la Révolution française et la première république* (Paris 1902). Brette published floor plans of the Hôtel des Menus Plaisirs converted into a meeting-place for the Estates General and then the Constituent Assembly, the Archbishopric, which the Constituent Assembly used temporarily, and finally the Manège, which was used until the Convention moved into the Tuileries Palace in May 1793. This book was to be volume 1 of a two-volume set, but volume 2 was never published.

6 Lemonnier, "La Mégalomanie dans l'architecture," 92–7.

7 The design is in the Bib. Nat., Estampes, Ha 56–E–31.

8 Pérouse de Montclos, *Etienne-Louis Boullée*, 182. The author is mistaken in saying that the constitution was to be inscribed on the façade: it is clearly the Rights of Man.

9 Bib. Nat., ms français 9153, 108v–109r.

10 The plans by Pâris are part of an album in the Arch. Nat., Cartes et Plans, N IV Seine 87, containing plans for a National Assembly by Pâris, Cathala, Combes, Mouillefarine, and Poyet. Pâris's designs are in fols. 2–4.

11 Ferdinand Boyer, "Les Salles d'assemblées sous la Révolution française et leur répliques en Europe," *Bulletin de la société de l'histoire de l'art français* (1952): 88–93.

12 Bib. Nat., Estampes, Ha 56, pls. 14, 15, 16.

13 Bib. Nat., ms français 9153, 109v.

14 Arch. Nat., Cartes et Plans, N IV Seine 87, fols. 6–10.

15 Arch. Nat., Cartes et Plans, N IV Seine 87, fols. 12–15, with copious notes.

16 *Gazette de France*, 23 juillet 1790.

17 There are various locations of this plan: Arch. Nat., Cartes et Plans, N IV Seine 87, fol. 5; Bib. Nat., Estampes, Va 250a; and Bib. Nat., Estampes, Coll. de Vinck, vol. 10, no. 1708. The catalogue of the Collection de Vinck has a long note about the project.

18 [Jean-Baptiste-Alphonse] Lahure, "Project d'un monument pour l'Assemblée Nationale," three plates, undated and unnumbered, in Van Cléemputte, ed., *Collection des prix que l'académie d'architecture proposoit et couronnoit tous les ans* (Paris, n.d.). In August 1790 the Académie d'architecture proposed as the subject for the Prix d'émulation "un édifice pour recevoir les assemblées nationales"– *Procès-verbaux de l'Académie d'architecture*, IX: 276 – but it is not clear whether this project was for this contest. According to the Archives de l'Institut, A 24, Lahure was a student in the Academy in 1786, but he is not mentioned in the proceedings.

19 The whole title of this plan is worth citing: Bernard Poyet, *Plan général des terreins et bâtimens situés entre la rivière et la rue St Honoré depuis le Pont Neuf, jusqu'aux Champs-Elisées … pour réunir dans la même enceinte le Palais de nos Rois, celui de l'Assemblée Nationale, le Louvre dont on feroit l'Hôtel de Ville et la Place de Louis XVI afin de réunir les pouvoirs Civil et Militaire et éviter la dispersion des différens Départemens qui rallentit le Service et constitue dans de plus grands frais. Présenté et Dédié à la Commune de Paris le 21 mars 1790*. Arch. Nat., Cartes et Plans, N IV Seine 87, fol. 11. Other copies are in Bib. Nat., Cartes et Plans, Ge C 3758, and Bib. Nat., Estampes, Ya 419 j, t 5, fol. 4.

20 Mangin père and M. Corbet, architecte, *Plan d'un projet d'embellissement nécessaire à une partie de la Ville de Paris entre les Champs-Elysées et la rue St Antoine sur laquelle sont projettés différens édifices, places, et monuments publics relatifs à la Nation … et présenté à l'Assemblée Nationale, l'an I*; Arch. Nat., N III Seine 1197. They presented this plan to the National Assembly on 14 April 1791, supporting it with a pamphlet, *Exposé et analyse du plan et projet présenté à l'Assemblée … le dit plan gravé dédié à Louis XV* [Paris, n.d.]. After Corbet's death, Mangin alone sent an appeal to the Legislative Assembly on 20 January 1792, *Pétition de Sr Mangin père … sur le plan dont il a fait hommage à l'Assemblée Nationale Constituante* ([Paris] 1792). Mangin made another appeal on 1 July 1792, *Adresse de M Mangin père à l'Assemblée nationale 1er juillet 1792* (Paris, n.d.).

21 Mangin and Corbet, *Exposé et Analyse*, 2 n 1.

22 Ibid., 3–4. Mangin returned to the economic advantages of his plan in subsequent pamphlets, *Réflexions d'un citoyen patriote, dont l'importance est telle qu'il peux en résulter deux ou trois-cent millions de bénéfice pour la Nation* ([Paris] 1792); and *Analyse des idées qui ont dirigées le citoyen Mangin père, architecte, dans la composition de son plan, dédié à la République française* (Paris, n.d.).

23 The republicanized version can be found in the Bib. Nat., Cartes et Plans, Ge C 3307; the Bib. Hist. de la Ville de Paris, B 12; and Bib. Mun. de Rouen, mss. 2137. In this revised plan the words "pour l'habitation de roi et de la Cour" have been replaced by "pour les diverses administrations de la République"; the National Assembly has given way to the Convention, and the royal emblems and medallions have disappeared. Also, collaborators are mentioned who do not appear in the earlier version: Cne M.-P. Vallet *scripsit* and J.-Ed. de la Porte *sculp*.

24 Michel Vovelle, *La Révolution française. Images et récit*, 5 vols. (Paris 1986), IV: 271, reproduces the elevation but mistakenly labels it "Vue de la principale entrée du palais Bourbon," perhaps because it is incorrectly labelled in the Musée Carnavalet. The elevation corresponds precisely with the ground plan in the Bib. Nat., where the site is clearly labelled, and with the pamphlet cited below in n 25.

25 Arch. Nat., Cartes et Plans, N II Seine 1–7, and Bib. Nat., Estampes, Va 269 i, microfilm H 49405. The project was explained in a pamphlet by the architect, *Détails pour servir d'instructions aux plans d'un Palais national, composés d'après le projet ayant pour titre "Considérations etc"* (Paris 1789). The project to which Rousseau refers was *Considérations sur l'établissement nécessaire à Assemblée et moyens d'ériger ce palais, avec une place, qui en ferait partie pour la statue du roi* (Paris 1789). This pamphlet, together with the one by Rousseau to which it is related, is in Arch. Nat., AD VIII 33.

26 Giraud, Avocat, *Place patriotique, avec un palais pour la permanence de l'Auguste Assemblée nationale, et de la description d'une fête annuelle pour le renouvellement du sermen civique, présentée à nos-seigneurs de la dite Assemblée* (Paris 1790), 23.

27 The ground-plan and a memoir by Thomas are in Arch. Nat., Cartes et Plans, N III Seine, 789–3. The architect may be Jean-François Thomas, a student who won grands prix in 1778, 1780, 1781, and 1785.

28 The design and explanation are in Arch. Nat., Cartes et Plans, N III Seine 585. A manuscript note says that Petit was a low-ranking officer connected to the Invalides and that he had drawn up two previous plans, one accepted by the king in 1788 and the other presented to the Commune in the same year as this one, that is in 1790.

29 Florentin Gilbert, *Adresse à tous les corps administratifs de la France et à tous les connoisseurs dans l'art de l'architecture et de la construction des travaux publics* (Paris 1790). Boyer did not find the design, but it is in the Bib. Nat., Estampes, Ef 105 rés. in-fol., tome III. Gilbert présenté the plan to the National Assembly on 30 March 1790, saying that he would publish an engraving of it as soon as he had enough subscribers.

30 Arch. Nat., Cartes et Plans, N III Seine, 789–3.

31 Armand-Guy Kersaint, *Discours sur les monuments publics, prononcé au conseil du département de Paris le 15 décembre 1791* (Paris 1792). This contains five memoirs signed by [Jacques] Molinos and [Jacques-Guillaume] Legrand.

32 *Arch. parl.*, vol. 24, 53f, and the *Moniteur*, vol. 8, no. 94, le 4 avril 1791, 30–1.

33 A.-C. Quatremère de Quincy, *Rapport sur l'édifice dit de Sainte-Geneviève fait au directoire du Département de Paris* (Paris 1791), 29. This was the first of three reports by Quatremère as work progressed into the Terror.

34 Quatremère described the new low-relief on pp 25–6. There is an engraving of it in the Musée Carnavalet and a sketch of it before it was destroyed in the Arch. Nat., Cartes et Plans, Versement d'architecture, LI, 21.

35 Musée Carnavalet, Top. Anon. GC, no. 3604. A note says "Projet de décoration pour le Panthéon vers 1791."

36 Charles Chaisneau, *Le Panthéon français, ou discours sur les honneurs publics décernés par la Nation à la Mémoire des Grands Hommes* (Dijon 1792). This undoubtedly was published before 10 August 1792 because Chaisneau envisaged honouring good kings and royal ministers such as Henry IV and Sully.

37 Ibid., 6–7.

38 A.-R. Mopinot [de la Chapotte], *Adresse à l'Assemblée Nationale* (Paris 1792). The author described himself as "Chevalier de Mopinot, ingénieur à la suite des armées, lieutenant colonel au premier régiment de cavalerie, ci-devant dauphin."

39 The letter, other documents, and drawings, envisaging the bridge decorated with the statues, are in Arch. Nat., F14 191b.

40 [Antoine-Laurent-Thomas] Vaudoyer, *Idées d'un citoyen français sur le lieu destiné à la sépulture des hommes illustres de France* [signed "Vaudoyer, 5 avril 1791"] (Paris, n.d.).

41 M.-C.-P. Le Sueur, *Projet d'utilité et d'embellissement pour la ville de Paris adressé aux sections* (Paris 1790). A note at the end of the pamphlet says it was presented to the primary assembly of the Section Faubourg St Denis on 14 October 1790. This rare pamphlet is in Arch. Nat., F¹⁴ 187ᵇ, doss. 17.

42 Ibid., under "Liberté."

43 *Municipalité de Paris, 10 septembre 1791*, a twenty-four-page brochure.

44 Bib. Nat., Estampes, Va 250a. Brullée, "Plan d'une partie du Canal royal de Paris et d'une place et d'un Palais National à construire sur les ruines de la Bastille … Aoust 1789."

45 Arch. Nat., DXXXVIII, carton 2, doss. 21, contains a memoir by Brullée dated 16 June 1792 that was apparently submitted originally to the Department of Paris, judging by a note on one of the folders. Later it evidently went to the Committee of Public Instruction of the Legislative Assembly, judging by another note on this document itself, but there is no mention of it in the proceedings of the committee edited by Guillaume.

46 *Annales patriotiques et littéraires*, no. DCLIII, 17 July 1790, 1693–4.

47 "Loi relative à l'Établissement d'un monument sur la place de la Bastille …, le 16–27 juin 1792 l'an 4ᵉ de la liberté," *Collection générale des lois* (Collection du Louvre), vol. IX, 421, loi no. 1807.

48 Arch. Nat., DXXXVIII, carton 5, doss. 65, dated 26 June 1792. The covering note says that the quatrain was composed nearly three years before at the end of 1789, at which time Duquesney had sent it to the president of the National Assembly and the mayor of Paris.

49 "Loi relative à la colonne qui doit être élevée sur les ruines de la Bastille … 13 juillet 1792, l'an IVᵉ de la liberté," *Collection générale des lois* (Collection du Louvre), vol. IX, 595, loi no. 1876.

50 "Décret portant que le coffre de fer déposé et enfermé le 14 juillet dernier … sera retiré," *Collection générale des décrets* (Collection Baudouin), 25 avril 1793, 150–1.

V THE REPUBLICANIZATION OF PARIS

1 *Arch. Parl.*, vol. 48, 2.

2 "Décret pour faire enlever les statues existantes dans les places de Paris du 11 août 1792," *Collection des décrets* (Collection Baudouin), 10 août–1 septembre 1792, no. 1325, 66.

3 *Arch. Parl.*, vol. 48, 115.

4 "Loi relative à la destruction des statues et monuments publics de bronze ou autres materières, et des monuments de la féodalité du 14 août 1792," *Collection générale des lois, proclamations* (Collection du Louvre), vol. X, août 1792, no. 2058, 283–4.

5 Arthur [Président], *Les Citoyens de la Section de la Place Vendôme, aux Marseillois* (n.p. [1793]).

6 Ibid., 7.

7 In 1793 there were decrees concerning removal of royal or feudal signs on 4 July, 1 August, 2 September, 9 September, 14 September, and 28 October.

8 For example, Arch. Nat., F¹³ 212, Bâtiments civils.

9 Arch. Nat., F17 1009ᴮ, no. 2064.

10 Stanley J. Idzerda, "Iconoclasm during the French Revolution," *American Historical Review* LX (October 1954): 13–24.

11 George Poisson, *Paris au temps de la Révolution* (Paris 1989), 100, 103, 114, with illustrations.

12 In promulgating the new calendar the Convention made its symbolic significance very clear: "Sur l'ère, le commencement de l'année, et sur les noms des jours, du 4 Frimaire an II," *Bulletin des lois*, Brumaire-Prairial an II, 57 ff.

13 *Arch. Parl.*, vol. 48, 2.

14 Gen. 2:19, 20.

15 Jault, *Projet d'une nouvelle nomenclature des rues de la Section de Bonne-Nouvelle, suivi de quelques vers républicains* (Paris, n.d. [10 Brumaire an II]).

16 Ibid., 5.

17 [Avril] *Convention Nationale. Instruction publique. Rapport au Conseil général de la Commune de Paris, sur quelques mesures à prendre en changeant le noms des rues. Imprimé en vertu de l'arrêté du Comité d'instruction publique le 17 nivôse l'an II* (Paris, n.d.).

18 *Almanach indicatif des rues de Paris, suivant leurs nouvelles dénominations, par order alphabétique. Précédé de l'énumération des quarante-huit sections et leurs chefs-lieux, d'un idée sommaire des differens comités du corps législatif, des bureaux du pouvoir exécutif, des autorités constituées etc.* (Paris, an III).

19 [Egid?] Verhelst, *Plan allégorique d'un jardin de la Révolution française et des vertus républicaines* (n.p., n.d.). A footnote says that the plan had been sent to the Committee of Public Safety on 16 Prairial an II.

20 An engraving of the plan and a lot of documents concerning it are in Arch. Nat., F¹³ 325ᵇ.

21 Migneron had also presented his project to the Academy of Architecture: *Procès Verbaux*, vol. IX, 126, 128, 131. The academy had appointed a commission that reported on 4 May 1784, but the minutes do not reveal the contents of the report. Migneron submitted models illustrating his methods in 1792: ibid., 312.

22 Arch. Nat., F¹³ 207, doss. 22.

23 In Christian symbolism three represents the Trinity and the spiritual world. Four stands for the four elements – earth, air, fire, and water – and the material world. Three plus four or three times four consequently represents a combination of the spiritual and the earthly, thus things human. Eight, on the other hand, signifies going one step beyond the purely human into a higher sphere. For this reason baptismal fonts have traditionally been octagonal.

24 Arch. Nat., F¹³ 207, doss. 22.

25 Arch. Nat., F¹⁴ 187ᵇ, doss. no. 63, mss dated 15 Ventôse an II. The project was presented to the Convention by the Jacobin Club and the Département des travaux publics, and referred to David on 11 Germinal an II and to Matthieu on 15 Germinal. M.-J. Guillaume, *Procès-verbaux du Comité d'instruction publique de la Convention nationale*, 6 vols. (Paris 1891–1907; table in two parts 1959), IV: 59, 80.

26 On the transition from the traditional cemetery to the "tomb in a park" idea culminating in the Père Lachaise Cemetery see Richard A. Etlin, *The Architecture of Death* (Cambridge, Mass. 1984).

27 *Moniteur*, no. 229, le 16 août 1792, 414. This monument survived for several years, as is revealed by the need to update the Declaration of the Rights of Man from time to time. On 24 Fructidor an II (13 August 1794) a decision of the Comité d'Instruction Publique ordered that the declaration of 1789 be replaced with that of 1793. On 29 Floréal an IV (19 May 1790) the Conseil d'examen des bâtiments civils ordered the declaration of 1793 effaced, but, expecting a plan for a new monument, did not order that the declaration of 1795 be put in its place: Arch. Nat., F²¹ 597, F¹³, 327–8, and F¹³, 503.

28 Mus. Carnavalet, Top. 40d.

29 *Moniteur*, no. 244, le 31 août 1792, 572. See the engraving "Pompe funèbre en l'honneur des martyrs de la journée du 10 dans le Jardin National le 26 août 1793," no. VII in *Collection de quinze estampes sur les principales journées de la Révolution*, by Helman and Monnet, Bib. Nat., Estampes, Coll. de Vinck, vol. 29, no. 4907.

30 Jean-Joseph Pithou de Lionville, *Description générale et historique des objets qui on servi à la pompe funèbre célébrée le 26 août aux Tuileries, pour honorer la mémoire des patriotes* (n.p., n.d.), 2–3. See too *Ordre et marche de cérémonie des Tuileries qui fera aujourd'hui, à trois heures après-midi, en honneur de nos frères morts en combattant pour la Liberté* (Paris [1792]).

31 Montesquiou-Fezensac, commander of the Army of the South, had entered Chambéry on 24 September 1792, and Savoy declared its independence soon afterwards, asking to form the eighty-fourth department.

32 The arrangements for the festival were described in the *Moniteur*, 9 octobre 1792, vol. 14, no. 283, 149.

33 The engraving, taken from the *Révolutions de Paris*, 13–20 octobre, no. 171, 166, is in Bib. Nat., Estampes, Coll. de Vinck, vol. 20, no. 3571.

34 The engraving "Exposition du corps de L. Michel Lepelletier sur le piédestal de la ci-devant statue de Louis XIV place des Piques le 24 janvier 1793," probably engraved by Allais, is in the Bib. Nat., Estampes, Coll. de Vinck, vol. 30, no. 5026.

35 On the reaction to Marat by various groups, and their manipulation of his image for political purposes, see Ian Germani, *The Metamorphoses of Marat*, PhD thesis, Queen's University 1983.

36 This move, which was contrary to the Convention's own ban on the Pantheonization of any individual until ten years after his death, came after David's presentation of his *Marat Assassinated* to his fellow deputies: *Arch. Parl*, vol. 79, 212. This decision was followed up by another on 25 November 1793 stating that Marat's remains should replace those of Mirabeau in the Pantheon and that on that day there should be a festival for all the Republic: ibid., vol. 80, 103. Six days later David, Romme, and Ste Foy were named commissioners for such a festival.

37 *Moniteur*, vol. 21, no. 358, 28 Fructidor an II (14 September 1794), 744.

38 On the ceremony surrounding his internment see Germani, *Metamorphoses*, 1: 72–5.

39 Marie Cerati, *Le Club des citoyennes républicaines révolutionnaires* (Paris 1966), 103–4.

40 The engraving cited below gives Martin's initials as J.-F., but according to Stanislas Lami, *Dictionnaire des sculpteurs*, his name was Gilles-François.

41 Bib. Nat., Estampes, Coll. de Vinck, vol. 32, no. 5321.

42 Ibid., no. 5322.

43 The artists can be identified by invoices for their work in Arch. Nat., F⁴ 2090.

44 The festival was reported in most newspapers, but the most complete accounts are the "Procès-verbal des monuments, de la marche, et des discours de la fête consacrée à l'inauguration de la constitution de la république française, le 10 août 1793," *Journal des débats et décrets* 49, no. 348–77 (Sept. 1793): 413–23, and the collection mentioned below in n 46.

45 Ibid., 418.

46 *Recueil complet de tout ce qui est passé à la Fête de l'Unité et l'Indivisibilité de la République Française* (Paris, n.d.). All the speeches were also published in the *Moniteur*, vol. 17, no. 224, 12 août 1793, 367–8.

47 "Procès-verbal des monuments," 421.

48 Bib. Nat., Estampes, Qb¹ août 1793.

49 See, for instance, the medallions showing six stations in the festival in the Bib. Nat., Estampes, Coll. de Vinck, vol. 45, fol. 35, no. 6171.

50 *Moniteur*, vol. 17, no. 224, 12 août 1793, 368.

51 "The placement of Hercules relative to Liberty is particularly relevant. The statue of Liberty came just before Hercules in the celebratory procession. By implication Liberty was important but representative only of a particular moment, a moment now passed": Lynn Hunt, "Hercules and the Radical Image in the French Revolution," *Representations* 1, no. 2 (Spring 1983): 95–117, quotation on 100–1. Later Professor Hunt argues that "The distant, feminine statue of Liberty represented a moderate republic now repudiated": ibid., 103.

52 "One of the most characteristic moments of this festival, and which can never be effaced from the memory of man … the moment when our common mother, Nature, presses from her fruitful breasts the pure and beneficial fluid of regeneration, is the one, citizens, which we have chosen for one of the faces of this medallion": Guillaume, *Procès-verbaux du Comité d'instruction publique* III: 288–91.

53 For a very detailed description of the palace under the Convention see Ferdinand Boyer, "Les Tuileries sous la Révolution," *Bulletin de la Société de l'histoire de l'art français* (1934):

54 *Arch. Parl.*, vol. 48, 109.

55 Ibid., vol. 49, 477–8.

56 Allais and Perrard-Montreuil worked together and published a pamphlet on their proposal, *Nouvelle salle de la Convention Nationale*, signed and dated 23 October 1792 ([Paris] n.d.).

57 There is an engraving of his plan, Bib. Nat., Estampes, Va 221. There is a photograph of the engraving in the Bib. Hist. de la Ville de Paris, B71.

58 *Moniteur*, vol. 13, no. 260, 16 septembre 1792, 704.

59 Boyer, "Les Tuileries," 202–8.

60 [Alexandre-] Pierre Vignon, *A la Convention nationale, sur la nouvelle salle dans le Palais des Tuileries*, (Paris 1792).

61 *Moniteur*, vol. 14, no. 301, 27 octobre 1792, 299.

62 *Arch. Parl.*, vol. 63, 193.

63 Declaration of the Rights of Man and the Citizen, 1793, article 32. There was no such article in the declaration of 1789.

64 Boyer, "Les Tuileries," 217. Boyer says that one of the statues was of "Publica" instead of Publicola, co-praetor with Lucius Junius Brutus, beside whom his likeness was placed.

65 *Moniteur*, vol. 15, no. 54, 23 février 1793, 526. Boyer reports that the young artist was named Favart, instead of Fleuriot.

66 *Moniteur*, vol. 18, no. 48, 8 novembre 1793, 361, and vol. 19, no. 107, 17 Nivôse an II (6 janvier 1794), 138.

67 Ibid., vol. 15, no. 90, 31 mars 1793, 836.

68 Ibid., vol. 18, no. 56, 26 Brumaire an II (16 novembre 1793), 429.

69 Boyer, "Les Tuileries," 223–5.

70 Ibid., 220–3.

71 *Arch. Parl.*, vol. 63, 193.

72 Boyer, "Les Tuileries," 228–9.

73 Ibid., 229–30.

74 *Arch. Parl.*, vol. 64, 140–1.

75 This petition does not appear in the *Arch. Parl.* but is quoted at length in their petition on 28 July, n 77 below.

76 *Arch. Parl.*, vol. 67, 660–2. A plan related to this contest is in Arch. Nat., Cartes et Plans, Versement d'Architecture, boîte 18, no. 1.

77 Ibid., vol. 69, 624–5. The motion was made by Dartigoëyte, not by David and Sergent, as Boyer reports.

78 H. Lapauze, ed., *Procès-verbaux de la Commune générale des arts de peinture, sculpture, et gravure, et de la Société populaire et républicaine des arts* (Paris 1903).

79 Thomas E. Crow, *Painting and Public Life in Eighteenth-Century Paris* (New Haven and London 1985).

80 James Leo Connolly Jr, *The Movement to Create a National Gallery of Art in Eighteenth-Century France*, PhD dissertation, University of Kansas 1962, available from University Microfilms.

81 *Décret qui fixe au 10 août l'ouverture du Musée de la République, 27 juillet 1793*, in *Collection générale des lois, proclamations et autres actes* (Collection du Louvre), vol. XV, loi no. 1292, 283.

82 Anon., project for transformation of the Louvre and the Tuileries, around 1793, Bib. Hist. de la Ville de Paris, B48.

83 Bib. Nat., Estampes, Coll. Hennin, vol. 133, no. 11667.

84 A.-C. Quatremère de Quincy, *Rapport fait au Directoire de Paris, le 13 novembre 1792, l'an première de la République Française, sur l'état actuel du Panthéon français; sur les changements qui s'y sont opérés; sur les travaux qui restent à entreprendre* (Paris [1792]).

The beginning of note 53 continues at the top of the right column:

197–262 (242–62 cover the period of the Directory). His account, however, is marred by a number of errors.

85 Quatremère de Quincy, *Rapport fait au Directoire du Département de Paris sur les travaux entrepris, continués ou achevés au Panthéon Français depuis le dernier compte, rendu le 17 Novembre, et sur l'état actuel du monument, le deuxième jour du second mois de l'an 2ᵉ*, (Paris [1793]).

86 *Rapport sur l'édifice dit de Sainte-Geneviève* [first report], 26.

87 Arch. Nat., F¹⁷ 1355, doss. 3.

88 Ibid. I have been unable to find the three maps mentioned in the documents.

89 Accounts submitted by artisans allow us to reconstruct the ephemeral architecture constructed for this fête: Arch. Nat., F⁴ 325 fol. 25; F¹³ 318-19; FI 1 84, doss. 2. The first scholar to reconstruct the layout was Werner Szambien, *J.-L.-N. Durand* (Paris 1984), fig. 49.

90 [Lesueur], Doorway for the Panthéon, Mus. Carnavalet, P.C. Dessins, D7792.

91 In Floréal an II a citizen by the name of Cizo Duplessis, "a sergeant volunteer of the National Guard," reminded the Committee of Public Safety that he had made a proposal for a Theatre of Morals in December 1789 but officials had turned it down: Arch. Nat., F¹⁷ 1010ᴮ, no. 2780.

92 De Wailly presented plans to the Committee of Public Instruction on 21 Frimaire an II – 11 December 1793 – which sent them to a Commission of Six. Later his plans and those of another architect were sent to the municipality of Paris, which approved de Wailly's plan: Guillaume, *Procès-verbaux*, III: 135, 390.

93 There are two sets of drawings showing the internal changes. One is in the Arch. Nat., Cartes et Plans, Versement d'Architecture, boîte 17. The other is in the Bib. de la Comédie Française, Carton Leclerc. The latter also has cross-sections and plans for a semicircular amphitheatre in front of the theatre.

94 Guillaume, *Procès-verbaux du Comité d'instruction publique*, III: 7 n 1.

95 *Moniteur*, vol. 21, no. 282, 12 Messidor an II (30 juin 1794), 96. The opening was on 9 Messidor.

96 On the geometry of the original plan of the theatre, the *place*, and the adjacent streets, see Monika Steinhauser and Daniel Rabreau, "Le Théâtre de l'Odéon de Charles de Wailly et Marie-Joseph Peyre 1767-1782," *Revue de l'art*, no. 19 (1973): 9-49, especially the diagram on 20, pl. 22. Rabreau, however, does not note the changed angle of the streets facing the theatre in the plans of 1793-94.

97 The suggestion by David is mentioned in the dossier containing a report by de Wailly to the Committee of Public Safety on 10 Frimaire an II (30 November 1793). Arch. Nat., F¹⁷ 1303, doss. 1, 2, 3.

98 Arch. Nat., F¹³ 1279, doss. 4.

99 *Moniteur*, vol. 21, no. 284, 14 Messidor an II (2 juillet 1794), 110-11.

100 Arch. Nat., F¹⁷ 1021⁶, doss. 4.

101 Ledoux evidently wanted to work on the collection of his designs and reflections eventually published as *L'Architecture considérée sous le rapport de l'art, des moeurs et de la législation* (Paris 1804).

102 *Moniteur*, vol. 20, no. 192, 12 Germinal an II (1ᵉʳ avril 1794), 94.

VI A VAST PLAN FOR REGENERATION

1 James A. Leith, *Media and Revolution: Moulding a New Citizenry during the Terror* (Toronto 1968), and Serge Bianchi, *La Révolution culturelle de l'an II: Elites et peuple 1789-1799* (Paris 1982).

2 *Moniteur*, vol. 20, no. 212, 2 Floréal an II (21 avril 1794), 263-4.

3 See, for example, Charles Poyet, *Projet proposé par Sᵗ Poyet … pour employer quarante mille personnes à la construction d'une place dédiée à la nation* (Paris, s.d.), and *Pétition présentée à la Convention par une réunion d'artistes* (Paris, s.d.). There are also a lot of appeals from artists in the Arch. Nat: F¹⁷ 1002, doss. 164; F¹⁷ 1009ᶜ, doss. 2272; F¹⁷ 1305, doss. 349, 535, and 604.

4 Arch. Nat., F¹⁷ 1326, doss. 11, nos. 284-8, and the covers of Détournelle's *Aux armes et aux arts … Journal de la Société républicaine des arts* (Paris 1794). See Appendix B.

5 The decrees were grouped in a pamphlet, *Arrêtés du Comité du salut public, relatifs aux monuments publics, aux arts et aux lettres* (Paris, n.d. [Floréal an II]), Bib. Nat., Lb⁴¹ 1092.

6 Jacques-Louis David, *Convention Nationale. Discours prononcé … dans la séance du 17 brumaire an II de la République* (7 novembre 1793) (Paris, n.d.). The final decree was approved by the Convention ten days later.

7 There were decrees on 1 and 4 April, 5 May, and 30 June 1793. Marcel Reinhard, *Nouvelle histoire de Paris: la Révolution* (Paris 1971), 370, dates the pivotal decree of 30 June 1793 as 1794. See *Décret qui approuve le programme du concours pour le plan de division du local compris entre les rues adjacentes du Palais National*, du 30 juin 1793, *Collection générale des lois, proclamations et autres actes* (Collection du Louvre), XV: 873-7, no. 1147. Several designs made in response to this decree can be located – for example, "Plan général du projet d'amenagement des abords du Louvre, des Tuileries, et de la place des Piques," Arch. Nat., Cartes et Plans, Versement d'architecture, boite no. XVIII, I; and "Rue de Rivoli. Projet d'amenagement du quartier situé entre la Seine, la Place de la Révolution la rue de la Révolution [Royale]," ibid., NIII Seine 853 (1-2). The last consists of two variants of the same plan.

8 Continuing the error of Marcel Reinhard, Pierre Lavedan, *Nouvelle histoire de Paris: histoire de l'urbanisme à Paris* (Paris 1975), 318, says that the Commission of Artists was formed in May 1794, instead of 1793. It could not have formed around Amelot in 1794 since he was imprisoned in October 1793 and died in prison the following year.

9 There are numerous articles on the Commission of Artists and the "Plan des artistes." For an account by the modern expert see Jeanne Pronteau, "Rapport sur les conférences en 1966-7 … sur le Plan de Verniquet 1791 et celui de la Commission des Artistes 1793-1797," *Ecole pratique des hautes études. Sciences historiques et philologiques. Annuaire 1967-1968*, 408-17.

10 It forms the first part of *Arrêtés du Comité de salut public relatifs aux monuments*, cited above in n 10.

11 The plan was published separately in Auguste Hubert, *Rapport sur l'embellissement du Palais et du Jardin national … présenté au Comité du salut public le 20 floréal* [l'an II] (Paris, n.d.).

12 The proceedings of the Comité pour l'embellissement du Palais et Jardin National are in Arch. Nat., série C, no. 364, plaquette I. For a brief account of its work, see Ferdinand Boyer, "Les Procès-Verbaux du Comité pour l'embellissement du Palais et du Jardin National des Tuileries (2 messidor-18 thermidor an II)" *Bulletin de la Société de l'histoire de l'art français* (1938): 261-77.

13 Arrêté du 3 Prairial an II (22 mai 1794), Alphonse Aulard, *Recueil des actes du Comité de salut public*, vol. 13, 667.

14 Mus. Carnavalet, GC Arch. A-D, D6470. An engraving of the plan was published by Delannoy's son, Marie-Antoine Delannoy, *Souvenirs de la vie et des ouvrages de F.-J. Delannoy* (Paris 1839), pl. I.

15 Mary Sheriff, "Comments on Revolutionary Allegory," *The Consortium on Revolutionary Europe 1987*, 683. The question is not, however, whether the People as Hercules represents a more radical phase of the Revolution (which seems indisputable) but whether Liberty was "repudiated," "rejected," and "replaced," as Lynn Hunt argues. See my own article, ibid., 631-45, esp. n 46.

16 James A. Leith, "The Birth of a Goddess: The Advent of Equality in the French Revolution," *The Consortium on Revolutionary Europe Proceedings 1988*, 119-32, pl. 628-39.

17 Arch. Nat., C, no. 364, plaquette I, 9 Messidor an II, 13.

18 Aulard, *Actes du Comité de Salut public*, vol. 14, 554–5, 9 Messidor an II (27 juin 1794). The decree is usually dated 28 June. The original is in Arch. Nat., AF II 80, in the handwriting of Barère.

19 On the paintings done for the contest see William Olander, *Pour transmettre à la posterité: French Painting and Revolution 1774–95*, PhD diss., New York University 1983, 2 vols.; University Microfilms, Ann Arbor 1985.

20 *Notice des ouvrages de sculpture, architecture et peinture, exposés aux concours qui ont eu lieu en vertu des décrets de la Convention Nationale, et des arrêtés du Comité de Salut public, soumis au jugement du jury des arts* (Paris, n.d.), Bib. Nat., Estampes, Collection Deloynes, no. 1724.

21 *Registre des inspecteurs de la salle*, Arch. Nat., Dᶜ xxxvᶜ, 1, 2, 3, hereafter cited as *Registre*. Proposals for sculpture are listed in Appendix D.

22 The prizes are listed in Portiez (de l'Oise), *Rapport fait au nom du Comité d'instruction publique sur les concours de sculpture, architecture et peinture ouverts par les décrets de la Convention nationale* (Paris, n.d. [décret de 14 Fructidor an III]). For the prize list see Appendix E.

23 Allais, Détournelle, and Vaudoyer, *Grands prix d'architecture*, pl. 23.

24 Ecole des Beaux-Arts, no. 1853.

25 Allais, Détournelle, and Vaudoyer, *Grands prix d'architecture*, pl. 41.

26 *Registre*, no. 1567. Another arch by Brongniart is in the collection of M Jacques de Sacy, inventaire no. 517. See the catalogue *Alexandre-Théodore Brongniart 1739–1813. Architecture et décor*, Musée Carnavalet 22 avril–13 juillet 1986, 225–7.

27 Lequeu entered a Temple to Equality, a column for the Place de la Victoire, two designs for a primary assembly, a justice of the peace, and this triumphal arch; *Registre*, nos. 1486, 1885, 2108. On 4 Vendémiaire an III, after the contest was closed, he entered a monument recalling the awful events of 14 Fructidor, making seven designs in all; ibid., no. 2445. His Temple of the Earth also seems to be related to this contest.

28 Allais, Détournelle, and Vaudoyer, *Grands prix d'architecture*, pl. 30.

29 Bib. Nat., Estampes, Ha 80a, 2ᵉ partie, no. 4.

30 Werner Szambien, *Les Projets de l'an II: concours d'architecture de la période révolutionnaire* (Paris 1986), 79.

31 Staatliche Graphische Sammlung, Munich, inv. nr. 27154.

32 Ecole des Beaux-Arts, prise en charge no. 18268.

33 Szambien, *Les Projets de l'an II*, 63–4, says that twelve columns of names on each side, totalling forty-eight, correspond to the number of sections in Paris. There are in fact fifteen columns on each face, perhaps one for each of the sixty units of the Parisian National Guard.

34 Szambien, *Les Projects de l'an II*, 62–3. Even on stylistic grounds the attribution seems dubious.

35 Ecole des Beaux-Arts, prise en charge no. 18269.

36 Musée Carnavalet, TGC Arch., Anon, D3681. Rabreau, "L'Architecture et la Fête," 252, reports incorrectly that this design is in the Ecole des Beaux-Arts.

37 The Mausoleum of Augustus was engraved for Lauro, *Antiquae urbis splendor*, 1612–28.

38 See, for example, Jean-Jacques Lequeu, mausoleum for great men to be built in the woods near the Hague, undated, and Jean-Nicolas Jomard, "Elyseum or Public Cemetery," design for the Grand Prix of 1799.

39 The copy is by Durand's student, Leo von Klenze, labelled "Unbekanntes Projekt: Tempel," Staatliche Graphische Sammlung, Munich, inv. nr. 27000.

40 Allais, Détournelle, and Vaudoyer, *Grands prix d'architecture*, pls. 26, 27, 28.

41 Ecole des Beaux-Arts, prise en charge no. 18268. The design is classified as anonymous, but can be identified by the no. 8, which also appears in the prize list.

42 Ibid., no. 18267. According to Guiffrey, the editor of the *Livrets* of the *salons*, his initials were C.P.R.

43 *Registre*, no. 1572.

44 Ecole des Beaux-Arts, no. 1843.

45 Ibid, prise en charge no. 18268.

46 The design, now in the Carnavalet Museum, TGC Arch., D8743, was published for the first time in the catalogue for the exhibition, *Le Temple. Représentations d'un art sacré* (Paris 1982), no. 234, but the editors did not connect it to the contest, nor did they decipher the acronym. The *Registre*, no. 1457, shows that Bonnet submitted a "plan, section et élévation d'un temple à l'Egalité." It is signed "A.F. [Phrygian bonnet] A.," obviously "A.-F. Bonnet, architecte."

47 Bib. Nat., Estampes, Ha 80b, p. 10.

48 Ibid., pl. 72b.

49 Szambien, *Les projets de l'an II*, 90–2, mentions the affinity between Lequeu's Temple of the Earth and his Temple to Equality, but adds that "this project was not however submitted during the contest." Szambien does not mention the note by the artist on the back.

50 Philippe Duboy, *Lequeu: An Architectural Enigma* (London 1986), 234–5, reproduces the design and the note on the back but does not discuss its relationship to the Temple to Equality or the Contest of Year II.

51 The decree establishing the worship of the Supreme Being was passed on 18 Floréal an II, 7 May 1794 – that is, more than three weeks before Lequeu submitted his project according to the date on the back.

52 *Notice des ouvrages*, 34, no. 27. This would seem not to be Lequeu's Temple to Equality, which we know was submitted on 13 Prairial an II – 1 June 1794 – according to the *Registre*, no. 1486.

53 The possibility that the date Lequeu later put on the back of the design is incorrect is strengthened by the fact that he was unquestionably wrong about the date of another design; see n 88.

54 *Registre*, no. 1850. The "14" pencilled on the design refers to the number among Temples to Equality under which it was listed in the *Notice des ouvrages*.

55 Ecole des Beaux-Arts, prise en charge no. 18261.

56 Allais, Détournelle, and Vaudoyer, *Grands prix d'architecture*, pls. 31, 32. The elevation also appears in Charles-Paul Landon, *Annales du Musée … Ecole française. Architecture* (Paris 1823–35), 15, pl. 8.

57 Musée Carnavalet, TGC, I, D8208, and Détournelle, *Recueil d'architecture nouvelle* (Paris, an XIII), pls. 52, 53. In Szambien, *Projets de l'an II*, 117–18, the descriptions do not match the illustrations, or the illustrations are mislabelled.

58 Ecole des Beaux-Arts, prise en charge no. 18257.

59 Ibid., prise en charge no. 18265.

60 Mus. Carnavalet, GC Arch., Anon., D8094. This is still classified as anonymous, although there can be no doubt about its authorship: *Registre*, no. 1553.

61 Nicolas Goulet, *Le Temple des lois et de la Liberté* (Paris, n.d.).

62 Allais, Détournelle, and Vaudoyer, *Grands prix d'architecture*, pls. 24, 25, 26.

63 Ecole des Beaux-Arts, nos. 1842, 1843.

64 Ibid., cit., prise en charge no. 18263.

65 Musée Carnavalet, TGC, I D3291, 1, 2. This can be identified by the entry in *Registre*, no. 1523. Percier was the only architect to enter a project for the banks of the Seine. Also, it has the "B" mentioned in the register. Szambien, *Les Projets de l'an II*, 75–8, attributes the design to both Percier and Fontaine. Only Percier's name is listed in the register, but both he and Fontaine won a prize of 4,000 *livres* under the rubric of embellishment for a project listed under no. 4 in the *Notice des ouvrages* as "a plan, cross-section, and elevation of arenas and a theatre for celebration of the triumphs of the Republic."

66 Ecole des Beaux-Arts, prise en charge no. 18272; *Registre*, no. 1880.

67 Weimar, Kunstsammlungen.

68 Bib. Nat., Estampes, Ha 80a, I, pl. 4.

69 Allais, Détournelle, et Vaudoyer, *Grands prix d'architecture,* pls. 33, 34; and Weimar, Kunstsammlungen.

70 J.-N.-L. Durand, *Précis des leçons d'architecture données à l'Ecole polytechnique* (Paris 1805), II: 7.

71 Ecole des Beaux-Arts, prise en charge no. 18258.

72 M. Ozouf, "Symboles et fonction des âges dans les fêtes révolutionnaires," *Annales historiques de la Révolution française,* no. 202 (1970): 569–93.

73 Allais, Détournelle, and Vaudoyer, *Grands prix d'architecture,* pl. 40.

74 Ecole des Beaux-Arts, no. 1850. Szambien, *Les Projets de l'an II,* 136, attributes this design to Durand and Thibault on stylistic grounds. The two architects won a prize for public baths, the one listed as no. 5 in the catalogue for the public exhibition, whereas it is no. 6 that best fits this design: "Plan, coupe et élév. de Bains publics en face des Invalides, sur l'avenue des Champs-Elysées, *avec explication*" (italics added). The design has a long explanation on the left. An artist listed as "Houet, architecte" submitted a plan for baths and fountains, with a slogan similar to but not quite the same as that of Durand and Thibault, "le bonheur d'être utile" (*Registre,* no. 1869). This is probably J.-C. Huet, who we know was a member of the Société républicaine des arts (see list in Détournelle, *Aux armes et aux arts,* reproduced in App. B, 320). If Huet is the "Houet" who competed for the Grand Prix in 1779, then like Durand he was a student of Leroy.

75 Détournelle, *Recueil d'architecture nouvelle,* pls. 52, 53.

76 Project by [Ch. S.?] Thierry, *Registre,* no. 1889.

77 Allais, Détournelle, and Vaudoyer, *Grand prix d'architecture,* pls. 35–7.

78 *Procès-verbaux de la première séance du jury des arts nommé par la Convention nationale et assemblé dans une des salles du Musée en vertu des décrets de 9 et 25 brumaire an II* (17 Pluviôse an II, 5 février 1794) (Paris, n.d.), 55.

79 Ecole des Beaux-Arts, prise en charge no. 18260.

80 *Registre,* no. 1528.

81 Ibid., no. 1500. Ecole des Beaux-Arts, no. 1851.

82 *Registre,* no. 1899.

83 Ibid., no. 1900.

84 Ibid., no. 2221.

85 Ibid., no. 1497.

86 Ibid., no. 1703.

87 Ibid., no. 1902. The project for an *enceinte* for the Pantheon does not appear in the register, but was listed in the *Notice des ouvrages,* 41, no. 2.

88 Duboy, *Lequeu,* reproduces both sides of the design on 243–4, then dates it 27 September 1793 instead of 26 September 1794, in the "Autobiography" on 353–4.

VII TOWARDS AN IDEOLOGICAL LANDSCAPE

1 *Décret relatif aux parcs, maisons, etc. portant les armoiries,* du 1er août 1793, in *Collection générale des décrets* (Colletion Baudouin), août 1793, 11.

2 *Décret qui prescrit un terme pour l'enlèvement des signes de royauté,* du 18 Vendémiaire [an II], ibid., octobre 1793 (Vendémiaire an II), 162.

3 *Décret qui ordonne de faire retourner les plaques de cheminées ou contrefeux portant des signes de féodalité,* du 21 Vendémiaire [an II], ibid., octobre 1793 (Vendémiaire an II), 191.

4 *Moniteur,* vol. 16, no. 154, 3 juin 1793, 538.

5 Laws confirming name changes began in the final sessions of the Legislative Assembly and continued under the Convention. See the *Collection générale des lois, proclamations, instructions et autres actes* (Collection du Louvre), vols. XI–XVI. Other name changes are mentioned in Arch. Nat., F^{17}1008^B–1008^C.

6 Arch. Nat., F^{14} 10259, 26. The designs are signed "Chabane ing."

7 Arch. Nat., F^{17} 1010^D, 3817. Enclosed with the letter was a placard announcing the name changes.

8 *Moniteur,* vol. 18, no. 46, 16 Brumaire an II, (6 novembre 1793), 344.

9 The *Moniteur* gives his name as E. Chamouleau, but it certainly must have been F. Chamoulaud, member of the Cercle Social, promoter of various humanitarian schemes and author of *Plan de la régénération des moeurs en France* (Paris, n.d.).

10 [Abbé Henri-B.] Grégoire, *Convention Nationale. Système de dénominations topographiques pour les places, rues, quais, etc. de toute les communes de la République* (Paris, n.d.), 3.

11 *Décret portant que les fleurs-de-lis marquées sur les milles qui bordent les routes, seront remplacées par le bonnet de la liberté,* du 20 septembre 1793, *Collection générale des décrets* (Collection Baudouin), septembre 1793, 203–4.

12 *Procès-verbal de l'Assemblée nationale* (Paris 1791–92), vol. IX, 491.

13 *Décret relatif aux arbres de la liberté,* du 30 pluviôse [an II], *Collection générale des décrets* (Collection Baudouin), Pluviôse-Ventôse an II, 8.

14 Arch. Nat., F^{17} 1005^B, 997. A similar idea was proposed by Geruzez, a *curé* from Sacy near Reims, "Monuments républicains: project d'un monument à élever dans chaque commune, en l'honneur de ceux qui sont morts pour la patrie," *La Feuille villageoise* VII, 4e année, no. 10 (1 Frimaire an II): 220–5.

15 "Suite de la séance du 28 Décembre," *Annales patriotiques et littéraires* CCCLXV (30 décembre 1792): 1632.

16 *Révolutions de Paris,* no. 217 (10–18 frimaire an II, 30 November-8 December 1793): 290. The engraving is also in the Bib. Nat., Estampes, Coll. Hennin, vol. 133, no. 11706.

17 I am indebted here to the insightful paper "The Lynching of the Tyrant," which Sergio Bertelli of Florence presented to the conference Revolutions in Comparison, held at UCLA 18–19 June 1988 as the introduction to that university's program for the 1989 bicentennial of the French Revolution.

18 The proposed statue does not show several other ingredients of the ritual of killing the tyrant – decapitation, castration, cutting off the right hand, and dragging through the streets – all inversions of the rituals of power.

19 Arch. Mun. Troyes, Délibérations municipales, 2 Frimaire an II.

20 A. Millin, *Voyage dans les départements du Midi de la France,* 5 vols. (Paris 1807–11), III: 485–6.

21 Arch. Mun. Nantes, D$^{1-2}$, Conseil Municipal, 11 July 1791. Renou, *Colonne de la Place Louis XVI,* 18–20, states incorrectly that the decision to put a statue of Liberty in the place of one of Louis XVI was made after 10 August 1792.

22 [J. La Vallée, J. Breton, and L. Brion], *Voyages dans les départements,* 13 vols. (Paris 1792–an X). The engraving by Fachot, an engineer, is in vol. VI, 8.

23 *Plan de la Ville de Nantes* by Coulon, an III.

24 Christian Pfister, *Histoire de Nancy,* 3 vols. (Paris-Nancy 1902–9), 3: 516–24.

25 *Pétition à la municipalité de Nancy* (n.d.,n.p.). The main argument of those who sought to save the statue was the beneficence of Louis XV and Stanislas.

26 *Journal de Nancy et des frontières,* no. 15, 98.

27 Ibid., no. 23, 180.

28 Arch. Nat., C273. Also Gustave Laurent, "Le Conventionnel Rühl à Reims. La Destruction de la Sainte-Ampoule," *Figures révolutionnaires champenoises,* 1ère série (Reims 1923): 91–122.

29 *Moniteur,* vol. 18, 13 octobre 1793, 100, report on the session of 16 Vendémiaire an II (7 octobre 1793).

30 *Relation de la fête civique qui doit avoir lieu à Reims le 23 octobre 1792* (Reims, s.d.). Bib. Mun. Reims, CR IV 917^2 MM.

31 Ibid.

32 Arch. Mun. Reims, R 216 FM, Délibérations du Conseil Général, minutes of 13 August 1792.

33 Arch. Mun. Reims, R 13 FM and R 14 FM, Délibérations du Club de Reims, minutes of 7, 9, 16, 21, 30 July and 4, 6, 10 August. The Conseil Général of the city approved the plans on 19 July: Arch. Mun. Reims, R 218 FM.

34 Mus. Carnavalet, PC Top., Projets relevés à caractère pittoresque, D 3602.

35 On 15 August a citizen expressed surprise at the Jacobin Club that the scroll inscribed with the names of the fallen had not yet been finished: Arch. Mun. Reims, R 14 FM.

36 Ordre de la marche qui aura lieu à Reims le 10 août 1793 (Reims, s.d.). Bib. Mun. Reims, CR IV 917⁴ MM. Another account appears in the Manuel de citoyen, contenant les évènemens politiques des années 1793 et 1794 [Reims], no. 44 (14 août 1793): 355–6. Ibid., CR V 1191 M.

37 Arch. Mun. Reims, C 829 FM, liasse 49.

38 Ibid., liasse 28.

39 Fête civique en l'honneur de la Raison … pour le 30 Frimaire [an II] (Reims, n.d.).

40 There are two versions, one labelled and the other not, in the Bib. Mun. Bordeaux, Fonds Delpit, série B, carton 13, #14.

41 Ibid., #18.

42 L. Lamothe, Le Jardin public et l'école d'équitation de Bordeaux (Bordeaux 1849).

43 Rapport fait en séance publique du conseil général de la commune, le 15 décembre 1792 sur les divers plans présentés par les artistes … imprimé par le délibération de 28 avril l'an second de la république française. Arch. Mun. Bordeaux, M3. The council's appeal to artists was issued on 20 November 1792, and the report was considered twice, once in December and again the following April.

44 Ibid., 22.

45 Georges-François Pariset, "L'Architecte Brongniart: ses activités à Bordeaux et à Réole 1793–1795," Bulletin et Mémoires de la Société archéologique de Bordeaux, (1951–62) LXII (1964): 181–239.

46 Gaston Ducaunnès-Duval, ed., Ville de Bordeaux. Inventaire-sommaire des archives municipales. Période révolutionnaire 1789–an VIII (Bordeaux 1910), vol. II, 55, session of the municipal council 7 Frimaire an II.

47 Jacques Silvestre de Sacy, Alexandre-Théodore Brongniart. Sa vie. Son Oeuvre (Paris 1940), 97.

48 Arch. Dép. Gironde, 3 L 346.

49 Jacques de Sacy, Brongniart, 97; Pariset, "L'Architecte Brongniart," 203–4.

50 Ducaunnès-Duval, ed., Archives Municipales, vol. II, 74, session of 7 Germinal an II.

51 This ground-plan is reproduced in colour in the catalogue Alexandre-Théodore Brongniart 1739–1813. Architecture et décor, Musée Carnavalet, 22 avril–13 juillet 1986, pl. no. 253, 222. In this catalogue the design is dated 1793, whereas it must have been done in the spring of 1794.

52 Pariset, "L'Architecte Brongniart," 210–12.

53 Ibid., 216.

54 Arch. Nat., F¹³ 1713.

55 Arch. Dép. Gironde, 4 L 123.

56 Arch. Nat., Cartes et Plans, F¹⁴ 10216, no. 6².

57 Ducaunnès-Duval, Archives Municipales, vol. II, 186, session of 3 Messidor an II. The club asked the municipality to open a subscription and appoint commissioners to finance the project, but the councillors replied that this was beyond their powers.

58 On his career, see Jean-Jacques Duthoy, "Un Architecte néoclassique: François Verly, Lille, Anvers, Bruxelles (1760–1822). Contribution à l'étude de l'architecture 'révolutionnaire,'" Revue Belge d'archéologie de l'art (Bruxelles 1972), 41 (1974): 119–50.

59 Odile Ramette, De la fête révolutionnaire. Essai sur le rôle et l'impact des manifestations festives, sur l'architecture et l'urbanisme à Lille dans la dernière décennie du XVIIIᵉ siècle, doctorat de 3ᵉ cycle, Université de Paris 1979.

60 Anon., "Le Temple de la Raison à Lille," Bulletin de la Société d'études de la province de Cambrai IV, (1902): 260.

61 Arch. Dep. Nord, L 5050 contains many documents concerning work on the temple during Brumaire, Frimaire, Nivôse, and Pluviôse an II, that is October through January of 1793–94.

62 Arch. Mun. Lille, 18.079. The deliberations of the municipal council are in 8 vols. covering 1790–1800 under the same cote.

63 It is not clear how far Corbet got in sculpting this figure. The plaster version was to be presented to a jury to decide if changes should be made. The records show that he was still working on it in September 1794: Arch. Mun. Lille, 17.957, doss. 2.

64 Arch. Mun. Lille, 18.079, vol. V, fol. 193, item 784, 23 Messidor an III. Parishioners asked for the material from the amphitheatre to be used in reconstructing the altar.

65 Arch. Dép. Nord, L 2122, Rés 333.

66 Ibid., L 5050.

67 Arch. Mun. Lille, 18.079, vol. IV, fol. 166, item 614.

68 Ibid., vol. V, fol. 54, item 254. 16 Nivôse an III (5 January 1795).

69 Arch. Mun. Lille, 17.982, doss. 10.

70 Moniteur, vol. 14, no. 302, 28 octobre 1792, 307–8.

71 Arch. Mun. Lille, 18.050, doss. 13. The end of the letter seems to be missing, along with the beginning of his speech.

72 Arch. Mun. Lille, 18.079, vol. II, vol. 185, item 728, 13 novembre an II.

73 Ibid., vol. IV, fols. 148–50.

74 Musée Hospice Comtesse 971-11-1, H2465.

75 Oeuvres de Jean-Jacques Rousseau, ed. Mussay Pathy (Paris 1829), XI: 169 (Lettre à M D'Alembert).

76 Duthoy, "Un architecte néo-classique," 135.

77 Mark K. Deming, La Halle au blé de Paris 1762–1813 (Bruxelles 1984). Compare the elevation by Verly on page 106 with views of the Halle au blé on pages 182–3.

78 Although this design is dated 29 Thermidor an II in the lower left-hand corner, Rabreau, "L'Architecture et la Fête," 244, dates it an VIII. On this and other parts of Verly's proposals see James A. Leith, "Entürfe für ein revolutionäres Zentrum. Verlys Pläne für Lille. Projects for a Revolutionary Centre. Verly's Plan for Lille," Berlin Architectural Journal, no. 7 (15 March 1983): 56–63.

79 Jacques-François Blondel, Cours d'architecture, 9 vols. (Paris 1771–79), I: 410–12.

80 Arch. Mun. Montpellier, Registre du Conseil général, vol. VI, 52.

81 Ibid., vol. VIII, 290.

82 Procès-verbal de la fête funèbre consacrée à la mémoire de Marat … par le peuple de Montpellier (Montpellier an II), 3–4, Bib. Mun. Montpellier, 11378.

83 Société populaire de Montpellier. Rapport fait au nom des comités des arts et de l'instructon réunis par Raisin Pagès. Sur le plan de la fête consacrée à l'Etre Suprême (Montpellier, an II), Bib. Mun. Montpellier, 11946.

84 Arch. Mun. Montpellier, Registre du Conseil général, vol. V, 26.

85 Bib. Mun. Montpellier, mss Soulier, Chronique de Montpellier, vol. I, 316.

86 Arch. Mun. Montpellier, Registre du Conseil général, vol. VII, 117.

87 Arch. Dép. Hérault, L 5501.

88 Sur le plan de la fête.

89 Louis Grasset-Morel, Le Temple de la Raison et les colonnes de la Liberté à Montpellier (Montpellier 1901).

90 Ibid., 10.

91 The catalogue previously cited, *Projets et dessins pour la Place Royale du Peyrou*, 67 and 84, contains an error. It dates Boisset's proposal from 18 Nivôse an II, the date on which he added it to the guidelines for the new Commission for the Amelioration of Agriculture and the Arts. The catalogue transcribes this date as 7 January 1793 instead of 7 January 1794. The Cult of Reason did not emerge until the fall of 1793. Moreover, in a letter from Montpellier to Lyon dated 22 Frimaire an II, that is 12 December 1793, Boisset mentions the project. Arch. Dép. Rhône, 42 L 106ᵉ, 84.

92 Arch. Dép. Hérault, L 2184.

93 Arch. Dép. L 1T/h9.

94 For example, *Annales patriotiques et littéraires*, 2 mars 1794, no. CCCCXXV, [1897]-8.

95 *La Société Populaire au citoyen* — (Montpellier, n.d.), Arch. Dép. Hérault, L 5523.

96 *La Société populaire régénérée des sans-culottes de la Commune à la Convention Nationale* (Montpellier, n.d.), Arch. Dép. Hérault, L 5523.

97 Arch. Dép. Hérault, L 2184.

98 Arch. Nat., Cartes et Plans, NIII Hérault 24.

99 Caisse Nationale des Monuments Historiques et des Sites, inv. 18823.

100 Arch. Nat., F¹³ 571.

101 One of the best accounts of Chinard's work is Salomon de la Chapelle, "Joseph Chinard, sculpture: sa vie et son oeuvre," *Revue du Lyonnais*, 5ᵉ série, vol. XXII (1897): 77–98, 209–18, 272–91, 337–57, 412–42, and vol. XXIII, 37–52, 141–57, 229–38. On the fronton see esp. vol. XXII: 209–12.

102 There is a copy of the medallion in the Musée Historique de Lyon. On the face are the two statues of Liberty and Equality, with the date August 1793 underneath. On the back is inscribed DESSIN DE L'OUVRAGE EN SCULPTURE QUE NOTRE CONCITOYEN CHINARD EXECUTE SUR LA FAÇADE DE LA MAISON COMMUNE. L'AN II.

103 *Etrennes géographiques et récréatifs, ou Almanach du diocèse de Lyon*, an XII.

104 *Bulletin du Département du Rhone-et-Loire. Imprimé par ordre du Comité général de Surveillance et du Salut Public*. Facsimile, following the original format, edited by Charavay fils ainé (Paris and Lyon 1845), no. 27, 3–4 September 1793, 2–3.

105 Arch. Dép. Rhone, 42 L 106ᵉ, 75 ff.

106 Pierre-Marie Gonon, *Bibliographie historique de la Ville de Lyon pendant la Révolution française* (Lyon 1844), note under no. 1570.

107 Gay, [architecte], "Fête de la Raison dans l'église Saint-Jean à Lyon," Bib. Mun. Garde-Dieu, Lyon, mss 2394-1.

108 *Fête à l'Etre-Suprême célébrée à Commune-Affranchie le 20 Prairial an II* (Lyon, n.d.), 6. Bib. Mun. Garde-Dieu, Lyon, 355975.

109 *Programme et description de la fête de l'Egalité à Commune-Affranchie le décadi 20 Ventôse an deuxième* (Lyon, n.d.). Bib. Mun. Garde-Dieu, Lyon 500570.

110 *Lettre du citoyen D???? au Citoyen M???? député à la Convention* (Lyon, n.d.) This is appended to the program cited above.

111 De la Chapelle, "Joseph Chinard," XXII: 284.

112 *Fête à l'Etre Suprême célébrée à Commune-Affranchie*, passim.

113 Tournon, *Plant [sic] de la fête de l'Etre Suprême*, Bib. Mun. Garde-Dieu, Lyon, Coll. Coste, no. 649.

114 The ceremony was delayed because the municipal council had been in the hands of a group considered counter-revolutionary from 24 July through 21 August 1793. The minutes are struck out for this period. On the plans for the fête see Arch. Mun. Aix-en-Provence, Déliberations du Conseil, LL 79, vol. 7, fols. 109 and 136.

115 Ibid., vol. 8, fols. 182–3.

116 Arch. Mun. Aix-en-Provence, M.I. article 49.

117 Arch. Mun. Aix-en-Provence, LL 81, vol. 9, fol. 35.

118 Quoted in Katrin Simons, *Jacques Réattu: Peintre de la Révolution française* (Paris 1985), 38

119 Arch. Dép. Vaucluse, série Fi.

120 The ten designs are in the Mus. Réattu, cat. 44, nos. 115–25. The design mentioned is no. 119. They are analysed in Simons, *Jacques Réattu*, 37–43.

121 Bib. Nat., Estampes, Qb¹, janvier 1793. See the catalogue of the exhibition *Charles de Wailly 1730–1798*, Caisse Nationale des monuments historiques et des sites (Paris 1979), 87.

122 Arch. Dép. Somme, La 1036.

123 The statue was commissioned on 9 Floréal an II, or 28 April 1794. Arch. Nat., F¹⁷ 1057.

124 Arch. Dép. Somme, 2 L I/19 and 2 L I/107.

125 Arch. Dép. Meurthe-et-Moselle, L 1694.

126 Bib. Nat., Estampes, Ha 80a, première partie, 33.

127 Duboy, *Lequeu*, 16, 353.

128 "La Commission des travaux publics aux artistes," le 18 Messidor an II, *Moniteur*, vol. 21, no. 296, 26 Messidor an II (14 juillet 1794), 201.

129 Ecole des Beaux-Arts, prise en charge no. 18265.

130 Goulet, *Le Temple des Lois*, 4.

131 *Commission de l'instruction publique. Architecture rurale* (Paris, n.d.).

132 *Inventaire*, no. 1955; *Notice des ouvrages*, 34–5, nos. 7–9.

133 *Inventaire*, no. 2260; *Notice des ouvrages*, 34, no. 3.

VIII DERADICALIZATION AND MILITARIZATION

1 Anon., "Le Temt [sic] découvre la verité … Le peuple représenté sous la figure d'Hercule, terressant [sic] l'hydre du Triumvirat," Bib. Nat., Estampes, Coll. Hennin, vol. 135, no. 163371.

2 *Moniteur*, vol. 21, no. 358, 28 Fructidor an II (14 septembre 1794), 744.

3 *Moniteur*, vol. 23, no. 142, 22 Pluviôse an II (10 février 1795), 416.

4 Paul Fassy, *Une page de l'histoire de Paris sous le Terreur: Marat, sa mort, ses véritables funérailles*, 2ᵉ éd. (Paris 1867), 40.

5 Marvin Carlson, *The Theatre of the French Revolution* (Ithaca 1966) 230–1.

6 Arch. Nat., C 364, plaquette 1. The committee met twenty times between 2 Messidor an II (20 June 1794) and 18 Thermidor an II (5 August 1794). An order of the Committee of Public Safety dated 16 Thermidor, read to the Committee for Embellishment two days later, suspended its work: Aulard, *Actes du Comité de salut public*, vol. 15, 630.

7 Arch. Nat., C 354, doss. 1851, report to the Inspectors of the Hall of the Convention.

8 Wilhelm Adolf Schmidt, *Tableaux de la Révolution française, publiés sur les papiers inédits du département et de la police secrète de Paris*, 3 vols. (Leipzig 1867–70), 2: 261–78.

9 *Décret qui ordonne que le monument élevé en forme de montagne devant la maison nationale ainsi que tous de ce genre élevés dans toute l'étendue de la République seront incessamment démolis et détruits*, 2 Ventôse an III, in *Décrets de la Convention Nationale*, Ventôse an III, décret no. 867.

10 The temple, with the Mountain in place, was inaugurated on 20 September 1794: Arch. Mun. Lille, 18.079, vol. IV, fol. 166, no. 614. It was dismantled in the spring of 1795, judging by discussion in the municipal council about the expenses in May of that year: ibid., vol. V, fol. 142 verso.

11 Arch. Mun. Lille, 18.079, vol. IV, fol. 148 verso and 150.

12 Bib. Nat., Estampes, Coll. Hennin, vol. 138, no. 12165.

13 Arch. Mun. Montpellier, Registre du Conseil Général, vol. X, 8.

14 Ibid., vol. XI, 33.

15 *Moniteur*, vol. 23, no. 110, 20 Nivôse l'an III (9 janvier 1795), 156–60.

16 Ibid., vol. 24, no. 248, 8 Prairial l'an III (27 mai 1795), 529.

17 Bib. mun. Avignon, Est., Atlas 14, no. 21, Coll. Esprit Requieu. See Claude Badet, *La Révolution en Provence: images et histoire* (Avignon 1889), 98.

18 *Registre,* under 9 and 10 Thermidor.

19 The terms of the election of the jury were laid down in the "Loi portant qu'il sera nommé un jury … 9 Frimaire an III [29 November 1794]," Arch. Nat., AD VIII 12. The jury was not elected until 20–22 Frimaire an II, 10–12 December 1794: Arch. Nat., F17 1281, doss. 7, no. 74.

20 Pierre-Théodore Bienaimé, *Rapport sur quelques abus introduits dans la répartition et l'exécution des travaux publics* (Paris, an III). It appeared in mid-January 1795.

21 *Extrait du procès-verbal des séances du jury des arts, ou rapport fait au Comité d'instruction publique sur les prix que le jury a décernés aux ouvrages de peinture, sculpture, et architecture,* signed by Léon Dufourny and dated 21 Prairial an III (9 June 1795), mss in Arch. Nat., F17 1057, doss. 3.

22 Louis-François-René Portiez, *Rapport fait au nom du Comité d'instruction publique sur les concours de sculpture, peinture, et architecture ouverts par les décrets de la Convention nationale* (Paris, n.d.). The decree was passed on 14 Fructidor an III, 31 August 1795.

23 *Extrait du procès-verbal des séances du jury des arts ou rapport fait au Comité d'instruction publique,* article 2e, Examen des programmes … , "De la sculpture."

24 Ibid.

25 Arch. Nat., F17 1281, doss. 10, nos. 168–9, contains an extract from the minutes of the jury of 27 Pluviôse an III, 15 February 1795, recording the discussion of the Rousseau project.

26 *Extrait du procès-verbal des séances du jury des arts, ou rapport fait au Comité d'instruction publique,* article 2e, Examen des programmes … , "De l'architecture."

27 Portiez, *Rapport fait au nom du Comité d'instruction publique,* 1-6.

28 *Prix décernés par le jury des arts aux ouvrages d'architecture, sculpture et peinture soumis à son jugement,* Fructidor an III: Bib. Nat., Estampes, Coll. Deloynes, vol. 56, no. 1737. There were also large one-page announcements for each genre: ibid., nos. 1734, 1735, 1736.

29 *Extrait du procès-verbal des séances du jury,* "Pour l'architecture, 1er Prix."

30 Arch. Nat., F17 1056, doss. 5.

31 Ibid., doss. 6, contains a table showing the original value in *assignats,* the reduced value, and the amount paid up to the end of year VI.

32 Ibid., doss. 7-10, contain files about payments to individual artists.

33 Mus. Carnavalet, D3918, D7694, D8179.

34 "Projet d'élever un cirque en pierre dans le Champ de Mars," *Décade philosophique, littéraire et politique,* no. 13, 10 Pluviôse an VI, 29 janvier 1788, 236.

35 "Projet de Labarre pour la restoration du Panthéon," ibid., no. 33, 30 Thermidor an VI, 17 août 1799, 372–3. The author thought that it would be better to spend money on a huge column on the Place de la Bastille than on strengthening the walls of the Panthéon.

36 "Vues sur le Panthéon Français et moyens de remédier aux effrayantes dégradations qui s'y manifestent par cit. Dewailly, architecte de l'Institut, avec une gravure," ibid., no. 9, 30 Frimaire an VI, 20 décembre 1797, 537-41.

37 Brongniart, plan for reinforcing the dome of the Pantheon, cross-section.

38 "Monument élevé dans la ville d'Auch," ibid., no. 13, 10 Pluviôse an VII, 29 janvier 1799, 243; "Lebreton … description d'un monument qui vient d'être érigé dans la promenade de Besançon," *Magazin encyclopédique,* V (1799): 384.

39 "Obélisque élevé dans la ville d'Auch," *La Décade philosophique,* no. 10, 10 Nivôse an VII, 55-6.

40 "Programme qu'on prépare pour approprier les églises aux solemnités Décadaires," ibid., no. 9, 30 Frimaire an VII, 20 décembre 1798, 555-6.

41 Arch. Nat., F13 729, doss. Loiret.

42 The design on four sheets is in Arch. Nat., F13 531, signed S. Far. The departmental officials approved the plan on 6 October 1794: Arch. des Yvelines, L 132, fol. 318. For background see F. Evrard, "Le Jeu de Paume de Versailles de 1786 à 1804," *La Révolution française* LXXIV (1921): 289–317, but Evrard did not find the design.

43 *Moniteur,* vol. 24, no. 240, 30 Floréal an III, 19 mai 1795, 481.

44 Arch. Nat., F13 1166, contains the elevation and a lot of documents on the project between Year III and 1811. For the subsequent history of the market, see Gabriel Vauthier, "Le Marché Saint-Honoré," *Bulletin de l'histoire de Paris et de l'Ile de France,* 57e année (1930): 84-8.

45 *Journal des debats et décrets,* vol. 74, no. 1133, 4 Brumaire an IV, 548.

46 "Directoire exécutif au ministre de l'Intérieur," 8 Floréal an IV, *Le Redacteur,* vol. II, no. 139, 3.

47 [Pierre] Benezech, *Ministère de l'Intérieur. Appel aux artistes* (Paris, Floréal an IV). Also the *Moniteur Universel,* no. 246, 6 Prairial an IV, 982–3.

48 Athanase Détournelle, *Recueil d'architecture nouvelle* (Paris, an XIII), pl. 64.

49 Boudhors, "Plan et coupe d'un Autel de la Patrie," Ecole des Beaux-Arts, no. 1808. The "4" scrawled on the upper right probably was the number given to it for reference in the contest. On the back a handwritten note says: "Description d'un projet d'autel de la patrie, dressé en exécution de l'appel aux artistes inséré par ordre du Ministre de l'Intérieur dans le numéro no. 246 du *Moniteur Universel* … dressé à Strasbourg le 28 prairial l'an IV de la République."

50 Musée Carnavalet, Top., PC 127A, and Alais, Détournelle, and Vaudoyer, *Grands prix d'architecture,* pls. 43, 44.

51 "Projet pour la Place de la Concorde à Paris. La Concorde reserrant les liens du faisceau de l'état," Mus. Carnavalet, P.C. Dessins, "Pozzi," D7991.

52 [Athanase] Détournelle and [Armand-Charles] Caraffe, "Elévation du monument à la Concorde," an V, and "Coupe du monument," Mus. Carnavalet, Top. PC 127 A.; pl. 65 and 66 in Détournelle's *Recueil d'architecture nouvelle.*

53 Détournelle and Caraffe, "Monument consacré à Humen, allégorie de l'Indivisibilité demandé par le gouvernement l'an IV," Bib. Nat., Estampes, Ha 78 pet. fol.; also pl. 18 in Détournelle, *Recueil d'architecture nouvelle.*

54 [Jean-Baptiste] Faivre, "Monument à ériger sur la place des Victoires. Sujet d'un prix proposé par le gouvernement en 1796 (l'an IV de la Rép.)," Allais, Détournelle, et Vaudoyer, *Grand prix d'architecture,* pl. 42.

55 "Nouvelles littéraires," *Magazin encyclopédique,* II (1796): 407.

56 "Tableau des prix distribués par l'Institut national dans sa séance générale du 5 Messidor an V, aux artistes qui, au jugement de la classe de littérature et beaux-arts, ont mérité des encouragements dans le concours que le gouvernement a fait ouvrir sur les projets d'embellissements pour les places de Paris," *Mémoires de l'Institut national des sciences et arts. Littérature et beaux-arts,* 5 vols. (Paris, an VI-an XII), I: 37-8.

57 *Procès-verbaux de l'académie des beaux-arts,* ed. Marcel Bonnaire (Paris 1937-43), I: 33-8, 69.

58 [Athanase Détournelle], "Histoire des concours en architecture, et coup d'oeil sur ceux qui ont lieu en France depuis Louis XV," *Journal des arts, des sciences et de la littérature,* an IX, no. 145, 145-8; no. 147, 193-7; no. 148, 217-21; no. 149, 241-4; no. 150, 265-8; no. 151, 289-93; no. 152, 313-18; no. 153, 346-53; and no. 154, 373-8. See esp. no. 151, 292.

59 Charles-Louis Corbet, *Lettre au Citoyen Lagarde, sécrétaire-général du Directoire Exécutif sur les esquisses et projets de monuments pour les places publiques de Paris, faits après l'invitation du ministre de l'intérieur* (Paris, an V).

60 Pierre-J.-B. Chaussard, *Monuments de l'héroïsme français* (Paris, n.d.).

61 This design was no. 4 in Sotheby's catalogue, *Important 19th-Century European Paintings, Drawings and Watercolours,* of items offered for sale on Thursday, 24 May 1984. The project was displayed in the Salon of 1795.

62 Szambien, *Les Projets de l'an II,* 57-8.

63 This is reported in his pamphlet, [Antoine] Voinier, *Projet d'un monument triomphal, en l'honneur des quatorze armées de la République,* (Paris, an III).

64 Mus. Carnavalet, G.C. Arch. E.-La., D6120.

65 Drawings of the project and documents about it are in Arch. Nat., F¹³ 870, including an unsigned printed pamphlet, *Description de la colonne à ériger à la Paix. Moyens de l'exécuter sans le secours du trésor public* (n.p., n.d.). An engraving later appeared in Charles-Paul Landon, *Annales du musée. Ecole française moderne. Architecture*, 2nd ed. (1834), pl. 59.

66 Arch. Nat., F¹³ 531, contains four dossiers on this project. The designs are scattered in Bib. Nat., Cabinet des Estampes, Va 234, the Bibliothèque de l'Opéra, the Bibliothèque historique de la ville de Paris, and the Bibliothèque municipale de Nantes.

67 Daniel Rabreau, "Un forum au coeur du Paris révolutionnaire. Le projet de Théâtre des arts de Charles de Wailly, 1798," *L'Ivre de Pierre* I (1977), 35–48. This article is well documented, but Rabreau seems to have missed the dossiers in the archives.

68 *Décade philosophique,* t. II, 30 Ventôse an VI, 559–60.

69 M. Bonnaire, *Procès-verbaux de l'Académie des Beaux-Arts* (Paris 1937), vol. I, 123–8, session of 13 Floréal an VI, 2 May 1798.

70 There are a lot of examples in Arch. Nat., F¹ᶜ I, 84–8, and F¹⁷ 1043, doss. I, nos. 8–10.

71 Girardet del. and l'Epine sculp., "Cérémonie funèbre en l'honneur du Général Hoche … célébrée au Champs de Mars le 10 Vendémiaire de l'an VI," Bib. Nat., Estampes, Coll. Hennin, vol. 140, no. 12369.

72 Girardet inv. et del. and Berthault sculp., "Entrée triomphale des monuments des sciences et des arts en France … le 9 et 10 Thermidor an VI de la République," Bib. Nat., Estampes, Coll. de Vinck, vol. 50, no. 6935.

73 François Cointeraux, *Paris tel qu'il était à son origine, Paris tel qu'il est aujourd'hui* (Paris, an VII).

74 On this contest see "Projets pour l'embellissement des Champs-Elysées à Paris", *La Décade philosophique*, no. 15, 30 Pluviôse an VII, 372.

75 Cointereaux, *Paris tel qu'il était*, 7.

76 Ibid., 15–16.

77 Anon., "La Trinité Républicaine," Bib. Nat., Estampes, Coll. de Vinck, vol. 51, no. 6949.

78 The drawing for the project is in the Cooper-Hewitt Museum in New York, acc. no. 1911-28-212. It was reproduced in Richard P. Wunder, *Extravagant Drawings of the Eighteenth Century from the Collection of the Cooper-Union Museum* (New York 1962), no. 17. The engraving, with a flap showing the alternative group for the top of the globe, is in the Bib. Nat., Estampes, DC 17, fol. 6. It was reproduced in Maurice Vloberg, *Jean Houël, peintre et graveur 1735–1813* (Paris 1930), 126, pl. XXXII.

79 Jean-Pierre-Louis-Laurent Houël, *Projet d'un monument public, que l'on pourroit élever au milieu d'une des places publiques de Paris* [Paris, an VIII]. This pamphlet seems to be very rare. A copy is in the British Library, 936.c.35 (35).

80 Ibid., 2.

81 *Loi qui ordonne la vente du Château Trompette, sur l'emplacement duquel il sera érigé un monument tromphal, du 21 Fructidor an V, Bulletin des lois,* vol. 18, bulletin 146, no. 1426.

82 The various decrees and instructions have been gathered in the Arch. Mun. Bordeaux, M2 (Liasse), 40

83 Arch. Nat., F¹³ 1711, Dossier Boussel. Pointing out that the contest called for a monument consecrated to both the triumph of French armies and the peace that resulted from it, Boussel remarked, "cette idée nous parait difficile à rendre, en ce qu'elle renferme deux objets dont les attributs sont differens."

84 *Concours pour le monument à élever sur l'emplacement du Château-Trompette à Bordeaux. Rapports faits au jury sur les 28 projets exposés en Ventôse an IX de la République.* Arch. Mun. Bordeaux VIII G 51, or Arch. Nat., F¹³ 1711, with a note saying it was distributed to the jury on 21 germinal an IX. Despite the title, there were thirty projects submitted.

85 Pietro Clochar presented two variants of his plan: *Mémoires explicatifs des objets contenus dans la première et deuxième distribution générale du terrain du Château-Trompette* (n.p.,

n.d.), Arch. Mun. Bordeaux, M2 #33. Despite the wealth of evidence available on this contest, Rabreau, "L'Architecture et la fête," 243, reports that Clochar's second plan was for the Contest of Year II.

86 [Pietro Clochar], *Colonne projetée "A la Victoire et à la Paix" dédiée aux armées de la terre et de la mer surmontée du Génie de la Guerre,* Arch. Mun. Bordeaux, XXI-N-18–20.

87 A dossier on this and other projects, including a ground-plan of this one, are in Arch. Nat., F¹³ 1711. Another copy of the ground-plan is in Bib. Nat., Estampes, Va 33, vol. 6.

88 Musée d'Aquitaine, 74.2.1, 78 1218.

89 Arch. Mun. Bordeaux, VIII G 40.

90 Arch. Nat., F¹³ 1713, doss. Ramelet. According to a memoir he was Jean Ramelet from Besançon.

91 F.-L. Aubry, *Projet d'un monument à la gloire des defenseurs de la patrie* (Douai, 12 Floréal an V [1ᵉʳ mars 1797]).

92 *Concours pour le monument à élever sur l'emplacement du Château-Trompette à Bordeaux. Rapport.* The design by Labarre is in Arch. Mun. Bordeaux, VIII G 51.

IX THE DREAM AND THE MEMORY

1 "Les deux statues de la Liberté à Toulon," *Bulletin de la Société des Amis*, no. 66 (1940): 201–2. The other statue of Liberty was one erected on the Champ de Bastille in Year IV, which seems to have been replaced by the one in front of the city hall.

2 E. Boudier, "Au sujet du monument élevé place d'Armes en 1793," *Bulletin de la Société historique et artistique de Suresnes* V (1933–34): 212–13.

3 Cited in Maurice Agulhon, *Marianne into Battle: Republican Imagery and Symbolism in France* (Cambridge 1981), 24.

4 This was pointed out forcefully by the report submitted to the emperor on the state of the arts by a group from the fine arts section of the institute in 1808: Arch. Nat., AD VIII 12, no. 45. The report was subsequently published: J. Lebreton, *Rapport sur les Beaux-Arts* (Paris, n.d. [1810]).

5 Boullée, *Architecture*, ed. J.-M.-Pérouse de Montclos, 49. Here I am indebted to the analysis of Rabreau, *L'Architecture et la fête*, 248.

6 Louis-Pierre Baltard, *Journal de l'Ecole Polytechnique*, Germinal an III, 15.

7 See Appendix A.

8 "Concours pour la construction d'un autel de la Patrie," *Magazin encyclopédique*, 2ᵉ an, 1796, vol. I, 411–12.

9 A synthesis of the revisionist literature has been made by William Doyle, *Origins of the French Revolution* (Oxford 1980).

10 For elaboration of this case see James A. Leith's contribution to a debate among Albert Soboul, William Doyle, and Leith on the origins of the Revolution held at the annual meeting of the Canadian Historical Association in 1981 and later published in the *Annales historiques de la Révolution française*, no. 4 (1982): 632–9.

11 Hunt, *Politics, Culture and Class,* 234–6.

12 Alphonse Aulard, *Le Christianisme et la Révolution française* (Paris 1927).

13 Mus. du Louvre, Département des peintures, Inv. 2405, MR 1165.

14 From Landon, *Annales du Musée, Ecole française moderne. Architecture*, 2nd ed. (Paris 1834), pl. 65–6 (114–15).

15 This is a phrase used by June Hargrove of the University of Maryland in describing her study of monuments to individuals in Paris since the Revolution.

16 A good way to compare the "plan des artistes" with later plans is to study the plates in Alphand, et al., eds., *Les Travaux de Paris 1789–1889. Atlas* (Paris 1889). Plate X provides a reconstruction of the Commission of Artists set up in 1793, and plates XI-XIV show the subsequent development of streets.

APPENDIX A

1 The tables in Leith, *The Idea of Art as Propaganda in France,* show that about 15.3 per cent of all works of sculpture and 28 per cent of all architectural designs were related to the Revolution, whereas only 12 per cent of engravings and 2.32 per cent of drawings and paintings, plus 10 per cent of the portraits, were related to contemporary politics.

2 These appear to be the plans mentioned in chap. 1, 33.

3 See his pamphlet on this project discussed in chap. 3, 102-3.

4 This appears to be the project discussed in chap. 7, 291-2, pls. 300-1.

5 This is discussed in chap. 5, 187, and reproduced in pl. 148.

6 This is probably the project discussed in chap. 6, 220-1, reproduced in pl. 164.

7 This is probably the project discussed in chap. 8, 327-9, reproduced in pl. 329.

8 This may be related to the project discussed in chap. 4, 142-3, reproduced in pl. 129.

9 Some of these are probably related to the plans discussed in chap. 8, 317-18, and reproduced in pls. 307-10.

10 These are doubtlessly the prize-winning projects for such temples discussed in chap. 6, 225-6, 232-3, reproduced in pls. 182-7, 204-7.

11 See the plates in Landon, *Annales du Musée,* vol. III, pls. 48-9.

12 This is undoubtedly the project he had submitted to the Contest of Year II, discussed in chap. 6, 242, reproduced in pls. 244-8.

APPENDIX B

1 Société populaire et républicaine des arts.

2 Arch. Nat., F17^{17} 1326, doss. II, nos. 284-5.

APPENDIX D

1 This is not listed in the *Registre,* but in papers of the Committee of Public Safety this work is described as a new submission to the contest: Arch. Nat., AF II 66, doss. 489, fol. 13.

APPENDIX E

1 Portiez (de l'Oise), *Rapport fait au nom du Comité d'instruction publique, sur les concours de sculpture, architecture et peinture ouverts par les décrets de la Convention nationale* (Paris, n.d.) [Décret du 14 Fructidor an III], Arch Nat. F^{17} 1056, no. 5. This is reprinted in Guillaume, *Procès-verbaux du Comité d'instruction publique,* vol. IV, 253-62.

2 *Notice des ouvrages de sculpture, architecture, et peinture exposés aux concours* (Paris, n.d.).

3 There is no reason given why this prize was higher than other "minimum" monetary awards in this category.

A GUIDE TO SOURCES

ARCHIVES

Archives Nationales

On documents relative to the arts in the Archives Nationales, see Mireille Rambeau, *Les Sources de l'histoire de l'art aux Archives Nationales ... avec une étude sur les sources de l'histoire de l'art aux Archives de la Seine par Georges Bailhache and Michel Fleury* (Paris 1955). Only the most important series related to projects for monuments, squares, and public buildings are listed below.

MANUSCRIPT DOCUMENTS

Series AF II. Conseil exécutif provisoire. Comités de la Convention. Especially valuable are cartons 66, 67, and 80, containing documents on public opinion, propaganda, museums, festivals, monuments, and public works, especially decrees of the Committee of Public Safety. The register AF II* 133–5 gives an overall view of the committee's decrees on monuments and public works.

Series C and CC. Assemblées nationales. A number of proposals for monuments, squares, and public buildings, many with plans attached, are found in the papers of the various Assemblies. C 364, plaquette 1, records the minutes of the Comité pour l'embellissement du Palais et Jardin National, which are very revealing about the government's plans in Year II.

Series D. Missions des représentants du peuple et Comités des Assemblées Nationales. Some of the papers of the deputies on mission concern destruction of symbols of the Old Regime and projects for monuments. D*xxxv^c, vols. 1, 2, 3, Registre du Comité des Inspecteurs de la Salle de la Convention, lists letters and other items delivered to the Convention, each of which was given a number, providing the key to authorship of many unsigned projects submitted in Year II, some of which had remained unidentified until recently.

Series F^{1c}. Esprit public. Especially useful are F^{1c} 87, containing material on the Dépôt des fêtes, a sort of arsenal of props, and about how to make festivals more appealing; and F^{1c} 115–17, containing documents on the laying of cornerstones and on public monuments.

Series F^{13}. Bâtiments civils. Especially useful are cartons 204, 205, 206, 207, 212, 312^b, 312^c, 313–17, 318, 319, 325^b, 505, 507, 513, 531, 707, 708, 739, 870, 871, 1279, 1400^b, 1711, 1712^a, 1712^b, 1713, 1716–18, and 1935–8, containing documents on work for festivals, urban planning, various *places* in Paris, the "Plan des artistes," suppression of feudal signs, proposals for monuments, and plans for provincial cities.

Series F^{14}. Travaux publics. This series contains many documents relative to the history of urbanism in Paris and the provinces. Cartons 187^b, 118, 191^b, and 194 contain evidence about the embellishment of Paris, projects for theatres, plans for the Louvre, for decoration of bridges, and for new squares. An inventory in the Salle des inventaires, 10 42 2, lists designs that are scattered throughout these cartons.

Series F^{17}. Instruction publique. Besides cartons containing the papers of the Comité d'instruction publique, the Commission des monuments, and the Commission temporaire des arts, all of which have been edited and published, cartons 1001, 1102, 1008^d, 1009^c, 1020, 1037, 1056, 1281, 1288, and 1303, containing documents on projects for monuments, art contests, prizes for artists, and on rural architecture, are very valuable.

Series O^1. Maison du Roi. Although this series contains for the most part documents on the Old Regime, it also extends into the Revolution. Cartons 1045–2805 contain documents on the Direction générale des bâtiments, the equivalent of a modern ministry of fine arts, concerned with royal buildings, public monuments, and the academies.

ICONOGRAPHICAL SOURCES

Cartes et Plans. Besides designs and maps scattered through the series described above, the department of Cartes et Plans contains many documents on monuments, squares, and public buildings. In 1960 a huge deposit of documents on public buildings was added, known as the Versement d'architecture. On all the holdings of this department see the excellent catalogue by Monique Hébert, *Catalogue général des cartes, plans et dessins d'architecture*, 4 vols. (Paris 1958–72).

Bibliothèque Nationale

Many designs are appended to printed books and pamphlets listed in the bibliography below, but most designs are in the Département des Estampes. There are some classified by the architect's name, while others are in the huge collections of images related to the history of France: the Collection de Vinck, the Collection Hennin, and the Collection Qb. Also, many designs have been incorporated into the enormous collection Topographie, where they can be found under the name of the city, then the street or square. Some designs are located in Cartes et Plans.

Bibliothèque historique de la Ville de Paris

In this library many designs are appended to books and pamphlets by the artists, but others not attached to such printed matter are classified by artist or, if anonymous, by topographical location. There are some uncatalogued designs kept in the underground level, to which it is almost impossible to gain access.

Carnavalet Museum

In this museum there is also a large department of prints and drawings. There is, however, no handy catalogue for locating designs for monuments and buildings. Some designs are classified by the name of the artist, others among architectural drawings or engravings, and still others according to their topographical location. A few monuments commemorating events are in the historical section.

Ecole des Beaux-Arts

The Ecole nationale supérieure des Beaux-Arts, to give it its full name, has a large collection of books and pamphlets on art, architecture, and urbanism, as well as a rich collection of prints, drawings, and paintings. Most of the designs done by students of architecture in the eighteenth century are located there. About half the surviving designs submitted to the Concours de l'an II are located here, many of them unidentified until recently.

Other Paris Collections

A few designs are located in the Archives de la Seine, the Bibliothèque de l'Arsenal, the Institut de France, the Musée des arts décoratifs, the Musée des arts et des traditions populaires, and the Musée du Louvre. In the latter such designs, especially some showing the ephemeral architecture of the Revolution, are located in the Cabinet des dessins.

Departmental Collections

In a typical departmental centre architectural designs and related documents are located in the departmental archives, the municipal archives, and the municipal library. Some more may be in an art gallery, a historical museum, or in the collection of a local archeological society. A. Betgé-Brezetz, *Guide des Archives de la Gironde* (Bordeaux 1973), can serve as a model for research in any other departmental centre.

PRIMARY PRINTED SOURCES

Collections of Laws and Decrees

None of the well-known collections of laws and decrees is actually complete when one is looking for items concerning monuments, public buildings, or urbanism. Moreover, the indexes and tables are very inadequate; consequently, it is advisable to search through several collections.

Archives parlementaires de 1787 à 1860. Paris 1867–. This is a compilation drawing not only on the minutes of the various assemblies but on information culled from newspapers. It contains many supplementary reports, pamphlets, and other items related to the debates, but unfortunately the first series, the one dealing with the Revolution, is still not finished.

Collection des lois depuis 1789 jusqu'au 22 Prairial an II formant le commencement du "Bulletin des Lois." 7 vols. Paris, an XII. This was intended to cover the period until the *Bulletin* began on 10 June 1794, but only goes to October 1791. There is an index located below, *Dictionnaire de législation.*

Collection générale des décrets rendus par l'Assemblée nationale (then ... *par l'Assemblée nationale législative;* and ... *par la Convention nationale*). 18 vols. in 19 parts for the Constituent; 6 vols. in 7 parts for the Legislative; 35 vols. for the Convention. Paris 1790–an IV. Known as the Collection Baudouin.

Collection générale des lois, décrets, arrêtés, sénatus-consultes, avis du Conseil d'Etat, et règlements d'administration publique depuis 1789 jusqu'au 1ᵉ avril 1814. 12 vols. Paris 1817–19. Known as the Collection Rondonneau.

Collection générale des lois et des actes du Corps législatif et du Directoire exécutif. 18 vols. Paris, an IV–an VIII. This is the sequel to the Collection Baudouin listed above.

Collection générale des lois, proclamation, instructions et autres actes. 6 vols. for the Constituent and Legislative; 12 vols. for the Convention; 5 vols. for the Directory. Known as the Collection du Louvre.

Dictionnaire de legislation, ou Table alphabétique des lois rendues depuis 1789 jusqu'à l'an VI. 7 vols. Paris an VIII–an IX. With a *Supplément* covering an VII to an X.

Pièces imprimées par ordre de la Convention nationale. 13 vols. Paris 1792–an IV.

Recueil des lettres, circulaires, discours et autres actes ... émanés ... du ministre de l'intérieur. 3 vols. Paris, n.d.

Table générale par ordre alphabétique de matières des lois ... depuis l'ouverture des Etats-Généraux ... au avril 1814. 4 vols. Paris 1816. By Rondonneau, but preceding his Collection listed above.

Newspapers

Annales patriotiques et littéraires.
Bulletin de littérature, des sciences et des arts. Paris, an III–an V.
Bulletin des lois
Chronique de Paris
Courrier du Bas-Rhin
Décade philosophique, littéraire et politique
La Feuille villageoise
Gazette de France
Journal de Nancy et des frontières
Journal de Paris
Journal polytechnique
Journal des débats et décrets
Magazin encyclopédique
Mercure de France
Moniteur Universel
Révolutions de Paris

Other Printed Material

Académie des beaux-arts. Procès verbaux de l'... Ed. Marcel Bonnaire. 3 vols. Paris 1937–43.

Académie des inscriptions et belles-lettres. Histoire et mémoires. 51 vols. Paris 1717–1809.

Académie royale d'architecture. Procès verbaux de l'... 1671–1793. Ed. Henry Lemonnier. 10 vols. Paris 1911–29.

Adresse des républicains de la Société des Amis de la Liberté et de l'Egalité de Morteau à la Convention Nationale, déclarant que leurs larmes ont coulé en abondance sur le martyr de la liberté, l'immortel Le Peletier, et que les colonnes élevées à sa mémoire éterniseront parmi eux le souvenir de son sacrifice au salut de la République. 10 février 1793.

Allais, G.-E., Détournelle, A., et Vaudoyer, A.-L.-T., eds. *Grands Prix d'architecture. Projets couronnés par l'Académie d'architecture et par l'Institut de France.* Paris 1806.

Allais, Guillaume-Edouard and Perrard de Montreuil, *Nouvelle salle de la Convention nationale.* Signed and dated 23 October 1792. [Paris], n.d.

Alliance de la Société des amis de la constitution et de l'égalité de Montpellier, avec la Garde Nationale de cette ville et la troupe de ligne y étant en garnison. Montpellier 1790.

Almanach indicatif des rues de Paris, suivant leurs nouvelles dénominations, par ordre alphabétique. Précédé de l'énumération des quarante-huit sections et leurs chefs-lieux, d'une idée sommaire des différens comités du corps législatif, des bureaux du pouvoir exécutif, des autorités constituées. Paris, an III.

Arnaud, Abbé. *Etablissement qui intéresse l'utilité publique et la décoration de la capitale.* Paris 1790.

Arrêtés du Comité de salut public relatifs aux monuments publics, aux arts et aux lettres. Extraits du registre des arrêtés. N.p., n.d. [Floréal, l'an II].

Arthur, [Président]. *Le Citoyens de la Section de la Place-Vendôme, aux Marseillais.* Imp. de la section, n.p., n.d. [1792].

Aubry, F.-L. (arpentier). *Projet d'un monument à la gloire des défenseurs de la patrie.* Douai, 12 Floréal an V.

[Avril,]. *Convention Nationale. Instruction publique. Rapport au Conseil général de la Commune de Paris, sur quelques mesures à prendre en changeant le nom des rues. Imprimé en vertu de l'arrêté du Comité d'instruction publique le 17 Nivôse l'an II.* Paris, n.d.

Baltard, [Louis-Pierre]. *Projet d'un monument à élever aux triomphes des Armées de la République et à la paix.* Bordeaux, n.d.

Barère, Bertrand. *Rapport fait au nom du Comité de salut public sur la suite des événements du siège d'Ypres, et sur les monuments nationaux environnans Paris.* Convention Nationale, 13 Messidor an II (1 juillet 1794). Paris n.d.

Baudouin, Jean. *Recueil d'emblèmes divers.* Paris 1638–39.

Benezech, [Pierre]. *Ministère de l'Intérieur. Appel aux artistes.* Paris, an IV.

[Berruer, Pierre]. *Projet de monument pour le Champs de Mars.* Paris, n.d.

Bienaimé, Pierre-Théodore. *Rapport sur quelques abus introduits dans la répartition et l'exécution des travaux.* Paris, an III.

Blondel, Jacques-François. *Cours d'architecture.* 9 vols. Paris 1771–79.

Blondel, Architecte [Jean-Baptiste]. *Observations de sieur Blondel, architecte et dessinateur du Cabinet du roi, sur le projet de la fête de la confédération patriotique du 14 juillet.* Paris 1790.

Boudard, J.-B. *Iconologie tirée de divers auteurs; ouvrage utile aux gens-de-lettres, aux poètes, aux artistes, et généralement à tous les amateurs des beaux-arts.* Parme et Paris 1759.

Boullée, Etienne-Louis. *Boullée's Treatise on Architecture.* Ed. Helen Rosenau. London 1953.

Boullée, Etienne. *Architecture. Essai sur l'art.* Ed. Jean-Marie Pérouse de Monclos. Paris 1968.

Briot, [Pierre-Joseph]. *Mesures du salut public, de pacification et de défense générale, proposées au Conseil des Cinq-Cents et renvoyées à l'examen de la commission des sept … séance du 12 Fructidor, an VII.* Paris, an VII.

Brullée, Jean-Pierre, Ingénieur. *Mémoire présenté à l'Assemblée Nationale … concernant l'offre de faire verser dans la caisse de la ville de Paris une somme de vingt millions … l'établissement d'un canal … et la construction, sur les ruines de la Bastille, d'une place Nationale.* Paris 1789.

Brullée, [Jean-Pierre]. *Mémoire sur les moyens de former des établissements d'utilité publique et d'en assurer les propriétés au profit de la nation sans être à charge au trésor national.* [Paris], 20 Brumaire an VIII.

Bulletin du Département du Rhone-et-Loire. Imprimé par ordre du Comité général de Surveillance et de Salut Public. Ed. Charavay fils ainé. [1793]; Paris and Lyon 1845.

Cambacérès, [Jean-Jacques-Régis de]. *Rapport et projets de résolutions sur un message du Directoire exécutif, du 11 ventôse, présentés … dans la séance du 18 ventôse.* Paris, an V.

Capelle, J.F. *Des temples de l'humanité ou les hospices régénérés, dans lesquelles tous les citoyens formant des compagnies de secours, participeront à l'exercice de la bienfaisance publique envers les malades indigens.* N.p., n.d.

Cathala, [Etienne-Louis-Denis]. *Projet d'une place sur l'emplacement de la Bastille, avec une colonne au milieu, semblable à celle de Trajan à Rome.* N.p. [1791].

Chaisneau, Abbé Charles. *Le Panthéon français, ou Discours sur les honneurs publics décernés par la nation à la mémoire des grands hommes.* Dijon: imp. de P. Causse 1792.

Chamoulaud, François. *Plan pour la régénération des moeurs en France, présenté en forme de pétition à la Convention Nationale, le quartidi 2ᵉ décade, brumaire 2ᵉ année.* Paris, n.d.

Chaussard, P[ierre-Jean-Baptiste]. *Monumens de l'héroïsme français: nécessité de ramener à un plan unique, et de coordonner à ceux déjà existans, les monuments qu'on propose d'élever à Paris sur l'étendue comprise entre les Tuileries sur l'étendue comprise entre les Tuileries et l'Etoile: Considérations générales et projet.* Paris, n.d.

Cizos-Duplessis, François. *Projet pour l'établissement d'un nouveau théâtre sous le nom de fêtes nationales, dédié aux districts de Paris.* Paris: Imprimerie de Cailleau 1789.

Clochar, Pietro. *Mémoires explicatifs des objets contenus dans la première et deuxième distribution générale du terrain du Château-Trompette.* N.p., n.d.

Cointeraux, François. *Ecole d'architecture rurale.* Paris 1791.

– *Paris tel qu'il était à son origine, Paris tel qu'il est aujourd'hui.* Paris, an VII.

Combes, [Louis]. *Projet d'un plan de division du terrain du Château-Trompette à Bordeaux, par le citoyen Combes, Architecte du Département de la Gironde et Associé-correspondant de l'Institut national.* Bordeaux, an VI.

Comité d'instruction publique de la Convention nationale. Procès-verbaux du … Ed. M.-J. Guillaume. 6 vols. Paris 1891–1907. Table in two parts. Paris 1959.

Commission des Monuments. Procès-verbaux de la … Ed. L. Teutey. 2 vols. Paris 1902–1903.

Commune générale des arts de peinture, sculpture, et gravure, et de la Société populaire et républicaine des arts. Procès-verbaux de la … Ed. H. Lapauze. Paris 1903.

Concours pour le monument à élever sur l'emplacement du Château Trompette à Bordeaux. Rapports fait au jury sur les 28 projets exposés en Ventôse an IX de la République. [Paris, an IX].

Confédération nationale du 14 juillet, ou description fidelle de tout ce qui a précédé, accompagné et suivi cette auguste cérémonie. Paris 1790.

Considérations sur l'établissement nécessaire à l'Assemblée nationale et moyens d'ériger le palais, avec une place, qui en ferait partie pour la statue de roi. Paris 1789.

Coquéau, C.-P. *Mémoire sur la nécessité de transférer et reconstruire l'Hôtel-Dieu de Paris suivi d'un projet de translation de cet hôpital.* N.p., 1785.

Corbet, Charles-Louis. *Lettre au Citoyen Lagarde, Secrétaire-Général du Directoire Exécutif, sur les esquisses et projets de monuments pour les places publiques de Paris, faits d'après l'invitation du ministre de l'intérieur; sur la statue de la Liberté, place de la Concorde, celle de J.-J. Rousseau aux Tuileries, celles du péristyle du Conseil des anciens; sur la composition du jury des arts, etc.; suivi d'une réponse au rapport contre les arts et les artistes, fait par le citoyen Mercier, aux Conseil des cinq-cents.* Paris, an V.

Daubermesnil, [François-Antoine]. *Projet de résolution … [to the Conseil des Cinq-Cents].* 29 Floréal an V. Paris, Floréal an V.

David, Jacques-Louis. *Convention nationale. Discours prononcé … dans la séance du 17 brumaire l'an II de la République.* Paris, n.d.

– *Convention nationale. Rapport fait à la Convention le 27 brumaire l'an II.* Paris, n.d.

Davy de Chavigné, François-Antoine. *Projet d'un monument sur l'emplacement de la Bastille à décerner par les Etats-généraux à Louis XVI, restaurateur de la liberté publique, et à consacrer à la patrie et à la liberté à la Concorde et à la loi, présenté à l'Académie royale d'architecture en sa séance du 8 juin 1789.* N.p., 1789.

Decomberousse, Benoit-Michel. *Discours prononcé … en présentant l'ouvrage et les plans du cit. Cointeraux relatifs à l'ancien état, à l'état actuel de Paris et aux embellissements dont il est susceptible.* Conseil des anciens, 14 Ventôse an 7 (1ᵉʳ mars 1799). Paris, an VII.

Delafosse, Jean-Charles. *Nouvelle iconologie historique.* Paris 1768.

Description de la fête de pacte fédératif, fixé par la ville avec le règlement de la police. Grande illumination. Paris, n.d.

Description de la fête nationale donnée par la Société populaire de Lille … le 30 brumaire an II … suivie de la liste des rues dont les noms sont changés. Lille 1883.

Description fidelle de tout ce qui a précédé, accompagné et suivi la cérémonie de la confédération nationale du 14 juillet. 2nd éd. Paris, n.d.

Desmarais, bibliothécaire de Rocroy. *Projet dont la grandeur la beauté, l'utilité, le produit et le peu de dépense ne peuvent être reconnus véritable qu'après en avoir fait la lecture.* Paris, n.d.

Détail de l'embellissement du jardin national. Paris: Leronge et Berthelot, n.d.

Détails des fêtes données au Champ-de-Mars, sur les ruines de la Bastille, à la Halle neuve et sur la Seine, le 18 juillet 1790. Paris, n.d.

Détails exacts de l'embellissement des jardins et de la Convention et autres lieux, pour le 20 prairial … suivi d'un superbe monument qui va être élevé sur le Pont Neuf réprésentant le peuple français terrassant le fanatisme, le royalisme, et le fédéralisme … Extraits du registre des arrêtés de comité du salut public 25 floréal an II. Paris, n.d.

Détournelle, Athanase. *Aux armes et aux arts! Peinture, sculpture, architecture, gravure. Journal de la Société républicaine des arts.* Paris [1794].

[Détournelle, Athanase]. "Histoire des concours en architecture, et coup d'oeil sur ceux qui ont eu lieu en France depuis Louis XIV." *Journal des arts, des sciences et de la littérature* (an IX): no. 145, pp 145–8; no. 147, pp 193–7; no. 148, pp 217–21; no. 149, pp 241–4; no. 150, pp 265–8; no. 151, pp 289–93; no. 152, pp 313–18; no. 153, pp 346–52; no. 154, pp 373–8.

Détournelle, Athanase. *Recueil d'architecture nouvelle.* Paris, an XIII.

Du Laurent, l'Abbé Hyacinthe. *Les Monuments publics, poème.* Paris 1753.

Du Morier, Joseph-Pierre. *Projet de cahiers lu au district assemblé en l'église Notre-Dame, précédé d'observations proposées à cette assemblée sur ses droits et sur sa convocation, et suivi d'une note relative à la réforme des moeurs, à l'éducation publique, à l'honneur.* N.p., n.d.

Durand, Jean-Nicolas-Louis. *Précis des leçons d'architecture données à l'Ecole polytechnique.* 2 vols. Paris, an X-XIII.

– *Recueil et parallèle des édifices anciens et modernes.* Paris, an VII-IX.

Dusaulx, [Jean]. *Discours prononcé à la Convention Nationale … par Dusaulx député de Paris.* Paris, Germinal an III.

Dussausoy, Maille. *Le Citoyen désinteressé ou diverses idées patriotiques concernant quelques établissemens et embellissemens utiles à la ville de Paris.* 2 vols. Paris 1767–68.

Etrennes géographiques et récréatifs, ou Almanach du diocèse de Lyon. An XII.

Faulcon, F.-M. *Anniversaire, ou journal de ce qui s'est passé pendant la semaine de la Confédération.* Paris 1790.

Fédération de la Garde Nationale, et des troupes de la ligne de la Ville d'Aix, en présence de Messieurs les Maire et Officiers Municipaux. [Aix-en-Provence] 1790.

Fédération des français dans la capitale de l'empire le 14 juillet 1790 … enrichi de toutes les inscriptions et allégories qui étaient autour de l'Autel de la Patrie, de l'arc de triomphe, de l'Hôtel de Ville, la Place Henri IV, les Champs-Elysées, la Bastille etc. Paris, n.d.

Fédération des français dans la capitale de l'empire, le 14 juillet, jour anniversaire de la révolution. Estampe de trois pieds de long sur deux de haut … Prospectus. Paris, n.d.

Fédération des François, 14 juillet 1790. Extrait des déliberations du Conseil Général de la Commune de Montpellier. Montpellier, n.d.

Fête à l'Etre-Suprême célébrée à Commune-Affranchie le 20 Prairial an II. Lyon, n.d.

Fête civique en l'honneur de la Raison … pour le 30 Frimaire [an II]. Reims, n.d.

Fête nationale qui sera célébrée aujourd'hui au Champ-de-Mars, aux Champs-Elysées, à la Halle et sur la place de la Bastille et feu d'artifice au Pont Neuf. Paris, n.d.

Fontaine, Pierre-François-Louis, and Percier, Charles. *Examen et Parallèle des Projets sur l'achèvement et la Réunion des Palais du Louvre et des Tuileries depuis l'an 1541 jusqu'en 1809.* Ms.

Gatteaux, [Nicolas-Marie]. *Projet d'un monument pour consacrer la Révolution.* Paris, n.d. [1790].

Gaucher, Charles-Etienne. *Iconologie, ou traité de la sciences des allegories.* 4 vols. Paris, n.d.

Geruzes, curé de Sacy près Reims. "Monuments républicains: projet d'un monument à élever dans chaque commune de la République, en l'honneur de ceux qui sont morts pour la patrie," *La Feuille villageoise* VII, no. 10 (15 frimaire an II): 220–5.

Gilbert, Florentin. *Adresse à tous les corps administratifs de la France et à tous les connoisseurs dans l'art de l'architecture et de la construction des travaux publics.* Paris 1790.

Giraud, Avocat. *Place patriotique, avec un palais pour la permanence de l'auguste Assemblée Nationale, et la description d'une fête annuelle pour le renouvellement du serment civique.* Paris 1790.

Gisors, Alexandre-Jean-Baptiste-Guy. *Projet de l'établissement de la Bibliothèque Nationale dans l'édifice ci-devant destiné à la paroisse de la Magdeleine.* Paris, an VII.

Goulet, Nicolas. *Le Temple des lois et de la Liberté.* Paris, n.d.

Grégoire, [Abbé Henri-B.] *Convention Nationale. Système des dénominations topographiques pour les places, rues, quais et de toutes les communes de la République … Imprimé par ordre du Comité d'instruction publique.* Paris, n.d.

Grobert, Joseph-François-Louis. *Description des travaux exécutés pour le déplacement, transport et élévation des groupes de Coustou. Imprimée et gravée par ordre du Gouvernement, présentée au Directoire Exécutif.* Paris, an IV.

Guyot, Raymond and Thénard, L. [Jean-François]. *Le Conventionnel Goujon.* Paris 1908.

Houël, Jean-Pierre-Louis-Laurent. *Projet d'un monument public, que l'on pourroit élever au milieu d'une des places publiques de Paris.* Paris 1799.

Hubert, Auguste. *Rapport sur l'embellissement du Palais et du Jardin national … présenté au Comité de Salut public le 20 floréal (an II).* Paris: [Imp. Nat.], n.d.

Idées patriotiques d'un citoyen. Ami des arts, relativement à la statue de bronze de la place de la Fédération [à Lyon] du 22 août. Lyon [1792].

Institut national des sciences et arts. Mémoires de l'…, Littérature et beaux-arts. 5 vols. Paris, an VI-XII.

Jansen, Hendrik. *Projet tendant à conserver les arts en France, en immortalisant les événements patriotiques et les citoyens illustres.* Paris, n.d.

Jault, *Projet d'une nouvelle nomenclature des rues de l'arrondissement de la section de Bonne Nouvelle, suivi de quelques vers républicains par citoyen Jault, membre de la Commune de Paris et du comité de vérification de la guerre.* [10 Brumaire an II], n.d.

Kersaint, Armand-Guy. *Discours sur les monuments publics, prononcé au Conseil du département de Paris, le 15 décembre 1791.* Paris 1792.

Laborie, Sieur, amateur. *Analyse d'un Temple de la Concorde dédié à Louis XVI.* Paris, n.d.

Lacombe de Prezel, Honoré. *Dictionnaire iconologique.* Paris 1756.

Lambert, Charles. *Motion en faveur des généraux des nos armées et moyen de conserver les monuments les plus precieux qui existent tant à Paris qu'aux environs de cette commune, en leur assurant une destination aussi utile qu'honorable pour la République.* [Paris], Brumaire l'an IV.

Landon, Charles-Paul. *Annales du Musée et de l'Ecole moderne des beaux-arts, recueil de gravures au trait d'après les principaux ouvrages … qui chaque année ont remporté les prix.* Tome I[-VIII]. Paris, an IX(1801)-an XIII(1805).

– *Annales du Musée et de l'école moderne des beaux-arts.* 2nd ed. Paris 1823-35.

Laugier, Abbé Marc-Antoine (ex-jésuite). *Essai sur l'architecture.* Paris 1753; 1755.

Lavallée, Joseph. *Notice historique sur Charles de Wailly, architecte … lue à la séance publique de la Société philotechnique, le 20 brumaire an VII.* Paris, l'an VII.

[La Vallée, J., Breton, J.-B.-J., Brion, L. père]. *Voyages dans les départements de la France, par une société d'artistes et gens de lettres; enrichi de tableaux géographiques et d'estampes.* Paris: Brion, 1792–an X (1802).

Lebrun, Jean-Baptiste-Pierre. *Réflexions sur le Muséum national.* N.p., n.d.

– *Observations sur le Muséum national … pour servir de suite aux réflexions qu'il a déjà publiées sur le même objet.* Paris 1793.

Ledoux, Claude-Nicolas. *L'Architecture considérée sur le rapport de l'art, des moeurs et de la législation.* Paris 1804.

Lenoir, Alexandre. *Description historique et chronologique des monuments de sculpture réunis au musée des Monuments français.* Paris, an VI.

– *Musée des Monuments français.* Paris 1800-06.

– *Notice historique des monuments des arts réunis au Dépôt national rue des Petits-Augustins.* Paris, an IV.

Le Sueur, M.C.P. *Projet d'utilité et d'embellissement pour la ville de Paris, addressé aux sections.* Paris 1790.

Lhote. *Au corps législatif. Château-Trompette. Développement du nouveau plan de distribution des emplacements du Château-Trompette, sous le rapport des avantages qu'il renferme pour le gouvernement, le trésor public, les habitans de Bordeaux, le commerce, le concessionnaire, et les acquéreurs partiel.* [Paris], n.d.

– *Aux armées. Monument à élever aux quatorze armées de la République, sur l'emplacement du Château-Trompette de Bordeaux. Programme.* [Paris], n.d.

– *Château-Trompette … Développement des dispositions adoptées dans le projet du Citoyen Lhote, Architecte à Bordeaux.* N.p., an V.

– *Nouveaux développements du monument à élever aux armées sur le terrain du Château-Trompette, d'après le plan du cit. Lhote.* [Paris], n.d.

Louis [Louis-Nicolas, "Victor"]. *Nouvelles observations du citoyen Louis, architecte, sur la place projetée pour la ville de Bordeaux.* N.p., n.d.

– *Réfutation des nouveaux développements du Citoyen Lhote, architecte, par Louis, aussi architecte, sur la place de la Paix projetée pour la ville de Bordeaux.* N.p., n.d.

– *Observations du Citoyen Louis sur un projet pour la ville de Bordeaux nouvellement proposé au corps legislatif.* N.p., n.d.

Mangin, Père [Charles]. *Adresse de sieur Mangin père à l'Assemblée nationale le mardi 1er juillet 1792.* Paris, n.d.

– *Analyse des idées qui ont dirigé le citoyen Mangin père, architecte, dans la composition de son plan, dédié à la République française, avec ses vues sur l'établissement d'un bureau, composé d'architectes consommés qui s'occuperaient exclusivement des domaines nationaux.* Paris, n.d.

Mangin, Père [Charles], et Corbet, architectes. *Exposé et analyse du plan et projet présenté à l'assemblée nationale par les sieurs Mangin, père, et Corbet, architectes … ledit plan gravé dédié à Louis XVI, Roi des François.* [Paris], n.d.

Mangin, Père [Charles]. *Pétition de S Mangin père, architecte; et supplément au mémoire instructif, sur le plan dont il a fait hommage à l'Assemblée Nationale Constituante, en avril 1791 sous le titre: d'Exposé et Analyse du Plan et Projet présenté à l'Assemblée Nationale.* Paris 1792.

— *Réflexions d'un citoyen patriote, dont l'importance est telle qu'il peut en résulter deux on trois-cent millions de bénéfice pour la Nation, en vendant les biens nationaux qui restent à adjuger dans le seul Département de Paris et même dans la Capitale seul.* [Paris] 1792.

Manuel du citoyen, contenant les événements politiques des années 1793 et 1794. Reims, n.d.

Mémoire explicatif d'un projet exposé au concours pour la distribution des terrains et du monument à élever sur l'emplacement du Château-Trompette à Bordeaux sous la devise "A la valeur des Armées francais." N.p., n.d.

Mercier, Louis-Sébastien. *Paris pendant la Révolution.* Nouvelle édition annotée. 2 vols. Paris 1862.

Millin, Aubin-Louis. *Voyage dans les départements du Midi de la France.* 5 vols. Paris 1807–11.

Ministère de l'intérieur. Concours ouvert pour le monument et les édifices à élever sur l'emplacement du Château-Trompette à Bordeaux. Extrait des Registres du Directoire exécutif, du 8 thermidor, an VII. Paris, an VII.

Ministère de l'intérieur. Liberté Egalité 9ᵉ division. Bâtiments civils. Champs-Elysées. Programme pour l'embellissement des Champs-Elysées. [Paris] Brumaire an VII.

Mopinot de la Chapotte, A.-R., Chevalier de. *Proposition d'un monument à élever dans la capitale de France, pour transmettre aux races futures l'époque de l'heureuse révolution qui l'a revivifiée sous le règne de Louis XVI.* Paris 1790.

Mopinot [de la Chapotte, A.-R., Chevalier de]. *Adresse à l'Assemblée nationale … mars 1792.* Paris [1792].

Morlet, Hypolite. *Mémoire sur le programme du second concours ouvert pour les projets relatifs au terrain [sic] du Château-Trompette à Bordeaux, avec détails sur les deux genres de projet qui paroissent plus sensiblement pouvoir résulter des données diverses de cette localité.* Bordeaux, an VII.

Normand, Charles, P.-J. *Recueil varié de plans et de façades, motifs pour des maisons de ville et de campagne, des monuments et des établissemens publics et particuliers.* Paris 1823.

Notice des ouvrages de sculpture, architecture, et peinture, exposés aux concours qui ont eu lieu en vertu des décrets de la Convention Nationale, et des arrêtés du Comité de Salut public, soumis au jugement du jury des arts. Paris, n.d.

Notices sur la nouvelle nomenclature des rues de La Rochelle par plusieurs citoyens de cette commune. La Rochelle, an III.

Ordre de la marche qui aura lieu à Reims le 10 août 1793. Reims, n.d.

Ordre et marche de cérémonie des Tuileries qui se fera aujourd'hui, à trois après-midi, en honneur des nos frères morts en combattant pour la Liberté. Paris [1792].

Palloy, Pierre-François. *Adresse et projet général … présenté à l'Assemblée Nationale et au roi des Français.* Paris 1792.

Patte, Pierre. *Mémoires sur les objets les plus importants de l'architecture.* Paris 1769.

— *Monuments érigés en France à la gloire de Louis XV.* Paris 1765.

Pétition présentée à la Convention Nationale par une réunion d'artistes. Paris: Imp. Nat., n.d.

Peyre, Antoine-Marie. *Projet de Bibliothèque dans le local du Luxembourg. Aux représentants du peuple composant le Comité d'instruction publique.* N.p., n.d.

Peyre, Marie-Joseph. *Oeuvres d'architecture.* Paris 1765.

Pithou de Lionville, Jean-Joseph. *Description générale et historique des objets qui ont servi à la pompe funèbre célébrée le 26 août aux Tuileries pour honorer la mémoire des patriotes.* N.p., n.d.

Plan de l'embellissement du jardin national dit Les Thuilleries, du Palais national de la Convention. Paris, n.d.

Pons [de Verdun]. *Corps législatif, Corps des Cinq-Cents. Rapport … au nom d'une commission spéciale sur le projet de monument aux victoires nationales du citoyen Poyet. Séance du 16 messidor an VI.* Paris, Messidor an VI.

Portiez (de l'Oise). *Rapport fait au nom du Comité d'instruction publique sur les concours de sculpture, architecture et peinture ouverts par les décrets de la Convention nationale.* Paris, n.d.

Poyet, [Bernard]. *Description de la colonne à ériger à la paix, moyens de l'exécuter sans le secours du trésor public, et reponses aux critiques faites sur la construction de ce monument.* Paris, n.d.

Poyet, Bernard. *Idées générales … sur le projet de la fête du 14 juillet.* Paris, 16 juin 1790.

[Poyet, Bernard.] *Mémoire sur la nécessité d'entreprendre de grands travaux publics pour prévenir la ruine totale des arts en France et pour occuper d'une manière utile les artistes et ouvriers de la Capitale.* N.p., 1790.

Poyet, Bernard. *Observations … sur les objections faites au Conseil des cinq-cents relativement au projet d'élever un monument national sur le terre-plein du Pont Neuf.* Paris, n.d.

— *Projet de cirque national et de fêtes annuelles.* Paris 1792.

— Poyet, Bernard. *Projet … pour employer quarante mille personnes … à la construction d'une place dédiée à la nation.* Paris, n.d.

— *Projets de monument à ériger pour la gloire et l'utilité de la République.* N.p., n.d.

Poyet, [Bernard]. *Projets de places et édifices à ériger pour la gloire et utilité de la République.* Paris, l'an VIII.

Prix décernés par le jury des arts aux ouvrages d'architecture, sculpture et peinture soumis à son jugement. N.p., Fructidor an III.

Procès-verbal de la fête civique que la municipalité et les citoyens d'Orléans ont célébrée le 14 juillet 1790. N.p., n.d.

Procès-verbal de la fête funèbre consacrée à la mémoire de Marat … par le peuple de Montpellier. Montpellier, an II.

Procès-verbal de la première séance du jury des arts nommé par la Convention nationale et assemblé dans une des salles du Muséum en vertu des décrets des 9 et 25 brumaire an II pour juger les ouvrages de peinture, sculpture, et architecture mis au concours pour obtenir le prix. Paris, n.d.

Programme d'une temple de l'Egalité. N.p., n.d. [a footnote is dated Prairial an II].

Programme et description de la fête de l'Egalité à Commune-Affranchie le décadi 20 ventôse an deuxième. Lyon, n.d.

Projet d'un monument à la gloire de Henri IV. N.p., n.d.

Pujoulx, Jean-Baptiste. *Paris à la fin du XVIIIᵉ siècle, ou Esquisse historique et morale des monuments et des ruines de cette capitale, de l'état des sciences, des arts et de l'industrie à cette époque.* Paris, an IX (1801).

Quatremère de Quincy, A.-C. *Rapport sur l'édifice dit de Sainte-Geneviève, fait au Directoire du Département de Paris.* Paris 1791.

– *Rapport fait au Directoire de Département de Paris, le 13 novembre 1792, l'an premier de la République Française, sur l'état actuel de Panthéon français; sur les changements qui s'y sont opérés; sur les travaux qui restent à entreprendre.* Paris, n.d.

– *Rapport fait au Directoire du Département de Paris, sur les travaux entrepris, continués ou achevés au Panthéon français depuis le dernier compte, rendu le 17 décembre 1792, et sur l'état actuel du monument, le deuxième jour de second mois de l'an 2ᵉ.* Paris [1793].

Raguin frères, Serruriers, Gardes-Nationales. *Adresse à l'Assemblée Nationale sur la construction d'une salle destinée à l'Assemblée.* N.p., n.d.

Ramel de Nogaret, Dominique-Vincent. *Discours … et programme pour le construction d'un galerie pour le Muséum … le transport de la Bibliothèque nationale dans celles-ci et l'établissemen des deux salles d'assemblée du corps léglislatif dans le Palais national.* Paris: Imp. Nat., n.d.

Rapport fait en séance publique du conseil général de la commune, le 15 décembre 1792 sur les divers plans présentés par les artistes … imprimé par le déliberation du 28 avril l'an second de la république française. Bordeaux, n.d.

Recueil complet de tout ce qui est passé à la Fête de l'Unité et l'Indivisibilité de la République française. Paris, n.d.

Recueil de différentes pièces extraites des procès-verbaux du jury qui a été nommé pour le jugement des ouvrages exposés aux Salons qui ont eu lieu depuis l'an II jusques et y compris l'an VI. Paris, an VIII.

Relation de la fête civique qui doit avoir lieu à Reims le 23 octobre 1792. Reims, n.d.

Ripa, Cesare. *Iconologia, overo descrittione dell'imagini universali.* Rome 1593.

Rousseau, [Pierre]. *Détails pour servir d'instructions aux plans d'un Palais national, composé d'après le projet ayant pour titre "Considérations etc."* Paris 1789.

Saint-Pierre, Jacques-Henri-Bernardin de. *Etudes de la Nature.* 3 vols. Paris 1784.

Sergent, Antoine-François [Sergent-Marceau]. *District de Saint-Jacques-l'Hôpital. Assemblée ordinaire du mercredi 10 février 1790. Monument à la gloire de Louis XVI.* [Paris] 1790.

Sobre le jeune, architecte. *Projet d'un monument à élever dans le Champ de la Fédération.* N.p., n.d.

Société populaire de Montpellier. Rapport fait au nom des comités des arts et de l'instruction réunis par Raisin Pagès. Sur le plan de la fête consacrée à l'Etre Suprême. Montpellier, an II.

La Société Populaire Régénérée des Sans-Culotes de la Commune à la Convention Nationale. Montpellier, n.d.

Songe patriotique, ou le monument et la fête. Paris 1790.

Soulavie, Jean-Louis. *Mémoires historiques et politiques du règne de Louis XVI.* Paris, an X-1801.

Teisserenc, [Abbé Etienne]. *Géographie parisienne, en forme de dictionnaire, contenant l'explication de Paris, ou de son plan, mis en carte géographique du royaume de France pour servir d'introduction à la géographie générale. Méthode nouvelle.* Paris 1754.

– *Plan de Paris mis en carte géographique du royaume de France divisé par les gouvernements des provinces.* Paris, n.d.

Thiac jeune, Bonfin fils, et Lacottee fils de l'ainé, architectes. *Mémoire explicatif du plan … pour la division du terrain [sic] du Château-Trompette.* Bordeaux, an v.

[Twiss, Richard.] *A Trip to Paris in July and August 1792.* London 1793.

Van Cléemputte, ed. *Collection des prix que l'académie d'architecture proposoit et couronnoit tous les ans, gravé au trait, imprimée sur papier propre à été lavé.* Paris, n.d.

Varenne, de (huissier de l'Assemblée Nationale). *Projet d'un monument à ériger pour le Roi et Nosseigneurs des Etats Généraux.* N.p., 1789.

Vaudoyer, [Antoine-Laurent-Thomas]. *Idées d'un citoyen françois sur le lieu destiné à la sépulture des hommes illustres de France. Signé Vaudoyer, 5 avril 1791.* Paris, n.d.

Vaudoyer, A.-L.-T., et Baltard, L.P., *Grands Prix d'architecture. Projets couronnés pars l'Académie royale des Beaux-Arts de France.* Paris 1818-28.

Verhelst, [Egid]. *Plan allégorique d'un jardin de la Révolution française et des vertus républicaines.* N.p., n.d.

– *Description d'un temple présenté au concours par le C. Werhelst [sic] sous le n° 2499.* Paris, n.d.

Viel de Saint-Maux, Jean-Louis. *Lettres sur l'architecture des anciens, et celle des modernes, dans lesquelles se trouve développé le génie symbolique qui présida aux monuments de l'antiquité.* Paris 1787.

Vignon, [Alexandre-]Pierre. *A la Convention nationale, sur la nouvelle salle dans le Palais des Tuileries.* Paris, an II.

– *Mémoire à l'appui des plans et projets présentés par le sieur Vignon pour l'établissement de l'Assemblée nationale et de ses bureau dans l'enceinte actuelle de la nouvelle église de la Madeleine.* Paris, n.d.

Villeneuve, Martin Couret de. *L'Ecole des Francs Maçona.* "Jerusalem" 1748.

Voinier, [Antoine]. *Projet d'un monument tromphal en l'honneur des quatorze armées de la République.* Paris, an III.

SECONDARY SOURCES

Agulhon, Maurice. *Marianne into Battle. Republican Imagery and Symbolism in France.* Cambridge 1981.

Alphand, Adolphe, et al., eds. *Les Travaux de Paris 1789-1889. Atlas.* Paris 1889.

Anonymous, "Le Temple de la Raison à Lille." *Bulletin de la Société d'études de la province de Cambrai* IV (1902).

Les Architectes de la Liberté 1789-1799. Cat. of an exhibition at the Ecole nationale supérieure des Beaux-Arts in Paris, October 1989 to January 1990.

Ars in Urbe. An exhibition of civic art from the Renaissance to present times in Europe and the United States as created and revealed by painters, sculptors, architects. New Haven: Yale University Art Gallery 1953.

Aulanier, Christiane. *Histoire du Palais et Musée du Louvre.* Paris 1948-64.

Aulard, Alphonse. *Le Christianisme et la Révolution française.* Paris 1927.

Badet, Claude. *La Révolution en Provence: images et histoire.* Avignon 1989.

Baratier, Edouard, ed. *Documents de l'histoire de la Provence.* Toulouse 1971.

Bardet, Gaston. *Naissance et méconnaissance de l'urbanisme.* Paris 1951.

Benoit, François. *L'Art français sous la Révolution et l'Empire. Les doctrines, les idées, les genres.* Paris 1897.

Bianchi, Serge. *La Révolution culturelle de l'an II. Elites et peuple 1789–1799.* Paris 1982.

Billington, James H. *Fire in the Minds of Men: Origins of the Revolutionary Faith.* New York 1980.

Biver, Marie-Louise. *Le Panthéon à l'époque révolutionnaire.* Paris 1982.

Bochot, Henri. *Catalogue des dessins relatifs à l'histoire du théâtre conservé au département des estampes de la Bibliothèque Nationale.* Paris 1896.

Boislisle, M.A. de. "Notices historiques sur les Place des Victoires et la Place Vendôme." *Mémoires de la Société de l'Histoire de Paris* XV (1888): 203.

Bordes, Philippe, and Michel, Régis, eds. *Aux armes et aux arts. Les Arts de la Révolution.* Paris 1989.

Bonnet, Jean-Claude. "Naissance du Panthéon." *Poétique. Revue de théorie et d'analyse littéraires,* no. 3 (1978): 46–65.

Boudier, E. "Au Sujet du monument élevé place d'Armes en 1793." *Bulletin de la Société historique et artistique de Suresnes* V (1933–34): 212–13.

Bournon, Fernand. *Histoire générale de Paris. La Bastille, histoire et description des bâtiments, administration, régime de la Prison, événements historiques.* Paris 1893.

Boyer, Ferdinand. "L'Architecte Guy de Gisors." *Bulletin de la Société de l'histoire de l'art français* (1930): 276–9.

– "Projets de salles pour les assemblées révolutionnaires." *Bulletin de la Société de l'histoire de l'art français* (1933): 170–83.

– "Les Tuileries sous la Convention et le Directoire." *Bulletin de la Société de l'histoire de l'art français* II (1934): 197–263.

– *Les Tuileries sous la Révolution.* Paris 1935.

– "Les Cinq-Cents au Palais-Bourbon." *Bulletin de la Société de l'histoire de l'art français* (1935): 59–82.

– "Les Procès-verbaux du Comité pour l'embellissement du Palais et du Jardin national des Tuileries (2 messidor–18 thermidor an II)." *Bulletin de la Société de l'histoire de l'art français* (1938): 261–77.

– "Les Salles d'assemblées sous la Révolution française et leur répliques en Europe," *Bulletin de la Société de l'histoire de l'art français* (1952): 88–93.

– "Le Directoire et la création des musées des départements." *Bulletin de la Société de l'histoire de l'art français* 1972 (1973): 325–30.

Bracco, Patrick and Lebovici, Elizabeth. "Architecture éphémère." *Encyclopédie Universalis,* supplément 1 (Paris 1980), 209–14.

Braham, Allan. *The Architecture of the Enlightenment: From Soufflot to Ledoux.* London 1980.

Breton, Ernest. "Histoire de la place de la Concorde à Paris 1748–1840." Extract from *Journal de l'Institut historique,* n.p, n.d.

Brette, Armand. *"Le Plan de Paris, dit Plan des Artistes." La Révolution française* XXXVI (1899): 277–81.

– *Histoire des édifices où ont siégé les Assemblées parlementaires de la Révolution française et de la première république.* Vol. I. Paris 1902. Vol. II never appeared.

– "Nouvelles observations sur le plan de Paris. dit 'des artistes.'" *Révolution française* XXXV, no. 6 (14 décembre 1903): 496–501.

Brongniart, Alexandre-Théodore, 1739–1813. Architecture et décor. Cat. of an exhibition, Musée Carnavalet, 22 April–13 July 1986.

Bruel, A. "Note sur le Grand Plan de Paris dit Plan des Artistes." *Mémoires de la Société d'Histoire de Paris* IV, 1877 (Paris 1878).

Buisson, S. "Le Plan des artistes 1794–1799." *Vie Urbaine,* nos. 55–7 (1950).

Bulletin du Musée Carnavalet, Collection révolutionnaire, nos. 1–2 (1968).

Calonne, Baron Albéric de. *Histoire de la ville d'Amiens.* 2 vols. Amiens 1899–1900.

Cantarel-Besson, Yveline. *La Naissance du musée du Louvre: la politique muséologique sous la Révolution.* Thèse 3e cycle, Hist. Art., Paris IV. 2 vols. Paris 1984.

Castelnuovo, El. "Arti e revoluzione: ideologie et politiche nella Francia revoluzionaria." *Richerche di Storia dell'Arte,* nos. 13–14 (1981): 5–20.

Cavaignac, G. "Monuments révolutionnaires." *Revue républicaine* III (1834): 129–75.

Cerati, Marie. *Le Club des citoyennes républicaines révolutionnaires.* Paris 1966.

Chapelle, Salomon de la. "Joseph Chinard, sculpteur: sa vie et son oeuvre." *Revue du Lyonnais,* 5e sér., XXII (1897): 77–98, 209–18, 272–91, 337–57, 412–42; XXIII (1897): 37–52, 141–57, 229–38.

Christ, Yvan. *Le Louvre et les Tuileries, histoire architecturale d'un double palais.* Paris 1949.

– *Paris des utopies.* Paris 1970.

Christ, Yvan, and Schein, Ionel. *L'Oeuvre et les rêves de Claude-Nicolas Ledoux.* Paris 1971.

Connolly, James Leo, Jr. *The Movement to Create a National Gallery of Art in Eighteenth-Century France.* PhD diss. University of Kansas 1962.

Cosneau, Claude. *Mathurin Crucy, 1749–1826, architecte nantais.* Cat. exhibition, Musée Dobrée. Nantes 1986.

Courteault, Paul. "L'Aménagement de la place des Quinconces, histoire d'une idée." *Revue philomathique de Bordeaux* (1914): 84–92.

– *La Place Royale de Bordeaux.* Paris 1923.

Culot, Maurice, et al. *Places et monuments.* Liège and Brussels: Institut français d'architecture 1984.

[Delannoy, Marie-Antoine.] *Souvenirs de la vie et des ouvrages de F.-J. Delannoy.* Paris 1839.

De la place Louis XV à la place de la Concorde. Exhibition, Musée Carnavalet, 17 mai–14 août 1982. Paris 1982.

Deming, Mark K., and Vaulchier, Claudine de. "La Loi et ses monuments en 1791." *Dix-Huitième Siècle,* no. 14, (1982): 117–30.

Despois, Eugène. *Le Vandalisme révolutionnaire. Fondations littéraires, scientifiques et artistiques de la Convention.* Paris 1868.

Dessins d'architecture du XVe au XIXe siècle dans les collections du musée du Louvre. Exhibition and catalogue ed. Geneviève Monnier. Paris 1972.

Douglas, Mary. *Natural Symbols: Explorations in Cosmology.* London 1970.

Duboy, Philippe. *Jean-Jacques Lequeu: un énigme.* Paris 1987.

Durkheim, Emile. *Elementary Forms of Religious Life.* Trans. J.W. Swain. London 1915.

Duthoy, Jean-Jacques. "Un architecte néoclassique: François Verly, Lille, Anvers, Bruxelles (1760-1822). Contribution à l'étude de l'architecture 'révolutionnaire.'" *Revue Belge d'archéologie et d'histoire de l'art* 1972 , vol. 41 (Bruxelles 1974): 119-50.

Duval-Juve, Joseph. *Montpellier pendant la Révolution.* 2 vols. Montpellier 1879-81.

Escuret, Louis-H. *La Colonne de la Liberté de Montpellier.* Montpellier 1955.

Etlin, R.A. "Architecture and the Festival of Federation, Paris 1790." *Architectural History,* XVIII, (1975): 23-42.

– *The Architecture of Death: The Transformation of the Cemetery in Eighteenth-Century Paris.* Cambridge, Mass. 1984.

Evrard, F. "Le Jeu de Paume de Versailles de 1786 à 1804." *La Révolution française* LXXIV (1921): 289-317.

Fassy, Paul. *Une page de l'histoire de Paris sous le Terreur: Marat, sa mort, ses véritables funérailles.* 2nd ed. Paris 1867.

Felkay, Nicole. "Un Monument Méconnu: le Jeu de Paume à Versailles." *Bulletin de la Société de l'Histoire de Paris et de l'Ile-de-France,* IIIᵉ année, 1984 (1986), 115-23.

Fortier, Bruno. *La Politique de l'espace parisien à la fin de l'Ancien Régime.* Paris 1975.

Fournel, François-Victor. *Le Patriote Palloy et l'exploitation de la Bastille.* Paris 1892.

Fournier, Edgard. *Suresnes, notes historiques.* Paris 1890.

Gallet, Michel. *Claude-Nicolas Ledoux: 1736-1806.* Paris 1980.

Gallet, Michel, ed. *Soufflot et son temps.* Paris 1980.

Geertz, Clifford. "Centers, Kings and Charisma: Reflections on the Symbolics of Power." *Culture and Its Creation. Essays in Honor of Edward Shils.* Ed. Joseph Ben-David and Terry Nicolas Clark. Chicago 1977, 150-71.

Giedon, Siegfried. *Space, Time and Architecture.* 3rd ed. Cambridge, Mass. 1956.

Germani, Ian. *The Metamorphoses of Marat.* PhD thesis, Queen's University 1983.

Gonon, Pierre-Marie. *Bibliographie historique de la Ville de Lyon pendant la Révolution française.* Lyon 1844.

Granet, Solange. *Images de Paris. La place de la Concorde.* Paris 1963.

Grasset-Morel, Louis. *Le Temple de la Raison et les colonnes de la Liberté à Montpellier.* Montpellier 1901.

Green, Christopher. "Alexandre Lenoir and the Musée des Monuments Français during the French Revolution." *French Historical Studies* XII, no. 2 (1981): 200-22.

Guitard, E.H. "Les Beaux-Arts à Toulouse pendant la tourment révolutionnaire." *Mémoires de l'Académie des Sciences, inscriptions et belle-lettres de Toulouse* CXXXV (1973): 265-76.

Harrington, K. *Changing Ideas on Architecture in the "Encyclopédie" 1750-1776.* Ann Arbor 1985.

Harten, E. "La Démocratisation de la culture dans les projets des musées pendant la Révolution française." *Les Droits de l'homme,* colloque de Grenoble, 1986. Grenoble 1988.

Hautecoeur, Louis. *Histoire de l'architecture classique en France.* Vol. V, *Révolution et Empire 1792-1815.* Paris 1953.

– *Mystique et Architecture. Symbolisme du cercle et de la coupole.* Paris 1954.

– "Les Places en France au XVIIIᵉ siècle." *Gazette des beaux-arts* (1975): 89-115.

Hermant, Daniel. "De la constestation à l'orthodoxie: la révolution culturelle en France après 1789." *Contrepoint,* no. 17 (1975): 166-77.

Herrmann, Wolfgang. *Laugier and Eighteenth-Century French Theory.* London 1962.

Hirschfeld, Gustave. *Arcs de tiomphes et colonnes triomphales de Paris.* Grenoble 1938.

Hollande, Maurice. "La 'Place Royale': sa réalisation à Reims." *La Champagne économique,* no. 12 (1957): 346-59.

Honour, Hugh. *Neo-Classicism.* London 1968.

Huard, G. "Alexandre Lenoir et la Muséum," *Bulletin de la Société de l'Histoire de l'Art français* (1940): 188-206.

Hunt, Lynn. "Hercules and the Radical Image of the French Revolution." *Representations* I, no. 2 (Spring 1983): 95-117.

– *Politics, Culture and Class.* Berkeley 1984.

Idzerda, Stanley D. "Iconoclasm during the French Revolution." *American Historical Review* XL (1956): 13-26.

Isambert, André. *Le Sens du sacré: fête et religion populaire.* Paris: Editions de Minuit 1982.

Jacques, Annie and Mouilleseaux, Jean-Pierre. *Les Architectes de la Liberté.* Paris 1988.

Jadart, Henri. *Du sort des monuments et des oeuvres d'art à Reims pendant et depuis la Révolution.* Paris 1909.

Kaufmann, Emil. "Three Revolutionary Architects: Boullée, Ledoux and Lequeu." *Transactions of the American Philosophical Society,* n.s., 42, pt 3 (1952): 431-564.

– *Architecture in the Age of Reason: Baroque and Post-Baroque in England, Italy and France.* Hamden, Conn. 1966.

Lacombe, Paul. "Les noms des rues de Paris sous la Révolution." *Revue de la Révolution* VII (jan-juin 1886): 100-11, 223-33, 280-91.

Lami, Stanislas. *Dictionnaire des sculpteurs de l'école française au dix-huitième siècle.* Paris 1910-11.

Lamothe, L. *Le Jardin public et l'école d'équitation de Bordeaux.* Bordeaux 1849.

Lankheit, Klaus. *Révolution et Restauration.* Trans. Jean-Pierre Simon. Paris 1966.

– *Der Tempel der Vernunft, Unveröffentlichte Zeichnungen von Boullée.* Basel-Stuttgart 1968.

Laredo, Dominique. "Deux exemples révolutionnaires en province: une colonne de la Liberté (1791) et un temple de la Raison (1793)." *Les Images de la Révolution française,* ed. Michel Vovelle. Paris 1988, 151-5.

Laurent, Gustave. *Les Fêtes révolutionnaires dans le département de la Marne et principalement à Reims et à Châlons sur Marne 1789-1800.* Reims 1899.

– "Le Conventionnel Rühl à Reims. La Destruction de la Sainte-Ampoule." *Figures révolutionnaires champenoises,* Ière série (Reims 1923): 91-122.

Lavedan, Pierre. "Les Places Louis XVI" *Vie urbaine*, n.s., no. 1 (1958): 1–30.
– *Nouvelle histoire de Paris: histoire de l'urbanisme à Paris.* Paris 1975.

Leith, James A. *The Idea of Art as Propaganda in France 1750–1799: A Study in the History of Ideas.* Toronto 1965.
– *Media and Revolution: Moulding a New Citzenry during the Terror.* Toronto 1968.
– "Nationalism and the Fine Arts in France, 1750–1789." *Studies on Voltaire and the Eighteenth Century* LXXXIX (1972): 319–37.
– "Le Culte de Franklin avant et pendant la Révolution française." *Annales historiques de la Révolution française*, no. 4 (1976): 543–71.
– "The Idea of the Inculcation of National Patriotism in French Educational Thought." *Education in the 18th Century*, ed. J.D. Browning. Publications of the McMaster Association for Eighteenth-Century Studies. Vol. VI. New York 1979, 59–77.
– "Space and Revolution: Architectural and Urban Planning during the Terror." *Consortium on Revolutionary Europe: Proceedings 1980.* 2 vols. Durham, NC, 1980, II: 28–43.
– "Desacralization, Resacralization, and Architectural Planning during the French Revolution." *Eighteenth-Century Life*, n.s. 3, VII (May 1982): 74–84.
– "Entwürfe für ein revolutionäres Zentrum, Verlys Pläne für Lille. Projects for a Revolutionary Centre. Verly's Plan for Lille," *Daidalos. Berlin Architectural Journal*, no. 7 (15 March 1983): 56–63.
– "Deradicalization and Militarization: Some Architectural Projects under the Directory." *Consortium on Revolutionary Europe: Proceedings 1985.* 29–44.
– "The Role of Architecture in the Propagation and Sanctification of the Law in the French Revolution." *Problemy teorii i filozofii prawa.* Lublin: Universytet Marii Curie-Sklodowskiej 1985, 139–51.
– "Symbolizing a New Era: Some Architectural Projects under the Constituent and Legislative Assemblies." *The Arts: Enjoyment and Expression.* Arts Research Seminar no. 5, Canada Council, May 1986, 127–37.
– "Planning Space for the Masses during the French Revolution." *Man and Nature* VI (Edmonton 1987): 225–67.
– "Symbols in Revolution: The Strange Metamorphoses of the Triangle during the French Revolution." *Symbols in Life and Art*, ed. J.A. Leith. Royal Society of Canada 1987, 105–18.
– "Le Sacré et l'architecture en l'an II." *Les Architectes de la Liberté.* Cat. of an exhibition at the Ecole nationale supérieure des Beaux-Arts in Paris, October 1989 to January 1990, 165–80.

Lejeaux, Jeanne. "Georges-François Blondel, dessinateur, graveur, et architecte." *Bulletin de la Société de l'histoire de l'art français* (1935): 85–9.

Lelièvre, Pierre. *Nantes au XVIIIᵉ siècle. Urbanisme et architecture.* Nantes 1942.
– "La formation du Muséum au Palais du Louvre." *Urbanisme et Architecture. Etudes écrites en l'honneur de Pierre Lavedan.* Paris 1954.

Lemagny, Jean-Claude. *Les Architectes visionnaires de la fin du XVIIIᵉ siècle.* Paris 1966.

Lemoine, Henri. *Le Démolisseur de la Bastille, la place de la Bastille, son histoire de 1789 à nos jours.* Paris: Perrin 1930.

Lemonnier, Henry. "La mégalomanie dans l'architecture." *L'Architecte* IV (1910): 92–7.

Lenôtre, Théodore-Gosselin, called G. *Les Quartiers de Paris pendant la Révolution 1789–1804.* Paris 1896.

Levallet-Haug, Geneviève. *Claude-Nicolas Ledoux 1736–1806.* Paris and Strasbourg 1934.

McLennan, A. "Politics and Aesthetics of Display: Museums in Paris 1750–1800." *Art History* VII, no. 4 (1984): 438–64.

Maindron, Ernest. *Le Champs de Mars.* Lille 1889.

Marcq, Michel. "Deux projets montrent comment, à la fin du XVIIIᵉ siècle, Lille s'honora d'un architecte de la trempe de Ledoux et Boullée." *La Voix du Nord*, no. 7195, mercredi, 16 août 1967, 6.

Marshall, Anthony J. "Symbols and Showmanship in Roman Public Life: The Fasces." *Phoenix* 38, no. 2 (1984): 120–141.

Mellon, Stanley. "Alexandre Lenoir: The Museum versus the Revolution." *Consortium on Revolutionary Europe: Proceedings 1979.* Gainesville, Fla, 1979, 75–88.

Mosser, Monique. "Le rocher et la colonne. Un thème d'iconographie au XVIIIᵉ siècle." *Revue de l'Art*, no. 58–9 (1983): 53–74.
– "Le Temple et la montagne: généalogie d"un décor de fête révolutionnaire." *Revue de l'art*, no. 83 (1989): 21–35.

Mosser, Monique, and Rabreau, Daniel. "L'Architecture des Lumières en France." *Revue de l'Art*, no. 52 (1981): 47–53.
– "Französiche Architekturmodelle im Zeitalter der Aufkläung." *Daidalos. Berlin Architectural Journal* 2 (1981): 83–97.

Mouilleseaux, Jean-Pierre. Les Colosses funèbres. Les pyramides éphémères de la Révolution française. FMR, éd. française, no. 21 (août 1989): 25–38.

Le Néoclassicisme. Dessins français de 1750 à 1825 dans les collections du Musée du Louvre. L' Exposition du Cabinet des dessins. Musée du Louvre. Paris, 14 juin-2 octobre 1972. Catalogue by Arlet Sérullaz. Paris 1972.

Le Néo-classicisme français: dessins des musées de province. Exhibition, Grand Palais, Paris 1975. Paris 1974.

Oeschlin, Werner. "Pyramide et sphère. Notes sur l'architecture révolutionnaire du XVIIIᵉ siècle et ses sources italiennes." *Gazette des Beaux-Arts* LXXVIII (avril 1971): 201–38.

Olander, William. *Pour Transmettre à la Posterité: French Painting and Revolution 1774–1795.* PhD diss., 2 vols., New York University 1983.

Ozouf, Mona. "Architecture et urbanisme. L'image de la ville chez C.-N. Ledoux." *Annales. Economies, Sociétés, Civilisations* (novembre-décembre 1966).
– "Symboles et fonction des âges dans les fêtes révolutionnaires." *Annales historiques de la Révolution française*, no. 202 (1970): 569–93.
– "Le Cortège et la ville. Les itinéraires parisiens des fêtes révolutionnaires." *Annales. Economies, Sociétés, Civilisations*, no.5 (1971): 889–916.

– *La Fête révolutionnaire, 1789–1799.* Paris 1976.

– "Le Panthéon." *Les Lieux de mémoire*, ed. P. Nora. Paris 1984.

Le Panthéon. Symbole des Révolutions. De l'Eglise de la Nation au Temple des grands hommes. Cat. of an exhibition at the Hôtel de Sully in Paris and the Centre Canadien d'Architecture in Montréal 1989.

Pariset, François-Georges. "L'Architecte Brongniart. Ses activités à Bordeaux et à la Réole 1793–1795." *Bulletin et Mémoires de la Société archéologique de Bordeaux* 1757–62 LXII (1964): 181–239.

– *L'Art néoclassique.* Paris 1974.

Parker, Harold T. *The Cult of Antiquity and the French Revolutionaries.* Chicago 1937.

Paulson, Roland. *Representations of Revolution 1789–1820.* New Haven and London 1983.

Penny, Nicholas. "Ampor Publicus Prosuit: Monuments for the People and of the People." *Burlington Magazine* CXXIX, no. 1017 (December 1987): 793–800.

Pérouse de Montclos, Jean-Marie. "L'Architecture à l'antique et la Révolution." *Art de France*, no. 4 (1964): 325–7.

– *Etienne-Louis Boullée 1728–1799. De l'architecture classique à l'architecture révolutionnaire.* Paris 1969.

– "Les traditions classiques et révolutionnaire dans l'urbanisme napoléonien." *Revue des monuments historiques*, no. 4 (1969): 67–79.

Pérouse de Montclos, Jean-Marie, ed. *Les Prix de Rome. Concours de l'Académie royale d'architecture au XVIIIᵉ siècle.* Paris 1984.

Pevsner, N., and Lang, S. "The Egyptian Revival." *Studies in Art, Architecture and Design* I (New York 1968).

Peysonn, Jean-Marc. *Le Mur d'enceinte des Fermiers généraux [à Paris] (1784–1791).* Thesis, Université de Paris I Panthéon-Sorbonne 1984.

Pfister, Christian. *Histoire de Nancy.* 3 vols. Paris-Nancy 1902–09.

Piranèse et les Français: 1740–1790. An exhibition at Rome, Dijon, and the Hôtel de Sully in Paris organized by the Académie de France in Rome. Intro. George Brunel. Rome 1976.

"Le Plan de Paris dit 'Plan des artistes.'" *La Révolution française*, 49 (juillet-décembre 1905): 176–9.

Poisson, George. "L'Art de la Révolution à Paris. Architecture et décors." *Gazette des Beaux-Arts* 76 (décembre 1970): 337–58.

Poulot, Dominique. "Naissance du monument historique." *Revue d'Histoire Moderne et Contemporaine* 32 (1985): 418–50.

– "Le Droit au musée: un choix du citoyen." *Les Droits de l'homme*, Actes du Colloque de Grenoble 1986. Grenoble 1988.

Projets et dessins pour la place royale du Peyrou à Montpellier. Exhibition cat. Montpellier 1983.

Pronteau, Jeanne. *Paris. Plan de la commission des artistes. Ecole pratique des hautes études. Sciences historiques et philologiques. Annuaire 1967–1968. Rapport sur les conférences en 1966–7 de Mme Jeanne Pronteau sur le plan de Verniquet 1791 et celui de la commission des artistes 1793–1797.* Paris: Sorbonne 1968.

– "Histoire de Paris [Projets entre 1740 et 1770]." *Annuaire. Ecole pratique des Hautes Etudes. IVᵉ section. Sciences historiques et philologiques* 1970–71, a. 103, 529–36.

– "L'Oeuvre architecturale de Edme Verniquet 1727–1804." *Annuaire. Ecole pratique des Hautes Etudes. IVᵉ section. Sciences historiques et philologiques* 1975–76, a. 108, 641–69.

– *Edme Verniquet.* Paris 1987.

Provence, Marcel. *Le Cours Mirabeau: trois siècles d'histoire.* Aix-en-Provence 1953.

Poullet, Marie-Françoise. "Les Places royales et l'aménagement urbain sous Louis XV." *Les Monuments historiques*, no. 120 (1982): 10–15.

Rabreau, Daniel. "Architecture des fêtes révolutionnaires." *Architecture d'aujourd'hui* (1975): 103–8.

– "Un forum au coeur de Paris révolutionnaire. Le projet de Théâtre des arts de Charles de Wailly, 1798." *L'Ivre de Pierre* I (1977): 35–48.

– "Architecture et fêtes dans la nouvelle Rome. Notes sur l'esthétique urbaine de la fin de l'Ancien régime et de la Révolution. Le Colisée. Le cirque. L'amphithéatre." *Les Fêtes de la Révolution.* Colloque de Clermont-Ferrand (juin 1974), ed. Jean Ehrard et Paul Viallaneix. Paris 1977, 357–75.

– "Architecture et art urbain." *L'Europe à la fin du XVIIIᵉ siècle.* Paris 1985.

– "L'Architecture et la fête." *Aux armes et aux arts. Les Arts de la Révolution*, ed. Philippe Bordes and Régis Michel. Paris 1989, 234–79.

Rabreau, Daniel, Deming, Marc K., Vernhes, Bernard, and Vaulchier, Claudine de. "Monuments civiques et éditaires à Paris à la fin de l'Ancien Régime (1763–1792)." *Revue de l'Art* (Paris), no. 52 (1981): 54–62.

Rabreau, Daniel, and Mosser, Monique, eds. *Charles de Wailly: peintre-architecte dans l'Europe des lumières.* Cat. exhibition, Paris, Hôtel de Sully 1979. Paris 1979.

Ramette, Odile. *De la fête révolutionnaire. Essai sur le rôle et l'impact des manifestations festives sur l'architecture et l'urbanisme à Lille dans la dernière décennie du XVIIIᵉ siècle.* Doctorat de 3ᵉ cycle, Université de Paris X, 1979.

Raval, Marcel, and Moreux, Jean-Charles. *Claude-Nicolas Ledoux 1736–1806.* Paris 1946.

Reinhard, Marcel. *Nouvelle histoire de Paris: la Révolution.* Paris 1971.

Renoul, J.-C. *Colonne de la place Louis XVI.* Nantes 1858.

Rocher-Jeauneau, M. *L'Oeuvre de Joseph Chinard au musée des Beaux-Arts de Lyon.* Lyon 1978.

Rondelet, A. *Notice historique sur la vie et les ouvrages de J.-N.-L. Durand.* Paris 1835.

Rosenau, Helen. "Claude Nicholas Ledoux." *Burlington Magazine*, no. 88 (July 1946): 162–8.

– "Architecture and the French Revolution: Jacques Lequeu." *Architectural Review*, no. 106 (August 1949): 111–16.

– "*Postscript on Lequeu.*" *Architectural Review*, no. 108 (October 1950): 264–7.

– "Boullée, architect-philosopher 1728–1799." *Architectural Review*, no. 111 (June 1952): 397–404.

– *The Ideal City in Its Architectural Evolution.* London 1959.

— *Social Purpose in Architecture. London and Paris Compared 1760–1800.*
London 1970.

— *Boullée and Visionary Architecture: Including Boullée's "Architecture, essay on art."*
London 1976.

Rykwert, J. *The First Moderns. The Architecture of the Eighteenth Century.*
Cambridge and London 1980.

Sacy, Jacques Silvestre de. *Alexandre-Théodore Brongniart 1739–1813. Sa vie – son oeuvre.* Paris 1940.

Sarazin, Charles. *La Place royale de Reims.* Reims 1911.

Schmidt, Théophile. *La Colonne de la Liberté de Montpellier élevée en 1791 et détruite en 1814.* Montpellier 1925.

Schmidt, Wilhelm Adolf. *Tableaux de la Révolution française, publiés sur les papiers inédits du département et de la police secrète de Paris.* 3 vols. Leipzig 1867.

— *Table alphabétique des matières contenues dans les trois volumes des Tableaux de la Révolution française.* Leipzig 1871.

— *Paris pendant la Révolution d'après les rapports de la police secrète 1789–1799.* Trans Paul Viollet. 4 vols. Paris 1880–94.

Schneider, R. *Quatremère de Quincy et son intervention dans les arts (1788–1830).* Paris 1910.

Sémiotique de l'espace. Colloque organisé à l'initiative du groupe 100 tête par le centre de mathématiques, méthodologie et informatique, 24–26 mai 1972. Paris: Gauthier 1979.

Sers, Philippe. *L'Architecture révolutionnaire.* Paris 1973.

Shils, Edward. *Center and Periphery: Essays in Macrosociology.* Chicago and London 1975.

Simons, K. *Jacques Réatteu. Peintre de la Révolution française.* Paris 1985.

Soulier, Vincent. *Chronique de Montpellier.* 2 vols. N.p. n.d. Bib. Mun. de Montpellier, ms 245.

Starobinski, Jean. *1789. Les Emblèmes de la Raison.* Paris 1973.

Steinhauser, Monika, and Rabreau, Daniel. "Le Théâtre de l'Odéon de Charles de Wailly et Marie-Joseph Peyre 1767–1782." *Revue de l'Art,* no. 19, (1973): 9–49.

Stern, Jean. *A l'ombre de Sophie Arnould, François Joseph Bélanger, architecte des Menus-Plaisirs, premier architecte de Comte d'Artois.* 2 vols. Paris 1930.

Symbolisme cosmique et monuments religieux. 2 vols. Catalogue of an exhibition, Musée Guimet, Paris, July 1952.

Szambien, Werner. *Jean-Nicolas-Louis Durand 1760–1834. De l'imitation à la norme.* Paris 1984.

— *Les Projets de l'an II. Concours de la période révolutionnaire.* Paris 1986.

— *Symétrie, goût, caractère: théorie et terminologie de l'architecture à l'age classique 1550–1800.* Paris: Picard 1986.

— "Le Style républicain." *Monuments historiques,* no. 144 (avril-mai 1986): 38–43.

— "Les Architectes parisiens à l'époque révolutionnaire." *Revue de l'art,* no. 83 (1989): 36–50.

Taillard, Christian. "De l'Ancien Régime à la Révolution: l'histoire exemplaire des projets d'aménagement au Château-Trompette à Bordeaux." *Revue de l'art,* no. 83 (1989): 77–85.

Le Temple: Représentations de l'architecture sacrée. Catalogue de l'exposition du musée national Message Marc Chagall, Nice, juillet-octobre 1982. Paris: Réunion des Musées Nationaux 1982.

Tuetey, Alexandre, and Guiffrey, Jean. *La Commission du Muséum et la création du musée du Louvre 1792–1793, documents recueillis et annotés.* Paris 1909.

Tulard, J., Fayard, J.-F., and Fierro, A. *Histoire et dictionnaire de la Révolution françoise.* Paris 1987.

Vatel, Charles. *Notice historique sur la salle du Jeu de Paume de Versailles.* Versailles 1883.

Vaulchier, Claudine de. "Projets pour l'Assemblée nationale: les ambitions déçues entre 1789 et 1792." *Revue de l'Art* 52 (1981): 54–61.

Vauthier, Gabriel. "Le Marché Saint-Honoré." *Bulletin de l'histoire de Paris et de l'île de France,* 57ᵉ année, (1930): 84–8.

Vidler, Anthony. *The Writing of the Walls. Architectural Theory in the Late Enlightenment.* Princeton 1986.

— *Ledoux.* Paris 1987.

Vloberg, Maurice. *Jean Houël, peintre et graveur 1735–1813.* Paris 1930.

Vogt, Adolf Max. "Die französische Revolution. Architektur und der Newtonismus." *21 Internationaler Kongress für Kunstgeschichte Bonn, 1964,* vol. 1 (1967): 229–32.

— *Russische und französische Revolutions Architektur 1917 1789. Zur Einwirkung des Marxismus und des Newtonismus auf die Bauweise.* Köln: Verlag M. Du Mont Schauberg 1974.

Vovelle, Michel. *L'Irrésistible Ascension de Joseph Sec, bourgeois d'Aix.* Aix-en-Provence 1975.

— *La Révolution française. Images et récits.* 5 vols. Paris 1986.

Wilhelm, J. "Un projet de Charles de Wailly pour l'aménagement du Salon du Louvre." *Bulletin du musée Carnavalet,* no. 1 (juin 1965): 3–13.

Wunder, Richard P. *Extravagant Drawings of the Eighteenth Century from the Collection of the Cooper-Union Museum.* New York: Lambert Spencer 1962.

Wunenburger, Jean-Jacques. *La Fête, le jeu, et le sacré.* Paris: J.P. Delarge 1977.

INDEX

Arnaud, J.M. Bordeaux   354
Archives de Vaucluse   300, 301
Archives Municipales, Nantes   257
Archives Nationales, Service Photographique   24, 25, 67, 68, 82, 83, 84, 88, 89, 90, 91, 93,
   94, 95, 96, 97, 98, 99, 100, 104, 105, 106, 108, 111, 112, 112, 127, 130, 131, 132, 133, 134, 135, 136,
   152, 154, 158, 159, 160, 270, 271, 272, 273, 274, 275, 282, 283, 292, 293, 294, 295, 317, 318, 319,
   320, 321, 322, 335, 336, 357
Bibliothèque Méjanes, Aix-en-Provence   63
Bibliothèque Municipale, Avignon   310
Bibliothèque Municipale, Lyon   297, 298
Bibliothèque Municipale, Reims   259
Bibliothèque Nationale, Service Photographique   2, 3, 4, 6, 7, 13, 14, 15, 16, 17, 18, 19, 20, 21,
   23, 27, 28, 29, 32, 33, 34, 35, 36, 37, 38, 39, 40, 41, 42, 43, 44, 45, 46, 47, 49, 50, 51, 53, 57, 62,
   64, 65, 66, 73, 74, 75, 76, 77, 79, 80, 81, 85, 86, 87, 101, 102, 103, 107, 114, 115, 116, 118, 119,
   120, 121, 122, 123, 124, 125, 126, 129, 137, 138, 139, 140, 141, 142, 146, 147, 149, 168, 170, 198,
   199, 200, 201, 202, 234, 235, 252, 253, 254, 255, 256, 303, 304, 305, 309, 315, 330, 331, 337, 338,
   340, 341, 343, 344, 346, 353
Bulloz, Paris   161
Caisse Nationale des Monuments Historiques et des Sites   284
Cooper-Hewitt Museum, N.Y.   345
Ecole Nationale Supérieure des Beaux-Arts, Service Photographique   163, 174, 175, 176, 177,
   178, 188, 189, 190, 191, 192, 193, 194, 203, 208, 209, 210, 211, 212, 213, 218, 219, 220, 221, 227,
   228, 229, 239, 240, 241, 249, 250, 251, 306, 307, 308, 324
Edimedia, Paris   109
Joubert, Luc, Bordeaux   260, 261, 262, 247, 348, 349, 350, 351, 352, 355, 356, 358
Josse, Hubert, Paris   48, 54, 55, 56, 70, 71, 72, 78, 128, 145, 148, 151, 153, 156, 157, 179, 180, 181,
   206, 222, 223, 224, 226, 258, 327, 333, 334, 339
Kunstsammlungen zu Weimar   230, 231, 232, 233, 236
Lauros-Giraudon, Paris   195, 196, 197, 316
Leith   1, 5, 31, 69, 143, 144, 150, 155, 162, 164, 169, 186, 187, 204, 205, 214, 215, 216, 217, 237,
   238, 244, 245, 246, 247, 248, 325, 326, 360
Montpellier, Mairie de   58, 59, 60, 61
Musée Carnavalet, Photothèque des Musées de Paris, ©, Spadem   26, 311, 312, 313, 314, 361
Musée des Beaux Arts, Lille   280, 281
Musée des Beaux-Arts, Lyon   296
Musée Réattu, Arles   302
New York Public Library, Photographic Service   207, 242, 243, 323, 328, 329
Pariset, Georges   263, 264, 265, 266, 267, 268, 269
Poteau, J. Lille   276, 277, 278
Réunion des Musées Nationaux   165, 166, 167, 359
Secrétariat Régional de l'Inventaire des Monuments et des Richesses Artistiques de
   Languedoc-Roussillon   285, 286, 287, 288, 289, 290, 291
Sotheby, New York   332
Staatliche Graphische Sammlung, Munich   171, 172, 173, 182, 183, 184, 185
Studio Gerondal, Lille   279
Terlay, Bernard, Aix-en-Provence   30, 299
Vallon, J. Montpellier   11, 12